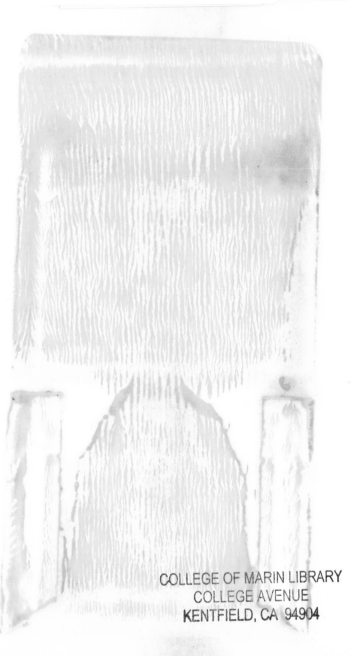

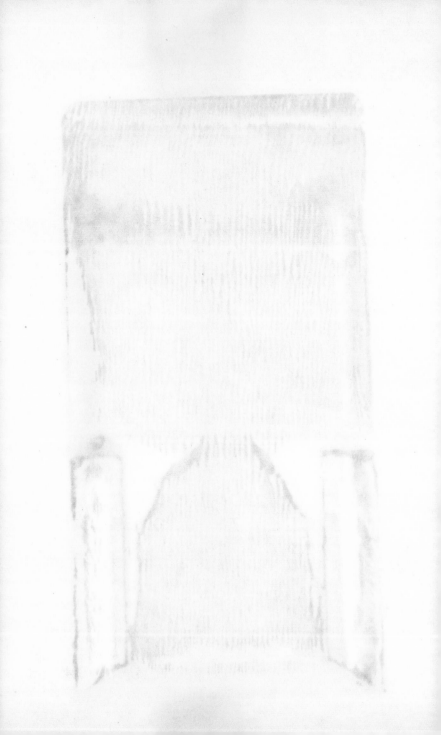

The Logical Structure of the World

Pseudoproblems in Philosophy

THE LOGICAL STRUCTURE
OF THE WORLD

PSEUDOPROBLEMS
IN PHILOSOPHY

BY RUDOLF CARNAP

Translated by
Rolf A. George

UNIVERSITY OF CALIFORNIA PRESS
BERKELEY AND LOS ANGELES 1969

University of California Press, Berkeley and Los Angeles, California

First published in German under the title *Der Logische Aufbau Der Welt*

This translation © 1967 by The Regents of the University of California
First Paper-bound Edition, 1969
Library of Congress Catalog Card Number: 66–13604
Printed in the United States of America

SBN   520-01417-0

PREFACE TO THE SECOND EDITION

Der Logische Aufbau der Welt was my first larger book, the first attempt to bring into systematic form my earlier philosophical reflections. The first version was written in the years 1922–1925. When I read the old formulations today, I find many a passage which I would now phrase differently or leave out altogether; but I still agree with the philosophical orientation which stands behind this book. This holds especially for the problems that are posed, and for the essential features of the method which was employed. The main problem concerns the possibility of the rational reconstruction of the concepts of all fields of knowledge on the basis of concepts that refer to the immediately given. By rational reconstruction is here meant the searching out of new definitions for old concepts. The old concepts did not ordinarily originate by way of deliberate formulation, but in more or less unreflected and spontaneous development. The new definitions should be superior to the old in clarity and exactness, and, above all, should fit into a systematic structure of concepts. Such a clarification of concepts, nowadays frequently called "explication," still seems to me one of the most important tasks of philosophy, especially if it is concerned with the main categories of human thought.

For a long time, philosophers of various persuasions have held the view that all concepts and judgments result from the coöperation of experience and reason. Basically, empiricists and rationalists agree in this view, even though both sides give a different estimation of the relative importance of the two factors, and obscure the essential agreement by carrying their viewpoints to extremes. The thesis which they have in common is frequently stated in the following simplified version: The senses provide the material of cognition, reason synthesizes the material so as to produce an organized system of knowledge. There arises then the problem of finding a synthesis of traditional empiricism and traditional rationalism. Traditional empiricism rightly emphasized the contribution of the senses, but did not realize the importance and peculiarity of logical and mathematical forms. Rationalism was aware of this importance, but believed that reason could not only provide the form, but could by itself (a priori) produce new content. Through the influence of Gottlob Frege, under whom I studied in Jena, but who was not recognized as an outstanding logician until after his death, and through the study of Bertrand Russell's work, I had realized, on the one hand, the fundamental importance of mathematics for the formation of a system of knowledge and, on the other hand, its purely logical, formal character to which it owes its independence from the contingencies of the real world. These insights formed the basis of my book. Later on, through conversations in Schlick's circle in Vienna and through the influence of Wittgenstein's ideas they developed into the mode of thought which characterized the "Vienna Circle." This orientation is sometimes called "logical empiricism" (or "logical positivism"), in order to indicate the two components.

In this book I was concerned with the indicated thesis, namely that it is in principle possible to reduce all concepts to the immediately given. However, the problem which I posed for myself was not to add to the number of general philosophical arguments which had already been advanced in support of this thesis. Rather, I wanted to attempt, for the first time, the actual formulation of a conceptual system of the indicated sort; that is to say, I was going to choose, to begin with, some simple basic concepts, for instance sensory qualities and relations, which are present in the raw material of experience; then I was going to formulate on this basis further definitions for concepts of various kinds. In order to handle this task, even if only in a few sample cases, it was necessary to have a logic available which was much superior to the traditional variety, especially as concerns the logic of relations. I could carry out my task thanks only to the modern logic which had been developed in the preceding decades, especially by Frege, Whitehead, and Russell; this logic contains a comprehensive theory of relations and their structural properties. Furthermore, through the definition of numbers and numerical functions on the basis of purely logical concepts, the entire conceptual structure of mathematics had been shown to be part of logic. I was much impressed by what this modern logic had already achieved, and I realized that further fruitful applications of its method were possible in the analysis and reformulation of concepts of all areas, including the empirical sciences. At the time, most philosophers did not even suspect the revolutionary importance of modern logic for philosophy and the investigation of the foundation of the sciences.

The system which is formulated in this book takes as basic elements the elementary experiences (§ 67). Only one basic concept is used, namely a certain relation between elementary experiences (recollection of similarity, § 78). It is then shown that the other concepts, e.g., the different senses, the visual sense, visual field places and their spatial relations, the colors and their relations of similarity, can be defined on this basis. It is certainly interesting that the restriction to a single basic concept is possible. However, nowadays this procedure appears to me to be too artificial. I should now prefer to use a larger number of basic concepts, especially since this would avoid some drawbacks which appear in the construction of the sense qualities (cf. the examples in §§ 70 and 72). I should now consider for use as basic elements, not elementary experiences, (in spite of the reasons which, in view of the findings of Gestalt psychology, speak for such a choice, cf. § 67), but something similar to Mach's elements, e.g., concrete sense data, as, for example, "a red of a certain type at a certain visual field place at a given time." I would then choose as basic concepts some of the relations between such elements, for example "x is earlier than y", the relation of spatial proximity in the visual field and in other sensory fields, and the relation of qualitative similarity, e.g., color similarity.

A system such as the one I have just indicated, as well as the one given in this book has its basis in the "autopsychological domain". However, in the book I have already indicated the possibility of another system form whose basic concepts refer to physical objects (§ 59). In addition to the three forms which are there given as examples for a physical basis (§ 62) I would now consider especially a form which contains as basic elements physical things, and as basic concepts observable properties and relations of such things. One of the advantages of this basis is the fact that relative to the properties and relations of the indicated sort, there is a greater degree of intersubjective agreement. All concepts which scientists use in their presystematic linguistic communication are of this sort. Hence a constructional system with such a basis seems particularly suitable for a rational reconstruction of the concept systems of the empirical sciences. In the discussions within the Vienna Circle, Otto Neurath and I subsequently developed the possibility of a unified system of concepts on a physical basis. This "physicalism" was presented in its first fairly rough form in several articles by Neurath and myself, which appeared in vols. 2–4 of *Erkenntnis* (1931–1934). Subsequently it has been modified and refined in several respects.

In the sequel I want to indicate in what respects I have changed my position since I wrote the *Aufbau*. I shall concentrate on the most important points. A detailed description of the development of my philosophical thought and position is given in my intellectual autobiography [Autob.]. (The expressons in [ ] refer to some of my later publications and to writings of other authors; cf. the "Bibliography 1961" below.)

One of the most important changes is the realization that the reduction of higher level concepts to lower level ones cannot always take the form of explicit definitions; generally more liberal forms of concept introduction must be used. Actually, without clearly realizing it, I already went beyond the limits of explicit definitions in the construction of the physical world. For example, for the correlation of colors with space-time points, only general principles, but no clear operating rules were given (§ 127). This procedure is related to the method of introducing concepts through postulates, to which I shall return later. The positivist thesis of the reducibility of thing concepts to autopsychological concepts remains valid, but the assertion that the former can be defined in terms of the latter must now be given up and hence also the assertion that all statements about things can be translated into statements about sense data. Analogous considerations hold for the physicalist thesis of the reducibility of scientific concepts to thing concepts and the reducibility of heteropsychological concepts to thing concepts. These changes have been explained in [Test.] § 15. In that article I suggested the so-called reduction sentences as a more liberal form for the introduction of concepts, which is especially suitable for dispositional concepts.

Later on I considered a method which was already used in science, especially in theoretical physics, namely the introduction of "theoretical concepts" through theoretical postulates and correspondence rules, and investigated the logical and methodological character of these concepts (cf. [Theor.]). The correspondence rules connect the theoretical terms with observation terms. Thus the theoretical terms are interpreted, but this interpretation is always incomplete. Herein lies the essential difference between theoretical terms and explicitly defined terms. The concepts of theoretical physics and of other advanced branches of science are best envisaged in this way. At present I am inclined to think that the same holds for all concepts referring to heteropsychological objects whether they occur in scientific psychology or in daily life.

A comprehensive exposition of our present physicalist position has been given by Feigl [Mental]; cf. also his article [Phys.] and my replies [Feigl] and [Ayer].

I am no longer satisfied with my discussion of the *extensional method* (§§ 43–45 of this book). The then customary version of the thesis of extensionality, as it was maintained by Russell, Wittgenstein, and myself, claimed that all statements are extensional. However, in this form the thesis is not correct. Hence I have later proposed a weaker version which claims that every nonextensional statement can be translated into a logically equivalent statement of an extensional language. It seems that this thesis holds for all hitherto known examples of nonextensional statements, but this has not yet been demonstrated; we can propose it only as a conjecture (cf. [Syntax] § 67; [Meaning] § 32, Method V). Fundamentally, the method which I have called the "extensional method" in § 43 simply consists in using an extensional language for the entire constructional system. This is unobjectionable. However, my description of the procedures is unclear in some points. One could get the impression that for the reconstruction of a given concept A through concept B it is sufficient that B have the same extension as A. Actually, a stronger requirement must be fulfilled: the coextensiveness of A and B must not be accidental, but necessary, i.e. it must rest either on the basis of logical rules or on the basis of natural laws (cf. my article [Goodman]). This condition is not mentioned in this book. However, it was my intention to formulate the reconstruction in such a way that the coextensiveness holds for any person (provided that he has normal senses and that circumstances are not "particularly unfavorable," §§ 70 and 72), hence is independent of the accidental selection of his observations and the course of his wanderings through the world. Hence the definitions of my system (to the extent in which they do not have to be disregarded as erroneous) fulfill the indicated conditions. For example, the characterization of the visual sense by the dimension number 5 rests upon the biologic-psychological laws which state that the visual sense is the only sense of a (normal, not color-blind) person for which the order of qualities has five dimensions.

I want to consider briefly the most important expositions and critical discussions of the *Aufbau*. Nelson Goodman has made the most thorough study of the problems dealt with in this book. In his book [Structure] he gives an explicit exposition of my theory, and a thorough and penetrating critical analysis, which even concerns itself with technical questions of the method used. He then describes the construction of his own system, which has essentially the same goal as my own, but deviates very considerably in some respects. In his contribution [Aufbau] Goodman briefly states his opinion about my system; I have replied to this in [Goodman]. Anybody concerned with the construction of a similar conceptual system will find valuable suggestions in Goodman's work even if he cannot agree with him in all points. Victor Kraft and Jørgen Jørgensen consider the *Aufbau* in connection with discussions of the positions of the Vienna Circle and logical empiricism. A more comprehensive exposition is given in Francesco Barone's book [Neopos.]. His pamphlet [Carnap] is a brief nontechnical summary for the nonspecialist. It also contains a bibliography of writings of other authors about various aspects of my philosophical views. Wolfgang Stegmüller ([Gegenw.] Chapter IX, sect. 5) gives a good account and discussion of the main ideas of my book, also of physicalism and related problems.

The article "Pseudoproblems in Philosophy," which is reprinted in this volume, appeared in 1928 at roughly the same time as the *Aufbau*. However, I did not write it until the end of 1927, the end of my first year in Vienna. Hence it shows a stronger influence of the Vienna discussions and Wittgenstein's book. It was written for the nonspecialist and hence is less technical than the *Aufbau*. The main theme is the aim of eliminating pseudoproblems from epistemology. To begin with, a general criterion of meaningfulness is formulated. Then this criterion is applied to the recognition of the heteropsychological. My position at the time represents an early phase of physicalism, about whose subsequent development I have made some general remarks above.

On the basis of this meaning criterion, several theses concerning reality are tested. It is shown that the thesis of realism, asserting the reality of the external world, as well as the thesis of idealism, denying this reality, are pseudostatements, sentences without factual content. The same is shown for theses about the reality or irreality of the hetero-psychological. This condemnation of all theses about metaphysical reality (which is clearly distinguished from empirical reality) is more radical than that in the *Aufbau,* where such theses were merely excluded from the domain of science. My more radical orientation was due, in part, to Wittgenstein's conception that metaphysical sentences are meaningless since they are in principle unverifiable. This position was held by the majority of the members of the Vienna Circle and other empiricists. On the other hand, the rejection of the theses of reality was not generally accepted. Wittgenstein had not explicitly included these theses among the metaphysical doctrines that were to be rejected; Schlick called himself a realist and accepted my position only later; Reichenbach did not share it at all. I myself have maintained these views even after the empirical meaning criterion had undergone several changes and had become considerably more liberal (cf. [Empir.] and [Ontol.]).

The *Aufbau* has not been available since the war, since not only the printed copies, but also the plates were destroyed in the war. I want to express my thanks to the publisher, Dr. Felix Meiner, for making the book available again. In behalf of myself and my friends I wish to thank Dr. Meiner for continuing to publish as long as possible our journal *Erkenntnis* in spite of all the political difficulties during the 1930's.

University of California, Los Angeles   RUDOLF CARNAP
March 1961

BIBLIOGRAPHY 1961

This is a list of those publications by myself and other philosophers to which I have referred in the preface. Bibliographies of Carnap, the Vienna Circle and logical empiricism can be found in Ayer [Posit.] 66 pages, Barone [Carnap] 4 pages, Del Pra, 17 pages, Feigl [Mental] 14 pages.

AYER, ALFRED J. (ed.)
>[Posit.] *Logical Positivism.* Glencoe, Illinois, 1958.

BARONE, FRANCESCO
>[Carnap] *Rudolf Carnap.* Torino, 1953. Reprinted from: *Filosofia,* 4 (1953), 353–392.

>[Neopos.] *Il neopositivismo logico.* Torino, 1953.

CARNAP, RUDOLF
>[Syntax] *Logische Syntax der Sprache.* Vienna, 1934.

>[Test.] "Testability and Meaning," *Philosophy of Science,* 3 (1936) 419–471; 4 (1937), 1–40. Also published separately, New Haven, Conn., 1950.

>[Meaning] *Meaning and Necessity.* A study in semantics and modal logic. Chicago (1947), 2nd rev. ed., 1956.

>[Empir.] "Empiricism, Semantics, and Ontology," *Revue Int. de Philosophie,* 4 (1950), 20–40. Reprinted in: [Meaning] 2nd ed.

>[Beob.] "Beobachtungssprache und theoretische Sprache," *Dialectica,* 12 (1958), 236–248. Reprinted in *Logica: Studia Paul Bernays dedicata.* Bibliotheque Scientifique, vol. 34. Neuchâtel, 1959.

[Einf.] *Einführung in die symbolische Logik,* mit besonderer Berücksichtigung ihrer Anwendungen. Vienna (1954), 2nd rev. ed., 1960.

[Theor.] "Theoretische Begriffe der Wissenschaft; eine logische und methodologische Untersuchung," *Zeitschr. f. philos. Forschung,* 4 (1960–1961), 209–233 and 571–596. Translated by A. Scheibal in: Feigl [Minn. St.] vol. 1, 38–76.

[Autob.] "Intellectual Autobiography." In: Schilpp.

[Replies] "Replies and Systematic Expositions." In: Schilpp.

[Ontol.] "My Views on Ontological Problems of Existence." [Replies] § 4.

[Feigl] "Herbert Feigl on Physicalism." [Replies] § 7.

[Ayer] "A. J. Ayer on Other Minds." [Replies] § 8.

[Goodman] "Nelson Goodman on *Der Logische Aufbau der Welt.*" [Replies] § 21.

DEL PRA, MARIO (ed.)

Rivista Critica della Storia di Filosofia 10 (1955), Fasc. V–VI (a double number on Rudolf Carnap).

FEIGL, HERBERT

[Empir.] "Logical Empiricism," in: D. D. Runes, ed., *Twentieth Century Philosophy.* New York, 1943. Reprinted and somewhat abbreviated in: H. Feigl and W. Sellars, *Readings in Philosophical Analysis.* New York, 1949, 3–26.

[Minn. St.] (ed. with others) *Minnesota Studies in Philosophy of Science,* vol. 1, 1956, vol. 2, 1958.

[Mental] "The 'Mental' and the 'Physical'." In [Minn. St.] vol. 2.

[Phys.] "Physicalism, unity of Science, and the Foundations of Psychology." In: Schilpp.

GOODMAN, NELSON

[Structure] *The Structure of Appearance.* Cambridge, Mass., 1951.

[Aufbau] "The Significance of *Der Logische Aufbau der Welt,*" In: Schilpp. Reprinted in: Sidney Hook (ed.), *American Philosophers at Work.* New York, 1956.

JØRGENSEN, JØRGEN

"The Development of Logical Empiricism." *Int. Encyclopedia of Unified Science,* II/9, Chicago, 1951.

KRAFT, VICTOR

Der Wiener Kreis. Der Ursprung des Neupositivismus. Vienna, 1950.

SCHILPP, PAUL A. (ed.)

The Philosophy of Rudolf Carnap. The Library of Living Philosophers. La Salle, 1965.

STEGMÜLLER, WOLFGANG

[Gegenw.] *Hauptströmungen der Gegenwartsphilosophie.* 2nd ed., Stuttgart, 1960.

PREFACE TO THE FIRST EDITION

What is the purpose of a scientific book? It is meant to convince the reader of the validity of the thoughts which it presents. However, this may not completely satisfy the reader; he may want to know, in addition, whence these thoughts came and where they lead, whether there are movements in other areas of inquiry with which they are connected. Only the book as a whole can demonstrate that the thoughts are correct. Here, outside of the framework of the theory, a brief answer to the second question may be attempted: what position in contemporary philosophy and contemporary life in general does this book occupy?

In the last few decades mathematicians have developed a new logic. They were forced to do this from necessity, namely by the foundation crisis of mathematics, in which traditional logic had proved an utter failure. It not only proved incapable of dealing with these difficult problems but something much worse happened, the worst fate that can befall a scientific theory: it led to contradictions. This was the strongest motive for the development of the new logic. The new logic avoided the contradictions of traditional logic, but aside from this purely negative virtue, it has already given proof of its positive capabilities, though only by examining and reëstablishing the foundations of mathematics.

It is understandable that the new logic has, to begin with, found attention only in the narrow circle of mathematicians and logicians. Its outstanding importance for philosophy as a whole has been realized only by a few; its application to this wider field has hardly begun. As soon as philosophers are willing to follow a scientific course (in the strict sense), they will not be able to avoid using this penetrating and efficient method for the clarification of concepts and the purification of problems. This book is to go a step along this road and to encourage further steps in the same direction.

We are here concerned, in the main, with questions of epistemology, that is with questions of the reduction of cognitions [1] to one another. The fruitfulness of the new method is shown by the fact that the answer to the question of reduction can be provided through a uniform reductional system of the concepts which occur in science. This system is much like a genealogy; it requires only a few root concepts. It can be expected that such a clarification of the relation of the scientific concepts to one another will also put in a new light several of the more general problems of philosophy. It will turn out that some problems are considerably simplified through the epistemological insights which are obtained in this way; others turn out to be mere pseudoproblems. But these additional tasks are only briefly mentioned in this book. Here is a wide, largely untilled, field which awaits our attention.

The basic orientation and the line of thought of this book are not property and achievement of the author alone but belong to a certain scientific atmosphere which is neither created nor maintained by any single individual. The thoughts which I have written down here are supported by a group of active or receptive collaborators. This group has in common especially a certain basic scientific orientation. That they have turned away from traditional philosophy is only a negative characteristic. The positive features are more important; it is not easy to describe them, but I shall try to give a loose characterization. The new type of philosophy has arisen in close contact with the work of the special sciences, especially mathematics and physics. Consequently they have taken the strict and responsible orientation of the scientific investigator as their guideline for philosophical work, while the attitude of the traditional philosopher is more like that of a poet. This new attitude not only changes the style of thinking but also the type of problem that is posed. The individual no longer undertakes to erect in one bold stroke an entire system of philosophy. Rather, each works at his special place within the one unified science. For the physicist and

---

[1] Erkenntnisse

the historian this orientation is commonplace, but in philosophy we witness the spectacle (which must be depressing to a person of scientific orientation) that one after another and side by side a multiplicity of incompatible philosophical systems is erected. If we allot to the individual in philosophical work as in the special sciences only a partial task, then we can look with more confidence into the future: in slow careful construction insight after insight will be won. Each collaborator contributes only what he can endorse and justify before the whole body of his co-workers. Thus stone will be carefully added to stone and a safe building will be erected at which each following generation can continue to work.

This requirement for justification and conclusive foundation of each thesis will eliminate all speculative and poetic work from philosophy. As soon as we began to take seriously the requirement of scientific strictness, the necessary result was that all of metaphysics was banished from philosophy, since its theses cannot be rationally justified. It must be possible to give a rational foundation for each scientific thesis, but this does not mean that such a thesis must always be discovered rationally, that is, through an exercise of the understanding alone. After all, the basic orientation and the direction of interests are not the result of deliberation, but are determined by emotions, drives, dispositions, and general living conditions. This does not only hold for philosophy but also for the most rational of sciences, namely physics and mathematics. The decisive factor is, however, that for the *justification* of a thesis the physicist does not cite irrational factors, but gives a purely empirical—rational justification. We demand the same from ourselves in our philosophical work. The practical handling of philosophical problems and the discovery of their solutions does not have to be purely intellectual, but will always contain emotional elements and intuitive methods. The *justification*, however, has to take place before the forum of the understanding; here we must not refer to our intuition or emotional needs. We too, have "emotional needs" in philosophy, but they are filled by clarity of concepts, precision of methods, responsible theses, achievement through coöperation in which each individual plays his part.

We do not deceive ourselves about the fact that movements in metaphysical philosophy and religion which are critical of such an orientation have again become very influential of late. Whence then our confidence that our call for clarity, for a science that is free from metaphysics, will be heard? It stems from the knowledge or, to put it somewhat more carefully, from the belief that these opposing powers belong to the past. We feel that there is an inner kinship between the attitude on which our philosophical work is founded and the intellectual attitude which presently manifests itself in entirely different walks of life; we feel this orientation in artistic movements, especially in architecture, and in movements which strive for meaningful forms of personal and collective life, of education, and of external organization in general. We feel all around us the same basic orientation, the same style of thinking and doing. It is an orientation which demands clarity everywhere, but which realizes that the fabric of life can never quite be comprehended. It makes us pay careful attention to detail and at the same time recognizes the great lines which run through the whole. It is an orientation which acknowledges the bonds that tie men together, but at the same time strives for free development of the individual. Our work is carried by the faith that this attitude will win the future.

Vienna   RUDOLF CARNAP
May 1928

TRANSLATOR'S PREFACE

A few remarks about some details of this translation are in order.

The German editions of the *Aufbau* contain no footnotes. All footnotes appearing in the present edition were added by me; most of them give the German original of certain expressions; two (in §§ 3 and 88) are based upon suggestions by Professor Carnap.

I have frequently omitted italics where the German text is spaced, since in German spacing is much more common as a mark of emphasis than italics are in English.

In the original, quotation marks are used for several purposes: to indicate the unusual employment of an expression, to mark out the first occurrence of a technical expression, or to show that a term is mentioned rather than used. Except for the last case, I have frequently deleted quotation marks, especially where they occurred in conjunction with spacing. I have italicized all expressions that are both spaced and enclosed in quotation marks in the German text. Neither quotation marks nor italics have been added.

The translation of several expressions warrants special mention. The word *'Beziehung'* has been translated either as 'relation' or as 'many place attribute', while *'Relation'* has been translated as 'relation extension'. An exception is 'basic relation' for *'Grundrelation'*, and 'theory of relations' for *'Relationstheorie';* other nontrivial exceptions are indicated in the footnotes. *'Aussage'* has been translated both as 'statement' and as 'proposition', whichever seemed more appropriate in a given context; *'Wesen'* is rendered both as 'essence' and as 'nature'; '. . . of physics' is the translation of *'physikalisch',* 'physical' that of *'physisch'.* Other translations have been listed in the index.

The summary of the *Aufbau* contained in Nelson Goodman's *Structure of Appearance* proved very helpful in preparing this edition. The present text follows Professor Goodman in the translation of some technical expressions, but deviates in others.

I wish to acknowledge my special debt to Professor Carnap, whom I could consult on a number of occasions; since he has not supervised the translation in detail, any translation errors are entirely my responsibility.

I also wish to express my gratitude to my colleagues at San Fernando Valley State College, where I did most of the work on this translation, for allowing me to use some of their reader funds for the preparation of the manuscript.

Special thanks are due to Mrs. Billie Kiger, not only for her efforts in preparing the manuscript, but also for her advice in stylistic as well as philosophical matters, and to Mrs. Patricia Poggi for reading the manuscript and making many valuable suggestions.

East Lansing, Michigan   R. A. G.
December 1963

CONTENTS

PART II. PRELIMINARY DISCUSSIONS

PART III. THE FORMAL PROBLEMS OF THE CONSTRUCTIONAL SYSTEM

The Logical Structure of the World

PART ONE

INTRODUCTION: OBJECTIVE AND PLAN OF THE INVESTIGATION

CHAPTER
A

THE OBJECTIVE

> The supreme maxim in scientific philosophizing is this: Wherever possible, logical constructions are to be substituted for inferred entities. RUSSELL

1. *The Aim: A Constructional System of Concepts*

The present investigations aim to establish a "constructional system", that is, an epistemic-logical system of objects or concepts. The word "object" is here always used in its widest sense, namely, for anything about which a statement can be made. Thus, among objects we count not only things, but also properties and classes, relations in extension and intension, states and events, what is actual as well as what is not.

Unlike other conceptual systems, a constructional system undertakes more than the division of concepts into various kinds and the investigation of the differences and mutual relations between these kinds. In addition, it attempts a step-by-step derivation or "construction" of all concepts from certain fundamental concepts, so that a genealogy of concepts results in which each one has its definite place. It is the main thesis of construction theory that all concepts can in this way be derived from a few fundamental concepts, and it is in this respect that it differs from most other ontologies.[1]

---

[1] Gegenstandstheorie

2. *What Does "Construction" Mean?*

In order to indicate more clearly the nature of our objective, the "constructional system", some important concepts of construction theory should first be explained. An object (or concept) is said to be *reducible* to one or more other objects if all statements about it can be transformed into statements about these other objects. (For the time being, the explanation in terms of the loose concept of "transformation" suffices. The following examples will make it sufficiently clear. The exact definitions of reducibility and construction will appear later; [2] they will not be given in terms of statements,[3] but of propositional functions.[4]) If *a* is reducible to *b*, and *b* to *c*, then *a* is reducible to *c*. Thus, reducibility is transitive.

> EXAMPLE. All fractions are reducible to natural numbers (i.e., positive integers), since all statements about fractions can be transformed into statements about natural numbers. Thus, for example, $3/7$ is reducible to 3 and 7, $2/5$ to 2 and 5, and the statement, "$3/7 > 2/5$", when transformed into a statement about natural numbers, turns into "For any natural numbers x and y, if $7x = 5y$, then $3x > 2y$." Furthermore, all real numbers, even the irrationals, can be reduced to fractions. Finally, all entities of arithmetic and analysis are reducible to natural numbers.

According to the explanation given above, if an object *a* is reducible to objects *b, c*, then all statements about *a* can be transformed into statements about *b* and *c*. To reduce *a* to *b, c* or to *construct a* out of *b, c* means to produce a general rule that indicates for each individual case how a statement about *a* must be transformed in order to yield a statement about *b, c*. This rule of translation we call a *construction rule* or *constructional definition* (it has the form of a definition; cf. § 38).

By a *constructional system* we mean a step-by-step ordering of objects in such a way that the objects of each level are constructed from those of the lower levels. Because of the transitivity of reducibility, all objects of the constructional system are thus indirectly constructed from objects of the first level. These *basic objects* form the *basis* of the system.

> EXAMPLE. A constructional system of arithmetical concepts can be established by deriving or "constructing" step-by-step (through chains

---

[2] See § 35.

[3] *Aussage*

[4] *Aussagefunktion*

of definitions) all arithmetical concepts from the fundamental concepts of natural number and immediate successor.

A theory is *axiomatized* when all statements of the theory are arranged in the form of a deductive system whose basis is formed by the axioms, and when all concepts of the theory are arranged in the form of a constructional system whose basis is formed by the fundamental concepts. So far, much more attention has been paid to the first task, namely, the deduction of statements from axioms, than to the methodology of the systematic construction of concepts. The latter is to be our present concern and is to be applied to the conceptual system of unified science. Only if we succeed in producing such a unified system of all concepts will it be possible to overcome the separation of unified science into unrelated special sciences.

Even though the subjective origin of all knowledge lies in the contents of experiences and their connections, it is still possible, as the constructional system will show, to advance to an intersubjective, objective world, which can be conceptually comprehended and which is identical for all observers.

3. *The Method: The Analysis of Reality with the Aid of the Theory of Relations*

The present investigations, as far as their method is concerned, are characterized by the fact that they attempt to bring to bear upon one another two branches of science that have so far been treated separately. Both branches have been developed independently to a considerable extent, but in our opinion they can make further progress only if they are conjoined. Logistics (symbolic logic) has been advanced by Russell and Whitehead to a point where it provides a *theory of relations* which allows almost all problems of the pure theory of ordering to be treated without great difficulty. On the other hand, the reduction of "reality" to the "given" has in recent times been considered an important task and has been partially accomplished, for example, by Avenarius, Mach, Poincaré, Külpe, and especially by Ziehen and Driesch (to mention only a few names). The present study is an attempt *to apply the theory of relations to the task of analyzing reality.* This is done in order to formulate the logical requirements which must be fulfilled by a constructional system of concepts, to bring into clearer focus the basis of the system, and to demonstrate by actually producing such a system (though part of it is only an outline) that it can be constructed on the indicated basis and within the indicated logical framework.

REFERENCES. The fundamental concepts of the theory of relations are found as far back as Leibniz' ideas of a *mathesis universalis* and of an *ars combinatoria*. The application of the theory of relations to the formulation of a constructional system is closely related to Leibniz' idea of a *characteristica universalis* and of a *scientia generalis*.

Logistics. The most comprehensive system of logistics is that of White-head and Russell. At the moment it is the only one which contains a well-developed theory of relations and therefore the only one which can be considered a methodological aid to construction theory. It is based on the pioneer work of Frege, Schröder, Peano, and others. It is contained *in toto* in [Princ. Math.]. An outline of the system with applications is given by Carnap [Logistik]. The concepts are explained (without symbolism) in Russell [Principles], [Math. Phil.], Dubislav [Wörterbuch]; with a different symbolism: Behmann [Math.]. A historical survey with a rich bibliography (up to 1917): Lewis [Survey].[5]

Applied theory of relations. Whitehead and Russell make some suggestions for the application of the theory of relations to nonlogical objects (without carrying them through in logical detail): Whitehead's "theory of extensive abstraction" and his "theory of occasions" in [Space], [Nat. Knowledge], [Nature]; Russell's construction of the external world [External W.], [Const. Matter], [Sense Data]. In questions of detail, construction theory diverges very considerably from Russell, but it, too, is based on his methodological principle: "The supreme maxim in scientific philosophizing is this: Wherever possible, logical constructions are to be substituted for inferred entities" [Sense Data] 155. We shall, however, employ this principle in an even more radical way than Russell (for example, through the choice of an autopsychological basis [§ 64], in the construction of that which is not seen from that which is seen [§ 124], and in the construction of heteropsychological objects [§ 140]). Carnap [Logistik] Part II, contains examples of the application of the theory of relations to various subjects (set theory, geometry, physics, theory of kinship relations, analysis of knowledge, analysis of language).

Construction theory. The most important suggestions for the solution

---

[5] Prof. Carnap suggests that it would be preferable to consult appropriate sections from his later work in symbolic logic, rather than the older [Logistik]; in particular his *Einführung in die symbolische Logik*, Vienna: Springer, 1954, and his *Introduction to Symbolic Logic and its Applications*, New York: Dover, 1958. Further literature can be found through: Alonzo Church, "A Bibliography of Symbolic Logic," *Journal of Symbolic Logic*, I (1936), and III (1938), and through reviews in subsequent issues of that journal.

of the problem as to how scientific concepts are to be reduced to the "given" have been made by Mach and Avenarius. In recent times, three different, independent attempts at a system of concepts have been made: Ziehen [Erkth.], Driesch [Ordnungsl.], Dubislav [Wörterbuch]. Only Dubislav's attempt has the form of a constructional system, since he is the only one who introduces chains of definitions. We will indicate agreements between our system and the just-mentioned systems on the few occasions when they occur, but our approach is, on the whole, quite different from those others because of the methodological tools which we shall employ.

There is also a connection with the goal which was proposed by Husserl, namely, his "mathesis of experiences" [Phänomenol.] 141, and with Meinong's theory of objects. More remotely connected are the classificatory systems of concepts (e.g., those of Ostwald, Wundt, Külpe, Tillich), since they do not derive concepts from one another.

4. *The Unity of the Object Domain*

If a constructional system of concepts or objects (it can be taken in either sense; cf. § 5) is possible in the manner indicated, then it follows that the objects do not come from several unrelated areas, but that *there is only one domain of objects and therefore only one science*. We can, of course, still differentiate various types of objects if they belong to different levels of the constructional system, or, in case they are on the same level, if their form of construction is different. Later on (III A), we shall show that the objects on higher levels are not constructed by mere summation, but that they are *logical complexes*. The object *state*,[6] for example, will have to be constructed in this constructional system out of psychological processes, but it should by no means be thought of as a sum of psychological processes. We shall distinguish between a *whole* and a *logical complex*. The whole is composed of its elements; they are its parts. An independent logical complex does not have this relation to its elements, but rather, it is characterized by the fact that all statements about it can be transformed into statements about its elements.

EXAMPLE. An analogy for the uniformity of objects and the multiplicity of different constructs[7] is found in synthetic geometry. It starts from points, straight lines, and surfaces as its elements; the higher constructs are constructed as complexes of these elements. The construction takes place in several steps, and the objects on the different levels

---

[6] Staat
[7] Gebilde

are essentially different from one another. Nevertheless, all statements about these constructs are ultimately statements about the elements. Thus we find different types of objects in this case, too, and yet a unified domain of objects from which they all arise.

5. *Concept and Object*

Since we always use the word "object" in its widest sense (§ 1), it follows that to every concept there belongs one and only one object: "its object" (not to be confused with the objects that fall *under* the concept). In opposition to the customary theory of concepts, it seems to us that the generality of a concept is relative, so that the borderline between general and individual concepts can be shifted, depending on the point of view (cf. § 158). Thus, we will say that even general concepts have their "objects". It makes no logical difference whether a given sign [8] denotes the concept or the object, or whether a sentence holds for objects or concepts. There is at most a psychological difference, namely, a difference in mental imagery.[9] Actually, we have here not two conceptions, but only two different interpretative modes of speech. Thus, in construction theory we sometimes speak of constructed objects, sometimes of constructed concepts, without differentiating.

These two parallel languages which deal with concepts and with objects and still say the same thing are actually the languages of realism and idealism. Does thinking "create" the objects, as the Neo-Kantian Marburg school teaches, or does thinking "merely apprehend" them, as realism asserts? Construction theory employs a neutral language and maintains that objects are neither "created" nor "apprehended" but *constructed*. I wish to emphasize from the beginning that the phrase "to construct" is always meant in a completely neutral sense. From the point of view of construction theory, the controversy between "creation" and "apprehension" is an idle linguistic dispute.

> We can actually go even further (without here giving any reasons) and state boldly that the object and its concept are one and the same. This identification does not amount to a reification [10] of the concept, but, on the contrary, is a "functionalization" of the object.

---

[8] Gegenstandszeichen
[9] repräsentierende Vorstellung
[10] Substantialisierung

CHAPTER

B

THE PLAN OF THE INVESTIGATION

6. *The Preliminary Discussions* (Part II)

The second part will be preparatory to the construction theory itself. Thus, the arguments given there do not presuppose the basic assumption of construction theory, namely, the possibility of a unified constructional system, but merely seek to clarify the scientific, or perhaps more exactly, the ontological [11] situation as it exists today.

In the first chapter (A) of Part II, the very important concept of a *structure* (in the sense of the purely formal aspects of a relation extension) will be explained, and its fundamental importance for science will be shown. It will be demonstrated that it is in principle possible to characterize all objects through merely structural properties (i.e., certain formal-logical properties of relation extensions or complexes of relation extensions) and thus to transform all scientific statements into purely structural statements.

In the second chapter (B), the most important *types of objects,* namely the physical, the psychological, and the cultural [12] will be briefly discussed as to their characteristics, differences, and mutual relations. We

[11] gegenstandstheoretisch
[12] das Geistige

will speak, not from the point of view and in the language of construction theory, but from the traditional viewpoint and in the (realistic) language of the empirical sciences. This discussion will give us, in a sense, a synopsis of the material which will be used in the formulation of the constructional system. This leads to a nonformal requirement which must be fulfilled, namely, the assignment of definite positions within the system for all the indicated objects.

7. The Formal Problems of the Constructional System (Part III)

The presentation of construction theory will begin with Part III. In the first chapter (A), the concept of construction will be discussed in more detail; in particular, it will be shown how it differs from composition by the summation of parts. It will be shown that the construction of an object must be given in the logical form of a definition: every object to be constructed will be introduced through its constructional definition either as a class or as a relation extension. Thus, in each step within the constructional system, one of these two forms will be produced. They are the *ascension forms* [13] of the constructional system. Others are not required.

In the second chapter (B), we shall undertake logical and factual investigations concerning the *object forms* and the *system form* of the constructional system. By the object form of a constructed object is meant the series of constructional steps which lead to it from the basic objects. We shall show in a general way how the object form can be established from the information found in the empirical sciences about this object, especially about its indicators.[14] By "system form" is meant the form of the system as a whole, i.e., the arrangement of the various steps in the system and the objects which are constructed by these steps. From the various logically and factually possible system forms, we shall select that one which best represents the epistemic [15] relations of the objects to one another.

In the third chapter (C), we shall treat of the problem of the *basis* of the constructional system, i.e., of basic objects of two essentially different kinds, namely, the *basic elements* and the *basic relations,* where the latter expression refers to the order which is initially established between the basic elements. We choose as basic elements of the system

---

[13] Stufenformen
[14] Kennzeichen
[15] erkenntnismässig

"my experiences" (more precisely, entities which initially have neither names nor properties, and which can be called terms of relations only after certain constructions have been carried out). Thus, we choose a system form with an "autopsychological basis". It will then be shown how it is possible to envisage these basic elements as unanalyzable units and nevertheless to construct those objects which are later on called the "properties" or "constituents" of these experiences through a procedure which is actually synthetic, but takes on the linguistic forms of an analysis. (We shall call this procedure "quasi analysis".)

The actual basic concepts of the constructional system, i.e., those concepts to which all other concepts of science are to be reduced, are not the basic elements, but the basic relations. This corresponds to a fundamental assumption of construction theory, namely, that *a system of relations is primary relative to its members*. We will choose the basic relations after certain nonformal [16] considerations. These considerations will already prepare the lower levels of the system by dealing with the question as to how and in what sequence the objects of the lower levels can be constructed, and what basic relations are required for the purpose. As it turns out, a very small number of basic relations, perhaps even only one, suffices.

In the fourth chapter (D), we shall discuss why and in what manner the constructions in the system outline (which constitutes Part IV) are given in four languages: namely, in the language of logistics, which is the proper language of the system, and in three translations which are to facilitate both the understanding of the individual constructions and the investigation into whether these constructions fulfill certain formal requirements. These three translations are: paraphrase of the constructional definitions in word language, the transformation of each definition into a statement indicating a state of affairs [17] in realistic language, and the transformation of each definition into a rule of operation on the basis of certain fictions which serve as an aid to intuition ("language of fictitious constructive operations").

8. *The Outline of a Constructional System* (Part IV)

In Part IV, some of the results of the preceding investigations are applied in practice; an outline of a constructional system is attempted. The lower levels of the system are given in great detail (Chapter A) by representing

---

[16] sachlich
[17] Sachverhaltsangabe

the individual constructions in symbolic form and translating them into three auxiliary languages (cf. § 7). We give this part in such great detail, not because its content is absolutely secure, but in order to give a very clear example of the point of the whole investigation and, in addition, to do some spade work on the problem of achieving a reasonable formulation of the lower levels. Using only one basic relation, we shall construct in this part, among other things, the sense qualities, the sense modalities, the visual sense, the spatial order of the visual field, the qualitative order of the color solid, and a preliminary time order.

In the second chapter (B), the constructions are given only in the word language, and no longer with the previous precision, but the individual steps are still clearly described. Here, the space-time world and the visual things in it, including "my body", as one of these visual things, the other senses (besides vision), and the other "autopsychological" entities, components, and states are constructed. The visual world is supplemented by the other senses until it becomes the sensory world, and this world is contrasted with the world of physics,[18] which is no longer concerned with sensory qualities.

In the third chapter (C), constructions are given in rough outline and only to the extent necessary to show that they can be carried out. In particular, we shall indicate the construction of the "heteropsychological" on the basis of "other persons" (as physical things) with the aid of the expression relation; the construction of the "world of the other person" and the "intersubjective world". Finally, the construction of cultural objects and values is also briefly indicated.

9. *The Clarification of Some Philosophical Problems* (Part V)

In Part V, we shall consider some of the traditional philosophical problems and show how construction theory can be used in order to clarify the problem situations to the extent to which they are part of (rational) science. The problems which are treated there are to serve only as examples of the method, and we shall not discuss them in great detail.

To begin with (Chapter A), some problems of essence [19] are discussed, especially the problems of identity, of psychophysical dualism, of intentionality, and of causality.

In Chapter B, we shall try to clarify the problem of psychophysical parallelism.

---

[18] physikalische Welt
[19] Wesensprobleme

Subsequently (C, D), the problem of reality is discussed. It is shown that construction theory is the common basis of the various philosophical positions which attempt an answer to this problem, namely, realism, idealism, and phenomenalism; it will also be shown that these positions differ from one another only where they go beyond construction theory; that is, in the field of metaphysics.

In the last chapter (E), the aims and limits of science are discussed, and their clear separation from metaphysics is demanded.

Summary

(The numbers given in parentheses refer to the sections of the book.)

I. INTRODUCTION: OBJECTIVE AND PLAN OF THE INVESTIGATION (1–9)

A. *The Objective (1–5)*

Construction theory engages in formal (logical) and substantive (epistemological) investigations which lead to the formulation of a constructional system. A constructional system is a system which (in principle) comprises all concepts (or objects) of science, not indeed as a classificatory, but as a derivational, system (genealogy): each concept is constructed from those that precede it in the system (1). A concept is said to be reducible to others, if all statements about it can be transformed into statements about these other concepts; the general rule for this transformation of statements for a given concept is called the *construction* of the concept (2). Logistics, in particular its most important branch, namely the theory of relations, serves as a methodological aid (3). Consequence of the possibility of a constructional system: all concepts are elements of one structure; hence, there is only one science (4). We take the constructional system to be, at the same time, the system of all *objects;* the only distinction between "concepts" and "objects" is a difference in modes of speech (5).

B. *The Plan of the Investigation (6–9)*

(A preliminary indication of the contents of the individual chapters)

PART TWO

PRELIMINARY DISCUSSIONS

CHAPTER

A

THE FORM OF SCIENTIFIC STATEMENTS

10. Property Description and Relation Description

In the following, we shall maintain and seek to establish the thesis that *science deals only with the description of structural properties of objects.* At the outset we shall define the concept of a structure. Afterward, in order to establish the thesis, we shall undertake an investigation concerning the possibility and meaning of structural descriptions. However, an actual proof for the thesis can be given only by demonstrating the possibility of a constructional system which is formal, but which nevertheless contains (in principle, if not in practice) all objects. We shall attempt this demonstration by formulating a constructional system in outline (Part IV).

In order to develop the concept of a structure, which is fundamental for construction theory, we make a distinction between two types of description of the objects of any domain; these we call property description and relation description. A *property description* indicates the properties which the individual objects of a given domain have, while a *relation description* indicates the relations which hold between these objects, but does not make any assertion about the objects as individuals. Thus, a property description makes individual or, in a sense, absolute, assertions while a relation description makes relative assertions.

EXAMPLES. A property description looks something like this: the domain is formed by objects *a, b, c; a, b, c* are persons. *a* is 20 years old and tall; *b* 21 years old, short, and thin; *c* is fat. A relation description looks something like this: the domain is formed by objects *a, b, c; a* is father of *b, b* the mother of *c, c* is the son of *b, a* is 60 years older than *c*.

No matter how many different forms both of the two types of description may assume, they are nevertheless fundamentally different from one another. From property descriptions, one can frequently draw conclusions concerning relations (in the first example, *b* is one year older than *a*); conversely, from relation descriptions, one can frequently infer something about properties (in the second example, *a* and *c* are male, *b* is female); however, the conclusion is then not equivalent to the premises, but contains less: the inference cannot be reversed. Thus, the fundamental difference remains. Frequently, both kinds of description are found together.

EXAMPLES. *Property descriptions:* Description of the set of conic sections through an account of the characteristics of the individual sections. Description of a curve through its coördinate equation, i.e., by giving the ordinate for each point on the abscissa. List of historical persons with a statement of the dates of birth and death for each of them.

Relation descriptions: Description of a geometrical figure which consists of points and straight lines through an indication of the relations of incidence. Description of a curve through its natural equation, i.e., through an indication of the position of each element of the curve relative to the preceding ones. Description of a group of persons by means of a genealogy, i.e., by giving their kinship relations.

We place such strong emphasis upon the difference between these two types of description because we shall maintain that they are not of equal value. Relation descriptions form the starting-point of the whole constructional system and hence constitute the basis of unified science. Furthermore, it is the goal of each scientific theory to become, as far as its content is concerned, a pure relation description. It can, of course, take on the linguistic form of a property description; this will sometimes even be an advantage; but it differs from a genuine property description in the fact that it can be transformed, if necessary, without loss into a relation description. In science, any property description either plays the role of a relation description except that it is in more convenient form, or else, if transformation is not yet possible, it indicates the provisional character of the theory in question.

EXAMPLE. In physics, we apparently have a property description when the color names ("blue", "red", etc.) are used. In present-day physics, descriptions of this kind are nothing but abbreviations, since they presuppose wave theory and since the color names can be translated into expressions of this theory (i.e., rates of oscillation). However, formerly, these property descriptions revealed the incomplete character of the theory of light, since they were not transformable into relation descriptions.

11. *The Concept of Structure*

There is a certain type of relation description which we shall call *structure description*. Unlike relation descriptions, these not only leave the properties of the individual elements of the range unmentioned, they do not even specify the relations themselves which hold between these elements. In a structure description, only the *structure* of the relation is indicated, i.e., the totality of its formal properties. (A more precise definition of structure will be given later.) By formal properties of a relation, we mean those that can be formulated without reference to the meaning [20] of the relation and the type of objects between which it holds. They are the subject of the theory of relations. The formal properties of relations can be defined exclusively with the aid of logistic symbols, i.e., ultimately with the aid of the few fundamental symbols which form the basis of logistics (symbolic logic). (Thus these symbols do not specifically belong to the theory of relations, but form the basis for the entire system of logic—propositional logic, the theory of propositional functions (concepts), the theory of classes, and the theory of relations.)

Let us now consider some of the most important of these formal properties.

A relation is called *symmetrical* when it is identical with its converse (e.g., contemporaneousness); otherwise, it is called *nonsymmetrical* (e.g., brother); a nonsymmetrical relation is called *asymmetrical* when it excludes its converse (e.g., father). A relation is called *reflexive* if, in the case of identity (within its field), it is always satisfied (e.g., contemporaneousness); otherwise, it is called *nonreflexive* (e.g., teacher). A nonreflexive relation is called *irreflexive* if it excludes identity (e.g., father). A relation is called *transitive* when it always holds also for the next member but one (e.g., ancestor); otherwise, *nontransitive* (e.g., friend). A nontransitive relation is called *intransitive* if it never holds for the next member but one (e.g., father). A relation is called con-

---

[20] inhaltlicher Sinn

nected if, between any two different members of the field, either it or its converse always holds (e.g., for a table group of six persons, the relation "one, two, or three seats to the left of"). A relation is called a *sequence* if it is irreflexive and transitive (and hence asymmetrical) and connected (e.g., "smaller than" for real numbers). A relation is called a *similarity relation* [21] if it is symmetrical and reflexive, and an *equivalence* if it is also transitive (cf. §§ 71, 73).

Other formal properties of relations are one-many–ness, many-one–ness, one-one–ness; specific number of elements in the field, of elements in the domain, of elements of the converse domain, of initial elements, last elements, etc.

In order to understand what is meant by the structure of a relation, let us think of the following arrow diagram: Let all members of the relation be represented by points. From each point, an arrow runs to those other points which stand to the former in the relation in question. A double arrow designates a pair of members for which the relation holds in both directions. An arrow that returns to its origin designates a member which has the relation to itself. If two relations have the same arrow diagram, then they are called *structurally equivalent,* or *isomorphic.* The arrow diagram is, as it were, the symbolic representation of the structure. Of course, the arrow diagrams of two isomorphic relations do not have to be congruent. We call two such diagrams equivalent if one of them can be transformed into the other by distorting it, as long as no connections are disrupted (topological equivalence).

12. *Structure Descriptions*

One can give a verbal description which is equivalent to an arrow diagram (where this diagram does not name the individual members) by listing all pairs for which the given relation holds, without, however, using any descriptions which have meaning outside of this list. For example, one can number the members arbitrarily and only for the purpose of producing the list. Such a list can be inferred from the diagram, i.e., it contains no more than the diagram; conversely, the list of pairs allows us to construct the diagram. Thus, the list of pairs, as well as the arrow diagram, gives the *complete* structure description.

If two relations have the same structure, then they are equivalent in all formal properties. Thus, all formal properties of a relation are determined if its structure is described. On the other hand, there is no general

---

[21] Ähnlichkeit

rule as to which formal properties suffice to determine the structure of a relation; it is the task of the theory of relations to investigate this question in detail. The graphic rendition of the structure of a relation by means of an arrow diagram is, of course, possible only if the number of members is finite. It must be possible to give an exact definition of the concept of structure and to indicate the structure of a given relation without the aid of diagrams. But, in this context, it is quite permissible to use the arrow diagram for the purposes of illustration, since, whenever such a diagram can be drawn, it precisely reflects the structure, and since it exhibits all the fundamental aspects of the general concept of structure.

We saw earlier that it was possible to draw conclusions concerning properties of individuals from relation descriptions. In the case of structure descriptions, this no longer holds true. They form the highest level of formalization and dematerialization. If we are given an arrow diagram which contains nothing but double arrows, then we know that it represents the structure of a symmetrical relation, but it is no longer evident whether it represents persons under the relation of acquaintance, or towns under the relation of direct telephone connection, etc. Thus, our thesis, namely that scientific statements relate only to structural properties, amounts to the assertion that scientific statements speak only of forms without stating what the elements and the relations of these forms are. Superficially, this seems to be a paradoxical assertion. Whitehead and Russell, by deriving the mathematical disciplines from logistics, have given a strict demonstration that mathematics (viz., not only arithmetic and analysis, but also geometry) is concerned with nothing but structure statements. However, the empirical sciences seem to be of an entirely different sort: in an empirical science, one ought to know whether one speaks of persons or villages. This is the decisive point: *empirical science must be in a position to distinguish these various entities;* initially, it does this mostly through definite descriptions utilizing other entities. But ultimately the definite descriptions are carried out with the aid of structure descriptions only. We shall give a detailed discussion of this in the sequel.

REFERENCES. The derivation of the concept of structure (or "relation number") is found in Russell [Princ. Math.] II, 303 ff. Russell also comments on the subject ([Math. Phil.] 53 ff.) and gives an indication of the importance of this concept for philosophy and science in general ([Math. Phil.] 61 ff.). Cf. also Carnap [Logistik] § 22.

Recently (in connection with ideas of Dilthey, Windelband, Rickert), a "logic of individuality" has repeatedly been demanded; what is desired here is a method which allows a conceptual comprehension of, and does justice to, the peculiarity of individual entities, and which does not attempt to grasp this peculiarity through inclusion in narrower and narrower classes. Such a method would be of great importance for individual psychology and for all cultural sciences, especially history. (Cf., for example, Freyer [Obj. Geist] 108 f.). I merely wish to mention in passing that the concept of structure as it occurs in the theory of relations would form a suitable basis for such a method. The method would have to be developed through adaptation of the tools of relation theory to the specific area in question. Cf. also Cassirer's theory of relational concepts [Substanzbegr.] esp. 299, and the application of the theory of relations (but not yet to cultural objects) in Carnap [Logistik] Part II.

13. *About Definite Descriptions*

A scientific statement makes sense only if the meaning of the object names which it contains can be indicated. There are two ways of doing this. The first of these is through *ostensive definitions;* the object which is meant is brought within the range of perception and is then indicated by an appropriate gesture, e.g., "That is Mont Blanc." The second consists of an unequivocal circumscription which we call *definite description.* A definite description does not indicate all properties of the object and thus replace concrete perception; on the contrary, it actually appeals to perception. Also, definite descriptions do not even list all essential characteristics, but only as many characterizing properties as are required to recognize unequivocally the object which is meant within the object domain under discussion. To give an example: the name "Mont Blanc" is used to indicate the highest mountain in the Alps, or the mountain so many kilometers east of Geneva. In order for the definite description to be successful, it is not sufficient that the describing sentence be meaningful. Rather, in the given object domain, there must be at least one object with the indicated properties and, secondly, there must be at most one such object. Thus, questions whether and what a definite description describes cannot be answered a priori, but only by reference to the object domain in question.

In most cases, as also in the examples given, a definite description indicates the relation of the object in question to other objects. Thus, it seems that the problem of the determination of objects is only pushed back one more step with each definite description, and that it can be finally resolved only through ostensive definitions. However, we shall presently see that, within any object domain, a unique system of definite descriptions is in principle possible, even without the aid of ostensive definitions. However, in a given case such a system may not be obtainable, and for a given object domain one cannot decide a priori whether or not it can be devised. It is of especial importance to consider the possibility of such a system for the totality of all objects of knowledge. Even in this case it is not possible to make an a priori decision. But we shall see later that any intersubjective, rational science presupposes this possibility.

REFERENCES. About definite descriptions, see Russell [Princ. Math.] I, 31 ff., 69 ff., 181 ff., [Math. Phil.] 168 ff.; Carnap [Logistik] §§ 7, 14.

14. *Example of a Definite Description Which is Purely Structural*

How can it be possible to give a definite description of all objects within a given object domain without indicating any one of them through an ostensive definition and without making any reference to an object outside of the given object domain? That there is such a possibility can be seen most easily by way of a concrete example which we shall give in great detail because of the importance of the general principle which it illustrates.

EXAMPLE. Let us look at a railroad map of, say, the Eurasian railroad network. We assume that this map is not a precise projection, but that it is distorted as much or more than the customary maps found in ticket offices. It does not then represent the distances, but only the connections within the network; (in the terminology of geometry): it indicates only the topological, not the metrical, properties of the network. The example of the railroad map has previously been used to clarify the concept of topological properties. It is equally well suited to clarify the closely related, but more general, logical concept of structural properties. We assume now that all stations are marked as points, but the map is not to contain any names nor any entries other than rail lines. The question now is: can we determine the names of the points on the map through an inspection of the actual railroad network? Since it is difficult to observe an actual railroad network, let us use in its stead a second map which contains all the names. Since our (first) map may be distorted more than the customary railroad maps, we will gain little by looking for characteristic shapes, for example, the long Siberian railroad. But there is a more promising way: we look up the intersections of highest order, i.e., those in which the largest number of lines meet. We will find only a small number of these. Assume that we find twenty intersections in which eight lines meet. We then count, for each such point, the number of stations between it and the next intersection on each of the eight lines, and we will hardly find two of the eight to coincide in all eight numbers. Thus, we have identified all twenty points. But if there are still two, or even all twenty, which have the same numbers, then all we have to do is to consider the connections between each of the eight neighboring intersections: whether or not they have direct connections, how many stations there are between them, how many lines meet in these neighboring intersections, etc. Given the network as it actually exists today: if we do all this, we will certainly not find any further coincidences. But if we are confronted with a network where even these characteristics do not allow us to differentiate, we would have to proceed, step by step, from the neighboring intersections to their neighbors, etc., in order to find still further characteristics for the main intersections. We proceed in this way until we find characteristics which no longer coincide, even if we have to survey our entire net. But once we have discovered the name for even one point on the map, the others are easily found, since only very few names qualify for the neighboring points.

But what happens if there are two intersections for which we cannot find any difference even after surveying the entire system? This simply means that there are two points with identical structural characteristics (homotopic points) as far as the relation to neighboring railroad stations is concerned. We would gather that this relation does not suffice to give a definite description of the objects of the given object domain. We would have to take recourse to ostensive definitions or to one or more other relations. To begin with, we would choose relations of similar kind: next to one another on the highway, on the telephone line, etc. However, in order to stay within the limits of purely structural statements, we must not mention these relations by name, but must represent them only through the arrow diagram of their total network. We must presuppose that by inspection of the geographic facts one can determine unequivocally whether a given network map represents the Eurasian highways or the telephone connections, etc. Through each of these further relations, we would then seek to describe first a few and then all the points of the network, analogously to the procedure employed with respect to the railroad connections. No one will suppose that there can still be two points which are homotopic under all of the relations we have introduced. However, such a case merely contradicts our notion of what actually exists, but is not altogether unimaginable. Thus, in order to solve the problem in principle, we must still pose the further problem: how can we produce a definite description if all of these relations do not suffice? So far we have utilized only spatial relations, since their schematic spatial representation on a map is both customary and easily understood. But we can also employ all other geographic relations and establish a connection between the various locations through relations between the numbers of inhabitants (not the numbers of inhabitants themselves), through economic processes, relations of climate, etc. If we are still left with two homotopic elements of the object domain, then we simply have two locations that are geographically indistinguishable. If we then move on to a new type of relation and take into account all historical relations between the locations, etc., we shall ultimately have used up all the concepts of the cultural as well as the physical sciences. If there should still be two locations for which we have found no difference even after exhausting all available scientific relations, then they are indistinguishable, not only for geography, but for science in general. They may be subjectively different: I could be in one of these locations, but not in the other. But this would not amount to an objective difference, since there would be in the other place a man just like myself who says, as I do: I am here and not there.

15. *The General Possibility of Structural Definite Descriptions*

From the preceding example, we can see the following: on the basis of a structural description, through one or more only structurally described relations within a given object domain, we can frequently provide a definite description of individual objects merely through structure statements and without ostensive definitions, provided only that the object domain is not too narrow and that the relation or relations have a sufficiently variegated structure. Where such a definite description is not unequivocally possible, the object domain must be enlarged or one must have recourse to other relations. If all relations available to science have been used, and no difference between two given objects of an object domain has been discovered, then, as far as science is concerned, these objects are completely alike, even if they appear subjectively different. (If the given assumptions are all fulfilled, then the two objects are not only to be envisaged as alike, but as identical in the strictest sense. This is not the place to give a justification for this apparently paradoxical assertion.) Thus, the result is that *a definite description through pure structure statements is generally possible to the extent in which scientific discrimination is possible at all;* such a description is unsuccessful for two objects only if these objects are not distinguishable at all by scientific methods.

Through the method of structural definite descriptions, it now becomes possible to assign unique symbols to empirical objects and thus to make them accessible to conceptual analysis.[22] On the other hand, it is precisely this assignment of symbols which allows the characterization of empirical objects as individuals. Thus, in this method lies the explanation for the "strange fact that, in cognition,[23] we correlate two sets, the elements of one of which are defined only through this correlation" (Reichenbach [Erk.] 38).

The purely structural definite descriptions which I have here discussed are closely related to the *implicit definitions* which Hilbert has used for his axiomatic geometry [Grundlagen] and whose general methodology and scientific importance have been discussed by Schlick [Erkenntnisl.] 29 ff. An implicit definition or definition through axioms consists in the following: one or more concepts are precisely determined by laying down that certain axioms are to hold for them. Of the axioms we require nothing but consistency, a formal-logical property which can be ascertained through purely logical considerations. Statements which can then be made about an object that has in this way been implicitly defined follow deductively from the axioms, i.e., through another purely logical procedure. Strictly speaking, it is not a definite object (concept) which is implicitly defined through the axioms, but a class of them or, what amounts to the same, an "indefinite object" or "improper concept"; cf. Carnap [Uneigentl.].

A structural definite description, in contradistinction to an implicit definition, characterizes (or defines) only a single object, to wit, an object belonging to an empirical, extralogical domain. (In the example of § 14, it was an individual railroad station in the object domain which consisted of the Eurasian railroad stations.) Thus, for the validity of such a description, it is not only required that the describing structure statements be consistent, but, in addition, the following empirical requirements must also be fulfilled: in the object domain in question, at least one object must exist which answers the description, and at most one such object must exist. Further statements about the object which has thus been described are then not all of them analytic, that is, deducible from the defining statements, as is the case with implicitly defined objects, but some of them are synthetic, namely, empirical findings within the object domain in question.

16. *All Scientific Statements are Structure Statements*

It becomes clear from the preceding investigations about structural definite descriptions that each object name which appears in a scientific

---

[22] Bearbeitung
[23] Erkenntnis

statement can in principle (if enough information is available) be replaced by a structural definite description of the object, together with an
indication of the object domain to which the description refers. This
holds, not only for the names of individual objects, but also for general
names, that is, for names of concepts, classes, relations (as we have seen
in the example of § 14, for the relation of road connections and so
forth). Thus, each scientific statement can in principle be transformed
into a statement which contains only structural properties and the indication of one or more object domains. Now, the fundamental thesis of
construction theory (cf. § 4), which we will attempt to demonstrate in
the following investigation, asserts that fundamentally there is only one
object domain and that each scientific statement is about the objects in
this domain. Thus, it becomes unnecessary to indicate for each statement
the object domain, and the result is that *each scientific statement can in
principle be so transformed that it is nothing but a structure statement*.
But this transformation is not only possible, it is imperative. For science
wants to speak about what is objective, and whatever does not belong to
the structure but to the material (i.e., anything that can be pointed out
in a concrete ostensive definition) is, in the final analysis, subjective.
One can easily see that physics is almost altogether desubjectivized, since
almost all physical concepts have been transformed into purely structural
concepts.

> To begin with, all mathematical concepts are reducible to concepts
> which stem from the theory of relations: four-dimensional tensor and
> vector fields are structural schemata; the network of world lines with
> the relations of coincidence and local time order is a structural schema
> in which only two relations are still named; and even these are uniquely
> determined through the character of the schema.

From the point of view of construction theory, this state of affairs is to
be described in the following way. The series of experiences is different
for each subject. If we want to achieve, in spite of this, agreement in the
names for the entities which are constructed on the basis of these experiences, then this cannot be done by reference to the completely divergent
content, but only through the formal description of the structure of these
entities. However, it is still a problem how, through the application of
uniform formal construction rules, entities result which have a structure
which is the same for all subjects, even though they are based on such
immensely different series of experiences. This is the problem of intersubjective reality. We shall return to it later. Let it suffice for the moment

to say that, *for science, it is possible and at the same time necessary to restrict itself to structure statements.* This is what we asserted in our thesis. It is nevertheless evident from what has been said in § 10 that scientific statements may have the linguistic form of a material relation description or even the form of a property description.

REFERENCES. Considerations similar to the preceding ones have sometimes led to the standpoint that not the given itself (viz., sensations), but "only the relations between the sensations have an objective value" (Poincaré [Wert] 198). This obviously is a move in the right direction, but does not go far enough. From the relations, we must go on to the structures of relations if we want to reach totally formalized entities. Relations themselves, in their qualitative peculiarity, are not intersubjectively communicable. It was not until Russell ([Math. Phil.] 62 f.) that the importance of structure for the achievement of objectivity was pointed out.

B

SURVEY OF THE OBJECT TYPES
AND THEIR RELATIONS

17. The Significance of Object Types for Construction Theory

In the present chapter (II, B), we do not undertake any new investigations, but merely give a survey of the different independent object types according to their familiar characteristic properties. We shall also discuss those relations between these types which have given rise to metaphysical problems (as, for example, the psychophysical relation), or are important for the logical-epistemic relation between the object types and therefore also for the problems of construction (as, for example, the expression relation).

The problem of object types and their mutual relations is of great importance for construction theory since its aim is a system of objects. The various differences and relations which can be indicated, and especially the differences between the various "object spheres", must somehow be reflected in the system that we are about to develop. This is an especially important test for our form of construction theory, since we subscribe to the thesis that the concepts of all objects can be derived from a single common basis.

When, later on, we give a presentation of construction theory, we shall not presuppose any of the factual results and problems of the present chapter, but will undertake the entire construction from the very beginning. There are only a few stages in the development of the system where we shall pay any attention to some of these facts. They will become the most important test when we judge our final result. On the other hand, the theory will lead to the conclusion that the *problems* which are discussed in the present chapter do not even occur in the newly developed system of objects; the obscurity and confusion which is the source of these problems did not arise because the facts themselves are complicated but because of certain traditional conceptual mistakes, which must be explained historically rather than by reference to the facts in question. (Objections against the assertions of this chapter should therefore be postponed until these assertions are later on employed in the formulation of the system.)

Thus, this chapter, even more than the preceding one (II, A) has a preparatory character, and can therefore be omitted without disturbing the context of construction theory which will be presented in the subsequent chapters. The only exceptions are the more fundamental discussions in §§ 20, 22, and 25.

18. *The Physical and Psychological Objects*

The concepts of the physical and the psychological are here to be taken in their customary sense, and therefore we will not give any explicit explanation, much less a definition, especially since both of them are in certain respects vague and, moreover, "logically impure" concepts (§ 29).

As examples of physical objects, we consider their most important type, namely, *physical bodies*. These are characterized especially by the fact that, at a given time, they occupy a given space (i.e., an extended piece of space). Thus, place, shape, size, and position belong to the determining characteristics of any physical body. Furthermore, at least one sensory quality belongs to these determining characteristics, e.g., color, weight, temperature, etc.

Since we take the word "object" here always in its widest sense (i.e., as something about which a statement can be made), we make no distinction between events and objects. To the *psychological objects* belong, to begin with, the acts of consciousness: perceptions, representations,[24] feelings, thoughts, acts of will, and so on. We count among them also unconscious processes to the extent to which they can be con-

---

[24] Vorstellungen

sidered analogous to acts of consciousness, for example, unconscious representations.

The psychological objects have in common with the physical ones that they can be temporally determined. In other respects, a sharp distinction must be drawn between the two types. A psychological object does not have color or any other sensory quality and, furthermore, no spatial determination. Outside of these negative characteristics, psychological objects have the positive characteristic that each of them belongs to some individual subject.

19. *Psychophysical Relation, Expression Relation, and Designation Relation*

The *psychophysical relation* holds between a psychological process and the "corresponding" or "parallel" process of the central nervous system. The theory which is advanced most frequently holds that all psychological objects belong to the domain of this relation, while the converse domain is formed by only a very small segment of the physical objects, namely, the processes in the nervous system of the living animal (or, perhaps, only the human) body.

Through voice, facial expressions, and other gestures, we can understand "what goes on within" a person. Thus, physical processes allow us to draw conclusions concerning psychological ones. The relation between a gesture, etc., and the psychological process we call the *expression relation*. To its domain belong almost all motions of the body and its members, in particular also the involuntary ones. To its converse domain belong part of the psychological objects, especially the emotions.

> Many physical objects which we utilize to understand other people and of which we say that they "express" something psychological, do not stand in the direct expression relation, as we have explained it, to that which they express, but rather in a more complex relation. This holds for all physical objects which are not processes of the body of another person. For example, it holds for pieces of writing and other artifacts, spoken words (i.e., the sound waves in the air), etc. There is a causal relation between these physical objects and the member of the domain of the expression relation proper, that is, the motions of the body. This causal relation is of such a nature that it preserves the characteristic features which carry the expression. Only because handwriting coincides in certain characteristic features with the motion of the hand can we use it in graphology as a sign of psychological facts. Thus, even

in these cases, we have to go back to the actual expression relation which holds between the motions of the hand (but not the marks on the paper) and the psychological events.

The expression relation must be carefully distinguished from the *designation relation*. This relation holds between those physical objects which "designate" and that which they designate, for example, between the sign "Rome" and the city of Rome. All objects, inasmuch as they are objects of conceptual knowledge, are somehow designated or, at least, can in principle be designated. Thus, to the converse domain of the designation relation belong the objects of all object types.

In some cases, the same physical object stands at the same time in an expression relation and in a designation relation to something psychological. In these cases, the relations must and can be well distinguished. For example, spoken words are, in any case, expression for something psychological, no matter what their content. For the sound of the voice, the speed, or the rhythm, but also the choice of the individual words and the style, betray something about the momentary psychological condition of the speaker. But, in addition to this, the words have a meaning. The difference between their expressive content and their meaning content is easily recognized, especially when the meaning concerns something other than psychological processes within the speaker.

20. *Correlation Problem and Essence of a Relation*

With each relation, there are connected two problems of a different kind; the difference between them is of special importance when the relation holds between objects of different object types. We call the *correlation problem* the question: between which pairs of objects does the relation hold? More precisely, what is the general law of correlation of the relation in question? The answer, then, has the following form: If the referent is of such and such a nature, then the corresponding relatum has such and such a nature (or vice versa).

> EXAMPLE. Let us consider the *designation relation* as it holds between written words and their meanings. Since natural languages do not have general rules which allow us to deduce the meaning of a word from its form, there is no way of indicating the extension of this relation except by enumeration of all its member pairs. If a basic language is already known, then this is done through a dictionary; otherwise, the answer takes on the form, for example, of a botanical garden, that is, a collection of objects, each of which has its name written on it.

If the meanings of the *words* are known, then the answer to the correlation problem of the designation relation for *sentences* can be solved through a general function, which, however, is usually very complicated. It is the syntax of the language in question cast in the form of a meaning rule. A meaning rule may (in an elementary case) have the following form: if a sentence consists of three words, a noun in the nominative case; a verb in the third person singular, present tense, active mood; and a noun in the accusative case, then it designates the state of affairs that the object of which the first word is the sign stands to the object of which the third word is the sign in the relation of which the verb is the sign.

From the correlation problem, we distinguish the *essence problem*. Here we do not simply ask between what objects the relation obtains, but what it is between the correlated objects, by virtue of which they are connected. The question does not ask for the constitution of the related object, but asks for the *essence* of the relation itself. Later on, on the basis of construction theory, we shall indicate the difference between science and metaphysics (§ 182), and we shall see that the essence problems belong to *metaphysics* (§§ 161, 165, 169).

EXAMPLE. The *causal relation* (i.e., the relation between cause and effect, as it occurs within physics) gives us a very clear example of the meaning of the essence problem in contradistinction to the correlation problem and the resulting division of labor between the special sciences and metaphysics. The question which cause is causally related to which effect (that is, the correlation problem), is the concern of physics. Its task is to find an answer to that question in the form of a general functional law (i.e., in the form: if the cause is of such and such a nature, then the effect is of such and such a nature). The answers which physics gives to this question are the natural laws. On the other hand, physics does not answer the question of what kind is the relation which obtains between two events that are related to one another as cause and effect. It does not tell us the nature of their connection, of "causal efficacy".

The problems of causality will be more precisely formulated and discussed subsequent to construction theory (§ 165).

The nature of the essence problem is closely connected with the concept of an *essential relation*.[25] By this is meant that which connects the members of a relation "essentially" or "really" or "actually", in contradistinction to the relation as a mere correlation which only points out the members that are so correlated. Later on it will be shown (§ 161)

[25] Wesensbeziehung

that the problem of essential relations as well as the essence problem of a relation can, within (rational) science, neither be resolved nor even posed. It belongs to metaphysics.

EXAMPLE. Especially in connection with the *problem of causality*, the concept of essential relations plays an important role. In discussions about the foundations of physics, one frequently finds the (erroneous) assumption, which is directed against certain positivistic or mathematicizing theories, that causality as a central concept of physics means not only correlation (i.e., mathematical function), but also an essential relation between the correlated processes, namely, the "effect", in the narrow sense, of one process upon the other.

21. *Problems of Correlation and Essence of the Afore-mentioned Relations*

The example of causality shows that the investigation of the correlation problem is the task of the special sciences. The same holds for the correlation problems of the earlier mentioned relations. Brain physiology, psychology, and psychopathology concern themselves with the correlation problem of the psychophysical relations. They attempt to ascertain what kind of physiological process in the central nervous system corresponds to a given psychological process, and vice versa. Very little has been done to solve this problem. The technical difficulties of such an investigation are patent; on the other hand, it is certainly not the case that there are fundamental obstacles, i.e., absolute limits to our knowledge of these matters. There has not been much research into the expression relation, even though it is very important for practical life, since our understanding of other persons depends upon it. However, we possess and utilize this knowledge, not in a theoretically explicit manner, but only intuitively ("empathy"). This is the reason why there is no satisfactory solution of the correlation problem of this relation. On the other hand, there are today promising beginnings to theories of physiognomics, graphology, and characterology. The correlation problem of the vast and variegated designation relation can hardly be resolved within a single theoretical system. In spite of the immense extension of the designation relation (written signs, signals, badges, etc.), there are fewer difficulties to be expected in this case than with the other discussed relations; at least, there will be no fundamental difficulties.

Thus we see that the correlation problems of the indicated relations will have to be solved within certain special sciences, and that no fundamental difficulties stand in the way of these solutions. On the other hand, the *essence problems* of these relations are a different matter. Since we are here concerned not with the *ascertainment,* but with the *interpretation* of facts, these questions cannot be empirically answered. Thus, their treatment is not among the tasks of the special sciences.

If, in connection with correlation problems, we encounter several competing hypotheses, between which we cannot decide, we can at least indicate which empirical data would be required to decide in favor of one hypothesis or another. On the other hand, no decisions have been made between various fundamentally opposed answers to essence problems, and apparently it is impossible to make such decisions: a depressing aspect for the impartial observer, since, even with the boldest hopes for future progress in knowledge, he cannot expect to find out which empirical or other sort of knowledge could bring about such a decision.

The question about the essence of the expression relation has received different, diverging, and even in part contradicting answers. The expressive act has sometimes been interpreted as the effect of the psychological facts that are expressed (thus, the problem has been pushed back to the essence problem of the causal relation), or else as its cause, or the two have been identified with one another. Occasionally, the expressed emotion is said to "inhere" in a special, unanalyzable way in the physical expression. Thus, the most divergent essential relations have been envisaged. The problem of the designation relation is somewhat simpler, since the connection between sign and signified object always contains a conventional component; that is, it is somehow brought about voluntarily. Only rarely has a special essential relation of "symbolizing" been assumed.

22. *The Psychophysical Problem as the Central Problem of Metaphysics*

The essence problem of the psychophysical relation can be called simply the psychophysical problem. Among the traditional problems of philosophy, it is the one which is most closely connected with the psychophysical relation, and, in addition, it has gradually become the main problem of metaphysics.

The question is this: provided that to all or some types of psychological processes there correspond simultaneous processes in the central nervous system, what connects the processes in question with one another? Very little has been done toward a solution of the correlation problem of the psychophysical relation, but, even if this problem were solved (i.e., if we could infer the characteristics of a brain process from the characteristics of a psychological process, and vice versa), nothing would have been achieved to further the solution of the essence problem (i.e., the "psychophysical problem"). For this problem is not concerned with the correlation, but with the essential relation; that is, with that which "essentially" or "fundamentally" leads from one process to the other or which brings forth both from a common root.

The attempted solutions and also their irreconcilable divergences are well known. The theories of occasionalism and of preëstablished harmony have perhaps only historical interest. Thus, there still remain, in the main, three hypotheses: mutual influence, parallelism, and identity in the sense of the two-aspect theory. The hypothesis of *mutual influence* assumes an essential relation between the two terms (i.e., a causal efficacy in both directions). The hypothesis of *parallelism* (in the narrowest sense, i.e., excluding the identity theory) denies the existence of an essential relation and assumes that there is only a functional correlation between the two types of objects (types of processes). Finally, the *identity theory* does not even admit that there are two types of objects, but assumes that the psychological and the physical are the two "aspects" ("the outer" and "the inner") of the same fundamental process. The counterarguments which are brought forth against each of these hypotheses by its adversaries seem to be conclusive: science generally assumes an uninterrupted causal nexus of all spatial processes; but this is not consistent with psychophysical mutual influence. On the other hand, one cannot see how a merely functional correlation, that is, a logical and not a real relation, can result in an experience which corresponds to the stimuli that impinge upon the senses. And the identity of two such different types of objects as the psychological and the physical remains an empty word as long as we are not told what is meant by the figurative expression "fundamental process" and "inner and outer aspects." (We do not wish to say anything against parallelism or the hypothesis of mutual influence as long as they are merely used heuristically, as working hypotheses for psychology. We are here concerned with metaphysical opinions.)

Three contradicting and equally unsatisfactory answers and no possibility of finding or even imagining an empirical fact that could here make the difference: a more hopeless situation can hardly be imagined. It could lead us to wonder whether the questions concerning problems of essence, especially the psychophysical problem, are not perhaps posed in a fallacious way. Construction theory will in fact lead to the conclusion that this is so. Once the constructional forms of the objects and the object types are found and their logical locations in the constructional system are known, and if furthermore the correlation problem of one of the above relations has been resolved, then we have found everything (rational) science can say about that relation. An additional question concerning the "essence" of the relation would lack any sense. It cannot even be formulated in scientific terms. The discussions of Part V will show this in more detail (§ 157 ff.).

23. *The Cultural Objects*

For philosophy, the most important types of objects, outside of the physical and the psychological ones, are the *cultural* (historical, sociological) *objects*.[26] They belong in the object domain of the cultural sciences.[27] Among the cultural objects, we count individual incidents and large scale occurrences, sociological groups, institutions, movements in all areas of culture, and also properties and relations of such processes and entities.

The philosophy of the nineteenth century did not pay sufficient attention to the fact that the cultural objects form an autonomous type. The reason for this is that epistemological and logical investigations tended to confine their attention predominately to physics and psychology as paradigmatic subject matter areas. Only the more recent history of philosophy (since Dilthey) has called attention to the methodological and object-theoretical peculiarity of the area of the cultural sciences.

The cultural objects have in common with the psychological ones the fact that they, too, are subject bound; their "bearers" are always the persons of a certain group. But, in contrast to the psychological objects, their bearers may change: a state or a custom can persist even though the bearing subjects perish and others take their place. Moreover, the cultural objects are not composed of psychological (much less physical) objects. They are of a completely different object type; the cultural objects belong to other object spheres (in a sense to be explained later on, § 29) than the physical and the psychological objects. This means that no cultural object may be meaningfully inserted into a proposition about a physical or a psychological object.

Later on, in the context of construction theory, we shall show in what way the assertion of the unity of the entire domain of objects of knowl-

---

[26] geistige Gegenstände

[27] Geisteswissenschaften

edge refers to the derivation ("construction") of all objects starting from one and the same basis, and that the assertion that the various spheres of objects are different means that there are different constructional levels and forms. Thus the two apparently opposing positions are reconciled (cf. § 41).

24. *The Manifestations and Documentations of Cultural Objects*

I wish to discuss here only the two most important relations between cultural and other objects, since knowledge of cultural objects, and thus their construction, depends entirely upon these relations. We call these two relations "manifestation" and "documentation".

A cultural object which exists during a certain time, does not have to be actual (i.e., manifested) at all points during this span. The psychological processes in which it appears or "manifests" itself, we shall call its (*psychological*) *manifestation*. The relation of the (psychological) manifestation of a cultural object to the object itself, we shall call the *manifestation relation* (more precisely: the psychological-cultural or, more briefly, the psychological manifestation relation).

> EXAMPLE. This relation holds, for example, between the present resolve of a man to lift his hat before another man, and the custom of hat-lifting. This custom does not exist merely during those moments in which somebody somewhere manifests it, but also during the times in between, as long as there are any persons who have the psychological disposition to react to certain impressions by greeting somebody through lifting their hats. During the times in between, the custom is "latent".

A physical object can also be the manifestation of a cultural one. Thus, the custom of hat-lifting manifests itself, for example, in the appropriate bodily motions of a certain man. But closer scrutiny shows that, even here, the psychological manifestation relation is fundamental. Thus we shall always mean the latter when we simply speak of the manifestation relation.

We call *documentations* of a cultural object those permanent physical objects in which the cultural life is, as it were, solidified: products, artifacts, and documents of a culture.

> EXAMPLES. The documentations or representations of an art style consist of the buildings, paintings, statues, etc. which belong to this style. The documentation of the present railroad system consists of all stationary and rolling material and the written documents of the railroad business.

It is the task of the cultural sciences to deal with the correlation problems of the manifestation and documentation relation. These sciences have to ascertain in which acts (in the physical and psychological sense) the individual cultural objects become overt and manifest themselves. In so doing they form, as it were, definitions for all the names of cultural objects. On the other hand, the documentation relation is of special importance for the cultural sciences, because the research into no longer existing cultural objects (and these, after all, form the larger part of the domain) rests almost exclusively upon conclusions drawn from documentation, namely, from written records, illustrations, things that have been built or formed, etc. But these conclusions presuppose that the documentation correlation (that is, the answer to the correlation problem of the documentation relation) is known. Thus, for the cultural sciences, the tasks of providing definitions, and of finding criteria for the recognition of their objects will be fulfilled by resolving these two correlation problems.

As with the relations which we considered earlier (§§ 21, 22), here, too, examination of the correlation problems is part of the task of the special sciences. The study of the essence problems, on the other hand, belongs to metaphysics. I do not wish to discuss at this time the attempted solutions of the essence problems (e.g., emanation theory, incarnation theory, psychologistic and materialistic interpretation). Here we find a situation very similar to that which held for the earlier essence problems: a struggle between divergent opinions, where there seems to be no possibility that a decision can be made through empirically obtained information.

25. The Multiplicity of Autonomous Object Types

After the physical, the psychological, and the cultural object types, I wish to give some examples of further autonomous object types. In the sequel, we shall reformulate the statement that each of these object types is "autonomous" by saying, more precisely, that they belong to different "object spheres" (§ 29). Later on, after we have given an account of construction theory, we shall have to ascertain whether the conceptual system which is based on this theory, namely, the "constructional system" (Part IV), provides a place for each of the object types which we have just mentioned.

Later (§ 41), we shall show that the assertion of the multiplicity of independent object types only apparently contradicts the thesis of the unity of the object domain.

EXAMPLES. *Logical objects:* Negation, implication, indirect proof. These are logical objects in the narrower sense, i.e., excluding the mathematical objects which are closely connected with them, but which, in accordance with the customary separation of the sciences, we shall not mention at this time. However, the boundary line is somewhat arbitrary. (The logical objects will later on be incorporated into the "constructional system" of concepts [they will be "constructed"] § 107.)

Mathematical objects: The number 3, the class of all algebraic numbers, the equilateral triangle. The triangle is here to be understood, not in the concrete-spatial, but in the mathematical-abstract, sense (construction of mathematical objects: § 107).

The object type of *spatial configurations:* The sphere, the equilateral triangle. Here, these expressions are not meant as expressions of abstract, nonspatial geometry, but in their ordinary, concrete-spatial sense (cf. mathematical objects). Physical objects are to be distinguished sharply from spatial configurations, since the latter lack the determinations of time, space, color, weight, etc. (construction of the spatial configurations: § 125).

The object type of the *colors:* grey, red, green. The colors do not have any determination of time or space (they are meant in the purely phenomenal sense); also, they are not, strictly speaking, determined as to color, weight, or other sensory qualities; this distinguishes them from physical objects. The difference between the colors and the psychological objects consists in the difference between the contents of a representation and the representation. (Construction of colors: § 118; in order to construct them as intersubjective objects, we would still have to apply to them the procedures of § 149. The same holds also for the constructions that are given below.)

The object type of *pitches: c, e,* the chord *c-e-g.* The object types of *odors* and *tastes* are also to be mentioned as independent object types, just as colors and pitches (construction of the sensory qualities: §§ 131, 133).

Biological objects: the oak, the horse. (Both of them are to be understood as species and not as individuals.) Such a biological object is not a sum of physical objects, but a complex of them; that is to say, a class; about the difference between a complex and a collection, cf. § 36, specifically between class and collection, § 37 (construction of biological objects: § 137).

Ethical objects: duty, obedience, ethical value (of an act). About the difference between these and psychological objects, cf. what has been said in connection with the colors (construction: § 152).

It can easily be seen that this list of object types can be continued, but it should suffice for our purposes. It shows that there is a multiplicity of object types, and it can be used to test the adequacy of a system of objects, in our case, of the constructional system.

Summary

II. PRELIMINARY DISCUSSIONS (10–25)

A. *The Form of Scientific Statements (10–16)*

A *property description* of a domain indicates the properties of the individual objects of that domain; a *relation description* indicates merely the relations between the objects. Construction theory views the latter as more fundamental (10). Two relations are said to be "isomorphic" or "of the same structure" if they agree in their formal properties, more precisely, if there is a one-to-one correspondence between them (to help visualize this: two relations are isomorphic if they have the same arrow diagram). That which is common to isomorphic relations (in the terminology of logistics: the class of these relations) is called their *structure* (11). A relation description is called a *structure description,* if the relations which occur are not themselves mentioned but only their structure is indicated. A structure description is given either through an (unnamed) arrow diagram or through a list of number-pairs. The structure description forms the highest level of formalization in the representation of a domain. Thesis: the representation of the world in science is fundamentally a structure description (12). By the *definite description* of an object is meant a unique characterization of that object, i.e., a characterization which allows an unequivocal identification of that object in the object domain in question (13). Thesis: every object of science can be uniquely characterized within its object domain through mere structure statements (14, 15). Hence it is in principle possible to transform all statements of science into *structure statements;* indeed, this transformation is necessary if science is to advance from the subjective to the objective: all genuine science is structural science [28] (16).

B. *Survey of the Object Types and Their Relations (17–25)*

In order to obtain a preliminary, very rough, division, we distinguish *physical, psychological,* and *cultural,* objects. The expressions "physical" and "psychological" are here taken in their customary sense; by "cultural" objects we mean objects of the cultural sciences (or *Geisteswissenschaften*): cultural or sociological events, states and entities (18, 23). The *psychophysical relation* is the relation between a psychological process and the parallel process in the nervous system. The *expression relation* is the relation between

---

[28] Strukturwissenschaft

a motion, a facial expression, or a vocal utterance of a person, and the psychological process which can be recognized in this utterance. The *designation relation* is the relation between a physical sign (written symbol, sound, badge, etc.) and that which is designated (19). For each relation there arises a *correlation problem* (which objects have this relation to one another?) and an *essence problem* (what is the nature of the relation? what is it that connects the correlated objects? (20). To investigate the correlation problems of the relations mentioned above is part of the task of science (namely of psychology and physiology; psychology and characterology; and various branches of semiotics, respectively). On the other hand, the solution of the essence problems of those relations does not consist in the ascertainment of facts, but in their interpretation; it is not a task of science. This is already indicated in the fact that various contradictory solutions have been proffered between which no (conceivable) experience could decide. Hence essence problems must be transferred from science to metaphysics; this is particularly obvious with the psychophysical problem (21, 22).

The psychological events in which a cultural object (cultural event) appears are called the latter's *manifestations;* the physical objects in which a cultural object is reflected are called its *documentations.* The correlation problem of these two relations is investigated in the cultural sciences, while the essence problem is again to be referred to metaphysics (24). The three indicated object types are merely the most important examples; there is a large number of other autonomous object types (25).

PART THREE

THE FORMAL PROBLEMS OF THE
CONSTRUCTIONAL SYSTEM

THE ASCENSION FORMS

26. *The Four Main Problems of Construction Theory*

The aim of construction theory consists in formulating a constructional system, i.e., a stepwise ordered system of objects (or concepts). The stepwise ordering is a result of the fact that the objects on each level are "constructed" from the objects of the lower levels in a sense to be made precise later. In the formation of such a system, the following four main problems are encountered. To begin with, a basis must be chosen, a lowest level upon which all others are founded. Secondly, we must determine the recurrent forms through which we ascend from one level to the next. Thirdly, we must investigate how the objects of various types can be constructed through repeated applications of the ascension forms. The fourth question concerns the over-all form of the system as it results from the stratified arrangement of the object types. We call these four problems the problems of *basis, ascension form, object form,* and *system form.* The problems of basis, object form, and system form are closely connected with one another. Their solutions are dependent upon one another, since the construction of the objects, and thus the form of the system, depends upon the choice of the basis, while the basis is chosen so as to allow the construction of all object types from it. On the other hand, the problem of the ascension forms depends less upon the efficacy which we require of the system as a whole and is also less complicated. While the basis of the system consists of extralogical entities which must be chosen from an unlimited number of candidates, the ascension forms must be chosen from a small number of logical forms, no matter what the content of the system. These forms will result from the concepts of a construction and of a logical complex. Of course, it is not antecedently obvious that one can make do with ascension forms as simple and as few in number (namely, two) as we maintain. This result will follow from later considerations concerning definition as a form of construction (§§ 38–40). A confirmation of this view can only be found in the actual formation of the constructional system itself (Part IV).

The problems of the basis, the object forms, and the system form will be dealt with in the later chapters of this part (B–D), where we must take into account empirical facts, namely, the properties and relations of objects which are investigated in the special sciences. Subsequently we shall consider the symbolic and linguistic forms which will be used to represent the constructional system (Chapter E). Here (in Chapter A), the formal-logical problem of the ascension forms is to be resolved.

27. *The Quasi Objects*

We can divide (linguistic) signs into those which have independent meaning and those which have meaning only in connection with other signs. Strictly speaking, only those (mostly complex) signs which designate a proposition, i.e., *sentences,* have independent meaning. Among the signs which are not themselves sentences and which occur in science only as parts of sentences, we wish to distinguish the so-called proper names, i.e., signs which designate a definite concrete individual object (e.g., "Napoleon", "moon") from the other parts of sentences. The traditional view is that the proper names have a relatively independent meaning and are thereby distinguished from the other signs. These other signs we call, after Frege, *incomplete symbols.*[29]

> It should be noted that this distinction is not logically precise. We make it to follow an established tradition and shall not attempt to give a more precise definition of the concept of "proper name". Perhaps there is only a difference in degree and the choice of a boundary line is arbitrary; at least, this seems to be the upshot of the later discussions on individual and general objects (§ 158).

---

[29] ungesättigte Zeichen

In the original usage of signs, the subject position of a sentence must always be occupied by a proper name. However, it proved advantageous to admit into the subject position also signs for general objects and, finally, also other incomplete symbols. This improper use, however, is permissible only when a transformation into proper use is possible, i.e., if the sentence can be translated into one or more sentences which have only proper names in their subject positions. More about this later. Thus, in improper use, incomplete symbols are used if they designated an object in the same way as an object name. One even speaks of "their designata", consciously or unconsciously introducing the fiction that there are such things. We wish to retain this fiction for reasons of utility. But, in order to remain perfectly aware of this fictional character, we will not say that an incomplete symbol designates an "object", but that it designates a *quasi object*. (In our view, even the so-called "general objects", e.g., "a dog" or "dogs" are already quasi objects.)

> EXAMPLES. If, for example, "Fido" and "Caro" are proper names of dogs, then the sentences "Fido is a dog" and "Caro is a dog" have the common constituent ". . . is a dog". This is an incomplete symbol (a propositional function, cf. § 28). Analogously, one finds as the common constituent of other sentences ". . . is a cat". This shares with the previous one the constituent ". . . is . . .", while the remainders ". . . a dog" and ". . . a cat" remain as incomplete symbols of a different sort. Let us now try to express the fact that all dogs are mammals. If we wanted to retain the sentence form ". . . is . . .", where the subject position is properly occupied by an object name, we would have to form the following complicated sentence: "it holds for all values of variable x that "x is a dog" implies "x is a mammal". Instead, we form a new sentence form by allowing ourselves to introduce an incomplete symbol into the subject position as if it were an object name. We say, "A dog is a mammal." In this sentence, no object name occurs, but we say about the incomplete symbol "a dog" that, while it does not designate an object, it designates a *quasi object* (since it occupies a position in the sentence as if it designated an object).
>
> If we want to get a more precise grasp of the indicated relations, then we will have to replace by logical symbols all those parts of the sentences which designate not extralogical entities, but logical relations. The meaning of these symbols becomes apparent through a comparison with the above-mentioned sentences ("logistic formulation of the logical skeleton," § 46). To begin with, we have the sentences, "Fido ε dog", "Caro ε dog", then the incomplete symbols ". . . ε dog" and ". . . ε cat" (or "x ε dog", and "x ε cat"); these designate propositional func-

tions. Furthermore, we have the incomplete symbols "dog" and "cat", which designate classes. In the sentence "dog ⊂ mammal", the class symbol is used like an object name. (About ⊂, cf. § 33.) Since all class symbols are introduced for precisely this purpose, it follows that all classes are quasi objects (§ 33).

The form of the sentence "dog ⊂ mammal", as containing no object symbols, only class symbols, can be justified only through the fact that it can be transformed into a sentence in which only proper names occur in the subject position, namely, into the above-mentioned sentence with variable *x*. Further investigation would show that the classes "dog" and "mammal" are complexes of individual animals (§ 36).

The "objects" of science are almost without exception quasi objects. Present-day nominalism would find this quite acceptable if it held merely for general concepts (cf. § 5), but it also holds for most individual objects of scientific investigation, as construction theory will show (cf. § 158 about individual and general objects).

The two *ascension forms* of construction which will be used in our system and which will be discussed in the sequel *are forms of quasi objects*.

REFERENCES. The theory of the incomplete symbols originated with Frege [Funktion], [Grundges.] I, 5; Russell gives extensive comments [Princ. Math.] I, 69 ff., [Math. Phil.] 182 ff. As indicated, our position is even more radical, but we cannot give a full account of the matter at this time.

The position which treats general objects as quasi objects is closely related to *nominalism*. It must be emphasized, however, that this position concerns only the problem of the *logical function* of symbols (words) which designate general objects. The question whether these designata have reality (in the metaphysical sense) is not thereby answered in the negative, but is not even posed (cf. VD).

28. *Propositional Functions*

If we delete from a sentence one or more object names (i.e., at first proper names, but then also names of quasi objects), then we say of the remaining incomplete symbol that it designates a *propositional function*. By introducing the deleted names as *arguments* into the blanks (the *argument positions*), we regain the original sentence. But, in order to produce some sentence, either true or false, we do not have to introduce precisely the deleted names, but can take others as long as they make sense together with the incomplete symbol. We call them *permissible arguments* of the propositional function. Instead of leaving the argument positions empty, it is better to mark them with the sign of a *variable*.

If the introduction of an object results in a true sentence, then we say that this object *satisfies* the propositional function. All other objects, as long as they are permissible arguments, result in a false sentence. A propositional function with precisely one argument position we call a *property* or *property concept*. All objects which satisfy this function "have" the property or "fall under" the (property) concept. A propositional function with two or more argument positions we call a (two-place or many-place) *relation* or a *relational concept*. Of the pairs, triples, etc., which satisfy this function, we say that the relation "holds for them" or "obtains" between them or the objects "stand in this relation" to one another. Thus every propositional function represents a concept, viz., either a property or a relation.

> EXAMPLES: Propositional functions: a. *Property*. From the sentence "Berlin is a city in Germany" results, by deletion of the subject term "Berlin", a propositional function with one argument position, namely, ". . . is a city in Germany" or "x is a city in Germany". It represents the property of being a city in Germany, or, more briefly, the concept "city in Germany". This incomplete symbol is turned into a true sentence by substituting the name "Hamburg", into a false sentence through substitution of the name "Paris", while substituting the word "moon" produces a meaningless string of words. Thus we say that Hamburg, but not Paris, falls under the concept "city in Germany"; while the object moon neither does nor does not fall under this concept, for the moon is not, unlike Berlin and Paris, a permissible argument of the function.
>
> b. *Relation*. From the sentence "Berlin is a city in Germany" results, by deletion of the two object names "Berlin" and "Germany", a propositional function with two argument positions, namely, ". . . is a city in . . ." or "x is a city in y". It represents the two-place relation between a city and the country in which this city lies. This incomplete symbol is turned into a true sentence by substituting the pair of names "Munich, Germany", into a false sentence through substitution of the words "Munich, England", and into a meaningless string of words by substituting the words "moon, Germany". Thus, Munich stands to Germany, but not to England, in the indicated relation, while one may not assert either that the relation holds, or that it does not hold, for the pair "moon, Germany".

29. *Isogeny; Object Spheres*

Two objects (and this always includes quasi objects) are said to be *isogenous* if there is an argument position in any propositional function for which the two object names are permissible arguments. If this is the case, then it holds for any argument position of any propositional function either that both names are permissible arguments, or that neither of them is. This is a consequence of the logical theory of types, which we cannot here discuss in detail. If two objects are not isogenous, then they are termed *allogeneous*.

> EXAMPLES. In Example a) of the preceding section, Hamburg and Paris turned out to be isogenous; the moon, on the other hand, was allogeneous relative to both Hamburg and Paris. In Example b), Berlin and Munich showed themselves to be isogenous, and also Germany and England. "Moon, Germany" was not a permissible pair of arguments. From this it does not follow that neither of them is a permissible argument for the position in question, but that at least one of them is not. Since Germany was a permissible argument for its position, it follows that the moon is not a permissible argument. Thus the moon is allogeneous relative to both Berlin and Munich.

By the *sphere* of an object we mean the class of all objects which are isogenous with the given object. (Since isogeny is transitive, the object spheres are mutually exclusive.) If every object of a given object type is isogenous with every object of another object type, then we call the object types themselves "isogenous". Correspondingly, we also speak of "allogeneous" object types. For *pure* object types, these are the only possible cases; that is to say, we call an object type pure, if all its objects are isogenous with one another, i.e., if the type is a subclass of an object sphere. All other types we call *impure*. Only the pure types are logically unobjectionable concepts; only they have classes as extensions (cf. § 32 f.). However, in the practical pursuit of science the impure types play an important role. Thus the main object types, namely, the physical, the psychological, and the cultural are impure types, as we shall see.

30. *"Confusion of Spheres" as a Source of Error*

If we wish to test whether or not two objects are isogenous, and if the statements about these objects are expressed in a word language, then we have to ascertain ultimately whether or not a string of words forms a meaningful sentence. This test frequently becomes quite complicated through a special sort of ambiguity of language. This ambiguity is frequently overlooked and has thereby caused considerable philosophical difficulties; in particular, it has very markedly retarded progress in the task with which we are presently concerned, namely, the formation of a conceptual system, and it complicates this task even now. We are here not concerned with straightforward ambiguity (homonymy) as it occurs, e.g., in such words as "cock", "spring", etc., nor with somewhat more subtle ambiguities as they occur in many expressions of ordinary life, of science and of philosophy, as, for example, in the words "representation", "value", "objective", "idea", etc. In our daily lives, we are well aware of the first type of ambiguity, while in philosophy we concern ourselves with the second, and we can thus avoid at least the more obvious mistakes. Let me explain, by way of example, the third type of ambiguity, the one which concerns us here. The expression "thankful" seems unambiguous when it is taken in its root sense (i.e., setting aside any use of the term in a metaphorical sense; this would fall under the second type of ambiguity considered above, e.g., when "thankful" is used relative to a task or work). However, we not only say of a person that he is thankful, but also of his character, of a look, of a letter, of a people. Now each of these five objects belongs to a different sphere. It follows from the theory of types that the properties of objects which belong to different spheres themselves belong to different spheres. Thus, there are five concepts, "thankful", which belong to different spheres, the confusion of which would lead to contradictions. However, generally speaking, there is no danger that we might draw an invalid conclusion since precisely the fact that these objects are of different spheres keeps us from misunderstanding which of the five concepts is meant. In general, using only one word for these different objects is innocuous, and therefore useful and justifiable. This ambiguity must be noted only if finer distinctions between concepts are to be made, distinctions which are important for epistemological and metaphysical problems. Neglect of the difference between concepts of different spheres, we call *confusion of spheres*.

REFERENCES. There has been no explicit recognition of the indicated type of ambiguity in logic. But it bears a certain resemblance to the multiplicity of "suppositions" of a word which the Schoolmen used to distinguish; cf. Erdmann [Bedeutung] 66 ff. It is more closely related to the *theory of types* which Russell has developed in order to overcome the logical paradoxes and which he has utilized in his logistic system [Types], [Princ. Math.], I, 39 ff., 168 ff., [Math. Phil.] 133 ff., cf. Carnap [Logistik] § 9. However, Russell has applied this theory only to formal-logical structures, not to a system of concrete concepts (more precisely: only to variables and logical constants, not to nonlogical constants). Our object spheres are Russell's "types" applied to extralogical concepts. Thus, the justification for making a distinction between the various object spheres and for claiming that there were five concepts, "thankful", in the preceding example is derived from the theory of types, even though the examples may not have sounded very persuasive since they were given in a word language. Although the theory of types is not generally accepted, none of its opponents has been able to produce a logical system which could avoid the contradictions (the so-called paradoxes) from which the older logic suffers, without using a theory of types.

That the indicated ambiguity can become a source of error in the investigation of isogeny is obvious from an inspection of the five objects of which thankfulness can be asserted and which one could erroneously presume to be isogenous on the basis of the criterion of § 29. The following example will make the matter more clear.

31. *An Application*

EXAMPLE. Let us investigate, to begin with, which objects are isogenous with a (definite, particular) stone. Sentences about this stone would be, for example, "The stone is red", "The stone weighs 5 kg.", "The stone lies in Switzerland", "The stone is hard". These sentences are unquestionably meaningful; it makes no difference whether they are true or false. Now we must substitute in these sentences the names of the objects we want to test, and must ascertain whether or not the sentences still have a meaning. It is of no concern whether the sentences become true or false. If we wish to apply the test to another stone or to a chicken, we will find that meaningful sentences result. Thus these objects are isogenous with the first stone (if we were to continue our investigation, we should find that they all belong to the sphere of physical bodies). On the other hand, the following list of objects which begins with the stone, does not contain any further object which is isogenous with the stone, for in no case do we obtain a meaningful sentence when we substitute the appropriate name for the name of the stone.

List of representative objects: (physical [30] objects): a particular stone, aluminum; (psychological objects): a (certain, particular) worry, the vivacity of Mr. N.; (cultural objects): the constitution of the Reich, expressionism; (biological objects): the Mongolian race, heredity of acquired traits; (mathematical and logical objects): the Pythagorean theorem, the number 3; (phenomenal [31] objects): the color green, a certain melody; (objects of physics [32]): the electrical elementary quan-

---

[30] physisch
[31] sinnesphänomenologisch
[32] physikalische Gegenstände

tum, the melting point of ice; (ethical object): the categorical imperative; (temporal object): the present day.

The following cases will show how the above-mentioned ambiguity (confusion of spheres) renders more difficult the test for isogeny and increases the likelihood of error: the sentences, "The stone is hard" and "The stone is red" seem to be meaningful also for aluminum, i.e., the first sentence true and the second false. Only the realization that the other two sentences about the stone ("It weighs 5 kg.", "It lies in Switzerland") are meaningless for aluminum shows that the two objects belong to different spheres. This leads to a more detailed investigation of the matter and leads to the recognition that the properties "red" and "hard" relative to a thing are not the same as the properties "red" and "hard" relative to a substance.

The example shows that it is frequently necessary to consider several different sentences in testing isogeny. Otherwise, one may be misled by the fact that words are frequently impure as far as spheres are concerned.

A more detailed investigation of the above list of objects would show that the indicated objects all belong to different spheres. One can show this for the first object, the stone, by means of the above-stated four sentences. We have already seen that some of these sentences seem to indicate isogeny with other objects on the list. Taken together, however, they show that the stone does not belong to the same sphere with any of the objects mentioned subsequently. There is no other object name on the list which would result even in apparently meaningful sentences in all four cases. The test for every other object on the list could be carried out accordingly.

The fact that the objects on the list belong to different object spheres means that each of them represents a different object sphere. Now the list can easily be extended at will in such a way that all further objects are also all from different spheres; thus we see that the number of different object spheres is large. At the moment, there is no way of telling whether this number is finite. In other words, not only is the number of object types which are coördinated with one another (e.g., as the species in a classification) very large, but also the number of object types which are *toto coelo* different from one another. (They are *toto coelo* different from one another in that each of them has its own *coelum,* its own object sphere.)

In the list of objects given above, several object types are represented by more than one object. Since these objects are not isogenous, this means that these object types are impure. It holds almost without exception that the traditional object types which are found in the sciences are almost always impure, i.e., they are not logically permissible concepts (e.g., physical, psychological, etc.).

32. The Extension of a Propositional Function

If two propositional functions stand to one another in such a relation that every object (or couple, triple, etc.) which satisfies the first also satisfies the second, then we say that the first *universally implies* the second. If two propositional functions stand to one another in a relation of mutual universal implication, then they are called universally equivalent or *coextensive*. Hence, coextensive propositional functions are satisfied by exactly the same arguments. If we assign the same symbol to propositional functions that are coextensive and if we from then on use only these new symbols, then we obviously disregard all points of difference between coextensive propositional functions and express only those factors in which they agree. Such a procedure we call an *extensional procedure;* the symbols which are the same for all coextensive propositional functions we call *extension symbols.* They have no independent meaning and they may be used only if we indicate for all sentence forms in which they are to be used how such sentences may be transformed into sentences in which extension symbols no longer occur; thus, in translating back, we replace these symbols by the appropriate propositional functions (more precisely, each extension symbol is replaced by any one of the coextensive propositional functions to which it was assigned). The extension symbols have no independent meaning, i.e., they are incomplete symbols (to an even higher degree than propositional functions). Nevertheless, in conformity with the customary usage, we speak of them as if there were objects which they designate. These objects we call *extensions.* Thus, extensions, too, are quasi objects. For example, we say of two coextensive propositional functions that they have the same extension (hence the word "coextensive"), since they have assigned to them the same extension symbol. Furthermore, if there are two propositional functions which are so related that each object (couple, triple, etc.) which satisfies the first also satisfies the second, then it is easily seen that the relation of universal implication is also fulfilled if each of these two propositional functions is replaced by another, coextensive, one. It is for this reason that we can express this relation with the aid of extension symbols; the symbol ⊂ between two extension symbols is defined as indicating the universal implication between the corresponding propositional functions. If we now speak again as if there were objects which are designated by extension symbols, we may say the sentence "$a \subset b$" means "(the extension) a is contained in (the extension) b." We call this relation between two extensions *inclusion* or *subsumption*.

Given a propositional function, we form a *symbol for its extension* by enclosing the propositional function in parentheses and by writing in front of it the appropriate variables with accents: $\hat{x}\hat{y}(. . . x . . . y . . .)$. We shall give examples during the following discussion of the two kinds of extensions, namely, classes and relation extensions.

33. *Classes*

The extension of a propositional function with only one argument position, i.e., the extension of a property, is called a *class*. Thus, coextensive properties have the same class. An object o which satisfies a given propositional function is called an *element* of the corresponding class, call it a. (In symbols, $o \, \epsilon \, a$); o "belongs to" class a (not "is included in"!). If a class a is included in class b (in the above-defined sense of subsumption), then a is called a *subclass* of b (in symbols: $a \subset b$).

> Let me briefly discuss some main concepts of the theory of classes. The class of objects which do not belong to a certain class a is called the "negate" or "complement" of a (in symbols, $-a$). $-a$, of course, does not comprise all remaining objects, but only the permissible but not satisfying arguments. To the "intersection" of two classes ($a \cap b$) belong all those objects which are elements of both a and b. To the "union" of two classes ($a \cup b$) belong those objects which are elements of at least one of them. The union of a class with its complement forms the object sphere of elements of this class, for it comprises all permissible arguments of the corresponding propositional function.

Classes, since they are extensions, are quasi objects. Thus the class symbols do not have independent meaning; they are merely aids for making statements about all the objects which satisfy a given propositional function without having to enumerate them one by one. Thus the class symbol represents, as it were, that which these objects, i.e., the elements of that class, have in common.

> EXAMPLE. Let us assume, for example, that the propositional function "x is a man" is satisfied by the same objects as the propositional function "x is a rational animal" and "x is a featherless biped." Thus

these three propositional functions are coextensive, and we assign to them the same extension symbol, e.g., ma (i.e., we define: $ma =_{df} \hat{x} \, (x$ is a man), cf. § 32). Since this is a propositional function with only one argument position, ma is a class symbol. Moreover, ma is an incomplete symbol; by itself it means nothing, but the sentences in which it occurs have meaning, since it is clear how this class symbol can be eliminated from them. For example, the sentence "$d \, \epsilon \, ma$" can be transformed into the sentence "d is a man" or "d is a featherless biped". Even though ma itself does not designate anything, one speaks of "the designatum of ma" as if it were an object. We want to be somewhat more cautious and call it a quasi object. It is "the class of all men", i.e., the extension of the propositional function "x is a man".

We must emphasize the fact that classes are quasi objects in relation to their elements, and that they belong to different spheres. This is important because a class is frequently confounded with the whole that consists of the elements of that class. These wholes, however, are not quasi objects relative to their parts, but are isogenous with them. We shall discuss the difference between classes and wholes, and the fact that elements belong to different spheres from their classes, more thoroughly in the sequel (§ 37).

REFERENCES. The theory of propositional functions and their extensions originated with Frege [Funktion] [Grundges.] (Frege calls them *Wertverläufe*) and was utilized by Whitehead and Russell in their system of logistics ([Princ. Math.], cf. also [Math. Phil.], 157 ff.). A good exposition is also found in Keyser [Math. Phil.] 49 ff.; Keyser gives an interesting elaboration of the concept of a propositional function in the form of his "doctrinal function" ("Theoriefunktion", 58 ff.). Cf. Carnap [Logistik] § 8.

Frege has already shown that extension symbols, and thus the class symbols, are *incomplete symbols* (cf. the quotations in § 27). According to Russell, it is irrelevant for logic whether or not there are actual objects which are designated by class symbols, since classes are not defined by themselves, but only in the context of total sentences ("no class theory"). More recently, Russell has expressed himself even more strongly and has called classes logical fictions or symbolic fictions [External W.] 206 ff., [Math. Phil.] 182 ff. This corresponds to our notion of classes as quasi objects. Furthermore, according to Russell, classes are sharply distinguished from their elements in that no statement can be meaningful for a class (i.e., either true or false), if it is meaningful for one of its elements (theory of types). This corresponds to our notion that classes and their elements belong to different spheres (§ 37).

34. *Relation Extensions*

The extension of a propositional function with several argument positions, i.e., of a relation [33] is called a *relation extension*.[34] Thus relation extensions stand in exact formal analogy to classes which are the extensions of propositional functions with only one argument position, i.e., properties. Hence we can here be somewhat briefer, since by virtue of the analogy some points will be clear without further explanation. Like classes, relation extensions are *quasi objects*.

Coextensive relations correspond to the same relation extension. A pair of objects x, y (the same holds for triples, quadruples, etc.) which satisfies a given propositional function and thus all propositional functions coextensive with it is called an *ordered pair* (or triple, etc.) of the relation extension which corresponds to the propositional function (xQy, where Q designates the relation extension). Since it is not generally permissible to interchange the argument positions of a propositional function, the different members of an ordered pair (or triple, etc.) must be differentiated. In an ordered pair (i.e., in the case of a two-place relation extension), we call them referent and relatum. Relation extensions have the capacity to produce order, and this capacity derives from the differentiation between their various argument positions. Hence the importance of the theory of relations for the exhibition of order in any subject area whatever.

Relation extensions are quasi objects. Nevertheless, in order to aid intuition, language treats them as if they were a third thing which is suspended between the two members. Through this reification, the linguistic expression becomes more graphic, and it is not often dangerous since we are for the most part conscious of it as a figurative and improper mode of speech. For the sake of simplicity, we follow common usage in this case as well and use symbols of relation extensions as if they were names of objects, but, in order to emphasize the improper mode of expression, we call them quasi objects.

Let us briefly indicate some main concepts of the elementary theory of relations. The class of the possible referents of a relation extension Q is called the "domain" of Q (in symbols: D'Q). The class of possible relata is called the "converse domain" (D'Q). If domain and converse domain are isogenous with one another, then the relation extension is

---

[33] Beziehung
[34] Relation

called *homogeneous*; in this case there exists a union of domain and converse domain, called the *field* of Q (C‘Q). The relation extension which holds for all Q pairs in opposite direction is called the *converse* of Q (Q̆). If *aPb* and *bQc* both hold, then there is a relation extension for *a* and *c*, called the *relative product* of P and Q (P|Q). *Powers of relations*: R^2 means $R|R$, R^3 means $R^2|R$, etc. R_{po} means the union of the powers (*power relation* or *chain*); R^0 means identity in the field of R.

The concepts of symmetry, reflexivity, transitivity, and connectedness have been explained above (§ 11). A relation extension is called *one-many* if, for each relatum, there exists only one referent; it is called *many-one* if, for each referent, there exists only one relatum. If both conditions are fulfilled, it is called *one-one*.

A relation extension R is called a *correlator* between two relation extensions P and Q if it establishes a one-one correspondence between the elements of P and the elements of Q such that to each pair of P there corresponds a pair of Q and vice versa. If such a correlator exists for two relation extensions P and Q, then P and Q are called *isomorphic* or *of the same structure*. This corresponds to our earlier graphic definition of structural equivalence with the aid of the arrow diagram. We now can give an exact definition of the structure or relation number [35] of a relation extension P: it is the class of relation extensions which are isomorphic to P. (Cf. the analogous definition of cardinal number, § 40.)

35. *Reducibility and Construction*

Above (§ 2), we have explained the concept of reducibility with the aid of the imprecise concept of the "transformation" of a statement. We must now indicate more precisely what is to be meant by a "transformation". To this end we can now utilize the concept of coextensiveness (or universal equivalence) of propositional functions (§ 32). We say that a proposition or propositional function is "exclusively about objects *a, b, . . .*" if, in its written expression, there appear as extralogical symbols only "*a*", "*b*", . . .; logical constants (§ 107) and general variables may also occur. If for each propositional function which is exclusively about objects *a, b, c* (where *b, c, . . .* may be absent) there exists a coextensive propositional function exclusively about *b, c, . . .* then *a* is said to be *reducible* to *b, c, . . .* Thus we can say more briefly but with less precision that *an object is said to be "reducible" to others, if all statements about it can be translated into statements which speak only about these other objects.*

---

[35] Relationszahl

In the simplest and most important case the object to be reduced occurs alone and without the other objects in the propositional function in question.

> EXAMPLE. "x is a prime number" is coextensive with "x is a natural number whose only divisors are 1 and x itself". The object (or concept) prime number is thereby reduced to these objects: natural number, 1, divisor.

The previously explained concept of a construction (§ 2) must now likewise be more precisely determined. By *constructing* a concept from other concepts, we shall mean the indication of its "constructional definition" on the basis of these other concepts. By a *constructional definition* of the concept a on the basis of concepts b and c, we mean a rule of translation which gives a general indication how any propositional function in which a occurs may be transformed into a coextensive propositional function in which a no longer occurs, but only b and c. In the simplest case, such a translation rule will consist in the prescription to replace a in all its occurrences by a certain expression in which only b and c occur ("explicit" definition).

If a concept is reducible to others, then it must indeed be possible in principle to construct it from them. However, if one knows that a concept is so reducible, one does not thereby know how it is constructed, since the formulation of a general transformation rule for all statements about this concept is a separate problem.

> EXAMPLE. The reducibility of fractions to natural numbers is easily understood, and a given statement about certain fractions can easily be transformed into a statement about natural numbers (cf. § 2). On the other hand, the construction, for example, of the fraction 2/7, i.e., the indication of a rule through which all statements about 2/7 can be transformed into statements about 2 and 7, is much more complicated (cf. § 40). Whitehead and Russell have solved this problem for all mathematical concepts [Princ. Math.]; thus they have produced a "constructional system" of the mathematical concepts.

36. *Complex and Whole*

If an object is logically reducible to others, then we call it a *logical complex* or, in brief, a *complex* of these other objects, which we shall call its *elements*. According to what we have said above (§§ 33, 34), classes and relation extensions are examples of complexes.

If an object stands to other objects in a relation such that they are its parts relative to an extensive medium, e.g., space or time, then we call the first object the *extensive whole* or, in brief, the *whole* of the other objects. The whole *consists* of its parts.

The difference between a complex and a whole must not be confounded with the difference between a "true whole" ("organic whole", "Gestalt") and "(mere) collection" (or "sum"); the second distinction is important for psychology and biology, but is not of the same fundamental importance for construction theory as the first one, since it is merely a differentiation between two types of wholes. Moreover, it is doubtful whether this second distinction is not actually a mere difference in degree, i.e., whether it is not perhaps the case that all wholes have, to more or less high degree, all properties which are generally attributed only to "true wholes". Perhaps there are no mere collections at all. However, no final decision can be made in this matter, since so far no sufficiently precise definition of true whole and *Gestalt* is available.

REFERENCES. Driesch ([Ordnungsl.] [Ganze] esp. 4) differentiates the *whole* (in the sense of the true or organic whole) from the *sum* by saying that it loses essential properties if a part is taken away from it. *Gestalt* theory is concerned with entities which are characterized by the fact that "properties and functions of a part depend upon its position in the whole to which it belongs" (Köhler [Gestaltprobl.] 514; cf. also Wertheimer [Gestaltth.]). The close connection between the two definitions is obvious; *examples* which fall under both definitions are: an organism as the whole of its members, a melody as the whole of its tones, a house as the whole of its stones. On the other hand, it is very difficult to find an example of a mere collection; even a stone as the collection of its molecules and a heap of stones as the collection of its stones are true wholes. It is questionable whether, for example, the totality of all the iron on earth could be called a mere collection.

To be sure, the concepts whole and complex are not mutually exclusive; but construction theory is especially concerned with those complexes which do not consist of their elements, as a whole consists of its parts. Such complexes we call *autonomous complexes*. Thus we differentiate a whole from an autonomous complex by the fact that in the former the elements are parts in the extensive sense; in the latter, they are not.

From the definition of construction and complex, it follows that, if an object is constructed from other objects, then it is a complex of them. *Thus all objects of a constructional system are complexes of the basic objects of the system.*

If we are concerned with a statement about a quasi object, i.e., a statement which is expressed in the form of a sentence in which an incomplete symbol occurs in a position where the sentence structure originally allows only an object name, then this use of the incomplete symbol must be defined; it must be possible to translate this sentence into another sentence, where we find only proper object names in argument (e.g., subject) positions. From this it follows that a quasi object which belongs to a certain object domain is always a complex of the objects of this domain; i.e., it is an autonomous complex and not the whole of its elements. For a whole is an object of the same object type as its elements. Since classes are quasi objects relative to their elements, it follows that they are autonomous complexes of these elements (cf. § 37); relation extensions are likewise autonomous complexes of their members.

37. *A Class Does Not Consist of Its Elements*

We say of a class and of a whole that they "correspond" to one another when the parts of the whole are the elements of the class. Since a whole can be divided into parts in various ways, there are always many classes which correspond to one whole. On the other hand, to each class there corresponds at most one whole, for the elements are uniquely determined through the class, and two objects which consist of the same parts are identical. Now, if a class were to consist of its elements (i.e., if it were identical with the whole that corresponds to it), then all those many classes which correspond to the same whole would be identical with one another. But, as we have seen, they are different from one another. *Thus, classes cannot consist of their elements as a whole consists of its parts.* Classes are quasi objects relative to their elements; they are complexes of their elements, and, since they do not consist of these elements, they are autonomous complexes of their elements.

The same holds for the mathematical concept of a *set*, which corresponds to the logical concept of a class. A set, too, does not consist of its elements. This is important to notice, since the character of a whole or a collection (or of an "aggregate") has erroneously been connected with the concept of a set ever since its inception (i.e., ever since Cantor's definition). In set theory itself, this notion does not generally have any consequences, but it seems to be the reason that the methodologically most advantageous and logically unobjectionable form of definition for the concept of power (or cardinal number), one of the central concepts of set theory, is frequently opposed (cf. § 41).

> EXAMPLE. One can envisage the organs or the cells or the atoms as parts of the whole *dog*. On the other hand, the class of the organs of

the dog, the class of its cells, the class of its atoms, are three different classes, each with different elements. Each of them has a different cardinality; consequently, they cannot be identical. All these different classes correspond to the whole which is the dog. Since these classes are not identical with one another, they can also not be identical with the whole which is the dog. They are of the same logical status because the various different partitions are of the same logical status; thus, it also cannot be that at least one of the classes is identical with the whole.

REFERENCES. Frege has already expressed very clearly the thesis of this section. "The extension of a concept does not consist of the objects which fall under the concept." [Krit.] 455. Russell has made the same point by calling attention to unit classes and null classes [Math. Phil.] 184. Cf. also the very pertinent remarks of Weyl [Handb.] 11.

Thus, not only is it not the case that a class is identical with the whole corresponding to it; it even belongs to a different sphere. As we have seen, extensions are quasi objects relative to their elements. Thus we see that it is part of the logical doctrine that an extension cannot be a permissible argument for the same argument position of the propositional function for which its elements are permissible arguments. *Nothing can be asserted of a class that can be asserted of its elements, and nothing can be asserted of a relation extension that can be asserted of its members.* (The well-known theorem of logic, that one cannot say of a class either that it does, or that it does not, belong to itself, is only a special case of this.)

Since a whole is isogenous with its parts while a class does not belong to the same sphere as its elements, it follows that a class is allogeneous to the whole that corresponds to it.

EXAMPLE. The difference between a wall as the whole of its bricks and the class of these bricks becomes especially clear through the fact that the wall is, but the class is not, isogenous with the bricks. This follows from an application of the criterion which employs propositional functions (§ 29). The propositional functions "x is made of burnt clay", "x is rectangular", "x is hard", are satisfied by a brick as well as by the wall; the propositional functions "x is of one color", "x is (spatially) small" are satisfied by a brick, and either they or their negations are satisfied by the wall. At any rate, for all five propositional functions, brick and wall are permissible arguments. On the other hand, the class of bricks is not a permissible argument for any of these propositional functions. It is a permissible argument for the propositional function "x has the cardinal number 100", "x is a subclass of the class of bricks in general"; for these, neither the wall nor a brick is a permissible argument.

38. *Construction Takes Place Through Definition*

If, in the course of the formation of the constructional system, a new object is "constructed", then this means, according to our definition of construction, that it is shown how statements about it can be transformed into statements about the basic objects of the system or the objects which have been constructed prior to the object in question. Thus a rule must be given which enables us to eliminate the name of the new object in all sentences in which it could occur; in other words, *a definition* of the name of the object must be given.

Now, two different cases must be distinguished. In the simpler case, a symbol can be introduced which is composed out of already known symbols (i.e., out of the basic symbols and other already defined ones) such that this symbol can always be put in the place of a new object symbol if this is to be eliminated. Here, the construction takes place by way of an *explicit definition:* the new symbol is declared to have the same meaning as the compound one. In this case, the new object is not a quasi object relative to certain of the older objects, since what it is can be explicitly indicated. Thus, it remains within one of the already formed object spheres, even if we should consider it as a representative of a new object type. We have already seen that the differentiation of types, unlike the opposition between spheres, is not logically precise but depends upon practical purposes of classification.

The second case arises when no explicit definition is possible. In this case, a special kind of definition is required, namely, the so-called "definition in use".

39. *Definitions in Use*

If no explicit definition is possible for an object, then its object name, given in isolation, does not designate anything in the manner of already constructed objects; in this case, we are confronted with a quasi object relative to the already constructed objects. However, if an object is to be called "constructed on the basis of the previous objects," then it must nevertheless be possible to transform the propositions about it into propositions in which only the previous objects occur, even though there is no symbol for this object which is composed of the symbols of the already constructed objects. Thus we must have a translation rule which generally determines the transformation operation for the statement form in which the new object name is to occur. In contrast to an explicit definition, such an introduction of a new symbol is called a *definition in use* (*definitio in usu*), since it does not explain the new symbol itself—which, after all, does not have any meaning by itself—but only its use in complete sentences.

> REFERENCES. Cf. Russell [Princ. Math.] I, 25, 69. The expression "implicit definition" is customary for an entirely different determination of objects through axiomatic systems and should be reserved for this purpose. (Cf. § 15). Occasionally, when one is concerned with the contrast between implicit and explicit definitions, both, definitions in use and explicit definitions proper, are called "explicit definitions in the wider sense."

In order for a translation rule to be applicable to all sentences of a certain sentence form, it must refer to propositional functions. It must equate with one another the expressions for two propositional functions, one of which contains the new object name, while the other contains only old ones, and both of which must contain the same variables. Under these conditions, the second expression is to be considered a translation of the first. A simple consideration shows that we have to proceed in this way. If the expression which contains the new symbol were not to contain any variables (i.e., if it were not the expression for a propositional function, but for a proposition, i.e., a sentence), then the rule would not hold for different sentences, but only for this one. And if this expression contains variables, then the translation which is prescribed by the rule must contain the same variables, since otherwise it would not tell us how, in the application to a sentence which is to be translated, the object names which occur in the argument positions are to be transferred to the new sentence.

> EXAMPLES. The form of an explicit definition is probably well enough known, but it is important that its distinction from a definition in use should become as clear as possible. If the number 1 and the operation + are known, then the other numbers can be defined explicitly: "$2 =_{df} 1 + 1$", "$3 =_{df} 2 + 1$", etc. ("$=_{df}$" is to be read as "equals by definition" or "is always replaceable by").
>
> *Definition in use.* Let us assume that the concepts of a natural number and of multiplication are known. The concept of *prime number* is to be introduced. The expression "prime number" cannot be defined

explicitly in the way in which we have previously defined the symbols "2" and "3". Thus it might seem as if a definition of the following form would be permissible: "prime numbers $=_{df}$ those numbers which . . ." or "A prime number $=_{df}$ a number which . . ." But a definition of this form only appears explicit; this deception is brought about by the linguistic forms which make it appear as if such expressions as "the prime numbers" or "a prime number" designate objects, since they use such expressions as subjects of sentences. Expressions such as "those which . . ." or "a . . ." are already (very useful) abbreviations for *definitions in use;* they correspond to the class symbols of logic. The prime number concept is not a proper object relative to the numbers 1, 2, 3, . . . Thus it can be defined only in use by indicating which meaning a sentence of the form "a is a prime number" is to have, where a is a number. This meaning must be indicated by giving a propositional function which means the same as the propositional function "x is a prime number," and contains nothing but already known symbols, and which could thus serve as a translation rule for sentences of the form "n is a prime number". Thus, we could define: "x is a prime number" $=_{df}$ "x is a natural number and has only 1 and x as divisors."

40. *The Ascension Forms: Class and Relation Extension*

We have seen that the construction of an object has to take the form of a definition. Now a constructional definition is either explicit or it is a definition in use. In the first case, the object to be constructed is isogenous with some of the preceding objects (i.e., no new *constructional level* is reached through it). *Thus, the ascension to a new constructional level takes place always through a definition in use.* Now, every definition in use indicates that a propositional function which is expressed with the aid of a new symbol means the same as a propositional function which is expressed only with the older symbols. By "same meaning", we mean that both propositional functions are satisfied by the same objects. A propositional function which is coextensive with another one (§ 32) is satisfied by the same objects as the latter; hence, in a contextual definition we can always replace the second propositional function by any other propositional function which is coextensive with it. Thus, a propositional function which is expressed with the aid of the new symbol is not associated with just a single, determinate, previously introduced propositional function f, but with all propositional functions that are coextensive with f; in other words, the new propositional function is associated with the extension of f. Thus, we can interpret the new propositional function purely extensionally: we introduce the new symbol as an extension symbol. Thus, through a constructional definition which leads to a new constructional level, we always define either a class or a relation extension, depending upon whether the defining propositional function has only one argument position or whether it has several of them. Let us illustrate both forms with examples from arithmetic.

EXAMPLE. 1. *Class*. The cardinal numbers (or powers) are defined in logic as classes of equinumerous classes (or "sets"). Two classes are said to be equinumerous if there exists a one-to-one correspondence between them. Thus, for example, all classes which have five elements are equinumerous; the class on the second level which has all these classes as elements is then called the "cardinal number 5". The development of arithmetic on the basis of this definition shows that this definition is formally unobjectionable and satisfactory, since it allows us to derive all arithmetical properties of cardinal numbers and does not lead to contradictions. Nevertheless, there has been much opposition to this definition, not from logical, but from easily understandable intuitive motives. For example, the class to which supposedly belong all the classes of five objects in the world seems to be so boundless and comprehensive that its identity with the clearly delineated arithmetical entity, the cardinal number 5, appears to be absurd. However, this illusion rests solely upon the intuitive substitution of the class by the corresponding whole, which we have discussed above (cf. § 37). While this substitution is frequently useful, in this case it leads to errors. Let us return to our example: the class of the fingers of my right hand is not the whole "my right hand", and the class of all such classes of five objects does not consist of all hands, feet, piles of five stones, etc. This boundless collection would of course be quite useless as an arithmetical entity. Rather, we cannot say what the class of the fingers of my right hand is, because this class is only a quasi object (i.e., an autonomous complex). A symbol introduced for it would not have any meaning by itself, but would only serve to make statements about the fingers of my right hand, without having to enumerate these five objects one by one (i.e., statements about that which they have in common, for example, the properties of form, color, and matter, which these five fingers share). Likewise, one cannot say what the class of all classes of five objects itself is (i.e., the class of those classes, the elements of which can be brought into a one-to-one correspondence to the elements of the class of the fingers of my right hand). It, too, is only a quasi object (i.e., an autonomous complex). If we introduce a symbol for it—for example, cl_5—this symbol does not designate a proper object, but merely serves to make statements about the elements of this class (i.e., about all classes of five objects) without having to enumerate them one by one, which, in this case, would not be practicable anyway, because their number is infinite. Now, if cl_5 is a symbol which allows us to make statements about all those properties which all classes of five objects have in common, then what could be the difference between it and the arithmetical sign "5" (for the cardinal number)? The cardinal number 5 is a quasi object, just as the class cl_5 is; the symbol "5" does not designate a proper object, but only serves to make statements about those properties which all possible classes of five objects have in common. Thus, we see that the indicated definition of cardinal number does not replace the cardinal numbers by other schematically constructed entities, which have a certain formal analogy with cardinal numbers, but that this definition meets precisely the arithmetical concept itself. It is only the rarely articulated, but frequently tacit, conception of classes as wholes or collections which has obscured this fact.

REFERENCES. Frege was the first to give the above-mentioned definition of cardinal number: [Grundlg.] 79 ff., [Grundges.] I, 57. Russell has independently rediscovered it in 1901, and has applied it to the foundations of mathematics: [Principles] 114, [External W.] 199 ff., [Math. Phil.] 11, [Princ. Math.] I.

Objections of the indicated kind were made against this definition, for example, by: Hausdorff [Mengenl.] 46, J. Koenig [Logik] 226 note, cf. Fraenkel [Mengenl.] 44. The earlier Russell, in his attempt to stay as close as possible to common usage, has been guilty, in spite of his "no-class theory", of being not decisive enough in rejecting the interpretation of classes as wholes [Princ. Math.], [External W.] 126. Lately, he has definitely emphasized the differences between a class and "a pile or collection," in our terminology, wholes or collections [Math. Phil.] 184. Nevertheless, he believes that, with this definition of cardinal numbers, he has to accept an oddity, only in order to gain a definite, unambiguous concept [Math. Phil.] 18. Our conception agrees with that of Weyl [Handb.] 11.

EXAMPLE. 2. *Relation extension.* We have seen above that fractions can be reduced to natural numbers and that they therefore must be envisaged as complexes of natural numbers (§ 2). This means that fractions are independent complexes, namely, quasi objects, for they can be defined as relation extensions of natural numbers. For example, "$2/3 =_{df} \hat{x}\hat{y}$ (x and y are natural numbers, and it holds that $3x = 2y$)".

41. *The Constructional Levels*

If, in a constructional system of any kind, we carry out a step-by-step construction of more and more object domains by proceeding from any set of basic objects by applying in any order the class and relation construction, then these domains, which are all in different spheres and of which each forms a domain of quasi objects relative to the preceding domain, are called *constructional levels*. Hence, constructional levels are object spheres which are brought into a stratified order within the constructional system by constructing some of these objects on the basis of others. Here, the relativity of the concept "quasi object", which holds for any object on any constructional level relative to the object on the preceding level, is especially obvious.

It is now clear how the two seemingly contradictory theses of the unity of the object domain (§ 4) and the multiplicity of independent object types (§ 25) are to be reconciled. In a constructional system, all objects are constructed from certain basic objects, but in step-by-step formulation. It follows from the construction on the basis of the same basic objects that statements about all objects are transformable into statements about these basic objects so that, as far as the logical *meaning* of its statements is concerned, science is concerned with only one domain. This is the sense of the first thesis. On the other hand, in its practical procedures, science does not always make use of this transformability by actually transforming all its statements. Most of the statements of science are made in the form of statements about constructed entities, not about basic objects. And these constructed entities belong to different constructional levels which are all allogeneous to one another. As far as the logical *f rm* of its statements is concerned, science therefore is concerned with many autonomous object types. This is the sense of the second thesis. The compatibility of these two theses rests on the fact that it is possible to construct different allogeneous levels from the same basic objects.

42. *Being and Holding* [36] (May be omitted)

Following an occasionally used terminology, one could speak of the different "modes of being" [37] of the objects of different object spheres. This expression is particularly apt to make clear that allogeneous objects are completely dissimilar and cannot be compared. Fundamentally, the difference between being and holding, of which so much has been made in recent philosophy, goes back to the difference between object spheres, more precisely, to the difference between proper objects and quasi objects. For, if a quasi object is constructed on the basis of certain

[36] Sein und Gelten
[37] Seinsarten

elements, then it "holds" for these elements; thus it is distinguished as something that holds from the elements which have being. That a relation (extension) "holds" between its members is familiar terminology; we are less accustomed to saying that a class "holds" for its elements, though the expression could here be used with the same justification, since the relationship is the same in both cases. Construction theory goes beyond the customary conception of being and holding by claiming that this contrast does not arise only once, that there is only one boundary between being and holding, but that this relationship, constantly repeated, leads from level to level: what holds for objects of the first level has a second mode of being, and can in turn become the object of something that holds of it (on a third level) etc. So far as construction theory is concerned, this is the logically strict form of the dialectic of the conceptual process. Hence the concepts being and holding are relative and express the relation between each constructional level and the succeeding one.

> EXAMPLE. Stepwise progress of construction, in which the relationship between being and holding recurs several times: Classes are constructed from things. These classes do not consist of the things. They do not have being in the same sense as the things; rather, they hold for the things. These classes, even though they hold of things, can now be envisaged as having a second mode of being. From them we can proceed, for example, to the cardinal numbers, which hold for these classes. (For the construction of cardinal numbers as classes of classes, cf. § 40.) Cardinal numbers belong to a third mode of being and allow us to construct the fractions as relation extensions which hold for certain cardinal numbers (cf. § 40). These fractions can also be reified [38], that is, they can be envisaged as belonging to a fourth mode of being, and can be made elements of certain classes which hold for them, namely the real numbers. The latter belong to a fifth mode of being, while the complex numbers, being relation extensions that hold for certain real numbers, belong to a sixth mode of being, etc.

This example involves only six steps, but it gives an idea that construction will lead to completely different kinds of objects if many such steps are taken. Eventually we shall arrive at objects which do not disclose, at first sight, nay for which it seems impossible, that they are constructed from the basic objects. Hence the appearance of paradox in Kronecker's saying that all of mathematics treats of nothing but natural numbers, and even more in the thesis of construction theory that

---

[38] vergegenständlicht

the objects of all sciences are constructed from the same basic objects through nothing but the application of the ascension forms of class and relation extension.

43. *An Objection Against the Extensional Method of Construction*

We have seen earlier that a constructional definition in the form of a definition in use (§ 39) consists in declaring that two propositional functions have the same meaning. We have furthermore considered (§ 40) that the propositional function so introduced can be determined only as far as its extension is concerned and that it is therefore sufficient to introduce, by way of a constructional definition, merely the extension symbol of the propositional function rather than the propositional function itself. Through this procedure, concepts are defined only extensionally. We therefore speak of an *extensional method* of construction. It is based upon the *thesis of extensionality*: in every statement about a concept, this concept may be taken extensionally (i.e., it may be represented by its extension [class or relation extension]). More precisely: in every statement about a propositional function, the latter may be replaced by its extension symbol.

One could now object that difficulties might result from the extensional method when one proceeds from an extensionally defined concept to statements about it and then to other concepts. For traditional logic does not subscribe to the thesis of extensionality: it claims that not all statements about a concept can be brought into the form of an extension statement.

REFERENCES. The above objection is related to the old distinction between *extensional* and *intensional logic*. However, there is no exact criterion as to when a statement concerns the extension or the intension of a concept. This distinction became important when the first systems of logic or symbolic logic (Boole, Venn, and Schröder) not only developed logic as merely extensional, but confined the field even more by taking subsumption to be the only statement form. Proceeding from Frege's theories, Russell then went beyond this narrow limitation: his system combines intensional with extensional logic. Frege was the first who made precise the much-discussed and age-old distinction between intension and extension of a concept by differentiating the concept as a function, the values of which are truth values, from its course of values [39] (in our terminology, "propositional function" and "extension"). Utiliz-

[39] Wertverlauf

ing this distinction, Russell developed intensional logic as the theory of propositional functions and extensional logic as the theory of extensions (classes and relation extensions). In this system, even extensional logic contains not only subsumptive statements but a large number of statements which differ from one another by the kind of predicate they have, while intensional logic is not bound to any definite statement form. According to Russell's earlier opinions, statements of intensional logic are not all translatable into statements about extensions: [Princ. Math.] I, 76 ff., [Math. Phil.] 187 f. Wittgenstein has attacked this position [Abhandlg.] 243 f., and subsequently Russell has been inclined to abandon it: Preface to Wittgenstein [Abhandlg.] 194 ff., [Princ. Math.] I² pp. xiv and 659 ff.

From a position which is closely related to that of Wittgenstein, we shall show that the indicated conception is in fact not tenable. We shall show the validity of the thesis of extensionality, so that any objection against the extensional method loses all force.

The *objection to the extensional method* is aimed not only at the constructional system with which we are here concerned, but philosophers who stand aloof from mathematics have made it a principal objection to any formal method which uses predominantly extensions, especially when it is concerned, as we are here, not with purely logical, but with epistemological, problems. Now, Russell's formulation of the difference between "extensional" and "intensional" statements has so far been the only attempt to give a clear account of the extension-intension problem. Thus, in spite of Russell's own scruples, it is the strongest weapon which we can hand our opponents so that a valid decision may be achieved.

A statement is called *extensional* if it can be transformed into an extension statement (class or relation (extension) statement); otherwise, it is called *intensional*. It is a necessary and sufficient condition for the extensionality of a statement about a propositional function f that we can replace f by any coextensive propositional function without changing the truth value of the statement. The *thesis of extensionality* states that all statements about any propositional function are extensional (i.e., that there are no intensional statements).

REFERENCES. Russell [Princ. Math.] I, 72 ff. and [Math. Phil.] 187 f.; both give examples for (apparently) intensional statements.

EXAMPLE. Let us consider the coextensive propositional functions, "x is a man" and "x is a rational animal". The following statement about the first of these propositional functions is to be evaluated with respect to its extensionality: " "x is a man" universally implies (i.e., for all values of its argument) "*x* is mortal" ". We do not have to investigate whether this statement is true or false. It retains, in any case, its truth value (i.e., it remains true or false) if, in place of "*x* is a man", we put the coextensive propositional function "*x* is a rational animal" or any other coextensive propositional function whatever. Thus the criterion is fulfilled and the implication statement in question is shown to be extensional. That it can in fact be transformed into an extension statement, more precisely, into a class statement, can easily be shown: "The class of all men is contained in the class of all mortals". (Here, the second propositional function has been transformed at the same time.)

As a counter-example, let us consider the following statement about the same propositional function: "I believe that "*x* is a man" universally implies "*x* is mortal" ". Here, we may not simply replace "*x* is a man" by some other coextensive propositional function. For one cannot conclude, from the given statement, whether my thinking and believing was at all concerned with other coextensive concepts, for example, with the concept, "rational animal". The above statement, "I believe that . . ." thus seems to be a nonextensional, i.e., intensional, statement about the propositional function, "*x* is a man". We shall later on return to this example and to the thesis of extensionality, but, at this point, I wish to introduce some new concepts which are required for the solution of this problem.

44. *The Distinction Between Sign Statements, Sense Statements, and Nominatum Statements*

In order to give a foundation for the thesis of extensionality and thus to justify the extensional method of construction, we have to introduce another, more general, classification of statements than the above-discussed distinction between extensional and intensional statements about propositional functions. This classification will be concerned not only with statements about propositional functions, but with statements about any objects whatever, as well as about statements and functions. We distinguish sign statements, sense statements, and nominatum statements.

This distinction is connected with the three different ways in which a sign may be used. We distinguish from the *sign itself*, on the one hand the *sense* which it "expresses" and on the other hand the *nominatum* which it "designates". (This distinction stems from Frege [Sinn], [Grundges.] I, 7.) If a sign is placed in the argument position of a propositional function, then it is not in itself clear what is meant as the argument for the propositional function, even if the sign and its nominatum are known. Though one can generally guess it from the context, we shall introduce some auxiliary symbols (only for §§ 44, 45) in order to make the distinction clearer and to indicate which of the three kinds is meant. If the *sign itself* is the argument of the propositional function, then we enclose it in quotation marks, e.g., " "7" is an Arabic number", " "5 + 2" consists of three constituents". We enclose the argument sign in brackets if its *nominatum*, i.e., that which is designated by it, is meant, as is usually the case. For example: "[7] is an odd number". But there is a third thing that could be meant by the sign 7. We shall distinguish it from the nominatum by calling it the *sense* of the sign and shall indicate it by pointed brackets, e.g., "I just had the representation [40] ⟨7⟩". What is meant by this becomes still more clear when we compare the substitutions which are possible in the three cases, if the truth value is to be preserved. In the case of the sign statement, very little variation is permissible. The above statement about "7" allows neither the substitution of "VII" nor of "5 + 2". On the other hand, in the sentence which contains the sign "⟨7⟩", we may replace it by "⟨VII⟩", for the *sense statement* asserts that I have a representation of the number seven, and this fact can be expressed equally well with any of the three signs ⟨seven⟩, ⟨7⟩, ⟨VII⟩. On the other hand, the statement, "I just had the representation ⟨5 + 2⟩" does not necessarily have the same truth value; it is not required that I should have had a representation of the sum of five and two. The *nominatum expression* shows itself least susceptible to change. In the sentences, "[7] is an odd number" or "[7] > 6", I may substitute [VII] as well as [5 + 2]. Consequently, we give the following definitions: by the *sign itself* we mean the written (or linguistic, etc.) figure; 7, VII, 5 + 2 are different from one another as far as the signs themselves are concerned; hence, in our nomenclature: "7", "VII", and "5 + 2" are different objects. By the *sense* of a sign we mean that which the intensional objects, i.e., representations, thoughts, etc., which the sign is to evoke, have in common. 7 and VII have the same sense, namely, the number seven as the content of a representation or thought; 5 + 2 has a different sense. Hence, ⟨7⟩ is the same as ⟨VII⟩, but ⟨5 + 2⟩ is something different. Likewise, ⟨the evening star⟩ is the same as ⟨*der Abendstern*⟩, but ⟨the morning star⟩ is something different; ⟨Scott⟩ is something different from ⟨the author of *Waverley*⟩. By the nominatum of a sign we mean the object which it designates; 7, VII, and 5 + 2 have the same nominatum, namely, the number seven (arithmeti-

---

[40] Vorstellung

cal equality is logical identity, as Frege [Grundges.] I, p. ix has shown);
[7], [VII], and $[5 + 2]$ are the same; further, [the morning star] and
[the evening star] are identical, likewise, [Scott] and [the author of
Waverley].

The difference between the sign itself, its sense, and its nominatum,
which has here been explained for signs which designate *objects* in the
narrower sense, also holds for sentences as signs for propositions and
for signs for propositional functions. We can be very brief because of the
analogy to what has gone before. Let us first consider *sentences*. The
sense of a sentence is the thought which it expresses. The nominatum of
a sentence is, according to Frege, its truth value, i.e., either truth or
falsity.

> EXAMPLE. Consider the following three sentences: A. Socrates is
> a man; B. *Socrates homo est;* C. $2 + 2 = 4$; call them A, B, C. A, B,
> and C are different from one another as signs (sentences); A and B
> have the same sense; A, B, and C have the same nominatum, i.e., the
> same truth value: truth. Statements about these sentences can be classi-
> fied as above: " "A" consists of four words" is a sign statement; neither
> B nor C may be substituted for A. "⟨A⟩ is a historical fact" is a sense
> statement. We may put ⟨B⟩, but not ⟨C⟩, in the place of ⟨A⟩.
> "[A] is equivalent to (i.e., has the same truth value as) $[1 + 1 = 2]$"
> is a nominatum statement. In this case we may substitute [B] as well
> as [C] for [A].

45. *Justification of the Extensional Method*

The most important case of this tripartition occurs with statements about
propositional functions. Let us choose the following as examples of
propositional functions: 1. x is a man, 2. x *homo est*, 3. x is a rational
animal. These three propositional functions are coextensive since they are
satisfied by the same values for x; thus, they have the same nominatum.
However, the sense of the first is identical only with that of the second,
not with that of the third. In a sign statement about the first one, e.g., " "x
is a man" consists of 7 letters", we can substitute neither the second nor
the third. "I believe that there are things which satisfy ⟨x is a man⟩"
is a sense statement; here we may substitute the second, but not the third,
propositional function, since my thinking and believing does not necessarily have to be concerned with the concept of a rational animal too.
"[x is a man] universally implies [x is mortal]" is a nominatum statement. In this case, we may substitute the second as well as the third

propositional function, or any other coextensive one. According to the previously stated criteria (§ 43), this nominatum statement is an extensional statement, while the sense statement is an intensional statement, about the propositional function: x is a man. The indicated sign statement does not deal with the propositional function at all, but only with its sign, i.e., a group of letters. Our considerations now show us that the nominatum statement and the sense statement are not really concerned with the same thing, for ⟨x is a man⟩ is not the same as [x is a man]. The difference is analogous to that between ⟨5 + 2⟩ and [5 + 2], i.e., between that which I represent to myself in connection with the sum of 5 and 2, and the number seven.

Thus our considerations have led to the following result: the distinction between extensional and intensional statements about a propositional function is not valid, for the statements in question are not about the same object. Only those statements which we have called extensional are concerned with the propositional function itself. The so-called intensional statements deal with something altogether different (e.g., a concept as the content of a representation or thought).

Thus the thesis of extensionality is valid: there are no intensional statements about propositional functions; what were taken to be such were actually not statements about propositional functions, but statements about their sense. Every statement that does not concern the sense of a propositional function, but the function itself, retains its truth value if any coextensive propositional function whatever is substituted; i.e., it can be stated in the form of an extensional statement.

Without giving further reasons, let me here indicate that this result can be extended. For the above argument holds not only for statements about propositional functions, but, according to our previous considerations, in an analogous way also for statements about statements and for statements about objects in the narrower sense. Thus we obtain the general result: *there are no intensional statements. All statements are extensional.* In every sentence, the sign which represents the object that is to be judged, whether it is an object in the narrower sense, or a statement, or a propositional function, or whatever, may be replaced by any sign which has the same nominatum, even if it has a different sense.

Since every statement about a propositional function can be brought into the form of an extensional statement, the possibility of making statements about propositional functions is not restricted in any way if we introduce for them merely their extensions. *Thus the extensional method of construction is justified.*

B

THE SYSTEM FORM

1. FORMAL INVESTIGATIONS

46. *The System Form Depends Upon Reducibility*

After having discussed the problem of the ascension forms and having found that the individual levels of the constructional system are to be erected by means of definitions using classes and relation extensions, we are now confronted with a second problem, namely, that of the "system form" (i.e., the over-all form of the constructional system). How are we to proceed with the step-by-step construction of our system, so that all the objects of science find a place in it? In the preliminary Chapter II B, we have already considered several object types. Now, the objects of the various types are to be brought into a system. The order in the constructional system is determined by the fact that an object a can be constructed on the basis of the objects $b, c, \ldots$ which precede it. In other words, a must be reducible to $b, c, \ldots$ (i.e., propositional functions about a must be transformable into coextensive propositional functions about $b, c, \ldots$)

For a precise application of this criterion, it would be required that the propositional functions with which we are concerned are given a logistic rendition, either in their entirety, or as far as their logical skeleton is concerned, or at least that they are given in logical form. We say that a statement or a propositional function has been given a *logistic rendition,* if it is expressed in logistic symbols. By the *logical skeleton* of a statement or a propositional function, we mean its logical structure.[41] Thus, we shall say of a statement that its logical skeleton has been given a logistic rendition, if all extralogical concepts are expressed by the customary words, while the logical relations between these extra-logical concepts, which constitute the skeleton, are expressed by logistic signs. We shall say that a statement is given in *logical form* if it is expressed entirely in words of the natural language, but in such words that there is a unique way, on the basis of either explicit or tacit agreements, of giving the skeleton in logistic rendition.

> EXAMPLE. Statement in natural language: "If somebody is a Negro, then he is also a man." Logical form: "If somebody belongs to the class of Negroes, then he also always belongs to the class of men". Logistic rendition of the logical skeleton: "(x): $x \in$ Negro. $\supset$. $x \in$ man"; logistic expression of the entire statement: "(x): $x \in ne. \supset . x \in ma$".

> REFERENCE. About the logical skeleton: Carnap [Logistik] § 42 ff., with examples for the logistic rendition of statements.

47. *The Criterion for Reducibility in Realistic Language*

The purpose of construction theory is to order the objects of all sciences into a system according to their reducibility to one another. Thus, later on, we shall have to inquire into the reducibility of the various object types. There will then arise the difficulty that we have to apply the criterion of reducibility to statements and statement forms which are given only in word language. In view of this task, it is advisable to express the criterion in still another form so that we no longer speak of propositional functions and their logical relations, but of states of affairs and their factual [42] relations. Thus, we translate it from the formal-logical, in this case the *constructional language,* into the language of facts, or *realistic language.* (About the difference between these two languages, see § 52.)

We now arrive at a *factual criterion* [43] *of reducibility* which is wanting

---

[41] formal-logische Form

[42] sachlich

[43] Sachverhaltskriterium

in logical strictness, but allows easier application to the empirical findings of the individual sciences. It is the following: We call an object *a* "reducible to the objects *b, c,* . . ." if, for any state of affairs whatever, relative to the objects *a, b, c,* . . . , a *necessary and sufficient condition* can be indicated which depends only upon objects *b, c,* . . .

We must now show that this criterion coincides with the one we gave earlier (§ 35). The coextensiveness of two propositional functions A, B, means: A universally implies B and vice versa (§ 32). Now, if A universally implies B, then this means that, in each case in which A is satisfied, B is also satisfied; in other words, that A is a sufficient condition for B; and if B universally implies A, then this means that B is never satisfied in any case in which A is not satisfied, so that A is a necessary condition for B. Thus, if A and B are coextensive, then A is a necessary and sufficient condition for B (and, at the same time, B is a necessary and sufficient condition for A, a point with which we are not here concerned). However, there seems to be a deviation in one point: the new criterion speaks of "states of affairs",[44] while the earlier one speaks of propositional functions. The question is whether a state of affairs is indicated through a propositional function or through a statement. Here we must make the following distinction: *individual* states of affairs are to be indicated through statements; *general states of affairs,* through propositional functions. Linguistic usage does not make a precise distinction between these two types. In the case of the reducibility criterion, we are concerned with general states of affairs, since only they allow us to speak of conditions. (The same holds for states of affairs which occur in natural laws.) Thus, the two criteria agree in this point also.

48. *The Basic State of Affairs Relative to an Object*

The factual criterion of reducibility offers still another difficulty which arises from the expression "any state of affairs whatever". Thus, strictly speaking, we would have to test the frequently very large number of possible states of affairs in which the objects might occur, in order to decide upon the reducibility of one object to another. However, it turns out that for each object there is a *basic state of affairs.* It occurs in any other state of affairs only in connection with this basic one. To put it more precisely and in constructional language: for every object, there is a *fundamental propositional function* such that all occurrences of the object can be expressed with the aid of this fundamental propositional

---

[44] Sachverhalt

function. For a property concept, the basic state of affairs is the occurrence of this property (fundamental propositional function: "x has the property . . ." or "x is a . . ."); for a relational concept, the basic state of affairs is the fact that the relation holds (fundamental propositional function: "x stands to y in the relation . . .").

In conformity with the extensional method of construction (§ 43), let a class symbol stand for a property concept, for example, say, c, and a relation (extension) symbol for a relational concept, say, Q; then the fundamental propositional functions are "$x \in c$" and "$x \, Q \, y$". It is in fact the case that every sentence in which the class symbol c occurs can be transformed in such a way that c occurs only in the context "$x \in c$", and every sentence in which the relation symbol Q occurs can be transformed so that Q occurs only in the context "$x \, Q \, y$".

Any definition, through which an object in the constructional system is constructed (i.e., its "constructional definition"), has to make use of the basic state of affairs for this object. The propositional function of the basic state of affairs is the definiendum; the propositional function which designates the necessary and sufficient condition for this basic state of affairs is the definiens, for two propositional functions are coextensive if one of them designates a necessary and sufficient condition for the other (§ 47). The juxtaposition of two coextensive propositional functions, the first of which contains, besides the variables, only one symbol which does not occur in the other one, can be viewed as a definition of this symbol (i.e., as a contextual definition § 39).

> EXAMPLE. Construction of an object with the aid of its basic state of affairs. The basic state of affairs of temperature equilibrium is: "x stands to y in the relation of temperature equilibrium." A necessary and sufficient condition for this is the state of affairs: "If bodies x and y are brought into spatial contact (either directly or through the mediation of other bodies), then they show neither increase nor decrease in temperature." Thus, these two propositional functions are coextensive. Hence, we could use them for the formulation of a definition for the object of the first propositional function, namely, temperature equilibrium: "We call "temperature equilibrium" that relation between x and y which is characterized by the fact that bodies x and y, if they are brought into (direct or indirect) spatial contact with one another, neither increase nor decrease in temperature." In the formulation of the constructional system, the object "temperature equilibrium" can be introduced (i.e., "constructed") in this way, provided that the other objects which are referred to in the definition have been constructed previously.

49. Indicators [45] and Conditions

According to the preceding considerations, the proof of the reducibility of an object is to be based on the determination of a necessary and sufficient condition for the basic state of affairs for that object. The question arises whether such a condition can be established for every basic state of affairs. To solve this problem, we introduce the concept of a *scientific indicator*. The indicator of a state of affairs is a sufficient condition for the state of affairs, but not every sufficient condition can be called an indicator. We shall use the term "indicator" only for such conditions as are ordinarily used to identify the state of affairs (i.e., which are usually recognized *before* the state of affairs).

> EXAMPLE. High air pressure and a high barometer reading are conditions for one another: if the air pressure is high, then the barometer reading is high; if the barometer reading is high, then the air pressure is high. But only in the second case do we call the condition an indicator.

Science usually gives indicators for many states of affairs of which it treats, especially for the elementary ones, of which the others are composed, that is, especially for those that are suitable as basic states of affairs as, for example, "This thing is an oak tree", "This thing is a coöperative purchasing corporation." True, the process of recognizing such a state of affairs (i.e., the presence of a certain concept) is frequently not based on these indicators, but is carried out intuitively, even in science. But even this intuitively recognized concept can be considered a fully determined scientific object only because such indicators *can* be given. In many cases, especially in the cultural sciences, when we are concerned, for example, with the stylistic character of a work of art, etc., the indicators are given either very vaguely or not at all. In such a case the decision as to whether a certain state of affairs obtains is not made on the basis of rational criteria but by empathy. Such empathy decisions are justly considered *scientific* decisions. The justification for this rests upon the fact that either it is already possible, even though very complicated in the individual case, to produce indicators whose application does not require empathy or else that the task of finding such indicators has been recognized as a scientific task and is considered as solvable in principle. A decision, which has been made through empathy or otherwise, which cannot *in principle* be subjected to a rational test

---

[45] Kennzeichen

through conceptual criteria would forfeit every claim to scientific status. Even the cultural sciences observe this limit to the admissibility of empathy decisions, if not explicitly, then at least in their practical procedures.

Thus we say that *in principle there are indicators for all scientific states of affairs.* That is to say, we have the task of determining an indicator for every scientific state of affairs, and in principle this task can be fulfilled. A more detailed analysis, which we must omit for lack of space, would show furthermore that, in principle, there is an *infallible and at the same time always present* indicator for any scientific state of affairs (i.e., an indicator which is present when and only when the state of affairs is also present). Such an indicator can always be produced by conjoining the various indicators for the individual cases; it is a necessary and sufficient condition for the state of affairs. *Thus, the construction of any scientific object can be carried out by producing such an indicator for its basic state of affairs.*

> EXAMPLE. The *indicator* from which the *rattlesnake* has derived its name is an infallible and always present indicator for the fact that an animal is a rattlesnake. Thus the following propositional functions are coextensive: "*x* is a rattlesnake" and "*x* is an animal which carries a number of rattles at the end of its body". With these propositional functions, the first of which expresses the basic state of affairs of the object rattlesnake, we can produce a constructional definition for the rattlesnake which, in the customary formulation, would read: "By "rattlesnake", we mean an animal which carries rattles at the end of its body."

50. *Logical and Epistemic Value*

If we transform a sentence about an object by replacing the object name by its constructional definition, then the intuitive meaning [46] of the sentence, and thus its epistemic value, is frequently changed. This could lead to weighty objections against the method of construction which I am here suggesting; therefore, I want to concern myself with the question, in what respects the transformed sentence agrees with the original one and in what respects it does not.

If *a* is reducible to *b, c,* then the propositional functions K, L, . . . about *a* are coextensive with the propositional functions K', L', which are exclusively about *b, c.* The *constructional transformation* (i.e., the

---

[46] der vorstellungsmässige Sinn

elimination of the object *a* with the aid of its constructional definition) consists in the transformation of the propositional functions K, L, . . . into K', L', . . . Since the former are coextensive with the latter, the constructional transformation of a propositional function leaves the extension unchanged (§ 32); in the case of a statement, the truth value remains unchanged (i.e., it remains either true or false). Let us summarize these two cases in the following way: a constructional transformation leaves the *logical value* of a propositional function, as well as of a statement, untouched. We contrast this logical value with the "epistemic value". A constructional transformation may, for example, turn a true, epistemically valuable statement into a triviality; in such a case, we say that the "epistemic value" has been changed. But, since the trivial statement is also true, the logical value has not changed. A *constructional transformation of a statement* (or propositional function) *always leaves the logical value, but not necessarily the epistemic value, unchanged.* (In contradistinction to translations from one natural language to another, these transformations do not have to preserve the intuitive content.) This is an essential characteristic of the constructional method: as regards object names, statements, and propositional functions, *it is concerned exclusively with logical, not with epistemic, value; it is purely logical, not psychological.*

> EXAMPLE. In § 49, we have given a constructional definition for the rattlesnake. Let us use this definition in order to carry out the constructional transformation of the following sentence: "This animal, which carries rattles at the end of its body, is a rattlesnake." The result is the following tautology: "This animal, which carries rattles . . . , is an animal which carries rattles . . .". The epistemic value of the original sentence has been lost in the transformation. On the other hand, the logical value has been retained: the truth value of the tautology is truth, just as was the case with the original sentence.

> REFERENCES. Our theory of indicators and definite descriptions is, on the whole, based on Russell's theory of descriptions; ([Princ. Math.] I, 181 ff., [Math. Phil.] 168 ff., [Description]). There is, however, a deviation which follows from our distinction between logical and epistemic value: we consider a definite description as equivalent with (of the same logical value as) the proper name of the object which is described; Russell's argument from triviality ([Princ. Math.] I, 70, [Math. Phil.] 175 f.) is no objection, since a triviality may have the same logical value as a statement with a positive epistemic value. This conception is related to the thesis of extensionality (§ 43 ff.).

51. *Logical Translation and Translation of Sense*

Constructional theory constructs an object by seeking an infallible and always present indicator for it (more precisely, for its basic state of affairs). This is claimed to be a definition of the object, but it does not seem to achieve what we generally require of a definition in the sense of a conceptual definition.[47] As such, it would have to indicate the essential characteristics of a concept, but these are frequently not contained in the indicator.

We can view a definition as a rule of substitution or replacement; it states that a certain sign (the definiendum) may be replaced in all statements by another (generally complex) sign (the definiens). We can require different kinds of invariance from such a translation. If we require that the translated statements have the same logical value as the original ones, but not necessarily the same epistemic value, then we speak of a *logical translation*. On the other hand, if we make the more comprehensive requirement that the translation leave invariant also the epistemic value is that, the sense of the statements (as, for example, in the translation of a text from one natural language to another), then we speak of a *translation of sense;* (in this case the logical value, too, remains necessarily unchanged). Since the construction of an object in the constructional system has always to do only with logical value and not with epistemic value (§ 50), a constructional definition which employs the indicator of an object and which thus produces a logical translation achieves exactly what we demand of it.

> REFERENCES. The concern with nothing but the logical value (truth value) for a constructional derivation agrees with Leibniz' definition of identity: *"Eadum sunt, quorum unum potest substitui alteri salva veritate."*

52. *Realistic and Constructional Language*

One could raise still another objection against the use of an indicator in a constructional definition. There seems to be a fundamental opposition between construction theory and the empirical sciences as concerns the conception of reality. For example, we construct heteropsychological objects [48] (i.e., the psychological occurrences in another person) on the

---

[47] Begriffserklärung
[48] das Fremdpsychische

basis of physical indicators, namely, expressive motions and bodily reactions, including linguistic utterances, of the other person. To this, one could object from a realistic viewpoint, that heteropsychological occurrences are in reality something different from the reaction behavior, which plays only the role of an indicator.

> EXAMPLE. Let us consider anger (here taken as something hetero-psychological, i.e., as the anger of another person, in contrast to one's own anger, which we assume to be already constructed). The constructional definition of somebody else's anger would be something like this: "anger of person A" means "state of the body of A characterized through such and such physical processes of this body or through a certain disposition to react to stimuli of such and such a kind through physical processes of such and such a kind" (where the type of process is characterized with the aid of processes of my own body when I am angry). Here, the realistic objection would run somewhat like this: "The physical behavior of the other person's body is not itself the anger, but only an indicator of the anger."

Let K stand for the physical reaction behavior which is the indicator of a certain heteropsychological process. The objection amounts, then, to the following: the concept of this heteropsychological process is not itself identical with K, and therefore requires its own symbol, for example, F. To this objection, we make the following reply: all scientific (though not all metaphysical) statements about F, especially all statements which are made within psychology itself, can be transformed into statements about K that have the same logical value. Now, since K and F satisfy the same propositional functions, they are to be considered as identical (as far as logical value is concerned). No meaning for F, which is not identical with K, can be given in scientific (i.e., constructable) expressions. (This question is connected with Leibniz' thesis of the identity of indiscernibles, cf. § 51; and also with the problem of introjection and with the metaphysical component of the problem of reality, § 175 f.).

The realistic language, which the empirical sciences generally use, and the constructional language have actually the same meaning: they are both neutral as far as the decision of the metaphysical problem of reality between realism and idealism is concerned. It must be admitted that, in practice, linguistic realism, which is very useful in the empirical sciences, is frequently extended to a metaphysical realism; but this is a transgression of the boundary of science (cf. §178). There can be no objection against such a transgression, as long as it influences only the mental representations which accompany the scientific statements; this transgression is objectionable only if it influences the content of the statements of science.

Let us emphasize again the neutrality especially of the constructional language. This language is not intended to express any of the so-called epistemological, but in reality metaphysical, doctrines (for example, realism, idealism, solipsism), but only epistemic-logical relations. In the same sense, the expression "quasi object" designates only a certain logical relationship and is not meant as the denial of a metaphysical reality. It must be noted that all real objects (and construction theory considers them as real to the same degree as do the empirical sciences, cf. § 170) are quasi objects.

Once it is acknowledged that the realistic and the constructional languages have the same meaning, it follows that constructional definitions and the statements of the constructional system can be formed by translating indicator-statements and other statements which are found in the realistic language of the empirical sciences.

Once realistic and constructional languages are recognized as nothing but two different languages which express the same state of affairs, several, perhaps even most, epistemological disputes become pointless.

53. *Summary. Method for Solving the Problem of the System Form*

The problem of the system form is expressed in the question: how can the different object types be brought into a system such that the higher ones can always be constructed from the lower ones (i.e., such that the former are reducible to the latter)? To solve this problem, we must inquire into the mutual reducibility of the various object types. To accomplish this end, we take into account the information available in the special sciences, and, with its aid, attempt to find for each object under investigation the various possibilities for necessary and sufficient conditions for the basic state of affairs of that object. We can proceed by asking the special science in question for an (infallible and always present) indicator of the basic state of affairs. But through this method we cannot find all necessary and sufficient conditions. For this method looks only in one direction; it proceeds from a given object to those other objects which are already known. In the system form which we shall later on choose for the constructional system, construction will generally proceed in this direction, since this system is intended to reflect the epistemological hierarchy of objects. Thus, we can frequently use the method of indicators. However, in order to see the possibilities of other system forms, we shall have to pay some attention to conditions other than indicators.

After having here developed a method for testing reducibility, this test is to be applied in the following, second, half of this chapter, to the most important object types. This will allow us to discern the various possible system forms.

REFERENCES. The investigation of the reducibility of one object to other objects corresponds to what has been called, in realistic language, "determination" of real objects from other real objects or from the given.[49] The methods and particular criteria which are to be used in such determinations have been discussed in great detail by Külpe ([Realis.] esp. Vol. III).

Construction theory can accept and utilize all the results of investigations about "realization",[50] for example, those of Külpe; but we must be careful not to substitute the metaphysical concept of reality for the purely constructional concept (cf. § 175 f.). In construction theory, we must exercise a methodological abstinence as far as the postulating of reality[51] is concerned (cf. § 64); thus it is advisable to use a neutral language: in construction theory, we translate the findings of the empirical sciences from the "realistic" language into the "constructional" language (cf. § 52).

2. MATERIAL INVESTIGATIONS

54. *Epistemic Primacy*

Using the method which has been developed in the first half of this chapter, we now have to investigate the relations of reducibility which obtain between the objects of knowledge. Frequently, these relations hold in different directions, so that they alone do not uniquely determine the order of the system.

The system form which we want to give to our outline of the constructional system is characterized by the fact that it not only attempts to exhibit, as any system form, the order of the objects relative to their reducibility, but that it also attempts to show their order relative to *epistemic primacy*. An object (or an object type) is called *epistemically primary* relative to another one, which we call *epistemically secondary*,

---

[49] "Bestimmung" der Realitäten aus anderen Realitäten oder aus dem Gegebenen
[50] Realisierung
[51] Realsetzung

if the second one is recognized through the mediation of the first and thus presupposes, for its recognition, the recognition of the first. Fortunately, the sequence of constructions which is required for the expression of epistemic primacy is maintained when the method of indicators is applied, since an indicator is epistemically primary relative to its object. However, we also wish to investigate here other directions which reducibility relations may take, so as to ascertain the various possible system forms.

The fact that we take into consideration the epistemic relations does not mean that the syntheses or formations of cognition, as they occur in the actual process of cognition, are to be represented in the constructional system with all their concrete characteristics. In the constructional system, we shall merely reconstruct these manifestations in a rationalizing or schematizing fashion; intuitive understanding is replaced by discursive reasoning.

55. Cultural Objects are Reducible to Psychological Objects

We have seen earlier that the manifestation relation holds between psychological and cultural objects, and the documentation relation between physical and cultural objects (§ 24). It is these two relations which mediate the recognition of cultural objects. Admittedly, not every cultural object must necessarily be immediately manifested or documented. There may be some which are based upon other cultural objects and whose recognition is mediated through the latter. But, even then, they are indirectly recognized through manifestation and documentation.

> EXAMPLE. We ascertain the religion of a given society through the representations, emotions, thoughts, volitions of a religious sort which occur with the members of this society; also, documents in the form of writings, pictures, and buildings are considered. Thus, the recognition depends upon the manifestation and the documentation of the object in question.

It is occasionally claimed that it is possible to recognize cultural objects without having to take a detour via psychological processes in which they manifest themselves or via physical documentation. But so far, such methods are not known to science and have not yet been applied. The cultural sciences recognize their objects, whether a custom, a language, a state, an economy, art, or whatever, not through discursive reasoning, but through "empathy" or *verstehen*. But this intuitive procedure, without exception, begins with manifestations and documentations. Furthermore, it is not merely the case that intuitive understanding, or empathy, is occasioned by the recognition of the mediating psychological or physical objects, but its content is completely determined through the character of the mediating objects.

> EXAMPLE. The awareness of the aesthetic content of a work of art, for example a marble statue, is indeed not identical with the recognition of the sensible characteristics of the piece of marble, its shape, size, color, and material. But this awareness is not something *outside* of the perception, since for it no content other than the content of perception is given; more precisely: this awareness is uniquely determined through what is perceived by the senses. Thus, there exists a unique functional relation between the physical properties of the piece of marble and the aesthetic content of the work of art which is represented in this piece of marble.

Our considerations show that all cultural objects are reducible to their manifestations and documentations, either directly or through the mediation of other cultural objects. However, the documentation of a cultural object necessarily takes place with the aid of a manifestation. For, if a physical object is to be formed or transformed in such a way that it becomes a document, a bearer of expression for the cultural object, then this requires an act of creation or transformation on the part of one or several individuals, and thus psychological occurrences in which the cultural object comes alive; these psychological occurrences are the manifestations of the cultural object.

From this it follows that the domain of objects to which the cultural objects are reducible can be narrowed down: *every cultural object is reducible to its manifestations, that is, to psychological objects.*

56. The Construction of Cultural Objects from Psychological Objects

The recognition that all cultural objects are reducible to psychological objects does not in itself determine whether or not we shall construct the former from the latter within the constructional system. It is imaginable that there are certain persuasions (for example, the theory which interprets the entire world process dialectically as the emanation of a spirit) which lead to the assumption that all psychological objects are reducible to cultural ones. Such a supposition would indicate the possibility of a construction in the opposite direction. We shall not investigate the correctness of this assumption at this time.

In the system form which we shall use for our outline of a constructional system, we shall construct the cultural objects from the psychological ones and not vice versa. The reason for this lies in the epistemic relation between the two object types as it is expressed in the method of science. We have seen earlier that manifestations of cultural objects (and, furthermore, also documentations, which, however, lead to manifestations) have the role of indicators; more precisely, the role of objects which mediate recognition, from whose characteristics alone science ascertains the characteristics of the cultural objects themselves. This establishes the epistemic primacy of the psychological objects over the cultural objects. Since we have previously laid down a principle, according to which we shall choose a system form for which the direction of construction is determined by epistemic primacy, it is now determined that, in our constructional system, the cultural objects are constructed from the others, and especially from the psychological objects, and not vice versa.

Natural science tends to the opinion that a state, a custom, a religion consists of the psychological processes in which the entity in question manifests itself, just as a piece of iron consists of its molecules. In opposition to this, the cultural sciences tend to consider such entities as entities of a special type, not just as a sum of psychological processes.

Construction theory claims indeed that cultural objects are reducible to psychological ones and constructs the former from the latter in one of its system forms. Nevertheless, it considers the position of the cultural sciences justified. Cultural objects are not compounded out of psychological objects. We have already emphasized their peculiar character and have shown, not only that they are widely different from psychological objects, but that they belong to another "object sphere" (§§ 23, 31).

Thus, construction theory agrees with the cultural sciences as far as the independence of the cultural object type is concerned. On the other hand, it fulfills a requirement which is emphasized especially in the natural sciences, namely, the requirement of an analysis of cultural objects (i.e., their reduction to other objects). However, by analysis we do not mean decomposition into constituents. "Reducibility" and "construction" have the previously defined meaning of translatibility of statements (§§ 2, 35). In principle, all statements about cultural objects can be transformed into statements about psychological objects. But this is to be taken in a very modest sense. We cannot reproduce the *sense* of a statement about cultural objects in statements about psychological objects. (It can be done sometimes, but not always.) When we claim that a transformation in the constructional sense is possible, we mean that a transformation rule is possible, the application of which will leave the logical value, though not always the epistemic value, unchanged. This has been discussed earlier (§ 50 f.).

REFERENCES. The question whether or not cultural objects can be resolved into psychological processes is a matter of dispute (cf., for example, Freyer [Obj. Geist] 53). According to our considerations, this question must be answered in the negative, if by resolution is meant the proof of composition out of constituent parts, but it is to be answered in the affirmative if by resolution is meant the proof of logical reducibility.

57. *Physical Objects are Reducible to Psychological Objects and Vice Versa*

Statements about physical objects can be transformed into statements about perceptions (i.e., about psychological objects). For example, the statement that a certain body is red is transformed into a very complicated statement which says roughly that, under certain circumstances, a certain sensation of the visual sense ("red") occurs.

Statements about physical objects which are not immediately about sensory qualities can be reduced to statements that are. If a physical object were irreducible to sensory qualities and thus to psychological objects, this would mean that there are no perceptible indicators for it. Statements about it would be suspended in the void; in science, at least, there would be no room for it. *Thus, all physical objects are reducible to psychological ones.*

For every psychological process, there is a corresponding "parallel process" in the brain, i.e., a physical process. There is a univocal correspondence between each property of the psychological process and some (even though entirely different) property of the brain process. Thus, every statement about a psychological object is translatable into a statement about physical objects. Since the correlation problem of the psychophysical relation (cf. § 21) has not yet been solved, the present state of science does not allow us to indicate a general rule of translation. However, for our present purposes, the logical existence of this rule (i.e., the fact that a correlation of this kind holds) allows us to draw the conclusion that *it is in principle possible to reduce all psychological objects to physical objects.*

REFERENCES. The indicated position of a thoroughgoing and univocal psychophysical correlation is maintained, for example, by Wundt [Phys. Psychol.] III, 752; opponents of this position are, for example, Becher [Gehirn] and Bergson [Materie]. A comprehensive bibliography about this problem is given in Busse [Geist]. Cf. also §§ 58, 59.

An entirely different kind of reduction of psychological to physical objects is based, not upon the almost altogether unknown psychophysical relation, but upon the *expression relation*. To the expression relation in the narrower sense (§ 19), we must here add another relation which one could call, for example, *reporting relation*. By this we mean the relation between a bodily motion and a psychological process, provided that this motion indicates through speech, writing, or other sign-giving the presence and the nature of the psychological process. An example is the relation between the speech motions of a man which form the sentence: "I am glad about the beautiful weather" and his gladness about the beautiful weather. Expressive motions,[52] including reports of this type, are the only indicators by which we can recognize the psychological processes in other persons, the *heteropsychological processes*. Now, every heteropsychological process is in principle recognizable, that is, it can either be inferred from expressive motions or else questions can be asked about it. (It can be reported.) Thus, every statement about a psychological object can be transformed into a statement about those indicators. Thus it follows that all psychological objects can be reduced to expressive motions (in the wider sense), i.e., to physical objects.

From the recognizability in principle of every kind of heteropsychological process and from the uninterrupted causal nexus [53] among physical processes, it follows that all types of psychological processes have physical parallels (in the central nervous system). (This runs counter to the position of Bergson and others; see below.) We shall not here concern ourselves with a proof for our contention; it is not as important for the system form which we are here using as it would be for a form with physical basis (§ 59).

58. *The Autopsychological and the Heteropsychological*

We now have to decide whether our system form requires a construction of the psychological objects from the physical objects or vice versa. Because of their mutual reducibility, it is logically possible to do either.

---

[52] Ausdrucksbewegungen
[53] geschlossene Gesetzmässigkeit

Hence, we have to investigate the epistemic relation between these two object types. It turns out that psychological processes of other subjects can be recognized only through the mediation of physical objects, namely, through the mediation of expressive motions (in the wider sense) or, if we assume a state of brain physiology which has not yet been reached, through the mediation of brain processes. On the other hand, the recognition of our own psychological processes does not need to be mediated through the recognition of physical objects, but takes place directly. Thus, in order to arrange psychological and physical objects in the constructional system according to their epistemic relation, we have to split the domain of psychological objects into two parts: we separate the *heteropsychological* objects from the *autopsychological* objects. The autopsychological objects are epistemically primary relative to the physical objects, while the heteropsychological objects are secondary. Thus, we shall construct the physical objects from the autopsychological and the heteropsychological from the physical objects.

Thus, the sequence with respect to epistemic primacy of the four most important object domains is: the autopsychological, the physical, the heteropsychological, the cultural. Thus, our system form requires an arrangement within the constructional system which corresponds to this sequence. For the moment, this gives us a rough indication of the overall form. We shall later discuss the arrangement of the individual object types within these major domains.

> REFERENCES. Especially Dingler [Naturphil.] has clearly shown the necessity for treating separately the autopsychological and the heteropsychological, especially when we are concerned with epistemological investigations ("autopsychology"—"allopsychology").
>
> Becher [Geisteswiss.] 285 ff. has shown against Scheler that the heteropsychological can be recognized only through a mediation of the physical. For a detailed proof that the heteropsychological is reducible to the physical and indeed that it is epistemically secondary, see Carnap [Realismus].

59. *A System Form with Physical Basis*

If it is not required that the order of construction reflect the epistemic order of objects, other system forms are also possible. The possibility of placing the basis of the system in the domain of the cultural objects is quite problematic. While it is in fact possible to envisage all psychological processes as manifestations of cultural entities, the difficulty, if not impossibility, of such a system form lies in the fact that one cannot suppose all properties of psychological processes to be determined through the nature of the cultural entities which are manifested in them. Thus there is no thoroughgoing reducibility of psychological objects to cultural ones.

Since all cultural objects are reducible to psychological, and all psychological to physical objects, the basis of the system can be placed within the domain of physical objects. Such a system form could be called *materialistic,* since a system of this form would seem the most appropriate from the standpoint of materialism. However, it is important to separate clearly the logico-constructional aspect of the theory from its metaphysical aspect. From the logical viewpoint of construction theory, no objection can be made against scientific materialism. Its claim, namely, that all psychological (and other) objects are reducible to physical objects is justified. Construction theory and, more generally, (rational) science neither maintain nor deny the additional claim of metaphysical materialism that all psychological processes are essentially physical, and that nothing but the physical exists. The expressions "essence" and "exists" (as they are used here) have no place in the constructional system, and this alone shows them to be metaphysical; cf. §§ 176, 161.

A materialistic constructional system has the advantage that it uses as its basic domain the only domain (namely, the physical) which is characterized by a clear regularity of its processes. In this system form, psychological and cultural events become dependent upon the physical objects because of the way they are constructed. Thus they are placed within the one law-governed total process.[54] Since the task of empirical science (natural science, psychology, cultural science) consists, on the one hand, in the discovery of general laws, and, on the other hand, in the explanation of individual events through their subsumption under general laws, it follows that from the standpoint of empirical science the constructional system with physical basis constitutes a more appropriate arrangement of concepts than any other. (For the basis problem of this system, cf § 62.) We cannot, at this time, give an explicit characterization of this system and its importance for science.

From an epistemological viewpoint (in contradistinction to the viewpoint of empirical science), we are led to another arrangement of concepts, namely, to a constructional system with autopsychological basis (§ 60).

---

[54] in das eine gesetzmässige Gesamtgeschehen

REFERENCES. The so-called *behavioral psychology* (the "behaviorism" of Watson, Dewey, and others; see the bibliography in Russell [Mind]) reduces all psychological phenomena to what can be perceived through the senses, i.e., to the physical. Thus a constructional system which is based upon this position would choose a physical basis. According to what we have said above, such a system would be quite possible and practicable. However, the further claim of behaviorism, namely, that this ordering of objects is also a correct reflection of the epistemic relations, would still remain problematic.

It could seem to be an open question whether in a constructional system with physical basis there is room for the domain of values. This doubt, however, has been removed by Ostwald [Werte] with his derivation of values of several types upon a basis of energetics (based upon the second principle of energetics with the aid of the concept of dissipation). From a philosophical standpoint, it must be admitted that there is a methodological justification and fruitfulness, not only for the experiential, "phenomenological", but also for the energistic derivation of values. (We shall employ the phenomenological method in the outline of our constructional system, cf. § 152.) The decision between the two is not a question of validity, but one of system form; the difference lies merely in the way in which the problems are posed and the concepts constructed. Science as a whole needs both theories to exhibit both directions of logical reducibility, just as it needs a behavioristic as well as an introspective psychology; in general, it needs both an experiential and a materialistic derivation of all concepts.

60. *System Forms with Psychological Basis*

It is possible to have a constructional system with a psychological basis. The logical justification for this system form is independent of any metaphysical standpoint and rests solely upon the above proof that all cultural as well as physical objects are reducible to psychological objects. Theories of a positivist, especially sensationalist, persuasion are generally grounded upon a system form with psychological basis. The fact that we, too, use such a system form, however, does not mean that we proceed from a sensationalist or positivist position. Any decision on problems of this type lies outside of construction theory, namely, as we shall show later, in the domain of metaphysics (§ 178).

In the main, we have to distinguish two system forms with psychological basis: with one of them, the basis lies in the domain of the psychological in general; with the other, only in the autopsychological domain. It follows from previous considerations that the first system form (regardless of its logical possibility) does not always allow a construction in the order of the epistemic relation. Thus, because of our intention to express the epistemic order of the objects, we must use only the system form with the autopsychological basis for our outline of the constructional system.

REFERENCES. Gätschenberger ([Symbola] 437 ff., esp. 451) shows the possibility of two "sublanguages", which correspond to (in our terminology) the system forms with psychological and physical basis respectively: the scientific "language of the postulated" [55] and the psychological "language of the given". Gätschenberger is of the opinion that a *pure* language of the given cannot be accomplished; however, by using such a language in our constructional system, we shall show that a system form with psychological basis can be achieved.

---

[55] des Geforderten

CHAPTER

C

THE BASIS

1. THE BASIC ELEMENTS

61. *The Two Parts of the Basis Problem: Basic Elements and Basic Relations*

The problem of the basis of the constructional system falls into two parts. At first we must decide which objects to take as *basic elements* (i.e., as objects of the lowest constructional level). However, if further construction is to be possible, still other objects must be placed at the beginning of the constructional system, namely, either classes ("basic classes") or relation extensions ("basic relations" [56]). For, if the basic elements were given as coexisting without properties and without relations, then no constructional step, through which we could advance beyond them would be possible. We shall proceed, as is explained later, by placing, not classes, but relation extensions, the *basic relations,* at the beginning of the constructional system. These, and not the basic elements, form the undefined basic objects (basic concepts) of the system, and all other objects of the system are constructed from them. As far as construction is concerned, the basic relations take precedence over the basic

---

[56] Grundrelationen

elements which are their members; generally speaking, construction theory considers individual objects as secondary, relative to the network of relations in which they stand.

Thus, we divide the basis problem into the quest for basic elements and the quest for basic relations.

62. *Possible Physical Bases*

As was shown above, there seem to be two possibilities for the over-all form of the constructional system, namely, a system form with a physical basis or one with a psychological basis (a system form with a cultural basis appeared unworkable). In order to gain a general view of the various possibilities for constructional systems, we shall deal with the basis problem as it occurs in these different system forms and not only as we find it in the form which we shall ultimately adopt. Concerning the choice of a *physical basis,* we shall briefly indicate, by way of example, three possibilities without thereby excluding others.

EXAMPLES. 1. One could choose as basic elements the electrons (including the protons, with positive elementary charges) and, as basic relations, the spatial and temporal relations between them. Properties of the electromagnetic field can then be defined through implication statements about the acceleration of electrons. The atoms of all chemical elements are constructed as certain constellations of electrons, and gravitation is constructed through implication statements about the acceleration of atoms. The derivation of the remaining constants and other concepts of physical science then no longer offers any principal difficulties since, in physics, they can all be reduced to magnetic fields, electrons, and gravitation. The perceptible physical things and properties can then easily be constructed from the things and properties of physical science, since they are uniquely determined by them.

2. We may choose as basic elements the space-time points of the four-dimensional space-time continuum and, as basic relations, their relative location in the continuum and the one-many relations between real numbers and space-time points which correspond to the individual components of the potential functions: the electromagnetic four-dimensional vector field and the tensor field of gravitation. According to the general theory of relativity in Weyl's formulation, all concepts of physical science can in principle be derived from these data. The electrons are constructed as locations of peculiar distributions of potentials [57] or as topological individuals through their relative locations; all other derivations take place as in (1).

---

[57] Potentialverteilung

3. We may choose as basic elements the world points, in the sense of elements of the "world lines" of physical points (on the basis of Minkowski's formulation). They are not identical with the space-time points of the second example, but stand in a many-one relation to them. As basic relations, we may here choose coincidence and local time-order. From this we have to construct at first all topological, but then also the metrical, determinations of the space-time world (cf. Carnap [Abhäng.], [Logistik] § 37; Reichenbach [Axiomatik]), and finally the vector and tensor field of the above-mentioned theory of Weyl; after this, the construction proceeds as above.

After we have constructed the physical objects by proceeding from such a physical basis, we can construct the other object types according to our earlier considerations concerning the reducibility of psychological objects to physical ones and of cultural objects to psychological ones (§ 55 ff.).

63. *Possible Psychological Bases*

In selecting a psychological basis, either of the following alternatives is possible: the autopsychological (or "solipsistic") or the general psychological [58] basis. With the autopsychological basis, the available basic elements are restricted to those psychological objects which belong to only one subject. As we have seen above, in this case the psychological domain must be divided into two constructionally different parts: from the autopsychological objects we first construct the physical ones, and only then can we construct the heteropsychological objects. If we choose the general psychological basis, then the psychological objects of all psychological subjects are taken as basic elements. This method has the advantage that the construction of the totality of psychological objects is easier; it is carried out in precisely the same way in which the autopsychological objects are constructed if we choose the autopsychological basis. If we select the general psychological basis, this construction completes the task of constructing all psychological objects, while, if we choose the autopsychological basis, we still have, after the construction of the physical, the entirely different and quite difficult task of constructing the heteropsychological. In both cases we have, in addition, the choice of different *types* of psychological objects as basic elements, for example, the undivided experiences (of all subjects or of the one subject) or the parts of these experiences, or certain kinds of parts of

---

[58] allgemeinpsychisch

experiences, for example, the sensations. We shall consider these possibilities when we discuss the autopsychological basis (§ 67), which we shall choose.

64. The Choice of the Autopsychological Basis

In spite of the indicated advantages of the general psychological basis, we choose the autopsychological basis for our constructional system. The most important reason for this lies in our intention to have the constructional system reflect not only the logical-constructional order of the objects, but also their epistemic order (§ 54). It is for the same reason that we excluded the system form with physical basis, various versions of which were logically possible. Occasionally, one encounters the opinion that, not autopsychological, but general psychological, objects form the basis even in the epistemic order of objects, but this position cannot be maintained in view of the fact that it is impossible to recognize heteropsychological objects without the mediating recognition of physical ones (§ 58).

The second reason for preferring a system form with an autopsychological basis is a formal-logical one. For, even if a constructional system with a general psychological basis reflected the epistemic order of objects, a system with an autopsychological basis still has the advantage that the totality of all objects is constructed from a considerably smaller basis.

The autopsychological basis is also called *solipsistic*. We do not thereby subscribe to the solipsistic view that only one subject and its experiences are real, while the other subjects are nonreal. The differentiation between real and nonreal objects does not stand at the beginning of the constructional system. As far as the basis is concerned, we do not make a distinction between experiences which subsequent constructions allow us to differentiate into perceptions, hallucinations, dreams, etc. This differentiation and thus the distinction between real and nonreal objects occurs only at a relatively advanced constructional level (cf. § 170 ff.). At the beginning of the system, the experiences must simply be taken as they occur. We shall not claim reality or nonreality in connection with these experiences; rather, these claims will be "bracketed" (i.e., we will exercise the phenomenological "withholding of judgment", ἐποχή, in Husserl's sense ([Phänomenol.] §§ 31, 32).

Within the autopsychological realm, the basis must be still more precisely delimited. The term "psychological" could perhaps be thought of as comprehending unconscious occurrences, but the basis consists only in conscious appearances (in the widest sense): all experiences belong to it, no matter whether or not we presently or afterward reflect upon them. Thus, we prefer to speak of the *stream of experience*. The basis could also be described as *the given,* but we must realize that this does not presuppose somebody or something to whom the given is given (cf. § 65). The expression "the given" has the advantage of a certain neutrality over the expressions "the autopsychological" and "stream of experience". Strictly speaking, the expressions "autopsychological" and "stream of experience" should be written in the symbolism introduced in § 75 as ᴾautopsychologicalᴾ and ᴾstream of experienceᴾ.

REFERENCES. Since the choice of an autopsychological basis amounts merely to an application of the form and method of solipsism, but not to an acknowledgment of its central thesis, we may describe our position as *methodological solipsism*. This viewpoint has been maintained and expounded in detail, especially by Driesch, as the necessary starting point of epistemology ([Ordnungsl.] esp. 23). I mention here some further adherents of this theory, some of whom apply the solipsistic method only in the initial stages of their systems and eventually make an abrupt jump to the heteropsychological. Since they do not, for the most part, employ any precise forms of construction, it is not always clear whether this transition amounts to a construction on the solipsistic basis, as is the case in our constructional system, or whether it is a desertion of that basis.

Von Schubert-Soldern ([Erkth.] 65 ff.) explicitly wants his solipsism to be taken, not in a metaphysical, but only in a "methodological" sense, ([Solipsismus] 49, 53), a fact that is frequently overlooked by his critics (Gomperz [Ereignis] 236 ff., Ziehen [Erkth.] 37, 39, 277 ff., Husserl [Phänomenol.] e.g. 316; necessity to intersubjectivize: 317. Dingler [Naturphil.] 121 f., Reininger [Psychophys.] 51, Jacoby [Ontol.]. Volkelt ([Gewissheit] 55 ff.) chooses a "monological" (that is to say, an autopsychological) starting point for the theory of knowledge and gives a good criticism of the not (or not purely) autopsychological starting point of Avenarius, Cornelius, Petzold, and Rehmke. However, the method which Volkelt uses to break through the limits of individual subjectivity differs considerably from our own. Russell ([External W.] 96 f., [Sense-Data] 157 f.) considers the construction of the physical from an autopsychological basis very desirable, but also very difficult and presently altogether unattainable.

In opposition to the systems mentioned above, many others do not apply methodological solipsism, and some oppose it explicitly. Mach ([Anal.] 19) is especially conspicuous for his non-autopsychological basis, since it does not seem to be in harmony with the rest of his views. I do not here wish to enumerate the opponents of an autopsychological basis, but wish to mention only Frischeisen-Köhler ([Wissensch.]). He takes as the epistemological subject, not the self, but "consciousness in general", to which the individual selves are phenomena. It must all the more be noted that even this opponent cannot escape placing the fundamental phenomenon [59] of cognition in the autopsychological domain: "To find a starting point for methodical reflection, we have to go back to personal experience" (p. 244); "The limitation of the given to the sphere of my own self cannot be denied" (p. 254); "Thus, from the beginning of my reflection, I have to rely upon my own, and only my own, self-consciousness." (p. 265). He especially emphasizes the independence of this fact from one's attitude vis-à-vis the realism problem: "There are no objects of experience which are common to a number of experiencing subjects. Even this sentence—no matter how paradoxical it sounds—is not based upon any hypothesis concerning the reality or nonreality of the outside world. In order to grasp it, we do not have to leave the basis of naïve realism." We are even in a position to save ourselves a discussion of the antisolipsistic position of Mach, Schuppe, and Cassirer by pointing to Frischeisen-Köhler's refutation of these views. It is all the more difficult to understand how Frischeisen-Köhler can still think, in spite of these admissions, that he cannot use an autopsychological basis for his theory of knowledge. The explanation probably lies in the fact that it seems almost impossible to proceed from an autopsychological basis to the cognition and construction of other subjects, of the heteropsychological, and of an intersubjective external world. It can be assumed that this was the main reason why some other philosophers, too (for example, Natorp, Rickert [System] 184 ff., and others) have chosen a non-autopsychological basis. Since construction theory removes the obstacles, indicating and clearing the way from an autopsychological basis to the heteropsychological and to an intersubjective world (cf. §§ 66, 140, 145–149), there should be no reason left for adopting any other basis.

65. *The Given Does Not Have a Subject*

The expressions "autopsychological basis" and "methodological solipsism" are not to be interpreted as if we wanted to separate, to begin with, the *"ipse"*, or the "self", from the other subjects, or as if we wanted to single out one of the empirical subjects and declare it to be the epistemological subject. At the outset, we can speak neither of other

---

[59] Urphänomen

subjects nor of the self. Both of them are constructed simultaneously on a higher level. The choice of these expressions merely means that, *after* the formulation of the entire constructional system, we shall find various domains which we call, in conformity with the customary usage, the domain of the physical, of the psychological (i.e., of the auto- and heteropsychological), and of the cultural. Any complete constructional system, no matter what its system form, must contain these domains. In order to characterize the differences between the system forms, we shall indicate in which of the object domains the basic elements are located after the formation of the system is completed. Before the formulation of the system, the fundamental elements are without properties and do not fall into specific domains; at this point, we cannot even speak of these domains and especially not of a differentiation between different subjects. In our system form, the basic elements are to be called experiences of the self *after* the construction has been carried out; hence, we say: in our constructional system, "my experiences" are the basic elements. (More precisely, in the terminology of § 75: ᴾmy experiencesᴾ.)

> This state of affairs can be explained through an analogy: if we construct from the numbers 1, 2, 3, . . . at first zero and then the corresponding negative numbers, then step by step the rational numbers, the real numbers, the complex numbers, then we shall finally characterize our starting point within the entire system of numbers by saying that we have chosen the real, positive integers as the initial elements. At the beginning of the construction, the designation of the elements as "real", "positive", and "integral" is meaningless. It makes sense only after the construction of the domains of the complex, negative, and fractional numbers, since it indicates the boundary toward these other domains.

Likewise, the characterizations of the basic elements of our constructional system as "autopsychological", i.e., as "psychological" and as "mine", becomes meaningful only after the domains of the nonpsychological (to begin with, the physical) and of the "you" have been constructed. Then, however, they are quite meaningful and indicate how this system differs from other system forms with general psychological or physical basis. These other basis descriptions are also meaningful, not for the basic elements as such, but only in view of the system as a whole. Before the formation of the system, the *basis is neutral* in any system form; that is, in itself, it is neither psychological nor physical.

Egocentricity [60] *is not an original property of the basic elements,* of the

---

[60] Ich-Bezogenheit

given. To say that an experience is egocentric does not make sense until we speak of the experiences of others which are constructed from "my" experiences. We even must deny the presence of any kind of duality in the basic experience, as it is often assumed (for example, as "correlation between object and subject" or otherwise). Frischeisen-Köhler writes, "Since the beginning of modern philosophy, it is a common feature of all theories that, in the data which must be considered presuppositions of all thought . . . two components may be separated." [Wissensch.] 190. These theories are the victims of a prejudice, the main reason for which is the subject-predicate form of the sentences of our language.

This egocentricity does not seem equally fundamental in the different sense modalities. To begin with, it seems to hold only for visual perceptions and seems to be connected with spatial disposition and the resulting awareness of distance. One can conclude this from the fact that the blind, on the basis of their tactile impressions, do not arrive at a subject-object dualism, a fact which is oftentimes obscured because the blind adopt the language of the sighted. Furthermore, the behavior of a blind man to whom sight has been restored shows that, to begin with, "optical impressions are not given to them in depth," since these blind are "still all impression." From this it follows that the experiences of all the sense modalities, even of sight, are originally simple, undivided experiences and that the self-object division is the result of a synthesis which is carried out in analogy to the spatial ordering in the synthesis of visual impressions.

REFERENCES. About the indicated experiences of blind persons: Wittman [Raum] 15 f., based upon Ahlmann [Opt. Vorst.].

Volkelt ([Gewissheit] 59 ff.) gives an especially clear account of the "neutral character" of experiences as basic elements: that they are "my" experiences and that they are "psychological" can, strictly speaking, be said about them only after the "you" and the "physical" have been recognized.

The following philosophers agree that the self is not implicit in the original data of cognition: Mach [Anal.] 19 ff., v. Schubert-Soldern [Erkth.] 65 ff., Nietzsche [Wille] §§ 276, 309, 367 ff.: "It is merely a formulation of our grammatical habits that there must always be something that thinks when there is thinking and that there must always be a doer when there is a deed." Aster ([Erkenntnisl.] 33), too, refers to the misleading influence of linguistic forms. Likewise Gomperz [Ereignis], following Wahle. Ziehen [Erkth.] 50 ff., 279, 445 ff., explicit rebuttal of Schuppe in [Schuppe]. Dingler [Naturphil.] 120 ff. Schlick [Erkenntnisl.] 147 f. Gätschenberger [Symbola] 151.

On the other hand, with our notion of the subjectless given, we deviate from various systems with which we agree in other important aspects: Schuppe (cf. Ziehen [Schuppe]); Natorp [Psychol.] 26 ff.; Driesch [Ordnungsl.] 19; Husserl [Phänomenol.] 65, 160; Jacoby [Ontol.] 169; Russell [Description] 210. We have already referred to Frischeisen-Köhler [Wissensch.]. The weakness of his position becomes especially apparent in the following admission (p. 196): " . . . thus the confrontation of subject and object, which we must assume with all its ramifications for the immediately given, is neither contained in the actual data of introspection, nor can it be conceptually apprehended. To impose this distinction upon the given—that is, to construe the given in analogy to thought—is to introduce a theoretical interpretation." Here, similar to § 64, the strange opposition between a fact which Frischeisen-Köhler admits and that which, in his opinion, "must be assumed." The reason for this lies presumably in the fact that Frischeisen-Köhler thinks it to be impossible—as do probably many other proponents of the egocentricity of the given—to advance from a subjectless starting point to the construction of experiences which contain the self. However, construction theory will show that it can be done.

66. *The Autopsychological Basis and the Problem of Objectivity*

If the basis of the constructional system is autopsychological, then the danger of subjectivism seems to arise. Thus, we are confronted with the problem of how we can achieve objectivity of knowledge [61] with such a system form. The requirement that knowledge be objective can be understood in two senses. It could mean objectivity in contrast to arbitrariness: if a judgment is said to reflect knowledge, then this means that it does not depend on my whims. Objectivity in this sense can obviously be required and achieved even if the basis for knowledge is autopsychological.

Secondly, by objectivity is sometimes meant independence from the judging subject, validity which holds also for other subjects. It is precisely this intersubjectivity which is an essential feature of "reality"; it serves to distinguish reality from dream and deception. Thus, especially for scientific knowledge, intersubjectivity is one of the most important requirements. Our problem now is how science can arrive at intersubjectively valid assertions if all its objects are to be constructed from the standpoint of the individual subject, that is, if in the final analysis all statements of science have as their object only relations between "my"

[61] Erkenntnis

experiences? Since the stream of experience is different for each person, how can there be even one statement of science which is objective in this sense (i.e., which holds for every individual, even though he starts from his own individual stream of experience)? The solution to this problem lies in the fact that, even though the *material* of the individual streams of experience is completely different, or rather altogether incomparable, since a comparison of two sensations or two feelings of different subjects, as far as their immediately given qualities are concerned, is absurd, certain *structural properties* are analogous for all streams of experience. Now, if science is to be objective, then it must restrict itself to statements about such structural properties, and, as we have seen earlier, it can restrict itself to statements about structures, since all objects of knowledge are not content, but form, and since they can be represented as structural entities (cf. § 15 f.).

A system form with an autopsychological basis is acceptable only because it is recognized that *science is essentially concerned with structure and that, therefore, there is a way to construct the objective by starting from the individual stream of experience.* Much of the resistance to an autopsychological basis (or "methodological solipsism") can probably be traced back to an ignorance of this fact, and many of the other expressions for the original subject (e.g., "transcendental subject," "epistemological subject," "superindividual consciousness," "consciousness in general") can perhaps be thought of as expedients, since from the natural starting point in the epistemic order of objects, namely, the autopsychological, no transition to the intersubjective realm seemed possible (cf. the quotations in § 64).

Only later, during the formulation of the constructional system itself, can we demonstrate the precise method for achieving objectivity in the sense of intersubjectivity (§§ 146–149). The preceding general remarks will suffice for the moment.

67. *The Choice of the Basic Elements: The "Elementary Experiences"*

After deciding to choose an autopsychological basis for our system (i.e., the acts of consciousness or experiences of the self), we still must determine which entities from this general domain are to serve as basic elements. One could perhaps think of choosing the final constituents of experience at which one arrives through psychological or phenomenological analysis (such as the most simple sensations, as in Mach [Anal.]), or, more generally, psychological elements of different types from which experiences can be formed. However, upon closer inspection, we realize that in this case we do not take the given as it is, but abstractions from it (i.e., something that is epistemically secondary) as basic elements. It must be understood that constructional systems which proceed from such basic elements are as much justified and practicable as, for example, systems with a physical basis. However, since we wish to require of our constructional system that it should agree with the epistemic order of the objects (§ 54), we have to proceed from that which is epistemically primary, that is to say, from the "given", i.e., from experiences themselves in their totality and undivided unity. The above-mentioned constituents, down to the last elements, are derived from these experiences by relating them to one another and comparing them (i.e., through abstraction). The more simple steps of this abstraction are carried out intuitively in prescientific thought already, so that we quite commonly speak, for example, of visual perceptions and simultaneous auditory perceptions, as if they were two different constituents of the same experience. The familiarity of such divisions which are carried out in daily life should not deceive us about the fact that abstraction is already involved in the procedure. This applies a fortiori to elements which are discovered only through scientific analysis. The basic elements, that is, the experiences of the self as units (which will be more precisely delineated in the sequel), we call *elementary experiences*.

REFERENCES. In opposition to the "atomizing" school of thought in psychology and epistemology, which postulates such psychological "atoms" as, e.g., simple sensations as elements, there is presently more and more emphasis on the fact that *"every state of consciousness is a unit* and is not, strictly speaking, analyzable." (Schlick [Erkenntnisl.] 143 f.; italics mine). In particular, there is more and more proof that, in perception, the total impression is primary, while sensations and particular feelings, etc., are only the result of an abstracting analysis. This position has already been clearly indicated by Schuppe [Erkth.] 41, also [Imman. Phil.] 17: "The thinking of the individual begins with total impressions which only reflection analyzes into their simple elements." Similarly, Cornelius [Einleitg.] 210 f., also Gomperz [Weltansch.], with his doctrine of the "total impression" (as the feeling of unity for the impression as a whole), emphasizes this point and clarifies it with examples. He also gives a historical survey of related earlier theories. He mentions William Hamilton, Schuppe, Nietzsche [Wille] and others. Reininger [Erk.] 370, makes similar statements and refers to Kant.

The position just discussed has been developed especially by *Gestalt theory.* (Cf. Köhler [Gestaltprobl.] and Wertheimer [Gestaltth.]. It has become methodologically fruitful, especially in psychology, not only by suggesting new ways of asking questions, but also by arriving at materially new findings through a change in outlook. From this theory, new and important aspects arise for areas other than psychology.

Modern psychological research has confirmed more and more that, in the various sense modalities, the total impression is epistemically primary, and that the so-called individual sensations are derived only through abstractions, even though one says afterward that the perception is "composed" of them: the chord is more fundamental than the individual tones, the impression of the total visual field is more fundamental than the details in it, and again the individual shapes in the visual field are more fundamental than the colored visual field places, out of which they are "composed". These psychological investigations have frequently been undertaken in connection with Gestalt theory. Cf. also Wittmann [Raum] e.g., 48 ff.; note on page 19 of that work an interesting quotation from F. W. Hagen, who maintained a similar position as early as 1844.

As closely related, we must also mention the philosophical position of Driesch, with its emphasis upon "totalities" (cf. especially [Ordnungsl.] and [Ganze]).

In choosing as basic elements the elementary experiences, we do not assume that the stream of experience is composed of determinate, discrete elements. We only presuppose that statements can be made about certain places in the stream of experience, to the effect that one such place stands in a certain relation to another place, etc. But we do not assert that the stream of experience can be uniquely analyzed into such places.

68. *The Elementary Experiences are Unanalyzable*

The elementary experiences are to be the basic elements of our constructional system. From this basis we wish to construct all other objects of prescientific and scientific knowledge, and hence also those objects which one generally calls the constituents of experiences or components of psychological events and which are found as the result of psychological analysis (for example, partial sensations in a compound perception, different simultaneous perceptions of different senses, quality and intensity components of a sensation, etc.). From this results a special difficulty.

We remember that class and relation extension are to be the only ascension forms of the constructional system (§ 40). Starting from any basic elements and basic relations, we can form only objects of the following kinds in the constructional system: on the first constructional level, classes of elements and relations [62] between elements; on the second level, only (1) classes of such classes, or classes of relations [62] of the first level, and (2) relations [62] between such classes, or relations [62] between relations [62] on the first level, or relations [62] between classes on the first level and elements, etc. It is obvious that construction, when carried out with the aid of these ascension forms is always synthetic, never analytic. Even if we were to suppose that the basic elements are themselves again classes of other elements, classes of "fundamental elements", we could not construct these fundamental elements with the aid of the given ascension forms. *The basic elements of the constructional system cannot be analyzed through construction.* Thus, the elementary experiences cannot be analyzed in our system since this system takes them as basic elements.

This fact agrees very well with our conception that the elementary experiences are essentially unanalyzable units, which has, after all, led us to choose them as basic elements. However, it could appear now that the previously indicated aim, namely, to construct, among other things, all objects of science and also the known psychological elements (i.e., the so-called constituents of experience), would now become unattainable. This difficulty is of fundamental importance for construction theory and requires, for its resolution, the development of a special constructional method. This is now to be discussed in more detail.

69. *The Problem of Dealing with Unanalyzable Units*

We overcome the difficulty which results from the fact that elementary experiences are unanalyzable by introducing a constructional procedure which, even though synthetic, leads from any basic elements to objects which can serve as formal substituents for the constituents of the basic elements. We call them formal substituents, because all assertions which hold for the constituents hold, in analogous form, also, for them. We call this procedure *quasi analysis*. (It is derived from the Frege-Russell "principle of abstraction": cf. the remark at the end of § 73.) It is of importance wherever we are concerned with unanalyzable units of any kind, that is, with objects which, in their immediate given-ness, do not exhibit any constituents or properties or aspects. These objects are given, as it

---

[62] Relation

were, only in point form and can therefore be treated only synthetically; nevertheless, as a result of our procedure, we can ascribe various characteristics to them. Properties and constituents are here taken to be the same thing; with psychological processes, for example, one cannot use the expression "constituent" in its original, spatial sense, but only in the sense of the equally figurative expression of "different aspects" or "characteristics".

If unanalyzable units of any kind are given and if we are to discuss them at all, then statements about them must also be given. We have previously divided the descriptions of objects through statements into property descriptions and relation descriptions (§ 10). The statements about unanalyzable units cannot be given as property descriptions, since this would amount to saying that we ascribe characteristics to these units, which would contradict the concept we have of them. The statements can only be pure relation descriptions. Let us investigate especially the case where the relation descriptions are given in extensional form, i.e., in the form of a pair list,[63] for example, through enumeration (or other characterization) of the pairs of correlated members (cf. §§ 32, 34). Notice especially the case where the unanalyzable units in question form the basic elements of the constructional system; in this case, the relation description is possible only in extensional form, since the basic relations [64] of a constructional system are given only in extension (§§ 43, 45).

Generally speaking, and without restriction to the particular problem of elementary experiences, quasi analysis is to achieve the following: unanalyzable units of any kind, a pair list of which is presupposed, are to be manipulated with the constructional ascension forms of class and relation extension (i.e., with synthetic methods) in such a way that the result is a formal substitution for proper analysis (i.e., the analysis into constituents or properties), which cannot be carried out in this case. Because of the required formal analogy between the results of quasi analysis and those of proper analysis, one can suppose that a certain formal analogy will obtain between these two procedures themselves. Thus, we investigate, to begin with, which formal characteristics we can find in the procedure of a proper analysis which proceeds on the basis of nothing but a pair list of the objects to be analyzed. Then we shall see that the desired procedure of quasi analysis can be developed analogously.

---

[63] Since only dyadic relations are discussed in the sequel, I have translated *"Relationsbeschreibung"* as "pair list", even though "list of n-tuples" would have been more precise.

[64] Grundbeziehungen

70. *The Procedure of Proper Analysis on the Basis of a Pair List*

In the case of proper analysis, we are concerned neither with points that
have no properties nor with unanalyzable units, but with objects which
have several constituents (or characteristics). Analysis consists in inferring these constituents, which are initially unknown, from other data,
e.g., from a pair list. Let us illustrate this with a simple example.

EXAMPLE. Let our aim be the analysis of a number of things, each
of which has one or more colors. Let there be altogether five different
colors. Let us define the relation of "color kinship" in such a way that it
is to hold for two things if these have at least one color in common.
Let the things be individually designated, for example, by numbers. Now
let us assume that we do not know of any of the things which colors it
has. All we have is a pair list (i.e., we know only the extension of the
relation of color kinship: we are told all pairs for which this relation
holds, but we are not told which color these two things have in common).
In other words, the relation extension of color kinship is completely
given (cf. §§ 10 and 34). Now, our task consists in inferring from these
data the distribution of colors. We cannot proceed by choosing one of
the things at random and determining all its color kin on the basis of
the pair list, for it does not follow that all these are color akin to each
other.

The task of analysis is attained once we succeed in determining the
"color classes". Let us call the class of all things which have a certain
color in common a "color class" (e.g., the class of the red [completely
red or also red] things, of blue things, etc.). There are, in all, five color
classes which partially overlap. What is the connection between the color
classes and the relation of color kinship? Now, two properties are characteristic for the color classes. The first of these they have always; the
second, most of the time, namely, when conditions are not especially
unfavorable. First of all, any two elements of a color class stand in the
relation of color kinship to one another (because the members of the pair
both have the color which determines the color class). Secondly, the
color classes are the largest possible classes all of whose members are
color-akin (i.e., there is no thing outside of a color class which stands
in the relation of color kinship to all the things in the class). (This second property can occasionally be absent, for example, if one of the five
colors is a "companion" of a second, i.e., if none of the things has the
first color without having the second also.) For example, if blue is a
companion of red, then the blue color class does not have this second
property, for a thing which is red but not blue does not belong to this

color class and is nevertheless color akin to all things in this class, since all of them are also red. If there are no systematic connections between the distributions of the different colors, then this unfavorable case, namely, that the second property is missing in a color class, becomes the less likely the smaller the average number of colors of the thing and the larger the total number of things is. Let us assume that in our case the unfavorable conditions are not fulfilled (i.e., that the color classes have both of the characteristic properties). Now we have to determine, on the basis of the pair list, those classes of things which have these two properties (in the terminology of logic: the *similarity circles* [65] relative to color kinship). This is possible because the two properties have been described only with reference to couples for which the indicated relation holds. The classes formed in this way will be the color classes. In this case, we will find five color classes without, of course, being able to determine which color belongs to each of them. Thus, we must assign arbitrary names to them, for example, $c_1 \ldots c_5$. Now if we remember that a class does not consist of its elements, but is a quasi object, whose symbol serves to express that which is common to the elements of a class (§ 37), then we can simply think of the color class c_1 as the common color of the elements of c_1. Thus $c_1 \ldots c_5$ designate the five colors. We do not know, of course, whether c_1 is red or green, etc. Now, if one of the things is an element of c_1 and of c_2, but not an element of any other color class, then we say of it that it has two colors (i.e., it bears the colors c_1 and c_2). In a similar way, we can make this determination for each one of the things. Thus, the analysis is complete; we have determined the constituents (or properties) of each element, even though we have not used the usual names for the qualities, but have only characterized them as common properties of certain elements, that is, as classes.

Thus, if a pair list is given whose relation extension signifies agreement in (at least) one constituent, then the procedure of proper analysis consists in establishing the *similarity circles* associated with the relation extension, that is to say, the classes which have the following two properties: any two elements of such a class are a pair of the given relation extension, and no element outside of such a class forms a pair of this relation extension with every element in that class. Classes which are formed in this way are then assigned to their elements as constituents (or properties).

---

[65] Ähnlichkeitskreise

71. *The Procedure of Quasi Analysis*

The procedure of quasi analysis for elements which are unanalyzable units (that is, which have neither constituents nor characteristics) stands in exact formal analogy to the indicated procedure of proper analysis. In order to be able to use quasi analysis, it must be presupposed that a pair list is given, whose relation extension R has the same general formal property as the relation extension which forms the basis of proper analysis. The latter (in our example, color kinship) indicates agreement in a constituent and hence is symmetrical and reflexive (i.e. it is a "similarity"; cf. § 11). If R is likewise symmetrical and reflexive, then we can proceed as with proper analysis; that is, as if R also meant agreement in a constituent. Thus, we form similarity circles with respect to R (i.e., those classes *c* which have the following two properties: each pair in *c* is an R pair; no element outside of *c* forms an R pair with every element in *c*). In this case, too, we envisage the similarity circles (which correspond to the color classes of our example) as common properties of the elements and hence assign them to these elements as characteristics. But since it is presupposed that these elements are unanalyzable units, they cannot, strictly speaking, have characteristics or constituents, nor can this be a case of proper analysis. It is for this reason that we designate the procedure as *quasi analysis* and the entities which we find through this procedure and which we assign to the elements, as "quasi characteristics" or *quasi constituents*. Thus, for example, if we have found the similarity circles q_1, q_2, . . . (i.e., if we have found for each such circle the list of elements which belong to it) and if a certain element belongs, for example, to the classes q_1, q_3, q_4, then we say: this element, although as an unanalyzable unit it does not have proper constituents, has three quasi constituents, namely, q_1, q_3, q_4. Thus, the quasi analysis has been carried out and meets the requirements which we have previously laid down for it (§ 69).

EXAMPLE. Let us clarify the significance of quasi analysis through an example. As a domain of unanalyzable units, we use the so-called "compound" chords. As a phenomenon, i.e., as it is given in sensation (in contrast to the viewpoint of physics and acoustics), a chord is a uniform totality which is not composed of constituents. It may seem to us as if the chord we hear when we strike the keys *c, e, g* of the piano has three parts; however, this is due only to the fact that the character of our perception is partially determined by the tone kinship of this chord with innumerable other chords which are already known to us: the chord c-e-g is akin to all the chords which (acoustically speaking) contain c (one of these may be c alone). Furthermore, our original chord is akin in tone to all chords which contain e and likewise to all which contain g. Thus, it belongs to three chord classes, and this brings about the impression that it has three parts.

Let us now assume that we have not been given any qualitative characterization, but only a pair list of the chords which one can hear, for example, in a piano, that is to say, a pair list on the basis of tone kinship. Since this relation extension is reflexive and symmetrical, we can apply the procedure of quasi analysis to it. On the basis of the given pair list (i.e., on the basis of the list of pairs which are akin in tone), we determine the similarity circles. These similarity circles stand in exact formal analogy to the color classes of the earlier example of proper analysis. With the aid of this analogy, one can easily convince himself that they are identical with the above-mentioned chord classes (i.e., with the classes of such chords which [acoustically speaking] coincide in a constituent tone). Thus, for each "constituent tone" (in the language of acoustics), whether or not it occurs among the chords in isolation, we obtain such a quasi analytic similarity circle (i.e., for example, the similarity circles, c, d, e, etc.). Now we assign to each chord those similarity circles to which it belongs as quasi constituents. Since the chord c-e-g is an element of similarity circles c, e, and g, we assign to it these three classes, namely, c, e, g, as quasi constituents. (The threefold sign (c-e-g) of this chord refers initially only to its origin, namely, the depression of three keys of a piano, and does not refer to a tripartition of the uniform chord.) We said previously that the chord c-e-g does not, properly speaking, consist of three parts and that the impression of tripartition which it makes upon a trained ear is due to the fact that it belongs to three chord classes. Now we see that this impression of tripartition is the result of an intuitively performed quasi analysis. In hearing the chord, we detect—provided that we have already heard a sufficient number of other chords—three constituents, not in the sense of parts, but in the sense of three different directions in which we can proceed from it to other chords (i.e., to entire chord classes which stand to one another in the relation of tone kinship).

As we here identify what is generally called the constituent tones of a chord with chord classes (i.e., with classes of chords), it is important to recall the character of classes as quasi objects (§ 37). A chord class is neither the whole nor the collection of its elements. Thus, it is not the chord phenomenon which would result if the chords of this class were to be sounded in some temporal sequence or other, or even all together. A chord class, as any class, is that which its elements have in common.

But this, again, is not to be understood in the sense of a common constituent, for the chords have none such. The "class" is not, properly speaking, an object. Its symbol merely serves to make those assertions which hold equally for all its elements. It is apparent, then, that the characteristic or, more precisely, the quasi characteristic, *c*, cannot mean anything but the mutual kinship of all the chords which (acoustically speaking) "contain" *c*. If one were to hear the chord *c-e-g*, without having previously heard any musical chords, one would hardly think of it as having three parts. Even though we say that we recognize the tone *c* as a constituent tone in the chord *c-e-g*, we should not think of it as a proper constituent of this chord, but only as a quasi constituent. Otherwise, one would come to the conclusion (which has indeed sometimes been maintained) that the chord *c-e-g* consists of the individual tones *c, e, g*, and, in addition to them, of something new which comprises the actual character of the chord. Thus we would assume four constituents, where in truth there is only an unanalyzable unit without any constituents.

The importance of the procedure of quasi analysis becomes evident when we recall that, in the position here maintained, the elementary experiences (i.e., the basic elements of the constructional system) are unanalyzable units and that many psychological, especially phenomenal,[66] objects, which traditional psychology thought of as being compounds, are likewise unanalyzable. In the case of such entities, one can apply the language of analysis (i.e., one can speak of their constituents or components, etc.), but one should never forget that he is, strictly speaking, concerned with quasi constituents, since these entities—as they were originally given—have no proper constituents. (Cf. the references to recent psychological positions, especially Gestalt theory, and to holistic notions in philosophy in § 67.) An example is the notion of chords as indivisible units, which we have just discussed at some length. In summary, analysis or, more precisely, quasi analysis of an essentially unanalyzable entity into several quasi constituents means placing the entity in several kinship contexts on the basis of a kinship relation, where the unit remains undivided.

72. *Quasi Analysis on the Basis of a Part Similarity Relation* [67]

The indicated procedure of quasi analysis treats the relation extension of a given pair list as if it meant agreement in a constituent part. Conse-

---

[66] sinnesphänomenal
[67] Teilähnlichkeitsrelation

quently, the results are called quasi constituents. There is still another form of relation description, which we can consider analogous to quasi analysis. It is not the relation of having constituents that are identical, but the relation of having constituents that are alike. This kind of relation description gives rise to a second type of quasi analysis which does not have the same general importance as the first, but which must be explained because it is later applied in the constructional system.

EXAMPLE. Let us again begin with a comprehensible example. Let a large number of things be of such a nature that each of them has one or several colors. Here a much larger number of things is required than in the case of the first type of relation description (§ 70). However, in this case, the number of different colors is not to be restricted to five, but a very large number of colors from all parts of the color solid are to occur. We call two things *color similar* if, among other colors, they each have a color which is similar to that of the other (i.e., which, on the color solid, has a distance from the other which is smaller than a certain arbitrarily chosen magnitude). As in the earlier example, no information about these things is to be given, except enumeration of the pairs of this relation (i.e., pair list). It is impossible in this case to determine directly the *color classes* (i.e., the classes of all and only those things which, among other colors, bear a certain color); this can be done only through a complicated procedure which we shall develop later. On the other hand, we can easily determine a different type of class, namely, the "color similarity circles". All else develops from them.

The largest possible parts of the color solid, which contain nothing but colors that are similar to one another, are spheres which partially overlap each other, and whose diameter is the arbitrarily fixed maximal distance of similarity (which may be different in different parts of the color solid). Thus, to these color spheres belong not things, but colors. The class of things which have one of the colors of a certain color sphere is called a *color similarity circle*. We can now easily see that the characterizing properties of the color similarity circles, as based on color similarity, are the same as those of the color classes as based on color kinship in the earlier example: any two things belonging to a color similarity circle are color similar; no thing which does not belong to a certain color similarity circle is color similar to all things belonging to this circle. Hence, the color similarity circles are the similarity circles based on color similarity. (As in the earlier case, it is again required that certain unfavorable conditions are not present if we are to arrive at a correct determination of these classes. For example, it must not be the case that a thing *a*, even though it does not bear any of the blue colors, on the basis of which other things form the color similarity circle *c*, is nevertheless "accidentally" color similar to all these things in c by being similar in a color other than blue to each thing that belongs to c. We shall later return to this point.)

So far, we have derived only the color similarity circles and not yet the color classes, but, as we have indicated in the earlier example, only the color classes can be envisaged as the representatives of the colors themselves and can, as such, be assigned to the things. Now, the color classes are to the individual places of the color solid what the color similarity circles are to the color spheres. Since the individual places of the color solid are the largest parts of the color solid, which remain always undivided in the mutual overlapping of the color spheres, we can determine the color classes correspondingly as the largest subclasses of the color similarity circles which remain undivided through the mutual overlapping of these circles.

As we can see from the example, quasi analysis on the basis of a part similarity relation P consists first of all in establishing similarity circles relative to P, just as in the previous case. In this case, the quasi constituents are derived from the similarity circles only indirectly, namely, as the largest subclasses which remain undivided by the mutual overlapping of the similarity circles. (This explanation is not altogether precise; we shall give a more precise one later on when we explain the application of this procedure [§§ 81, 112].)

In view of the formal analogy of the first step in this second type of procedure with the first type of procedure, we can always carry out this step without having to decide antecedently whether the relation extension of a given pair list, to which we want to apply quasi analysis, is to be construed as part identity (i.e., agreement in a quasi constituent) or as part similarity (i.e., approximate agreement in a quasi constituent). After the first step has been carried out, the decision can easily be made, for similarity circles behave toward one another in an entirely different way in the first case than in the second. In the second case, there is a multiple mutual overlapping of similarity circles. Thus they can be put into one or more systems, such that those similarity circles which are close to one another in the system have a large number of elements in common. In the first case, on the other hand, similarity circles are either mutually exclusive (namely, if their elements each have only one quasi constituent) or else they have only insignificant parts in common with one another and, even then, an order does not generally result from this fact. Thus, if we do not know whether a given similarity relation Q is to be envisaged as part identity or as part similarity, then we must investigate the similarity circles on the basis of Q as to whether they show mutual overlappings characteristic of the first or of the second case. In the first case, the similarity circles themselves must be taken as quasi constituents. In the second case, the quasi constituents must be derived from the similarity circles, namely, as the largest subclasses which are not divided through the overlapping of the similarity circles.

73. Quasi Analysis on the Basis of a Transitive Relation

For a relation extension R, on whose basis a quasi analysis is carried out, we have so far presupposed only that it is symmetrical and reflexive. The indicated procedure is independent of the property of transitivity (about this concept, cf. § 11). In the examples which we have discussed so far, we were concerned with relation extensions which were neither transitive nor intransitive. However, the case of a quasi analysis on the basis of a *transitive* relation extension deserves special treatment, for precisely this case obtains frequently in the formation of concepts in various different fields, and, moreover, it is of a special formal simplicity. The classes which are to be formed as quasi constituents fulfill, in this case too, the previously indicated conditions, but they can be defined also in another, simpler way. Since in this case R is transitive, symmetrical, and reflexive (i.e., an "equivalence", § 11), it follows that no element outside of a similarity circle can be akin to any element within the similarity circle, for then it would have to be akin to all other elements of the similarity circle, and thus, contrary to our assumption, would have to belong to it. From this it follows, first, that if R is transitive, then the similarity circles do not have any elements in common. Of the two conceptions of a relation extension which were discussed in § 72—part identity and part similarity—only the first can obtain in this case: the similarity circles of R must here themselves be considered the quasi constituents; in this case, we shall call them *abstraction classes* of R. It follows, moreover, that the class of elements which stand to any given element in the relation (extension) R forms an abstraction class. Hence, the abstraction classes and thus the quasi constituents can here be defined as the (non-empty) classes of elements which are akin to a given element.

REFERENCES. The procedure of quasi analysis in this simplest case of a transitive relation extension corresponds to the "principle of abstraction", which was first explicitly mentioned by Russell ([Principles] 166; cf. also Frege [Grundlg.] 73 ff.). It had been used previously by Frege and then by Whitehead and Russell for the construction of the cardinal numbers (cf. § 40). Cf. Couturat [Prinz.] 51 ff.; Weyl [Handb.]

9 f., there also a reference to Leibniz; Carnap [Logistik] § 20. Whitehead and Russell have also referred to the extramathematical applicability of the principle and have used it for their constructions; cf. Russell [External W.] 124 ff.

74. *About Analysis and Synthesis*

Later on, in the formulation of the lower levels of our outline of the constructional system, we shall illustrate the application of the procedure of quasi analysis to the elementary experiences as basic elements. Then we shall see how this procedure puts us in a position, for example, to construct the different sense modalities and, within the sense modalities, the various sensory qualities, without disclaiming the unanalyzable character of elementary experiences.

Many epistemological systems (especially the positivistic ones) which are otherwise closely related to our constructional system have used, not experiences themselves, but sensory elements or other constituents of experiences as basic elements, without paying heed to their character as abstractions. The reason for this was perhaps that it seemed impossible to construct all objects of psychology and, among them also, those "constituents of experiences" if experiences themselves were chosen as basic elements. After we have shown, through the procedure of quasi analysis, that this impossibility is only apparent, there seems to be no reason for any epistemological position (and this holds especially for a positivistic one) why elementary experiences should not be acknowledged to have the character of unanalyzable units and why they should not be taken as basic elements.

In order to avoid any misunderstanding, let me emphasize again that, with the conception of elementary experiences as unanalyzable units, we do not brand a psychological statement, such as "this experience (or this act of consciousness) consists of a visual perception with such and such constituents, of an auditory sensation, of a feeling with such and such components, etc." as false or even meaningless. All we assert is that in such a statement the expression "constituents" refers only to quasi constituents. In other words, we say that every so-called constituent relates to the experience as the chord class c in the above example (§ 71) to the chord c-e-g, namely, as an entity which is constructed through kinship relations, that is, a "quasi constituent".

REFERENCES. Our position is closely related to that of Cornelius: "The value of such an analysis does not consist in the recognition of every single state of consciousness—no analysis of these can be possible —but in the recognition of regular connections between various such states." [Einleitg.] 314. Cf. also the quotations in § 67.

If class and relation extension are acknowledged as the only constructional steps (§ 68), then the *methodological unanalyzability* of the basic elements follows for any constructional system, and, from the choice of the essentially unanalyzable elementary experiences (§ 67) follows a *materially determined* [68] *unanalyzability*. From this arise the following consequences with respect to the general relationship between analysis and synthesis of scientific objects, which we assume to be constructed according to our constructional system. Since every object of science is constructed from the basic elements, to analyze it means to trace back the procedure of construction from the object itself to those elements which are required for its construction. Any analyzing beyond this point will have to take on the form of quasi analysis, since proper analysis is no longer possible. The same holds when the object to be analyzed is not a constructed entity, but a basic element. Now, quasi analysis leads to entities which we have called quasi constituents (in order to stay close to established usage, which calls them constituents). But this is done by forming classes of elements and, furthermore, relation extensions of these classes; hence, by way of synthesis, not analysis. We can therefore say: *Quasi analysis is a synthesis which wears the linguistic garb of an analysis.*

Since the basic elements are not accessible to proper analysis, but only either to quasi analysis or to other constructional procedures, all of which are synthetic, it follows, if we concentrate not upon the linguistic expression but upon the actual nature of the procedure, that these elements are accessible exclusively to synthesis and not to analysis. All other objects are synthetic entities constructed from the basic elements and analyzable only to the point where these basic elements are reached again. *Analysis is possible only if, and to the extent in which, synthesis has preceded; it is nothing but a retracing of the path of synthesis from the final structure to intermediate entities and finally—if the analysis is "complete" in the sense of construction theory—to the basic elements.* To be sure, an analysis is then not yet "complete" in the scientific sense, but its continuation is then a quasi analysis (i.e., a new synthesis).

---

[68] inhaltlich bestimmt

2. THE BASIC RELATIONS [69]

75. The Basic Relations as Basic Concepts of the System

We have realized earlier (§ 61) that, to lay down the basis of a constructional system, we need not only the basic elements, but also certain
initial ordering concepts,[70] since otherwise it is not possible to produce
any constructions starting from the basic elements. The question whether
these first ordering concepts are to be given the form of classes ("basic
classes") or of relation extensions ("basic relations") remained at first
open. But after the basic elements were chosen (§ 67) and the elementary experiences which were chosen turned out to be units unanalyzable in principle, it appeared that any assertion about them would have
to have the form of a pair list (§ 69). From this it follows that (one or
more) *basic relations* must be chosen as the first ordering concepts. These
basic relations, and not the basic elements, form the undefined basic
concepts of the system. The basic elements are constructed from the
basic relations (as their field).

> REFERENCES. Cassirer ([Substanzbegr.] 292 ff.) has shown that a
> science which has the aim of characterizing unique entities through
> contexts of laws without loss of individuality must utilize, not class
> ("generic") concepts, but *relational concepts,* since these can lead to
> the formation of series and thus to the establishment of systems of
> ordering. Since one can easily make the transition from relations to
> classes, and since the opposite is possible only very rarely, it follows that
> it is relation extensions which must initially be posited.
>
> Thus, two entirely different and frequently hostile philosophical posi-
> tions have the merit of both having discovered the necessary basis of the
> constructional system. Positivism has emphasized that the only material
> of cognition consists in the undigested experientially given. It is here that
> we have to look for the basic elements of the constructional system.
> Transcendental idealism, especially the Neo-Kantian school (Rickert,
> Cassirer, Bauch), has justly emphasized that these elements do not
> suffice. Order concepts, our basic relations, must be added.

We want to determine the basic relations in such a way that they are
isogenous (§ 29) to one another (i.e., that they are all of the same level,
§ 41). In fact, the terms of each of the basic relations are never to be

---

[69] Grundrelationen
[70] Ordnungssetzungen

anything but elementary experiences. In order to form the basic relations, we must now consider which relations between the elementary experiences are to be considered fundamental. We are not here concerned with the quest for psychologically fundamental relations or relations which are of especial importance for the processes of consciousness. Since the basic relations are to serve as the basis for the construction of all objects (of cognition), they must be chosen in such a way that, through them, all recognizable states of affairs can be expressed. According to our detailed discussion (§§ 50, 51), expressibility is to be understood only in the sense of a definite description; here we pay attention only to logical and not to epistemic value, nor are we concerned with the question whether, in the actual occurrence of a process of cognition, a state of affairs which can be expressed through certain basic relations [71] is actually derived from these basic relations. It happens occasionally that a certain state of affairs is fundamental and cannot be reduced to simpler ones, as far as the psychology of cognition is concerned, while it is logically dependent upon others in such a way that it can be constructed from them and that it therefore does not have to be postulated as a basic relation. We shall later on find examples for this.

In searching for the basic relations, we have to pay especial attention initially to the requirements of the construction of physical objects (i.e., we shall test our findings by applying them to facts of perception). Whether we need other basic relations for the construction of objects of higher levels (heteropsychological or cultural), we shall consider afterward. The present investigations whether certain relations are required as basic relations and especially whether they are sufficient for the demands that we put upon them can only be provisional. The correctness and appropriateness in the choice of the basic relations can be confirmed only through the fact that, in the formulation of the constructional system, the most important constructions, upon which all else rests, can be carried out with the aid of the chosen basic relations. This logical performance is the essential criterion for the basic relations. On the other hand, an investigation of whether a certain relation is fundamental as far as the psychology of cognition is concerned has mostly heuristic value.

In order to discuss which relations are meant as basic relations and what entities can be constructed from them, we have to speak of the experiences in the customary *factual language*,[72] in this case, the *lan-*

---

[71] From here to the end of §75, "basic relation" is a translation of *"Grundbeziehung"*.

[72] Sachverhaltssprache

guage of psychological analysis: we have to speak of their constituents, of sensations, of the various senses, of quality, intensity, etc. In using these expressions, we do not mean to suggest that these constituents, etc., are presupposed for the construction. This would lead to a vicious circle. The only purpose of these expressions is to *indicate* certain known states of affairs, especially fundamental relations between the elementary experiences. This can only be done in a mode of expression as it is customary in the discussion of experiences and their relations, hence, in the *language of psychology*. In Chapters C and D we shall enclose, for clarity's sake, expressions which are to be understood in this way in p-symbols (e.g., ᵖqualitiesᵖ). If an expression does not belong to the factual language, that is, if it is not meant in the sense of customary usage, but relates to the constructional system (hence, to a constructional definition, which either has already been given or the formulation of which is intended) or else, if it relates to an undefined basic concept of the system, then it will be enclosed in c-symbols (e.g., ᶜqualitiesᶜ). (We shall not use this symbolism in headings and in reference remarks.)

EXAMPLES. When we speak of ᵖconstituents of experiencesᵖ, then this does not contradict the notion of ᶜelementary experiencesᶜ as unanalyzable units, for by the expression "ᵖconstituentsᵖ", we mean the commonly understood entities. We express through the p-symbols that we have adopted this nomenclature without wanting to express the contention that we are here concerned with actual constituents. It is after all one of the problems to be dealt with, to find out what these entities actually are, namely, how they can be constructed and how they are then to be described in constructional language.

The expression "ᶜsensation qualitiesᶜ" or "ᶜqualitiesᶜ" will be used to refer to the ᶜquality classesᶜ as soon as these classes are constructed or at least when the type of their construction has been indicated (§ 81). On the other hand, the expression "ᵖsensation qualitiesᵖ" or "ᵖqualitiesᵖ" shall mean what is commonly intended by this word. This distinction is necessary in order to be able to deal with the question of whether the constructed ᶜqualitiesᶜ are really of such a nature that they can represent the known ᵖqualitiesᵖ, e.g., the ᵖsensation qualitiesᵖ. We must likewise make a distinction between ᶜtime orderᶜ and ᵖtime orderᵖ, etc.

The ᵖelementary experiencesᵖ are the known ᵖtotal objects of psychologyᵖ, the ᵖprocesses of consciousnessᵖ. The ᶜelementary experiencesᶜ are propertyless, pointlike arguments of relations. The ᵖelementary experiencesᵖ have ᵖconstituentsᵖ, e.g., ᵖsensation qualitiesᵖ. The ᶜelementary experiencesᶜ have ᶜquasi constituentsᶜ, e.g., ᶜsensation qualitiesᶜ or ᶜquality classesᶜ to which they belong as elements to classes.

76. Part Identity

In order to be able to construct the physical world, we need certain ᴾconstituents of elementary experiences, especially sensations with their determinations of quality and intensity, later on also spatial and temporal order which must refer back to certain characteristics of sensations which themselves do not have to be of a spatial or temporal nature in the proper senseᴾ.

The ᴾconstituents of elementary experiencesᴾ will have to be quasi constituents, since in our system the ᶜelementary experiencesᶜ are indivisible units. ᴾEvery sensation quality, whether it is a color, a tone, a fragrance, etc.ᴾ, will have to be a ᴾcommon property of those elementary experiencesᴾ in which it occurs as a ᴾconstituentᴾ (i.e., as a quasi constituent). This ᴾcommon propertyᴾ is constructionally represented as the class of the appropriate ᶜelementary experiencesᶜ ("ᶜquality classᶜ"). Above, we have discussed in some detail the fact that a class is not the whole or the collection of its elements, but a property which they have in common (§ 37). This class could be constructed, for example, for every ᴾsensation qualityᴾ through the procedure of quasi analysis on the basis of the relation of ᴾagreement of two elementary experiences in such a qualityᴾ. Thus we consider that relation which ᴾholds between two elementary experiences, x and y, if and only if in x there occurs an experience constituent a and in y an experience constituent b such that a and b agree in all characteristics,[73] namely, in quality in the narrower sense, in intensity, and in the location sign [74] which corresponds to the place in the sensory field, provided that the sense modality in question has these characteristics. Thus, two color sensations agree with one another if they agree in hue, saturation, brightness, and in location sign (i.e., in the place in the visual field); likewise, two (simple) tones, if they agree in pitch and loudnessᴾ. The just-discussed relation of ᴾagreement of two elementary experiences in an experience constituentᴾ is a kind of part identity; we call it, in brief, "ᴾpart identityᴾ". For the logistic formulation of the constructional system, we assign to this relation the symbol "Pi", so that "x Pi y" means: ᶜthe elementary experiences (i.e., the elements of the constructional system) x and y are part identicalᶜ; and this means ᴾthe elementary experiences x and y are part identicalᴾ (in the previously indicated sense). Since one can envisage the relation of ᴾpart identityᴾ

---

[73] in allen Bestimmungsstücken
[74] Lokalzeichen

as a fundamental fact of cognition, it seems reasonable to introduce the relation "Pi" as a basic relation. But we shall see later on that this is not very useful, since it can be derived from another relation which is likewise required for construction, but which itself cannot be derived from ᵖpart identityᵖ.

We have already seen that, from ᵖpart identityᵖ, we can either derive, through quasi analysis, the ᵖsensation qualitiesᵖ, or, if these can be obtained from another basic relation, one can conversely derive ᵖpart identityᵖ from the ᵖsensation qualitiesᵖ. In our construction we shall employ this second method.

Among the ᵖsense modalitiesᵖ we always wish to include the ᵖdomain of the emotionsᵖ.[75] This holds not only for the above explanation of ᵖpart identityᵖ, but also for the subsequent investigations. We do not wish to assert thereby (but we also do not wish to deny) that ᵖemotions are sensationsᵖ. However, we need a short expression for ᵖthe domains of constituents of experiences which are either the sense modalities or the domain of the emotionsᵖ. In this context we always mean by ᵖ*sensation qualities*ᵖ also the ᵖqualities of emotionsᵖ (cf. § 85).

77. Part Similarity

The dimensions ᵖof the sensation qualities of a sense modality, namely quality solid,[76] (e.g., color solid, tone scale), intensity scale, and sensory field (e.g., visual field, tactile field) are not recognizable on the basis of the relation of part identityᵖ (i.e., they are not constructable from ᶜpart identityᶜ). These orders rest upon ᵖproximity relationsᵖ, and the latter are not derived from ᵖpart identityᵖ: ᵖtwo color sensations of almost identical hues have, relative to part identity, the same relation to one another as two entirely different color sensations, nay, even as a color sensation and a tone sensationᵖ. Thus, even if we had already introduced ᶜpart identityᶜ as a basic relation, we would still have either to introduce ᵖthe approximate agreement of two elementary experiences relative to some characteristic of two constituentsᵖ, itself as a basic relation, or else we would have to introduce another basic relation, from which this relation is derivable. We call this relation ᵖpart similarityᵖ, and, for the purposes of its logistic manipulation, we assign to its extension the symbol Ps. ᵖTwo elementary experiences x and y are called "part similar" if and only if an experience constituent (e.g., a sensation) a of

---

[75] das Gebiet der Gefühle
[76] Qualitätskörper

x and an experience constituent b of y agree, either approximately or completely, in their characteristics (quality in the narrower sense, intensity, location sign)ᵖ.

By the expression "ᵖsimilarityᵖ", in contrast to "ᵖpart similarityᵖ", we here mean the corresponding relation between ᵖqualities of sensationsᵖ (even though this word has generally a wider meaning). To this relation, we assign the logistic extension symbol Sim. We say, for example, that ᵖtwo color sensations a and b are similarᵖ (a Sim b), ᵖif they agree approximately or completely in hue, saturation, brightness, (or hue, white content, black content) and location sign (i.e., place in the visual field); two elementary experiences x and y in which similar color sensations a and b occur are, then, part similarᵖ (x Ps y). (For the relation between ᵖqualities of sensationsᵖ which corresponds to ᵖpart identityᵖ, we do not need a new term nor a special sign, since this relation is identity itself). We want to take the relation extension Sim and thus also Ps as reflexive so that ᶜevery elementary experience is said to be part similar both to itself and to those elementary experiences with which it is part identical, and every sensation quality is similar to itselfᶜ.

78. Recollection of Similarity as Basic Relation [77]

We could use ᶜpart similarityᶜ as basic relation, but, instead, we shall rather take one of its constituent relations [78] from which it is easily derivable. This constituent relation is also epistemically more fundamental. ᵖIf it is recognized that two elementary experiences x and y are part similar, then a memory image of the earlier of the two, of say, x, must have been compared with ᵖ. This ᵖprocess of recollectionᵖ is not symmetrical; the occurrence of x is different from that of y. Thus, the ᵖresult of this cognitionᵖ is more precisely represented through an asymmetrical relation than through the symmetrical relation extension of ᶜpart similarityᶜ. We shall introduce this asymmetrical relation as basic relation; we call it ᶜrecollection of similarityᶜ and assign it the symbol Rs. "x Rs y" or "ᶜrecollection of similarity holds between x and yᶜ" means: "ᵖx and y are elementary experiences which are recognized as part similar through the comparison of a memory image of x with yᵖ". We can express this more briefly as "ᵖthe elementary experiences x and y are connected through recollection of similarityᵖ". (By "ᵖrecollectionᵖ" we do not here mean only the ᵖreproduction of an already faded experienceᵖ, but also the

---

[77] Grundbeziehung
[78] Teilrelation

^{p}retention of a just preceding experience, for example, a perception, which has not yet vanished but still has vivid aftereffects^p.)

From the indicated meanings of ^{p}part similarity and recollection of similarity^p, the following ^{c}derivation of part similarity from recollection of similarity^c results: ^{c}two elementary experiences x and y are called part similar (Ps) if the relation of recollection of similarity (Rs) holds either between x and y or between y and x^c. ("Derivation" means construction without strict form. The construction of ^{c}part similarity^c within the constructional system, which corresponds to this derivation, is carried out in § 110.)

Thus, while Ps can be derived from Rs, the opposite is not possible. If the difference in direction is once blotted out through a symmetrical relation, then it cannot be reintroduced by constructional methods. The difference in direction is important for the construction of time order; we shall later on derive time order from Rs without having to introduce a new basic relation. This is the main reason why we chose Rs and not Ps as basic relation.

79. *The Possibility of Further Derivations*

(In the following, we shall use the p- and c-symbols for psychological and constructional language only in special cases.)

In order to determine whether we have to introduce any basic relations other than recollection of similarity, we have to investigate the possibilities of further derivations from Rs and Ps. As we have mentioned earlier, it is not possible to derive part similarity (Ps) from part identity (Pi). However, the opposite derivation of Pi from Ps is possible, so that Pi does not have to be introduced as a basic relation.

For the derivation of Pi from Ps, the following simple method seems to present itself. We shall see that it is not successful. Two sensation qualities, a, b, are identical if and only if a is similar (Sim) to the same sensation qualities as is b. Sim and identity are relations which hold between sensation qualities; between elementary experiences, we have the corresponding relations Ps and Pi, respectively. Thus, one could think that part identity Pi should be defined in such a way that it holds between two elementary experiences x and y if and only if x stands in the relation Ps to the same elementary experiences as y. However, this definition would be inappropriate. For, it should after all hold, for example, that x Pi y, if in the elementary experiences x and y the same hue is found at the same place of the visual field. However, in this case, the indicated definition will fail most of the time. If, for example, x has another hue a at a different place of the visual field and y does not have a hue which is similar to a, then x is part similar to all elementary experiences in which a similar hue is in the place of a; but this does not hold for y. Thus, our tentatively formulated definition is here not fulfilled.

This attempted derivation shows the following: given a relation between elementary experiences which depends (as Pi and Ps) upon certain constituents of elementary experiences; if we want to ascertain whether such a relation holds, we shall have to consider upon *which* constituent it depends that the relation holds in a particular case. It is very easy to make mistakes in the various constructions of the lower levels if no proper attention is paid to this point. In this connection, it must also be noted that Pi is not transitive, as is usually the case with relations of identity or agreement (§ 11). The agreement of two elementary experiences in a *definite* constituent is indeed transitive, but not Pi as agreement in *any* constituent (cf. the nontransitivity of color kinship in the example of § 70).

The desired derivation of Pi from Ps cannot be carried out immediately. Rather, with the aid of the procedure of quasi analysis, we must derive from Ps first the "similarity circles" and then the "quality classes". From these we can then easily obtain Pi.

80. *Similarity Circles*

Let us apply to Ps the procedure of quasi analysis of the second type, which we discussed earlier (§ 72), i.e., quasi analysis on the basis of a part similarity relation (extension). We thereby determine the similarity circles based on Ps; from now on, let us call these simply *similarity circles* without any qualifying phrase, since similarity circles based on other relations will occur only rarely. Thus, by "ᶜsimilarity circlesᶜ", we understand those classes of elementary experiences which have the following two properties: any two elementary experiences of such a class are part similar to one another (Ps); if an elementary experience is part similar to all elementary experiences of such a class, then it belongs itself to that class. (The construction of similarity circles within the construction system is carried out according to this definition in § 111.) The second step of quasi analysis based on Ps will determine quasi constituents which we shall call *quality classes* (§ 81).

In order to understand the significance of the derived ᶜsimilarity circles and quality classesᶜ relative to the ᴾconstituents of experiencesᴾ, let us introduce a spatial symbolization of elementary experiences and their constituents, which we shall initially take to be sense impressions. Let us represent the sensation qualities through points; proximity of two points in space is to represent the relation of similarity (Sim) between the qualities in question. Thus, we obtain a connected spatial array as a spatial representation for each sense modality. The tone sensations form a two-dimensional array, since in them we differentiate pitch and loudness in them. Visual sensations do not form a three-dimensional array; this would merely correspond to the customary color solid, where the three dimensions, hue, saturation, and brightness, or hue, white content, and black content, are represented; rather, they form a five-dimensional array, since the location signs—which themselves form a two-dimensional manifold—also count as characteristics. Since a five-dimensional order is unintuitive, let us imagine a two-dimensional order, which depends upon the relations of the location signs (i.e., upon the order of the visual field); and let us furthermore imagine a set of three-dimensional color solids, one of which corresponds to each place of that two-dimensional order. Every point of the above-mentioned order represents a sensation quality (in the widest sense, cf. §§ 76, 85); we correlate to it those elementary experiences in which the sensation quality in question occurs. Since, in an elementary experience, several qualities occur at the same time, every elementary experience is correlated to various quality points, within different sense modalities as well as within the same sense modality.

Let us now consider a sense modality whose spatial representation is to have the dimension number n. Within this sense modality, we find n-dimensional spheres, whose diameters correspond to the largest distance that allows two sensation qualities to be still similar (Sim) at that place of the sense modality. Through comparison with the example of § 72, whose "color spheres" correspond to these n-dimensional quality spheres, we recognize easily that a similarity circle is the class of those elementary experiences which are assigned to the points of such an n-dimensional quality sphere. These similarity circles do not exclude one another, but frequently show a partial overlap. Here, we have to distinguish two different types of overlap, which we could perhaps describe as "essential" and "accidental". If two similarity circles correspond to two partially overlapping quality spheres, which then of course belong to the same sense modality, then the similarity circles show a corresponding overlap; this we call *essential overlap*. On the other hand, if two similarity circles correspond to mutually exclusive quality spheres, then they can nevertheless have elementary experiences in common, since each elementary experience corresponds to various quality points.

This "accidental" overlap can even occur between similarity circles of different sense modalities.

81. The Quality Classes

We can also envisage the just-mentioned overlapping of similarity circles as mutual dissections. Since the quality points are the largest parts which remain undivided in the mutual overlapping of quality spheres, the classes of elementary experiences which correspond to these points are the largest subclasses of the similarity circles, which remain always undivided through *essential* overlappings. Now each such class of elementary experiences which correspond to one point can be isolated through such dissections of overlapping.[79] For, for any two different quality points, one can always find a third one such that it is similar (Sim) to one but not to the other (i.e., one can thus always find a similarity circle which includes the elementary experiences of the one, but not of the other).

In addition, we have to consider the dissection through *accidental* overlapping of similarity circles. To gauge their effect, let us consider a concrete example.

> EXAMPLE. Let the classes a, b, be two similarity circles of the visual sense. Let us restrict ourselves only to two individual places of the visual field in order that we should not have to cope with a five-dimensional array, but only with three-dimensional arrays. The three-dimensional color solids which correspond to each of these visual field places we envisage, for simplicity's sake, not as continuous, but as discrete (i.e., as being composed of a finite number of discrete points). Let us refer to the color solids which correspond to the two visual field places as the first and the second color solid. Let the similarity circle a include all those elementary experiences which correspond to five definite points of the first color solid; these five points are then in proximity to one another in the color solid; assume that they lie within the range of the blue hues. In like fashion, let b be a similarity circle of five red hues of the second color solid. If, in an elementary experience, one of those blue hues is found in the first visual field place, then it will not ordinarily be the case that one of those red hues will be found at the second visual field place. Nevertheless, this can happen in certain cases, which, however, will form only a small fraction of all those cases in which the blue or else the red hues occur at their visual field place. This means that there may be some elementary experiences which belong to the similarity circle a as well as

---

[79] Überdeckungszerschneidungen

b; let us assume that they are the elementary experiences x, y, z. We are here concerned with an accidental overlap between a and b; it cannot be an essential overlap in this case, since a and b belong to different color solids and furthermore to different color ranges within the color solids. x corresponds to one of the five quality points of a; let us call the class of elementary experiences which correspond to this point q. Let y correspond to the same and z to a different point of a; thus, x and y are elements of q, but z is not. The class q represents a sensation quality of the visual sense, namely, a certain blue hue at a certain visual field place, for this sensation quality is a common property of the elements of q. Classes of this kind we call *quality classes*. Now, the quality class q of the similarity circle a is dissected by the similarity circle b, since only x and y and no other elements of q belong to b. The part of q which is cut off through the accidental overlapping of a and b is here only very small relative to q itself.

We have seen previously that quality classes (i.e., the classes of elementary experiences which are assigned to a given quality point) are not divided by an essential overlapping of similarity circles. We have now shown that they may be divided through an accidental overlapping. However, in this case, the part which is split off is generally (i.e., if special conditions do not obtain; see below) very small relative to the quality class as a whole and especially relative to the similarity circle. We can easily see this in the above example, and this result can be generalized without difficulty. Here then lies the difference between accidental and essential overlap, for, in the latter case, any piece of a similarity circle that is split off includes at least an entire quality class (i.e., a not inconsiderable fraction of the similarity circle or of one of its parts).

Since quality classes can be determined with the aid of essential overlapping of similarity circles and since these overlappings can be distinguished from accidental overlappings by the indicated characteristic, we now can provide a definition of quality classes. It contains two conditions; the first corresponds to the fact that quality classes are not divided by essential overlappings of similarity circles (i.e., overlappings which cut off more than only very small parts); the second condition is that quality classes should be the largest possible classes with the indicated property. (If the definition did not contain the second condition, then every subclass of a quality class would fulfill the definition.) The definition reads: a class c of elementary experience is called a *°quality class°* if c is totally contained in any similarity circle which contains a considerable part of c and if for every elementary experience x which does not belong to c there exists (at least) one similarity circle which contains c but to which x does not belong. (Construction of quality classes in the constructional system, § 112.)

We have previously seen that the ^{c}quality classes^c are constructional representations of ^{p}sensation qualities^p (in the widest sense, including the emotion qualities, etc.). Thus, we shall sometimes call them, in brief, "qualities".

In constructing similarity circles and quality classes, we must pay especial attention to the fact that the construction does not have to reflect the actual process of cognition, but that it is only a rational reconstruction which must lead to the same result.

> We have mentioned here and earlier (§ 72) that the application of the method of quasi analysis leads to the desired result only if special "unfavorable conditions" do not obtain. These unfavorable conditions could consist, for example, in the fact that certain ^{p}qualities^p always or frequently occur together with certain others. This would lead to irregularities in the derivation of ^{c}quality classes^c and later on in the division into ^{c}sensory classes^c and in the ^{c}Sim-order^c within the sensory classes. However, a more detailed investigation, which we have to omit for lack of space, shows that these interferences in the concept formation through quasi analysis can occur only if circumstances are present under which the real process of cognition, namely, the intuitive quasi analysis which is carried out in real life, would also not lead to normal results.

82. *Does One Basic Relation Suffice?*

We have seen earlier that the assignment of two elementary experiences to the same quality point—in other words, their membership in the same quality class—means that they have an identical constituent (i.e., that they are part identical [§ 76]). Thus, we can easily derive part identity (Pi) from quality classes: two elementary experiences are called *part identical* (Pi) if there is a quality class to which both of them belong. (For the construction of Pi, see § 113.) If we had introduced Pi as a basic relation, then we would derive the quality classes through quasi analysis from Pi. Here we actually proceeded in the opposite direction. Since we have just derived the quality classes from the similarity circles, which in turn were derived from part similarity (Ps), the desired derivation of Pi from Ps has been accomplished. Thus, the relation Pi, which is important for further derivations, does not have to be introduced as a basic relation.

So far, we have derived two relations between elementary experiences, namely, Pi and Ps, from the basic relation Rs. Furthermore, two kinds of classes of elementary experiences, namely, the similarity circles and the quality classes, have been derived. The latter are especially important since they represent the first constituents of elementary experiences, namely, the qualities of sensory perceptions and emotions (and perhaps even of other kinds, if there are such; cf. § 85). Now we must derive a further division of these qualities into the various domains, for example, of sensation qualities and sense modalities. Furthermore, for the individual sense modalities we have to derive a separation of the qualitative order (in the narrow sense) from the order of the sensory field, upon which the spatial order rests. Then we shall have to derive this spatial order itself and a temporal order. With the aid of the qualitative, the spatial, and the temporal order, the world of physical objects is then to be constructed, and finally the further object domains, especially the heteropsychological and the cultural.

The derivations themselves are discussed in the following, the third chapter of this part, and are then given in Part IV in the outline of our constructional system. As far as the problem of basic relations is concerned, we must here anticipate a result of later discussions, namely, that, *even for the further derivations, no new basic relation seems to be required.* Our primary objective is the treatment of the logical, not the content problems of the constructional system; thus, the exposition of the constructional system which is given in the sequel is only an outline, whose main purpose is to show the practical applications of the various formal principles and of the entire constructional method in an example. It is for this reason that we cannot make a definite assertion, but only a conjecture, to the effect that *recollection of similarity* (Rs) *suffices as basic relation for a constructional system with autopsychological basis.* In any event, the investigations show that a very small number of basic relations suffices and that we require as basic relations only relation extensions of elementary experiences and no relation extensions on higher levels. (Cf. the theses in § 156.)

83. *The Basic Relations as Categories* (May be omitted)

By categories are meant the forms of synthesis of the manifold of intuition [80] to the unity of the object. Now neither this explanation (which is not a definition) nor the various traditional tables of categories make it

---
[80] Anschauung

sufficiently clear what is meant by "categories". Since the concepts in our constructional system are clearer than those of the traditional systems, we ask what is there in the constructional system as a system of the synthesis of objects which corresponds to the categories? In construction theory, the manifold of intuition is called "the given", "the basic elements". The synthesis of this manifold to the unity of an object is here called the construction of this object from the given. Thus, the forms of this synthesis would be the constructional forms, of which we have distinguished several (§ 26). One could perhaps mean by "category" our ascension forms. Then we could say that, in our constructional system, we have only two categories, namely, class and relation. But perhaps we are in better agreement with established usage (which is not very clear) if we call the basic relations categories. The following fact would seem to support this: in a certain sense, every statement about any object is, *materialiter*, a statement about the basic elements. But, *formaliter*, it is a statement about the basic relations. Also, the agreement is easy to see when we consider a constructional system where the analysis has not been carried as far as in the present attempt and where, therefore, a larger number of basic relations is introduced.

In an earlier draft of the constructional system, the following five relations were proved to be sufficient basic relations (if we can speak of a proof in the sketchy exposition of that system): (central) part identity (somewhat narrower than Pi in the present system, § 76), (central) part similarity (somewhat narrower than Ps in the present system, cf. § 77), the serial relation of intensity scales (here constructed only after the visual things, § 131), the recollection relation (somewhat more general than the basic relation Rs in the present system, § 78), proximity in the sensory field (more general than Proxpl for visual field places in the present system, § 89). It must be noted that the recollection relation leads immediately to the construction of a (preliminary) time order (in a similar way, Er leads to Er_{po}, § 87), and proximity in the sensory field leads to the construction of a spatial order, namely, at first to the order within the sensory field which must already be called "spatial", later on to the proper spatial order of the physical world (like Proxpl in the present system, § 89).

One can see a certain similarity between the indicated five basic relations of the earlier draft and the categories which occur in some category systems, namely, identity, similarity, intensity, time, and space. Thus, we can envisage the problem of the basic relations in construction theory as the problem of categories.

We have advanced the conjecture (§ 82) that Rs suffices as a basic relation. It is, namely, the case that the five basic relations of the earlier draft can be, in part, derived from one another. Indeed, it appears that they can all be derived from a single one. As a statement about categories, this would have to be expressed in the following way: the five above-mentioned categorial forms are not the actual (fundamental) categories, but they are in part reducible to one another; *the number of (genuine) categories is very small; perhaps there is only a single category.*

D

THE OBJECT FORMS

84. Derivations as Preparation for Construction

Of the four main problems of construction theory (§ 26), only the last one, namely, that of the object forms, remains to be treated. This problem, more than any of the others, is predominantly concerned with the material content of the constructional system. Since we are here mainly concerned with the clarification of the logico-methodological aspect of construction theory, we will not be able to find a ready solution for it at this time. To begin with, we shall investigate, for the most important objects of the lower constructional levels, how they are determined by the basic relation and the already derived objects and thus how they can be constructed from these. The constructions themselves of these and other objects will then be given in the next section, in the outline of the constructional system. Thus the derivations which we are about to give here are in preparation for the constructions themselves. These derivations concentrate mostly upon the material aspect of the problem, while the later constructions will have to show how these material relationships are to be fitted into the logical forms which are to be used in the formulation of the constructional system. Since we are concerned merely with an outline, this process of fitting the material into the logical forms amounts to no more than an application, by way of example, of the methodological forms to those material relationships of the objects themselves. It is the methodological forms with which we are mostly concerned; we assert their validity and utility. On the other hand, the content which we use for our examples is not asserted to be conclusively established. Should the empirical sciences (for the lower constructional levels, this means especially the phenomenology of perception and psychology) come to the conclusion that the relations of objects are different from what we are here supposing, then these different relations must be expressed according to the same methodological principles in appropriate constructional forms. This means that we are here formulating basic relation(s) and object forms only with reservations. On the other hand, the formulation of the basic elements and especially of the system form and the ascension forms belongs to the thesis of our construction theory (cf. the theses in § 156).

Thus the following investigations serve, on the one hand, as a preparation for the following part, for the outline of the constructional system. On the other hand, they should contribute to the support of the conjecture advanced in the preceding section, namely, that a single basic relation suffices for the construction of all objects.

85. *The Sense Classes*

After the quality classes have been derived (§ 81), a relation of similarity (Sim) between them can be defined in a simple way. Two qualities are similar if, and only if, every elementary experience in which the first occurs is part similar to every elementary experience in which the second occurs. Thus, we define: two quality classes a and b are called *similar* (a Sim b) if every element of a is part similar (Ps) to every element of b (construction of Sim in the constructional system: § 114).

With the aid of the relation Sim, we can now proceed with a division into sense modalities. This division must be based upon qualities and not on elementary experiences, since any of the latter may belong to several sense modalities at the same time. Two qualities belong to the same sense modality, if and only if, there is a sequence of qualities between the two such that each quality in the sequence is similar to the next quality in the sequence. (For example, between any two tones, we can form such a chain of Sim pairs, but not between a tone and a fragrance.)

If we call a class which is formed by the qualities of one and the same sense modality a *sense class*, then the sense classes are formed through quasi analysis on the basis of the relation of connectibility through such Sim-chains (construction of sense classes: § 115).

We shall find as ᶜsense classesᶜ not only the classes of visual qualities, auditory qualities, thermal qualities, etc., but also the emotions; this is due to the meaning of the basic relation Rs and to the reasons advanced in § 76. If psychology were ever to demonstrate the existence of psychological entities other than sensations and emotions, entities which could not be reduced to either sensations or emotions, such as, for example, thoughts, volitions, or whatever, then the basic relation would also refer to the similarities between these entities; their ᴾqualitiesᴾ would be constructed as ᶜquality classesᶜ, and their domain or domains would be constructed as sense classes. Thus, no kind of psychological process lies outside the framework of constructable entities.

86. *The Characterization of the Visual Sense*

After the division of the qualities into sense classes has been derived, we can investigate the order of the qualities within each of these sense classes. Indeed, we can envisage Sim as the proximity relation which determines this order. If a proximity relation exists for a given domain, then the *dimension number* (Dn) of the domain is thereby determined (at the moment, we shall not concern ourselves with the definition). Thus every sense class has a certain Dn relative to Sim. We have mentioned above that the sense class of tone sensations has Dn 2, that of the visual sense, of color sensations, Dn 5 (§ 80). For the senses of the skin, the location signs are orderable in two dimensions. Since their qualities are furthermore differentiable through intensity and perhaps also through a quality series, the Dn of each of them (tactile sense, sense of warmth, sense of cold, sense of pain) is 3 or 4. The Dn of the other senses, including the domain of the emotions, is for some of them 2, for others 3.

The most important factor in this connection is that the quality order of the visual sense has a Dn which is different from that of all other senses. Thus it is possible to characterize, construct, give a definite description of, this sense, which is more important for the construction of physical objects than any of the others. The *constructional definition* reads simply: that sense class, for which the order of qualities relative to Sim has the Dn 5, is called the *visual sense* (construction: § 115).

It may seem paradoxical at first sight that we here give a "definition" of the visual sense, indeed, a definition on the basis of such an inessential property as the Dn, which does not have the slightest connection with the special phenomenal peculiarity of the visual sense and its difference from all other sensations. Such an objection, whether it is stated or whether it is merely a subconscious sentiment, rests upon a confusion of the aim of a constructional definition with that of a conceptual definition in the ordinary sense. We have mentioned earlier (§§ 50, 51) that we require of a constructional definition a regard only for logical, not for epistemic, value. For, a translation which is carried out with the aid of a constructional definition as translation rule has to guarantee nothing but the invariance of the truth value of the statements, and not also the invariance of the sense. If we assume that the psychological statement which we have used for our definition, namely, that the Dn of the similarity order for the visual sense, but for no other sense, is 5, then it is quite obvious in the present case that every statement about the visual sense remains true or false if, for the words "visual sense", we substitute "the sense whose similarity order has the Dn 5".

87. *The Temporal Order*

In our perception of physical things, we recognize not only properties in their qualitative and intensive differences, but also spatial and temporal relations. Let us first concern ourselves with the temporal relations. It is easy to see that the temporal determinations of the physical world go back to the recognition of the temporal relation between elementary experiences. The question now arises whether the temporal relation between elementary experiences must be introduced as a basic relation. It turns out, however, that it can be derived from recollection of similarity (Rs). After all, Rs includes a temporal relation: from x Rs y, one can conclude that x is temporally earlier than y. However, we cannot in this way decide for every pair of elementary experiences which of them is temporally earlier; we can make this decision only for part similar elementary experiences. But, because of the transitivity of the time relation, we can infer from such pairs the temporal order of many other pairs. For the construction of the temporal sequence, the recognition of the temporal relation of temporally near elementary experiences is especially important, and such temporally near elementary experiences are in many, perhaps in most, cases, part similar. For, if any sensation quality remains constant or varies continuously during a certain time interval, all temporally near elementary experiences in this time span are part similar to one another.

From the basic relation Rs, we cannot construct an uninterrupted temporal sequence. Nevertheless, we can construct a preliminary temporal order (about its construction, cf. § 120), which we shall have to supplement with the aid of the regularity of physical processes which cannot be done until after the construction of physical objects. Not only here, but also in the actual process of cognition, the time ordering of experiences which is based upon "time perception" is incomplete and becomes a completely ordered sequence only through inferences on the basis of known psychological and especially physical regularities.

88. Derivation of Visual Field Places

We have seen that the visual sense can be differentiated from the other senses without any new basic concept, solely through the dimension number 5 of the similarity order of its qualities. Although we have constructionally introduced this five-dimensional order, we did not thereby introduce the three-dimensional order of the color solid, nor the two-dimensional order of the visual field. The derivations which we have made so far do not enable us to differentiate the various dimensions. If, for example, two qualities, *a, b,* of the visual sense are similar (Sim) to one another in *color type* (i.e., in hue, saturation, and brightness) and if they also belong to two proximate visual field places, briefly, *places,* and if two other qualities *c, d,* are similar to one another by belonging to the same place and by agreeing approximately in color type, then both pairs are called, without distinction, "Sim-pairs", and cannot be distinguished on the basis of their behavior relative to Sim. We call two qualities (without reference to their color types) *place identical* if they agree in their location sign (i.e., if they belong to the same place); correspondingly, we call two qualities *color identical* (without reference to their place) if they agree in color type. Our task is now to derive one of these two relations, either place identity or color identity, from relations that have already been derived. The other one will easily result in either case from the first.

The *derivation of place identity* (Plid) is indeed possible. It rests mainly upon the circumstance that (different) place-identical qualities cannot appear simultaneously in the same elementary experience. This fact can be expressed through the already available derivations. For, in the language of construction theory, it corresponds to the fact that certain pairs of quality classes have no elementary experience as a common element, hence, that they are mutually exclusive quality classes (relation Excl). But Excl is only a necessary, not a sufficient, condition for

Plid. There may be pairs of visual qualities which belong to different places and which never happen to occur together in one experience. Thus we cannot simply define Plid through Excl. On the other hand, we can be sure that all Plid-pairs are found among the Excl-pairs. Thus, the task consists in sorting those unknown pairs out of the known pairs, but this is not immediately possible. However, the following method accomplishes our aim. If Plid had already been derived, we could define the (visual field) places as abstraction classes (§ 73) of Plid (i.e., as the largest possible classes of place identical qualities). If we form instead (through quasi analysis according to § 71) the similarity circles[81] of Excl, then the desired place classes are either identical with them or subclasses of them.

> It might seem as though this would not help us at all, as though we had only exchanged the earlier difficulty of sorting out the correct Plid-pairs from the Excl pairs for the new difficulty of sorting out the desired place-classes from the similarity circles [81] of Excl. In reality, however, the conditions are here quite different. In the earlier case, we had no reason to suppose that the Excl-pairs were, for the most part, also Plid-pairs. On the other hand, the probability that those similarity circles [81] are very much more comprehensive than the place classes which are contained in them is considerably smaller for the following reason: in order to make an erroneous assignment through quasi analysis of an element to a place class, it does not suffice that this element should have the relation Excl to one or more elements of the place, but it would have to have this relation to all elements of the place; this follows from the definition of similarity circles.[81] Looked at from another point of view: there are two necessary conditions for an erroneous assignment of an element to a given place class, namely, first, that the visual field place in question should be unoccupied in at least one elementary experience and, secondly, that the element to be assigned, which actually belongs to a different place, should occur only in such experiences as leave that other place unoccupied. For, in all other cases, the relation Excl would not obtain.

Through a more detailed investigation, one can show the following: if unoccupied places do not occur too frequently, then the number of Excl-pairs may still be considerably larger than the number of Plid-pairs; nevertheless, the probability that the similarity circles [81] of Excl surpass the place classes considerably is relatively very small. Incidentally, one

---

[81] The first German edition reads *"Abstraktionsklassen"* at the indicated places. The change is due to Prof. Carnap; it follows Prof. Goodman's observation that, since Excl. (*Fre*) is a nontransitive relation, there can be no abstraction class of Excl.

can see at once whether a similarity circle [81] is a proper place class by noticing that none of its elements belongs to another similarity circle.[81] Elements whose membership is doubtful betray themselves through repeated occurrence; one ought to make them the subject of a special investigation after the preliminary place classes have been constructed and have been brought into a proximity order. We cannot concern ourselves here with the relatively difficult procedure of this investigation (the determination of the similarity relations between certain quality classes of proximate places), but, through it, we could construct the definitive place classes. For our purposes, it is satisfactory to have shown the possibility of dividing the visual qualities into place classes through a simple procedure, even though this division holds only approximately (i.e., with the possible exception of individual visual qualities which cannot be assigned a place with this simple procedure [construction of place classes, § 117]).

89. *The Spatial Order of the Visual Field*

From the just-derived place classes, Plid is derivable, namely, as membership in the same place class (construction: § 117).

The introduction of place classes, which represent the visual field places, does not in itself lead to the spatial ordering of the visual field; this results only from the relations between the places, which, however, can now easily be derived.

Two places are called proximate places (Proxpl), if a quality of one of them is similar to a quality of the other (construction § 117). (We do not say "all qualities" since it is not impossible that at a given place qualities of certain color types do not occur.) Proxpl is the fundamental relation for the spatial order of the visual field. Thus, for example, the statement that the visual field is two dimensional is a statement about a certain formal property of Proxpl. (Thus, it does not mean that the visual field is like a surface in the phenomenal sense.)

REFERENCES. The literature does not seem to contain any attempts at the construction of the initial spatial order, that is, of the two-dimensional order of the visual field. The two systems which otherwise give the most detailed description of the individual constructions, namely, Ziehen [Erkth.] and Driesch [Ordnungsl.] skip over this construction even though it already requires a very considerable number of steps (even if

---

[81] See preceeding note.

one does not take only one basic relation, but a special basic relation for spatial ordering; they also omit the construction of three-dimensional space from the two-dimensional visual field order, which has repeatedly been discussed by others (cf. the references in § 124).

90. *The Ordering of Colors*

For the ordering of colors, which we frequently represent graphically in the form of the color solid, we do not need any further basic relation. The color order can be derived from the place classes and the proximity relation (Proxpl). For any two different colors, *f*, *g*, there is at least one color which is similar to *f*, but not to *g*. From this it follows: if *s*, *t*, *u*, are three neighboring places and if the quality *a* belongs to *s*, and the quality *b* to *t*, and if *a* and *b* have a different color type (this word comprises the dimensions of hue, saturation, and brightness), then it is not the case that both of them are similar to the same qualities of *u*. On the other hand, if *a* and *b* are both similar to the same qualities of *u*, then *a* and *b* must have the same color type, and vice versa: if they have the same color type, then the similar qualities in *u* must also be of that color type. Thus, this behavior of *a* and *b* can be used for a definition of "color identity in proximate places". From this we can derive the relation of color identity for arbitrary places (Colid): it holds between qualities *a* and *b* if, between *a* and *b*, there exists a chain of qualities such that each has to the next the relation of "color identity in proximate places" (construction: § 118).

The colors (in the sense of color types) result now simply as abstraction classes of Colid (construction: § 118).

In analogy to the relation of proximate places, we define here as *proximate colors* (Proxcol) two colors *f* and *g* if they are of such a kind that a quality of *f* is similar to a quality of *g*. (Generally speaking to each quality of *f*, there will be at least one similar quality in *g*, and vice versa, namely, a quality that occurs in the same or in a proximate place; however, for reasons similar to those given in connection with Proxpl we do not want to found our definition upon this fact.) The ordering of colors which depends upon Proxcol, we call *color solid*. The three-dimensionality of the color solid can be expressed analogously to the two-dimensionality of the visual field as a formal property of Proxcol (construction: § 118).

91. *Objections to the Given Derivation of the Visual Field Order and the Color Order*

Through the indicated derivations, we have divided the five-dimensional similarity order (i.e., the order based on similarity [Sim]) of the visual qualities into the two-dimensional order of the (visual field) places and the three-dimensional order of the colors. This division was possible because of the fact that the two relations of place identity and color identity are formally different from one another in that various color-identical qualities can occur in the same elementary experience, but not different place-identical qualities. One could object to this that the difference between the relation of two different colors in the same place and the relation of two identical colors in different places is not a merely formal difference, but a difference in quality or essence. It could be argued that, if only one basic relation is introduced, one cannot do justice to this essential difference, and that it is thus necessary to use several basic relations, among which there would have to be represented a qualitative and a location relation. It is indeed the case that the question as to the number of necessary basic relations has not yet been conclusively resolved. But, even if we were to introduce further basic relations, the difference between place identity and color identity does not belong to the given, but would have to be derived, for it is not a difference between pairs of elementary experiences themselves, but between pairs of qualities; the qualities would still have to be derived (namely through quasi analysis), and the same would hold a fortiori for that difference. Admittedly, the difference would, in this case, go back to different relations between elementary experiences which would be immediately given as different. Suppose that the difference between the two orders, which we have established through formal properties of the respective relations, is instead traced back to a qualitative difference between color and location sign (for the "places" must depend upon "location signs" of some sort). It must then be pointed out that, even in this case, these two quality determinations, with whose intuitively comprehensible difference we are here concerned, have the same status. But their role, for the construction of knowledge,[82] is nevertheless altogether different. One of the two determinations, the location sign, serves as the foundation of the "principle of individuation". It determines a preliminary ordering of places, upon which the spatial ordering ultimately rests. That this func-

---

[82] Erkenntnisaufbau

tion can be fulfilled by only one of the determinations is due precisely to that formal property of place identity through which we have separated it from color identity, namely, that nonidentical, place-identical qualities cannot occur in the same experience. Thus the separation of the two orders which we have carried out rests upon a formal, but not at all inessential, difference, namely, upon the difference in those properties on which the roles of the two determinations for the recognition of reality are based, namely, the role of that which orders (location sign) and of that which is being ordered (colors). We shall later on examine further considerations which are connected with this difference and with its role as a principle of individuation (§ 158).

92. *Other Possibilities for a Derivation of the Visual Field*

The indicated method for the derivation of the order of the visual field places is not the only one which is possible. It could be argued that only one kind of construction could be the correct one, since only one of them can properly reflect (more precisely: rationally reconstruct) the process of cognition as it takes place in the normal individual under normal circumstances. The reason for the multiplicity of possibilities lies in the fact that the real process of cognition, which we shall call *intuitive* in contrast to the rational reconstruction, is overdetermined.[83] Hence, the possibility and necessity of a plurality of determinations each of which would be sufficient by itself.

In the above-stated method of derivation of the visual field (§ 89), we have used only the similarity of the location sign of proximate visual field places. It is possible that this factor, even though it is always present, is not fundamental as far as the psychology of cognition is concerned. It could be that, fundamentally, the location signs are not comparable and that they do not exhibit relations of similarity to one another. It could be the case that certain pairs of location signs are marked as similar pairs only through an association due to a change in color quality which results upon a small motion of the eyes. It could also be the case that, from the viewpoint of the psychology of cognition, we should think of the origin of the relations between visual field places in a different way, namely, as connected with the kinesthetic sensations of the eye muscles. A different constructional derivation of the visual field order could be based upon such an assumption.

Let us discuss a third possibility of the derivation of the visual field

---

[83] überbestimmt

order because it raises a point which is of general importance. This derivation, compared to the previous ones, assumes a good deal less as given. We could take as given only what occurs in the visual focus and disregard all that is seen indirectly. However, in this case, we must assume as possible that two (or more) color types which have a common boundary (or meet in a point) can be sensed simultaneously in the visual focus, while we have previously claimed that to one place of the visual field there corresponds always only one color type. The colors which occur in this case form, to begin with, a one-dimensional order which is due to their temporal relations. We can easily arrive at higher orders, at a sort of visual field, by utilizing, in addition, the kinesthetic sensations of the eye movements. However, it is possible, even in this case, to do without the kinesthetic sensations, even though this makes the construction considerably more difficult. While we would then not have a visual field, the construction would lead to a two-dimensional order, just as in the derivations which we have discussed earlier. (We can easily convince ourselves of this fact if we think of the series of visual point sensations which we have when the eye is moved but the surroundings are unchanged.)

It is remarkable that in all cases (even though in different ways) there results at first a two-dimensional order, from which only later a three-dimensional order is constructed, namely, the order which we take to be the spatial order of physical reality. Once physical reality is fully constructed, we can go backward, interpreting the various two-dimensional orders and "explaining" their two-dimensionality from a certain property of physical reality which includes essentially certain physiological things and processes. We can then explain, from the two-dimensional order of the retinal organs, the fact that the visual field turns out to be two dimensional in the first type of derivation (i.e., on the basis of the location signs). For the construction with the aid of eye movements, the explanation goes back to the fact that the eye can be moved in two dimensions relative to the head. Finally, we have shown the possibility of a construction of the two-dimensional order of the visual field on the basis of visual point sensations, without any reference to sensations of eye movement. We have done this predominantly for the following reason: this third possibility, which leaves out of consideration the relations of location signs, shows that the actual reason for the two-dimensionality of the local order of the seen lies neither in the constitution of the retina nor in the nature of the eye movement; rather, the reason for this (always from the viewpoint of the completely constructed, three-dimensional, physical world) lies in the fact that the light rays which fall upon one point form a bundle of rays of second degree and are therefore ordered two-dimensionally. On the other hand, the constitution of the visual organ, as far as the arrangement of the nerve endings and its type of mobility are concerned, can be considered of practical value in view of this fact, since it facilitates the recognition of the two-dimensional order, but it is not absolutely necessary for the construction of this order.

93. The "Sensations" as Individual Constituents of Experiences

Above, we have constructed quality classes as classes of elementary experiences which represent the constituents of elementary experiences as quasi constituents. If two elementary experiences belong to the same quality class, then we say that the two experiences agree in a certain constituent. If we wish to differentiate the two like constituents of the two elementary experiences, then it does not suffice just to characterize them as to quality, but we must, in addition, identify the elementary experience to which they belong. Only a constituent which is so characterized is an individual, strictly unique constituent in the proper sense. In contrast to a constituent which is characterized only as to its quality (i.e., only as to how it is represented in a quality class), we wish to call it a "sensation". Actually, we choose this word only for the sake of brevity (according to what has been said above [§§ 76, 85], it also refers to simple emotions). Consequently, we would have to define a sensation as an ordered pair consisting of an elementary experience and a quality class, to which the experience belongs. (ᴾThe quality is a constituent of the experienceᴾ; ᶜthe experience is an element of the qualityᶜ.)

Simultaneity of constituents of experience relates to sensations: two sensations are called "simultaneous" if the elementary experiences (i.e., the referents of the pairs) are identical (construction of sensations and simultaneity: § 116).

> REFERENCES. Sensations properly belong to the object domain of psychology; qualities, on the other hand, belong to the domain of phenomenology or the theory of objects [84]; there they are called "objects of sensation": Meinong [Gegenstandsth.] 512, [Stellung] 8 ff.

It must be noted that, in our constructional system, we do not construct the qualities from the sensations (perhaps as classes of sensations, as certain positivistic theories would have it), but, vice versa, the sensa-

---

[84] Gegenstandstheorie

tions are constructed from the qualities. These qualities, of course, are then constructed from elementary experiences (thus fulfilling a general tenet of positivism). We mentioned, as one of our basic tenets, that the individual constituents of an elementary experience do not stand out in the individual experience, but are gained only through abstraction, namely, by placing the experience into orders which comprise other experiences also. It is a consequence of this that sensations are constructed from quality classes and not vice versa. *An individual experience, taken by itself, is unanalyzable. Experiences, taken as a manifold, can be compared and ordered, and only through their order result the (quasi) constituents of the individual experiences.*

94. Prospect of Further Derivations

We now have given derivations for the most important objects of the lower levels (i.e., we have determined how they may be constructed); thus we have determined their "object form". In doing so, we have used the relation extension of recollection of similarity as the only basic relation. Let us take a brief look at the derivation of some further objects, paying particular attention to whether new basic relations are required.

An especially important step in the constructional system is the construction of the three-dimensional spatial order, i.e., of visual space, from the two-dimensional order, namely, the visual field. Here are constructed, for the first time, things which belong to "reality" (in the sense of "outside world"). In the actual process of cognition, tactile and muscle sensations play an important role. However, the construction can be carried out with the aid of visual sensations alone. It will turn out that, for this construction, no new basic relation is required. We shall give a brief indication of this derivation to show that it can be carried out.

The visual sensations (as individual constituents of experiences) are arranged in a one-dimensional sequence (time sequence) of three-dimensional structures [85] (spaces) in a way that can be inferred from the temporal sequence of spatially ordered visual fields (of the individual experiences), where it is assumed that what is seen retains its characteristics of color, shape, and position, except where changes are either seen or inferred by analogy. We shall later on determine the construction of the space-time world more precisely (§§ 125–127). The "visual

---

[85] Gefüge

things" result from certain characteristically coördinated "world lines" of this four-dimensional structure (§ 128).

It must be noted that, for the construction of visual things and of three-dimensional space, we need neither the senses other than the visual sense nor the components of the visual qualities (hue, saturation, brightness), which, after all, have not yet been distinguished from one another through the derivations which we have given so far. Although this circumstance does not result in an economy in basic relations, it makes possible a methodological simplification of construction.

In the actual process of cognition, the three-dimensional character of things seems to be immediately given, at least in the case of persons whose consciousness is fully developed. There are cases, however, where the spatial order is the result of an ordering activity; this shows that the construction is not a mere fiction, but a rational reconstruction of actual processes. In the case of spatial ordering, this can of course be shown only if special difficulties keep the synthesis in the actual process of cognition, which corresponds to the construction, from proceeding as quickly and unconsciously as is usually the case. This is, for example, the case in the orientation of blind persons (cf. the interesting remarks of Ahlmann [Opt. Vorst.]).

From the indicated constructions, we shall then proceed to further constructions. Among the visual things, "my body" stands out through certain characteristics (§ 129). With its aid, we can give individual definite descriptions of the most important other senses, having identified, up to this point, only the visual sense (§§ 129, 131). Furthermore, the various components of the qualities which are represented in the quality classes can then be derived (e.g., quality in the narrower sense, intensity, location sign). In this way, we shall finally construct all the psychological entities of the autopsychological domain—in the derivations which have been discussed or sketched so far, we have been concerned only with this domain, and not with the heteropsychological domain. We shall also be able to divide these autopsychological entities into main areas ("sense classes") and discern their components (§ 131 f.). The construction of the autopsychological domain does not require any further basic relations.

We have to construct, then, the "perceptual things" by an assignment of the qualities of the other senses to the visual things (§ 133 f.). We shall construct the "world of physics" with the aid of the "world of perception" (§ 136). In such a way, we can construct the entire domain of physical objects.

The possibility of the construction of the heteropsychological objects follows from the earlier discussions concerning the reducibility of these objects to physical objects (§§ 57, 58); the possibility of the construction of cultural objects follows from the consideration concerning their reducibility to psychological objects (§§ 55, 56). Later on, we shall return to the construction of the heteropsychological objects (§ 140) and the construction of cultural objects (§ 150 f.) without, however, indicating their precise object forms. Nevertheless, it will become clear that, even for the construction of these object types, *no new basic relations are required.*

E

FORMS OF REPRESENTATION FOR A CONSTRUCTIONAL SYSTEM

95. *The Four Languages*

It is useful to give several parallel forms of representation or "languages" for the constructional system, in order to facilitate its comprehension and examination. In representing the outline of our constructional system in the next part, we shall use four languages, which are different from one another, partly only in form, but partly also as concerns their sense. By difference in sense, we mean a difference in the ideas [86] which different persuasions may connect with the constructional formula of an object which is otherwise neutral as far as sense is concerned. Thus, it is a difference in sense (or epistemic value) where the logical value remains the same (§ 50).

The basic language of the constructional system is the symbolic language of logistics. It alone gives the proper and precise expression for the constructions; the other languages serve only as more comprehensible auxiliary languages. However, in the following outline we shall give only the construction of the lower levels in this language. The reason for this does not lie in the fact that the objects of higher type offer particular difficulties of expression for this language, but in the fact that the problem

---

[86] Vorstellungen

of constructing the higher objects has itself not been solved with precision and that these constructions therefore can be given only in bold outline. As soon as the content of the construction of any object is precisely known, there are no difficulties in the way of a logistic formulation. This basic language of logistics we shall discuss in somewhat more detail in § 96, and we shall explain the most important symbols in § 97.

The other three languages offer nothing but translations from this basic language of logistics. To begin with, we shall give, after each constructional definition, a simple *paraphrase in word language* (cf. § 98). Then follows a translation into the *realistic language* customary in the empirical sciences. Its main purpose is to facilitate testing the correctness of the *content* of the construction (i.e., whether or not the constructional definition actually refers to the familiar object to which it purports to refer (§ 98)). Finally, we have used a *language of fictitious constructive operations*,[87] in which the construction is envisaged as a rule for a constructive operation. Its main purpose is to facilitate the intuitive recognition of the *formal* correctness of the construction (i.e., the testing of whether each constructional definition is operative,[88] that is, not ambiguous, not empty, and purely extensional) (§§ 99, 101, 102).

REFERENCES. Gätschenberger [Symbola] gives an explicit discussion of the relation between different languages which deal with the same state of affairs. His considerations can be used to facilitate the understanding of the multilingual technique which we are using here. The basic language of our constructional system forms a sketch for a unified language such as is demanded by Gätschenberger; it also has the algorithmic properties which Gätschenberger desires. However, we do not wish to make the claim that this sketch solves the problem of the unified language; rather, the problem is clarified as through an example, and the method for its solution is given.

96. *The Symbolic Language of Logistics*

The actual language of the constructional system is the symbolic language of logistics. The construction of the individual objects (of the lower levels), as well as some statements ("theorems") as examples, are given in "logistic formulation" (§ 46). There are two reasons for the application of this symbolic language. To begin with, a constructed object must clearly be distinguished from the corresponding object of

---

[87] Sprache einer fiktiven Konstruktion
[88] konstruktiv

daily life or of science. We have already shown the necessity for this distinction in the preceding chapter and have occasionally tried to make it obvious through special auxiliary symbols (p-symbols, c-symbols [§ 75]). The application of the symbolism, however, is more important for the attainment of a second desideratum: we must demonstrate that all objects are reducible to the basic objects (i.e., that all sentences about further objects are transformable into sentences which contain only logical signs and signs for the basic objects). It is obvious that the value of a constructional system stands or falls with the purity of this reduction, just as the value of an axiomatic exposition of a theory depends upon the purity of the derivations of theorems from axioms. We can best insure the purity of this reduction through the application of an appropriate symbolism. An application of the word language, without special symbolism, would guarantee this purity only if there were a system of the concepts of logistics in the word language, especially of the theory of relations, which is the most important part of logistics as far as the constructional system is concerned. Such a word system is not available, and one may doubt whether it will ever be developed, since the advantages of the symbolic treatment are obvious to everyone who is concerned with the theory of relations. The advantages are the same that we find in mathematics when we use the symbolism rather than expressing all mathematical equations and operations in a word language.

However, the system of constructions must not only be "pure" (i.e., free of unnoticed conceptual elements), but also formally accurate. In order for a constructional definition to fulfill its object-constructing function, it must be neither ambiguous nor empty, that is, it must not designate more than one, but it must also designate at least one, object (in the most general sense, including the quasi objects, i.e., either an individual, or a class, or a relation extension). If we formulate the definition in the word language, then this requirement is very difficult to fulfill (as is the related desideratum of "operativeness" of the construction, § 102, which we shall introduce in connection with the language of constructive operations). On the other hand, this requirement is easily and almost automatically fulfilled when we apply an appropriate symbolism, for example, when we apply the logistic forms for the introduction of classes or relation extensions and for definite descriptions of individuals. It is a fact of logistics that these forms guarantee unequivocalness and logical existence, for they have been created with these desired properties in view.

97. *Explanation of Some Logistic Symbols*

Knowledge of logistics is not a precondition for an understanding of construction theory nor for an understanding of the outline of a constructional system which is given below, since all logistical formulas which are introduced at that place are translated into the word language. Nevertheless, let us here indicate the meaning of those logistical symbols which will be used later, to the extent to which they have not already been explained earlier.

REFERENCES. For a more detailed exposition of logistics, cf. Carnap [Logistik]. For further references, cf. § 3.

EXPLANATION OF LOGISTIC SYMBOLS

Constants: classes with lower case, relations with capital, initial letter.

Variables: classes: α, β, . . . ; relations: P, Q, R, . . . ; in general: x, y, z.

Statements: $\sim$: negation; $\supset$: implication; one or several dots: conjunction (also substitute for parentheses); $=$ (or I): identity; $=_{df}$: definition symbol.

Propositional functions (§ 28): if fx is a propositional function, then (x) . fx means: "fx holds for every x"; $(\exists x)$. fx means: "there is an x for which fx holds."

Classes (§ 33): $\alpha \cap \beta$: intersection; $\alpha \cup \beta$; union; $\alpha \subset \beta$: subsumption; $\alpha - \beta$: remainder. α Ex β: "α and β have no element in common." $\exists ! \alpha$: "α is not empty"; $[x]$ or $\iota'x$: the class whose only element is x. If μ is a class of classes, then s'μ is the union of the μ-classes. Every class α has a cardinal number Nc'α (§ 40). The customary symbols are used for numbers, e.g., $>$, / (fraction sign).

Relations (§ 34, 11): Let Q, R be relation extensions. $\cap$, $\cup$, $\subset$ mean the same as with the classes (we omit the dot for the sake of simplicity). $\overrightarrow{R}'x$: the referents of x in R. R $\upharpoonright$ α: the relation which results from R if its converse domain is restricted to α; R $\vartriangleright$ α: the relation which results from R if its field is restricted to α. $\alpha \uparrow \beta$: the relation which holds between every element of α and every element of β. $x \downarrow y$: the relation whose only pair is x, y. as, sym, refl: the class, respectively, of asymmetrical, symmetrical, and transitive relations.

Quasi analysis (§§ 71, 73): Simil'R: the class of similarity circles based on R. Abstr'R: the class of abstraction classes based on R. Topology: Dnp (n, α, x, U): α has, in element x, the dimension number n

relative to a neighborhood relation U. Vicin'Q: the neighborhood rela-
tion, which is determined by the (proximity) relation Q. n Dnhomvic
Q: the field of Q has the homogenous dimension number n relative to
Vicin'Q.

98. Paraphrase in Word Language and Realistic Language

For each symbolic construction formula, we shall give a paraphrase in
words. However, this paraphrase is not to be envisaged as a strict formulation of the construction. Its purpose is to indicate the sense of the
formula in a more understandable, if less precise, manner. On the other
hand, the last two languages each give a new sense for each construction.

According to a symbolism which we used earlier (§ 75), the paraphrase in the word language should be enclosed in c̆-symbols, while the
realistic language corresponds to the expressions which we have previously marked by p-symbols. For each construction, we shall indicate
in realistic language the state of affairs on which it is based.

The introduction of a new symbol through a constructional definition
has a certain economic value; namely, the constructed entity can from
now on, in further statements and constructions, be designated with a
simple symbol instead of the complex constructing expression. In addition, the constructed entity is to be envisaged as a rational reconstruction
of an entity which has already been constructed in a partly intuitive,
partly rational way in daily life or in the sciences; thus, the name this
object bears in daily life guides the choice of the symbol. Hence, the
definition contains, among other things, also an assertion, namely, that a
certain familiar object, as far as its rational concept is concerned, can be
derived from such and such basic concepts in such and such a way. It
must be admitted that it is sometimes not easy to realize that a given
constructed entity corresponds in fact to a certain familiar object. The
schematic construction formulas seem at first strange, but it is also
difficult to recognize in a map the schematic representation of a land-
scape. The recognition of this agreement is facilitated by the translation
of the construction of an object into the realistic language, for this
translation expresses the fact that the indicated object, and only this
object, possesses certain properties as distinguishing characteristics.

99. The Language of Fictitious Constructive Operations

The individual constructions will be translated into a fourth language,
into the language of fictitious constructive operations. Here, the con-

structional definitions are not envisaged as acts of naming (as in the first and second languages) or as descriptions of familiar objects (as in the third language), but as operating rules for a constructive procedure. We shall presently describe in some detail certain appropriate fictions; once these fictions are introduced, the constructions can be expressed, as it were, as palpable processes, and thus the translation into this language satisfies best the desire for intuitive obviousness. This obviousness not only facilitates understanding, but also has heuristic value. While the realistic translation, through the continued contact with the facts of science, regulates the constructions with respect to their content, the language of constructive operations has a regulating effect with respect to their form. It precludes an attempted construction, as it were, automatically during the preliminary considerations, if the new object does not have a purely formal connection with the already constructed objects; in such cases, an operative formulation of a construction is altogether impossible (i.e., we cannot give it the form of an operating rule for the formation of an inventory list).

Appropriate fictions are chosen by keeping in mind the purpose of the constructions as rational reconstructions of the recognition of objects. This reconstruction is to reflect the formal structure of the formation of objects.[89] Hence, we shall introduce, to begin with, the fiction of a temporal separation between the experience of the raw material of cognition and our acting upon this material. Thereafter, we introduce the fiction of the retainability of the given (§ 101). As an overriding fiction, we assume that we have the task of providing a given subject A with rules for step-by-step operations through which A can arrive at the construction of certain schemata ("inventory lists") which correspond to the individual objects that are to be constructed (§ 102). If a constructional definition can be translated into such an operating rule, then we can be certain that the construction is purely extensional, as construction theory requires of each construction.

In the sequel (§ § 100–102), we shall give a more detailed description of the presuppositions and the method of the language of constructive operations. It must be emphasized that *the constructional system itself has nothing to do with these fictions;* they are related only to the fourth language, whose purpose is purely didactic, namely, to provide illustrations.

---

[89] Gegenstandsbildung

100. *Construction as Rational Reconstruction*

The "given" is never found in consciousness as mere raw material, but always in more or less complicated connections and formations. The synthesis of cognition, i.e., the formation of entities, or representations of things and of "reality", from the given, does not, for the most part, take place according to a conscious procedure.

> EXAMPLE. In looking at a house, we perceive it immediately and intuitively as a corporeal object; we imagine its unperceived back side, its continued existence while we are not looking at it. We recognize the determinate, familiar house; yet most of the time no explicit mental deductions are carried out.

In science, too, synthesis, the formation of objects, and cognition take place, for the most part, intuitively and not in the rational form of logical deductions.

> EXAMPLE. In perception, the botanist forms the object of an individual plant as a physical object, without thereby engaging in any conscious thinking activity; most of the time, he recognizes intuitively this thing as a plant of such and such a species.

The fact that the synthesis of cognition, namely, the object formation and the recognition of, or classification into, species, takes place intuitively, has the advantage of ease, speed, and obviousness. But intuitive recognition (e.g., of a plant) can become useful for further scientific work only because it is possible to give, in addition, the indicators (of the particular species of plant), to compare them with the perception and thus to give a rational justification of intuition.

The constructional system is a rational reconstruction of the entire formation of reality, which, in cognition, is carried out for the most part intuitively. In reconstructing the recognition of the plant, the botanist has to ask himself what, in the actual act of recognition, was really perceived and what was apperceptive synthesis? [90] But these two components which are united in the result he can separate only through abstraction. Thus, in rational reconstruction, construction theory has to distinguish, by means of abstraction, between the purely given and the synthesis; this division must be made, not only for the individual case, but for the entire conscious process.

---

[90] Verarbeitung

101. *The Fiction of the Separation and the Retainability of the Given*

The fourth language, namely, the language of "fictitious constructive operations", has the purpose of illustrating the constructions. In connection with it, we wish to make the assumption that a certain subject A is to be given operational rules as to how objects are to be formed from the given. Now we have just seen that it is necessary for construction theory to carry out in abstraction a separation between the purely given and the synthetic components (i.e., the constructional forms). In the present context, this is expressed as the fiction of the temporal separation of the given from the synthesis; during the first part of his life, A merely absorbs the given, without working upon it, and then, in the second part of his life, he synthesizes the retained material according to the rules which we have given him, without absorbing, during this part of his life, any more of the given. The only fictitious assumption concerning the experience (i.e., the contents of the first part of A's life) is the abstraction from all synthetic aspects. The further fictions are concerned only with the second part of his life. Here we ascribe certain abilities to A so that he is in a position to carry out this synthesis, and finally we also deny him certain bits of information so that the synthesis takes place only within the framework which is determined through the constructional method. We think of all synthetic elements, and thus of all thought processes, as separated from the experiences only for the purpose of this auxiliary language of fictitious construction. It is understood that, in construction proper, all content which occurs in experiences must be reflected in the constructions; thus, the acts of thought must also be constructed (cf. § 85).

In order to be able to apply the indicated fictional separation, we have to assume a further fiction, namely, that the given which has been experienced is not forgotten, but that A retains it in his memory, or that he makes a protocol of it, since otherwise there would be no material to be synthesized in the second part of his life. This fiction of the retainability of the given deviates from reality in various ways. To begin with, in real life, many things are forgotten, and, furthermore, we do not generally retain in our memory the raw given, but high-level, synthesized elements,[91] for example, physical or heteropsychological objects.

In construction, it is not essential to reproduce the process of cognition

---

[91] Verarbeitetes hoher Stufe

in all its aspects. During the discussion of the problem of the basic relations, we have already explained that, of the many relations which hold between the experiences, we postulate only the smallest number necessary to be able, in principle, to construct reality from them. "In principle" means that we shall disregard the question whether the construction of an individual object requires much or only a little material. As it were, each construction must be understood in the following way: "This object can be constructed in such and such a way from the given, provided only that a sufficient supply of the given is available." In the language of constructive operations, this aspect of the construction is to be expressed through the fiction that A does not forget anything of the given.

There is another assumption which is connected with the fiction of the retainability of the given, namely, that each element of the given (each elementary experience) is identically retained, so that, during the synthesis, it can be utilized more than once and can be identified each time as identically the same. In our fiction, we could express this, for example, by saying that each individual elementary experience is provided with an arbitrary, but permanent, token, for example, an (arbitrary) number.

102. *The Fiction of the Basic Relation Lists*

We realized earlier (§ 75) that construction theory may assume, as its initial material for the constructional system, not a property description, but merely a pair list of the elementary experiences which is based on the basic relation of the constructional system. In the language of constructive operations, this assumption is expressed by saying that, of the elementary experiences which A has in the first part of his life, A may not retain or record the individual properties of these elementary experiences, but only the pair list based on the basic relations. This is to say, A may retain an *inventory list of each basic relation* as a list of the number pairs of those elementary experiences between which the basic relation in question holds; thus, in our constructional system, A may retain nothing but the pair list of the only basic relation Rs. Constructions of impermissible (namely, not purely "operative" or "extensional") form cannot be expressed as operational rules; herein lies the regulative value of the indicated fiction.

The constructional system is a rational reconstruction of a process of cognition whose results are already known. Consequently, we add to the fiction of this language of constructive operations the assumption that, even though A does not know all of reality, it is known to us, since we have to give A his rules of procedure. It is only on the basis of this knowledge that we know which constructional steps are appropriate for each level and to which entity each of them leads, even though we do not know of what nature A's experiences are. Thus, for the purposes of this fiction, we assume that we know the sense [92] of the basic relation(s) so that, starting from it (them), we can lead A to the entities which we have in mind. On the other hand, we are not familiar with the basic relation list(s) of A. This fiction forces us to formulate constructions as operational rules independently from the individual subject. A, on the other hand, is familiar only with his relation list(s), but not with the sense of the basic relation(s).

The utility of the fictions which we have introduced has now become clear. They help us to maintain and examine the conceptual purity of the operational rules and thus of the constructional definitions. It is absolutely necessary that this purity be strictly maintained, either with the aid of such fictions or otherwise. Philosophical discussions which are somehow concerned with constructions frequently make the mistake of not restricting themselves to those data which may occur in the construction of an object.

Thus the translation of each construction into the language of constructive operations has the form of a rule. A uses this rule to produce, step by step, the inventory list of each constructed object, starting with his inventory list of the basic relation(s). If the object is constructed as a class, then the inventory list states the elements of the class; in the case of a relation extension, it states the member-pairs. A furnishes all constructed objects with individual, but arbitrary, tokens, for example, numbers, so that they may be mentioned in further lists. After the formation of each new inventory list, A is to produce supplemental entries.[93] That is to say, for each object, A produces, in addition to the inventory list, which is immediately given in its final version, also an *object description,* which is constantly enlarged through supplemental entries from later constructions. The supplemental entries of the inventory list of a class consist in attaching to the object description of each of its elements the information that this element belongs to this class. We have discussed examples of this in connection with quasi analysis, where certain classes were assigned to their elements as quasi constituents. The supplemental entries of the inventory list of a relation consist in the following: in the object descriptions of each of its members, it is noted

---

[92] Beziehungssinn
[93] Rückübertragung

to which other members it stands in this relation (extension) and which other members stand in this relation (extension) to it. Thus, the inventory list and object description of an object in the language of constructive operations correspond to what, in realistic language, is called definite description and characterization of an object. The definite description gives only necessary and sufficient characteristics for the determination that precisely this object is present. The characterization mentions all further known properties and relations of the object. The subsequent applications will clearly show how the inventory lists and object descriptions are to be formed (IV, A, § 108 ff. always under the heading "fictitious operation").

The question now arises whether it is always possible to translate a constructional definition into such an operating rule concerning the formation of an inventory list of a new object from the inventory lists of the basic relation(s) and the previously constructed objects. This requirement of operativeness of the constructions is easily fulfilled if the logistic language is used; the constructional definitions must have the form of extensional definitions. From the logical theory of extensions, it follows that the inventory list of a newly defined concept can be formed if this concept is defined as an extension (i.e., class or relation extension) and if the inventory lists of the other concepts which are mentioned in the definition are known. (About the concept of extension, cf. § 32; about the extensional method of construction, cf. §§ 43, 45.)

103. *About the General Rules of Construction*
(§§ 103 to 105 may be omitted)

System form and object forms of the constructional system are empirically determined; i.e., these forms depend upon reality and the individual objects which are presupposed as empirically known. However, when we are confronted on a given level with a certain empirical situation, then we may proceed in such and such a way or ways and in no other way; this must depend upon certain formal properties in the actual process of cognition as well as in the corresponding constructional system which is its reconstruction. *Thus each constructional step can be envisaged as the application of a general formal rule to the empirical situation of the level in question.* By empirical situation, we mean the properties of the already constructed entities which, even though formal, are nevertheless given only empirically. For example, we find through empirical investigation whether a certain constructed relation is transitive or not, etc., or whether or not two classes partially overlap, etc. The formal rule, however, is not itself empirical inasmuch as it represents an implication which holds, not only for a special level, but for each place of the constructional system.

These general rules could be called a priori rules, since the construction and cognition of the object is logically dependent upon them. However, we cannot become conscious of these rules except through abstraction from already formed or constructed experiences. Since the constructions of the individual objects are, for the most part, known with only very little precision, we are not in a position to carry out this abstraction (the constructional system which is sketched in the sequel gives the construction of individual objects only for the lower levels and, even in these cases, only in an experimental way, while the constructions of the higher levels are merely indicated). However, the rules are not to be designated as "a priori knowledge", for they do not represent knowledge, but *postulations*.[94] In the actual process of cognition, these postulations are carried out unconsciously. Even in scientific procedures, we are rarely conscious of them and they are rarely made explicit.

104. *Tentative Formulation of Some Construction Rules*

A system of general constructional rules (i.e., of rules which hold for any level) cannot yet be given for the reasons indicated above. Let us nevertheless attempt to formulate some such rules in order to show what is meant by "general rules" and what they would have to look like. These formulations have the character merely of a tentative example. (Concerning the terminology of the theory of relations, cf. §§ 11, 34.)

1. If any relation [95] is given (no matter whether it is a basic relation or a constructed relation on any level), then its domain, its converse domain, and (if possible, i.e., if the relation is homogeneous) its field is constructed. (We shall later apply this rule in the construction of elex, § 109.)

The purpose of rules 2 through 7 consists in making possible a quasi analysis according to rules 8 and 9; these rules form the complete disjunction of all cases of homogeneous relations. (For the application of quasi analysis, according to § 71, symmetry and reflexivity of the relation are required; for the simplest form, according to § 73, we also require transitivity.)

---

[94] Festsetzungen
[95] "relation" for *"Relation"* throughout § 104

2. If a homogeneous relation P is given which is neither symmetrical nor reflexive, we construct the relation Q as the union of P, its converse, and of P^0. Q is then symmetrical and reflexive, so that rule 7, 8, or 9 becomes applicable. (This rule is used in the construction of Ps, § 110.)

3. If a nonsymmetrical, reflexive relation P is given, we construct Q as the union of P and its converse. In this case, Q is symmetrical and reflexive, so that rule 7, 8, or 9 becomes applicable.

4. If a symmetrical, nonreflexive, nontransitive relation P is given, whose chain (power relation) becomes trivial (i.e., holds for all pairs of its field), we construct Q as the union of P and P^0. In this case, Q is symmetrical, reflexive, and nontransitive, so that rule 7 or 8 becomes applicable.

5. If a symmetrical, nonreflexive, and nontransitive relation P is given, whose chain does not become trivial (cf. rule 4), we construct Q as the chain (including identity) of P. In this case, Q is symmetrical, reflexive, and transitive, so that rule 9 can be applied. (This rule is applied for Colid, § 118.)

6. If a symmetrical, nonreflexive, transitive relation P is given, we construct Q as the union of P and P^0. In this case, Q is symmetrical, reflexive, and transitive, so that rule 9 can be applied.

7. If a symmetrical, reflexive, and nontransitive relation P is given, whose chain does not become trivial (cf. rule 4), we construct Q as the chain of P. In this case, Q is symmetrical, reflexive, and transitive, so that rule 9 can be applied. (This rule is applied in the construction of *sense*, § 115).

8. If a symmetrical, reflexive, and nontransitive relation Q is given whose chain becomes trivial (cf. rule 4), we apply *quasi analysis* (according to § 71) to Q, i.e., we construct the class of similarity circles of Q (used for similcirc, § 111; place, § 117).

9. If a symmetrical, reflexive, transitive relation Q is given, we apply *quasi analysis* (in the simplest form, according to § 73) to Q, i.e., we construct the class of abstraction classes of Q (used for sense, $analys_1$, color, §§ 115, 116, 118).

10. If the similarity circles of Q which result through quasi analysis according to rule 8 or 9 do not overlap or overlap only very little, then we consider them quasi constituents of their elements.

11. On the other hand, if the similarity circles of Q overlap to a considerable extent and in a systematic order, then we determine the quasi constituents by constructing the largest possible subclasses of the similarity circles of Q which (aside from small pieces) are not divided through the mutual dissections of the similarity circles of Q; cf. § 72 (used for qual, § 112).

12. If, among the quasi constituents which are formed on the basis of

Q according to rule 10 or 11, there are pairs such that all elements of the referent stand in the relation Q to all elements of the relatum, then we construct the relation S which is determined through these pairs as the proximity relation between the quasi constituents (used for Sim, § 114).

13. On the basis of the relation S, which is constructed according to rule 12, we divide the quasi constituents into connected areas by constructing the abstraction classes of the S-chain (used for sense, § 115).

14. On the basis of S (according to rule 12), we determine the properties of order of the quasi constituents within each of the connected areas (according to rule 13), especially the dimension number.

15. If the order of one of the areas (according to rule 14) deviates in certain general properties (e.g., dimension number) from those of all other areas, then this area is marked out through a constructional definition (used for sight, § 115).

105. *The Problem of Deducing the Construction Rules*

Now the question arises whether the general construction rules, of which we have tentatively given a few examples, could perhaps all be derived from a supreme principle and what the nature of this principle could be. We can here only raise this question, not answer it, since we have not even formulated the general rules themselves. We cannot even assert with assurance the existence of such a supreme principle.

In a certain sense, the method for the determination of the principle of construction is analogous to the determination of the single world formula for the physical processes. In both cases, we must proceed inductively from experience. In our case, we must abstract from the individual constructive steps which are found in the constructional system general rules for such steps, for example, the rules of the indicated examples. Furthermore, we must attempt to condense groups of such rules into more general rules (for example, rules 2 through 7 of the above examples into a more general rule of roughly this form: a homogeneous relation is to be transformed in as simple a way as possible, so that quasi analysis becomes applicable to it), until a single, most general rule results. If, in physics, the world formula were already known, then all the individual natural laws could be derived deductively without reference to experience. In exactly the same way, *all the general constructional rules could be deduced from the supreme principle of construction* without reference to experience, i.e., without reference to any concrete construction within the constructional system. But here, as there, the supreme principle is not known, but forms, for the time being, only a goal for research, a goal of which we do not even know whether it can be reached. In a deductive system of physics, we would identify the individual formally deduced laws and forms of invariants [96] with empirically known natural laws and object types, for example, chemical elements. In the same way, in a deductive constructional system, the particular, formally deduced entities would be identified with certain empirically known objects (things, properties, relations, events).

Even if the supreme principle of construction were already known, we still would have a further task, namely, to ascertain why it should be necessary, in view of the contribution of cognition to the larger context of life's purposes, that experiences are formed into objects in just the way expressed in the constructional system, in the general rules of construction and, most succinctly, in the supreme principle of construction. Given the present state of our knowledge, this teleological problem of the formation of knowledge can be attacked, not as a whole, but only in some of its details. Thus one could concern himself, for example, with the tendencies to reify [97] and attribute causal efficacy, which become noticeable at the higher levels of construction. At present, we shall deal no further with this problem.

Summary

III. THE FORMAL PROBLEMS OF THE CONSTRUCTIONAL SYSTEM (26–105)

A. *The Ascension Forms (26–45)*

Frequently, signs are introduced in order to make it possible to speak about objects of a certain type in an abbreviated way, where the sign in question does not designate an object (of that type). In such a case, one often speaks of the sign as if it designated an object of a new type, even though, strictly speaking, it designates nothing; if this is the case, we will say that the sign designates a *quasi object* ("quasi" relative to the object type given in the first place) (27). From a sentence, which is the sign of a proposition, we generate the sign of a *propositional function* by introducing variables, or blanks, in the place of partial signs; we can then substitute "arguments" in the "argument positions". Each propositional function represents a concept: if it has one argument position, it represents a property;

---

[96] Stabilitätsformen
[97] Substantialisierung

if it has several, a relation (28). Upon substitution of a "permissible" argument, a (true or false) sentence is generated; if other substitutions are made, a meaningless sign is produced. If two objects are permissible arguments for one and the same argument position of any propositional function, then they are called "isogenous", otherwise "allogeneous". The *object sphere* of an object is the class of all objects that are isogenous with it (29). An object type is called "pure" if all its objects are isogenous with one another. Most ordinary object types are impure: no logically unobjectionable concepts correspond to them. In ordinary language (even in science), almost every word designates several concepts from different spheres. The "confusion of spheres" creates many logical, and consequently also philosophical, perplexities (30, 31).

Propositional functions which are satisfied by the same arguments are called "universally equivalent" or "coextensive". To such functions are assigned identical "extension symbols". Such a symbol is said to designate the *extension* of a function. Hence extensions are quasi objects (32). The extension of a property is called a *class,* that of a relation, a *relation extension.* Thus class and relation extension are quasi objects (relative to the elements of the class and the terms of the relation extension, respectively) (33, 34). A concept *a* is *constructed* from *b, c* by producing its "constructional definition", i.e., by producing a translation rule which indicates for all cases how a propositional function about *a* can be transformed into a coextensive propositional function about *b, c*. If such a rule exists, then *a* is said to be reducible to *b, c* or to a "(logical) complex" of *b, c*. Hence, class and relation extension are complexes of their elements or members, respectively (35). An (extensive) whole is isogenous with its parts no matter whether it is a "true whole" ("organic whole", *Gestalt*) or a mere "collection". Since a class and its elements are allogeneous, it follows that it is not the whole, let alone the mere collection, of its elements; rather, it is a quasi object which serves to represent that which the elements have in common (36, 37).

The simplest case of a constructional definition of *a* out of *b, c* consists in the indication of an expression in terms of *b, c* which is equivalent with *a*: *explicit definition.* If such a definition is impossible, then a rule must be given for the translation of entire sentence forms (propositional functions) in which *a* occurs into *b, c*: *definition in use* (both forms are called "explicit definitions in the wider sense" to distinguish them from implicit definitions) (38, 39). In the formulation of a constructional system we speak of ascending to a new level whenever an object allogeneous to the preceding objects is constructed. This can take place only through definitions in use. Through such a definition, an extension symbol, i.e., the sign of a class or relation extension, is introduced. *Hence class and relation extension are the ascension forms* of the constructional system (40). Through repeated and sometimes intermixed application of the ascension forms we construct, within the constructional system, all objects out of the basic objects of the system; hence the unity of the object domain (due to the unity of the system) and, on the other hand, the plurality of (allogeneous) object types which follows from the multiplicity of construction forms (41). The relation being-holding obtains between each constructional level and the next higher one (42). Against the *extensional method* of construction theory (each concept is represented by an extension) the objection is raised that there may be statements about concepts which cannot be expressed with the aid of the extension symbol of the concept, namely, "intensional statements". The objection is overcome through the *thesis of extensionality*: there are no intensional, but only extensional, statements (i.e., statements that can be transformed into statements about extensions) (43, 45). This thesis is founded upon the distinction between "sign statements", "sense statements", and "nominatum statements"; it turns out that the extensional and the allegedly intensional propositions about a concept are not concerned with the same object (44).

B. *The System Forms (46–60)*

1. FORMAL INVESTIGATIONS (46–53)

The problem of the system form: how to formulate the constructional system so that all scientific objects find a place in it? (46). To solve this problem, the reducibility relations of the objects must be investigated. In the realistic, or matter of fact, language which is customary in the empirical sciences, "a is reducible to b, c" means the same as "for each state of affairs relative to a (b, c), a necessary and sufficient condition can be indicated which depends upon b and c alone" (47), or "there is an infallible and always present indicator which can be expressed through b and c". Since, in principle, science can produce such an indicator for every concept, it follows that all scientific objects are constructable (48, 49). The "constructional transformation", i.e., the transformation of a statement or propositional function with the aid of a constructional definition is a "logical translation", not a "translation of sense"; that is to say, it leaves the *logical value* unchanged (namely, the truth value of a proposition or the extension of a propositional function), but not always the *epistemic value* (50, 51).

2. MATERIAL INVESTIGATIONS (54–60)

An object a is called epistemically primary relative to b (where b is called epistemically secondary) if the recognition of b presupposes that of a. For our outline of the constructional system we wish to choose the *epistemic system form*: each object is constructed out of those other objects which are epistemically primary relative to it. Hence, in addition to their reducibility, the epistemic primacy of the object types must also be investigated (54). The cultural objects are not only reducible to, but are also recognized through, their manifestations and documentations. However, all documentations are reducible to manifestations; thus, all cultural objects can in the end be reduced to psychological ones and are epistemically secondary with respect to them (55, 56). All *physical* objects are (either directly or through the mediation of other physical objects) reducible to sensory qualities (of acts of perception). On the other hand, all psychological objects are reducible to physical objects (either through the psychophysical relation or through the expression relation) (57). Hence there are several possible system forms: the basis (the domain of the basic objects) is either physical or psychological. We must divide the psychological objects into two classes with respect to epistemic primacy: the *autopsychological* objects are epistemically primary relative to the physical objects, while the *heteropsychological* objects are secondary to them. Hence, in the epistemic system form, the most important object types occur in the following sequence: *autopsychological, physical, heteropsychological, and cultural objects* (58). There exists another system form with physical basis (materialistic system form) (59). The basis of the epistemic system form lies in the autopsychological domain; still another system form has a general-psychological basis (60).

C. *The Basis (61–83)*

1. THE BASIC ELEMENTS (61–74)

The basic objects from which all others are constructed are the *basic relations;* their members are called *basic elements* of the system (61). The epistemic system form, which we have chosen, has its basis in the autopsychological domain ("methodological solipsism") (64). However, the concept of the "self" does not belong to the initially given (65). In spite of the autopsychological basis, cognition can achieve an intersubjective, objective status (66). As basic elements within the autopsychological domain we must choose the *elementary experiences* (67), which are taken as unanalyzable units (68). Nevertheless, concept formation must arrive at the so-called constituents of experiences. The method required for this is *quasi analysis.* Essentially, it is a synthetic procedure clad in the language of analysis. It leads to structures which are substitutes for the constituents (there actually are no constituents), and which are therefore called *quasi constituents.* Quasi analysis consists in the following: the (unanalyzable) objects are placed in various kinship structures on the basis of a relation description; the various structures to which an object belongs are then its "quasi constituents" (69–71). Depending upon the formal properties of the relation on which it is based, quasi analysis takes different forms. The simplest form occurs in connection with transitive relations: *Principle of abstraction.* In this case the quasi constituents are called "abstraction classes" (72–74).

2. THE BASIC RELATIONS (75–83)

Two elementary experiences are called "part identical" if they agree in one part, "part similar" if they approximately agree in one part. It must be presupposed that these two relations are recognizable in any perception (76, 77). However, as basic relation we choose the asymmetrical relation, *recollection of similarity*, which corresponds to part similarity and contains in it the direction of time: this relation obtains between experiences x and y if x and y are recognized as part similar through a comparison of y with a memory image of x. From this basic relation, part similarity can be derived in a rather simple fashion (78). Through the application of quasi analysis to recollection of similarity, "similarity circles" can be derived (80), and "quality classes" can be derived from the similarity circles. The quality classes represent the sensory qualities (including emotions). Part identity is easily derived from the quality classes (81). A survey of further derivations leads to the supposition that *no other basic relation is required* (82). In a sense, the basic relations correspond to the "categories" of traditional philosophy (83).

D. *The Object Forms (84–94)*

The problem of object forms: in which form are the individual objects to be constructed? Object forms are here considered only by way of example; they do not properly belong to the thesis of construction theory, which concerns itself only with the choice of basis, system form and ascension forms (84). The objects of the lowest levels have already been mentioned and their derivability has been investigated; the following additional objects are derivable from them: the relation of similarity between quality classes; the sense classes as classes of qualities of the individual sense modalities (85); the definite description of the visual sense with the aid of its dimension number (86); the preliminary time order (87); the visual field places and their order in the visual field (88, 89); the colors and their order in the color solid (90–92). The constructional separation of the visual field order and the order of colors depends upon a formal difference between the two orders: it is impossible that in a single experience two different colors should appear at the same visual field place, but two visual field places can very well have the same color. Because of this formal difference, it is possible that the visual field order and the spatial order which results from it, but not the color order, can serve as the principle of individuation for reality (91). It is furthermore possible to derive the sensations in the sense of individual constituents of experiences (93). From the indicated objects it is possible to derive the other objects of the autopsychological domain, from these the physical, and then the heteropsychological and cultural objects (94).

E. *Forms of Representation for a Constructional System (95–105)*

The constructional system consists of a structure of definitional chains. The conceptual purity of this structure can best be safeguarded through the use of a symbolism. Hence, in the structure which we have formulated as an example, the symbolism of logistics is used as basic language. Parallel translations into three other languages serve to further the ease of understanding (95). The logistic language is based on the system of Russell and Whitehead, since this is the only system which possesses a detailed theory of relations (96, 97). The first translation is a paraphrase (of the individual constructional definitions and theorems) into ordinary word language; secondly, we give a translation into the realistic language, which describes the states of affairs at hand (98). The fourth language is the language of fictitious constructive operations: here each constructional definition is expressed as an operating rule in a constructive procedure (99). We imagine, in this case, that the "given" is presented in the form of a "list of the basic relations", i.e., a number-pair list of the basic relations; the operating rules lead from this list to further "inventory lists" for all objects (102). Hence, in this fiction, the contents of the given experiences is separated from their synthesis; we must make the additional fictitious assumption that the given can be indefinitely retained (101). The formulation of the constructional system does not attempt to represent the way in which the various experiential contents are experienced, but rather it is to be an account only of the logical relations which are contained in them; this is done through a *rational reconstruction* of the synthesis of the contents of experience, which in actual experience is for the most part intuitive (100). Once the individual objects are constructed, an additional (here unsolved) problem arises: the constructions should be recognized as special applications of general formal rules (103–105).

PART FOUR

OUTLINE OF A CONSTRUCTIONAL SYSTEM

A

THE LOWER LEVELS:
AUTOPSYCHOLOGICAL OBJECTS

106. *About Form, Content, and Purpose of this Outline*

In the following, we shall give a tentative version of the lower levels of
the constructional system (Chapter A); the higher levels, we shall merely
suggest (Chapters B and C). By and large, Chapter A comprehends the
autopsychological objects; Chapter B, the physical objects; and Chapter
C, the heteropsychological and cultural objects.

The constructional forms which we shall apply correspond to the
results of the preceding investigations (Part III); according to III, A, we
use class and relation extension as ascension forms; according to III, B,
we use a system form with autopsychological basis; according to III, C, 1,
we use as basic elements the elementary experiences; and, according to
III, C, 2, we use recollection of similarity as the only basic relation; the
object forms of the lower levels correspond to the derivations in III, C, 2,
and III, D.

The form of exposition results from what we have developed in the
preceding chapter (III, E). In particular, each construction is at first
given as a definition in the basic logistic language (under the heading
"construction"); then follows the translation into the three auxiliary
languages: paraphrase, realistic language, and language of fictitious

constructive operations (under the headings "paraphrase", "realistic state of affairs", "fictitious operations"); then follow statements about the constructed entities and explanations.

The statements or theorems of a constructional system are divided into two different types (the following are given as examples for theorems: Th. 1–6 in §§ 108, 110, 114, 117, 118). The first type of theorem can be deduced from the definitions alone (presupposing the axioms of logic, without which no deduction is possible at all). These we call *analytic* theorems. The second type of theorem, on the other hand, indicates the relations between constructed objects which can be ascertained only through experience. We call them *empirical* theorems. If an analytic theorem is transformed into a statement about the basic relation(s), a tautology results; if an empirical theorem is thus transformed, it indicates empirical, formal properties of the basic relation(s). Expressed in the realistic language, this means that the analytic theorems are tautological statements about concepts (these statements are not necessarily trivial, since the tautology may become apparent only after the transformation, as is the case with mathematical theorems); the empirical theorems express an empirically ascertained state of affairs.

> REFERENCES. In Kantian terminology, the analytic theorems are analytic judgments a priori; the empirical theorems are synthetic judgments a posteriori. It is the contention of construction theory that there are no such things as the "synthetic judgments a priori" which are essential for Kant's approach to epistemological problems.

As concerns the content of our constructional system, let us emphasize again that it is only a tentative example. The content depends upon the material findings of the empirical sciences; for the lower levels in particular, upon the findings of the phenomenology of perception, and psychology. The results of these sciences are themselves subject to debate; since a constructional system is merely the translation of such findings, its complete material correctness cannot be guaranteed. *The actual purpose of our exposition of construction theory is to pose the problem of a constructional system, and to carry out a logical investigation of the method which will lead to such a system; the formulation of the system is not itself part of the actual purpose.* We have nevertheless formulated some levels of the system and have indicated further levels. We have done this mostly to illustrate the problem, rather than to attempt a beginning of its solution.

107. *The Logical and Mathematical Objects*

Even before the introduction of the basic relation(s), we must construct the *logical objects,* or objects of pure logistics. Once the basic concepts of any object domain are introduced, e.g., the basic relation(s) of the constructional system, pure logistics is transformed into applied logistics; this holds in particular for the theory of relations. It is not necessary here to give an explicit account of the system of pure logistics.

> REFERENCES. A complete version of this system has been given by Russell and Whitehead [Princ. Math.], including the mathematical objects. Cf. the bibliography about logistics in § 3 and the explanation of logistic symbols in § 97.

The following basic concepts are required: incompatibility of two statements and validity of a propositional function for all arguments. Then the further connectives for two statements and negation are constructed as the first logical objects from the basic concepts; also, identity and existence. Then classes and relation extensions with their respective connectives are introduced, and finally all objects of the general theory of relations. (Cf. § 25 for the independence of logical objects from psychological and physical objects.)

Mathematics forms a branch of logistics (i.e., it does not require any new basic concepts). It is not necessary here to give an account of the formation of the system of mathematical objects; let us merely recall its main levels.

On the basis of the logical objects, we construct at first the arithmetical objects: cardinal numbers (cf. § 40); then the general relation numbers [98] (or "structures," cf. § 11), which are less frequently employed in mathematics; as a special type of the latter, we then construct the ordinal numbers. For each type of number, we construct its connectives; furthermore, the (general) series, the rational numbers, the real numbers, the vectors, etc.

Geometrical objects, too, are purely logical objects, i.e., they can be constructed within the system of logistics with the indicated basic concepts. By "geometry" we mean here purely mathematical, abstract geometry which is not concerned with space in the ordinary sense of the word, but concerned with certain multidimensional ordered structures which are also called "space", or, more precisely, "abstract space".

---

[98] Relationszahlen

Intuitive, phenomenally spatial objects form a special object domain; they belong to the real objects and can be constructed only later, after the introduction of the basic relation(s) of the constructional system (§ 125).

> REFERENCES. The derivability of geometrical concepts from logistics has been demonstrated through the investigations of Pieri, Peano, Huntington, Russell, Veblen, and others. A comprehensive discussion with bibliography has been given by Couturat [Prinz.], Chapter VI. Cf. also the examples of geometrical systems in Carnap [Logistik]. Volume IV of Whitehead and Russell's [Princ. Math.], which was to give a detailed statement of the derivation of geometry from logistics, has not yet appeared.
>
> About the difference between the so-called "space" of the pure theory of relations and the actual space of intuition, see Carnap [Raum]. (See also the bibliography on the subject in [Raum], 78 ff.) Keyser [Math. Phil.] gives an explicit account of the logical sense of abstract geometry as a mere theory *form* (theory function, "doctrinal function"); cf. also Weyl [Handb.].

It is important to notice that the logical and mathematical objects are not actually objects in the sense of real objects (objects of the empirical sciences). *Logic (including mathematics) consists solely of conventions* concerning the use of symbols, *and of tautologies* on the basis of these conventions. Thus, the symbols of logic (and mathematics) do not designate objects, but merely serve as symbolic fixations of these conventions. Objects in the sense of real objects (including quasi objects) are only the basic relation(s) and the objects constructed therefrom. All signs which have a definite meaning are called *constants* and are thus distinguished from the *variables* (§ 28). The *logical constants* are signs for logical objects; the *nonlogical constants* are signs for real objects (concepts of an object domain).

108. *The Basic Relation* (Rs)

Basic relation: Rs

Paraphrase: Recollection of similarity (cf. § 78).

Realistic state of affairs: x and y are elementary experiences, where a recollected representation of x is compared with y and found to be part similar to it (i.e., x and y are found to agree approximately in a constituent, § 78).

Fictitious operation: The only material which A has for synthesis is the *basic relation list,* the inventory list of Rs. This list contains pairs of terms of the relation extension, each argument designated by an arbitrary but determinate token (number), cf. § 102. This list is known only to A, not to us. On the other hand, only we, but not A, know the sense of the basic relation (as it has been given in § 78). Without knowing this sense, A can ascertain, from his basic relation list (i.e., empirically), the theorem Th. 1 below; this theorem states that no pair occurs in both orders of members (*a, b* and *b, a*) in that list. For each of the arguments of the basic relation, A begins an *object description.* These descriptions will later on grow in content; for the time being, A merely uses his basic relation list to ascertain for each member to which member it stands in the basic relation and which members stand to it in that relation. This way of using the basic relations list for object descriptions corresponds to supplemental entries as they occur in connection with objects which are constructed later on.

Theorem: Th. 1 Rs ϵ as (empirical).

Paraphrase: Rs is asymmetrical.

109. *The Basic Elements* (elex)

Construction: elex $=_{df}$ C'Rs

Paraphrase: The Rs-members are called *elementary experiences.*

Realistic state of affairs: The recollection of similarity holds between elementary experiences; thus, since they are arguments of the basic relation, they are the basic elements (§ 67).

Fictitious operation: A forms the *inventory list* of class elex as the number list of all members which occur in the basic relation list. The supplemental entries are here rather trivial, since A enters into the object description which he has previously started (§ 108) for each element the remark that it belongs to the class elex.

110. *Part Similarity* (Ps)

Construction: Ps $=_{df}$ Rs $\cup$ Řs $\cup$ Rs°

Paraphrase: Two elementary experiences x and y are called *part similar* if the relation Rs holds either between x and y or between y and x or if x and y are identical Rs-members.

Realistic state of affairs: If a recollection of similarity holds between elementary experiences x and y, then a part of x is similar to a part of y and a part of y is similar to a part of x (cf. §§ 78, 77).

Fictitious operation: A forms an inventory list of the relation Ps by entering all pairs of the Rs list; furthermore, also the converse pairs (i.e., in addition to *a, b,* always also *b, a*) and finally all identity pairs of members of the list (*a,a; b,b;* etc.). In this case, the supplemental entries consist in the following: after having previously begun his object descriptions (§ 108), A now uses the Ps list to supplement them by noting in each object description of a member of Rs (i.e., an elementary experience) to which others it stands in the relation Ps.

While A ascertains the *empirical theorems* on the basis of his list, the *analytic theorems* follow from the definition, thus do not require any confirmation through the inventory list. For example, Th. 2 and Th. 3 follow directly from the construction of Ps.

Theorems: Th. 2. Ps ϵ sym (analytic).

Th. 3. Ps ϵ refl (analytic).

Paraphrases: Ps is symmetrical; Ps is reflexive.

111. *Similarity Circles* (similcirc)

Construction: similcirc $=$ $_{Df}$ Simil'Ps

Paraphrase: The similarity circles based on Ps (which are formed through quasi analysis) are briefly called *similarity circles.*

Explanation: The indicated construction consists in the application of quasi analysis (§ 71) to Ps according to the derivation in § 80. According to Th. 1 and Th. 2, Ps has the properties required for this purpose, namely, symmetry and reflexivity.

Realistic state of affairs: Let us determine, in any quality domain, the largest possible class of qualities which are all in proximity of one another and thereafter the class of elementary experiences in which these qualities occur; then any two of these elementary experiences are part similar to one another, and no elementary experience outside of these is part similar to all of them (cf. § 80).

Fictitious operation: A is to compose the inventory list for all classes of elementary experiences which are similarity circles based on Ps. For this purpose, A determines at first all classes of part similar experiences; he starts with the unit classes of elementary experiences which belong to those classes because of the reflexivity of Ps. Then he forms the classes of two members by taking the pairs from the relation list of Ps; then he forms classes three of members, etc. Finally, he erases from his list all subclasses of other classes on the list. The remaining classes are the desired similarity circles. A now numbers the classes which he has found in order to be able to mention them individually. (This numbering has nothing to do with the numbering of elementary experiences.) He then enters all these class numbers into the inventory list of the class "similcirc"; into the inventory list of each of the classes which he has found, he enters the numbers of the elementary experiences which belong to it. Supplemental entries of similarity circles: A enters into the object description of each elementary experience the similarity circles to which it belongs (he designates the similarity circles by the newly introduced numbers).

112. *Quality Classes* (qual)

Construction: qual $=_{Df} \hat{a} \{(\gamma) : \gamma \epsilon \text{similcirc} . \text{Nc}'(a \cap \gamma) / \text{Nc}'a > \frac{1}{2}$
$. \supset . a \subset \gamma :. (x) : x \sim \epsilon a . \supset . (\exists \delta) . \delta \epsilon \text{similcirc} .$
$a \subset \delta . x \sim \epsilon \delta\}$

Paraphrase: A class k of elementary experiences is called a *quality class* if k is totally contained in each similarity circle which contains at least half of it, and if, for each elementary experience x which does not belong to k, there is a similarity circle in which k is contained, but to which x does not belong (according to the derivation in § 81).

Realistic state of affairs: The classes of elementary experiences which have a certain constituent in common are the largest classes which remain undivided when the similarity circles are divided through mutual partial overlapping, except for the splitting off of insignificant parts (cf. § 81).

(In translating the constructional language into the realistic language, we must observe the circumstance, which has been repeatedly mentioned, that a class does not consist of its elements [§ 37]. Thus, a quality class is not the whole or the collection of the individual experiences which belong to it, but it is a quasi object which represents that which its elements [i.e., the elementary experiences] have in common.)

Fictitious operation: For each pair of similarity circles which have a considerable part (at least half of one of them) in common, A forms the intersection and the two remainder classes. The resulting classes, if they have a considerable part in common with any other similarity circle, are again divided, etc., until classes are reached which are not divided through any similarity circles in the indicated way. These are the desired quality classes. After A has thus produced the inventory list for each quality class (i.e., a list of numbers of those elementary experiences which belong to the indicated class), he then numbers the quality classes which he has found, in an arbitrary way. We who know the sense of the basic relation, and thus also the sense of the constructed entities, know that the quality classes are the individual visual qualities, tones, fragrances, etc., but we do not as yet have a way of telling A whether a given quality class that he has formed is a tone, let alone which definite tone it represents. Eventually, we must come to the point where we can give him such information even though we do not know his inventory lists. For this is precisely the central thesis of construction theory, that each object about which a meaningful scientific statement can be made can be constructed. In the constructional language, this thesis is confirmed by the fact that we can later on convey to A the above-mentioned identifications.

The *inventory list* of the class "qual" lists the individual numbers which have been given to the quality classes. A produces the *supplemental entries* on the basis of the inventory lists of the individual quality classes by entering into the object description of each elementary experience the quality classes to which it belongs.

113. *Part Identity* (Pi)

Construction: $Pi =_{Df} \epsilon \upharpoonright qual \mid \check{\epsilon}$

Paraphrase: Two elementary experiences are called *part identical* if there is a quality class to which both belong.

Realistic state of affairs (trivial): If there exists a quality which occurs in each of two elements, then these two elements agree in a constituent (cf. §§ 76, 82).

Fictitious operation: Translation into the language of constructive operations is here and in the sequel generally no longer necessary; the previously given examples should suffice. The method remains the same; we give A a rule, on the basis of which he produces the inventory list of the new object; then he carries out the supplemental entries for the preceding objects which participate in the new object, whereby the object descriptions are more and more enriched.

114. *Similarity Between Qualities* (Sim)

Construction: $Sim =_{Df} \hat{a} \hat{\beta} \{a, \beta \epsilon qual . a \uparrow \beta \subset Ps\}$

Paraphrase: Two quality classes are called *similar* if each element of one of them is part similar to each element of the other.

Realistic state of affairs: It follows from the sense of part similarity that two qualities are similar to one another (i.e., that they are in qualitative proximity), if and only if each experience in which one of them occurs is part similar to each experience in which the other occurs (§§ 77, 85).

Fictitious construction: The supplemental entries of Sim are produced. This starts the object descriptions of the individual quality classes.

Theorem: Th. 4. Sim ϵ sym $\cap$ refl (analytic).

Paraphrase: Sim is symmetrical and reflexive.

115. *Sense Classes and Visual Sense* (sense, sight)

Construction: sense $=_{df}$ Abstr'Sim$_{po}$

Paraphrase: The abstraction classes of the Sim-chain are called *sense classes*.

Explanation: The construction takes place through quasi analysis (simplest form, § 73). The Sim-chain is transitive; also, according to Th. 4, symmetrical and reflexive.

In § 119, we shall translate the definition of sense back into an expression using Rs; the derivation relation of sense is given in § 121.

Realistic state of affairs: Two qualities can be connected through a series of qualities, where one quality is always similar to the next, only if they belong to the same sense modality (§ 85).

Fictitious operation: Once A has formed the inventory list of the class *sense,* whose elements are the sense classes, we know that one of the sense classes is that of the visual qualities; one, of the fragrances, etc., and that there is also one for the emotions (cf. §§ 76, 85); we have no way of informing A which is which. On the other hand, A is not permitted to give us the inventory lists of these individual classes. Thus our fiction makes explicit the narrow boundaries within which we must solve the problem of identifying the individual sense modalities or at least of identifying the visual sense which is basic for the further constructions.

Construction: sight $=_{df}$ $\hat{a}$ { $(\exists \lambda)$. $\lambda \epsilon$ sense . Dnp $(5, \lambda, a,$ Vicin' Sim)}

Paraphrase: The class *sight* (the *visual sense*) includes all those quality classes in which one sense class has the dimension number 5 relative to Sim (more precisely, relative to the neighborhood relation which is determined by Sim; cf. Carnap [Logistik] § 34b).

Realistic state of affairs: The visual field is a two-dimensional order of places such that a color of the three-dimensional color solid can be correlated to each of these places. The Sim-order of the other senses has a smaller dimension number (cf. § 86).

116. *Sensations* (sen) *and the Divisions of an Elementary Experience*

Construction: sen $=_{df} \hat{Q} \{(\exists x, a) . a \epsilon \text{qual} . x \epsilon a . Q = x \downarrow a\}$

Paraphrase: An (ordered) pair, consisting of an elementary experience and a quality class to which the experience belongs, is called a *sensation*. (Concerning this expression, cf. § 93.)

Realistic state of affairs: Cf. § 93.

Construction: Simul $=_{df} (\check{D} \mid D) \mathrel{\triangleright} \text{sen}$

Paraphrase: Two sen-pairs with the same referent are called *simultaneous* sensations.

Realistic state of affairs: Two individual constituents of experiences ("sensations") are simultaneous if they are constituents of the same experience (cf. § 87).

Divisions: According to earlier considerations (§ 93), we have to distinguish between the *individual* and *general* constituents of experiences (sen as contrasted with qual). Let us designate a class which contains the constituents of an elementary experience as its "division class"; thus we have to distinguish *two types of division classes* which we designate by div_1 and div_2.

Construction: $\text{Div}_1 =_{df} \text{Abstr'Simul}$

Paraphrase: The abstraction classes on the basis of Simul are called "division classes of the first type". Thus, the class of sensations of an elementary experience is such a class.

Realistic state of affairs: The sensations (in the general sense of an individual constituent of an experience) which are simultaneous with a given sensation are sensations of the same experience.

Construction: $\text{Div}_2 =_{df} \hat{\lambda} \hat{x} \{x \epsilon \text{elex} . \lambda = \hat{a} (a \epsilon \text{qual} . x \epsilon a)\}$

$\text{div}_2 =_{df} D'\text{Div}_2$

Paraphrase: The class λ of those quality classes to which the elementary experience x belongs is called the *division class of x of the second type* ($\lambda = \text{Div}_2\text{'}x$); such a class is called a *division class of the second type*.

117. *Visual Field Places and Visual Field* (place, Plid, Proxpl)

Construction: Excl $=_{df} (\text{Ex} \cup \text{I}) \mathrel{\triangleright} \text{Sight}$

place $=_{df} \hat{\chi} \{\exists! \chi : (\exists \lambda) . \lambda \epsilon \text{Simil'Excl} . \chi = \lambda - s' (\text{Simil'Excl} - [\lambda])\}$

Paraphrases: Excl designates (only here, and only for the sake of abbreviation) the relation extension "exclusive or identical" between quality classes of the visual field. A class of quality classes of the visual field is called a "visual field place" or, briefly, *place,* if it is not empty and if it includes those elements of a similarity circle λ of Excl which belong only to λ but not to other similarity circles of Excl.

Realistic state of affairs: Cf. § 88. (The places which are here constructed do not necessarily amount to a complete disposition of the qualities of the visual sense. According to earlier considerations, it is possible that the places of some exceptional qualities remain undetermined.)

Construction: Plid $=_{df} \epsilon \upharpoonleft$ place | $\check{\epsilon}$

Paraphrase: Quality classes of the visual sense are called *place identical* if they belong to the same place class.

Construction: Proxpl $=_{df} (\check{\epsilon} | \text{Sim} | \epsilon) \downharpoonright$ place

Paraphrase: Place classes are called *proximate places* if a quality class of one of them is similar to a quality class of the other.

Realistic state of affairs: Two visual qualities are similar to one another if and only if they belong to the same or to proximate visual field places (cf. § 89).

Remark: The Proxpl-*order is the visual field.*

Theorem: Th. 5. 2 Dnhomvic Proxpl (empirical).

Paraphrase: The order of the places on the basis of Proxpl (more precisely, on the basis of the neighborhood relation which is determined through Proxpl) has the homogeneous dimension number 2; that is to say, *the visual field is two dimensional.*

Fictitious operation to Th. 5: On the basis of the inventory list of Proxpl which A has produced, he can determine the dimension number of the Proxpl-order (this possibility shows very clearly that the dimension number is not a spatial property, but a property which belongs solely to the theory of relations, and that it is defined in a purely extensional way). In this way, A finds empirically that this dimension number equals 2.

118. *Colors and Color Solid* (Colidprox, Colid, color, Proxcol)

Construction: Colidprox $=_{df} \hat{a} \hat{\beta}$ {($\exists \chi, \lambda, \mu$) . χ Proxpl λ . χ Proxpl μ .

$$\lambda \text{ Proxpl } \mu . a \epsilon \chi . \beta \epsilon \lambda . \mu \cap \overrightarrow{\text{Sim}'}a = \mu \cap \overrightarrow{\text{Sim}'}\beta\}$$

Colid $=_{df}$ Colidprox$_{po}$

Paraphrase: 1. Two quality classes, α, β (of the visual sense) stand to one another in the relation of *color identity in proximate places* (α Colidprox β), if the place of α and the place of β are proximate places and if there is a place μ which is proximate to α and to β such that the quality classes of μ that are similar to those of α and its quality classes that are similar to those of β are the same. 2. The Colidprox-chain is called *color identity* (Colid).

Realistic state of affairs: Cf. § 90.

Construction: color $=_{df}$ Abstr'Colid

　　　　　　　Proxcol $=_{df}$ ($\check{\epsilon}$ | Sim | ϵ) $\rangle$ color

Paraphrase: 1. The abstraction classes of Colid are called "color classes" or, briefly, *colors*. 2. Two colors are called *proximate colors* if a quality class of one of them is similar to a quality class of the other.

Remarks: The construction of Proxcol is precisely analogous to that of Proxpl (§ 117). In general, there is a certain analogy between the division of visual quality classes into places and their division into colors, and hence a correlation between the class *place* and the class *color,* between Plid and Colid, between Proxpl and Proxcol. However, the construction formulas show an analogy only for the third of these pairs of correlations, but not for the first two. This has to do with the fact that the relation Plid is derived from the class *place* (§ 117), while, inversely, the class *color* has been derived from the relation Colid. This disanalogous behavior of the two orders in the formalism of the construction goes back to the fact that the spatial order is a principle of individuation, while the color ordering is not. Formally, this shows itself in the fact that, in an experience, two different qualities may well belong to the same color, but not to the same place. It may be recalled that it was this formal difference which allowed us to carry out the constructional separation of the two orders (cf. §§ 88, 91).

The Proxcol-order is the color solid (cf. § 90).

Realistic states of affairs: Cf. § 90.

Theorem: Th. 6. 3 Dnhomvic Proxcol (empirical).

Paraphrase: The order of the colors on the basis of Proxcol has the homogeneous dimension number 3; that is to say, *the color solid is three dimensional.*

119. *Example of a Retranslation of a Definition and a Statement*

Construction theory contains the thesis that *each scientific concept is either a class or a relation extension, which can be expressed through the basic relation(s) alone.* In order to make the sense of this thesis quite clear, let us consider as an example the concept of a sense class (sense). Let us form, for this concept, an expression which (aside from logical constants) contains only the symbol "Rs" of the basic relation. To begin with, according to the constructional definition of sense (§ 115), we have the identity:

$$\text{sense} = \text{Abstr'Sim}_{po} \qquad (1)$$

Since every definition is a rule of replacement, which allows us to replace in any context the definiendum by the definiens, we can replace in (1) Sim by its definiens (§ 114). The result is:

$$\text{sense} = \text{Abstr'}(\hat{a}\,\hat{\beta}\,\{a,\,\beta \in \text{qual} \cdot a \uparrow \beta \subset \text{Ps}\})_{po} \qquad (2)$$

Here we replace qual by its definiens and then similcirc and finally also Ps. The final result is:

$$\text{sense} = \text{Abstr'}(\hat{a}\,\hat{\beta}\,\{a,\,\beta \in \hat{\zeta}\,((\gamma) : \gamma \in \text{Simil'}(\text{Rs} \cup \text{Řs} \cup \text{Rs}^\circ)\cdot\text{Nc'}(\zeta \cap \gamma)\,/\,\text{Nc'}\zeta > \tfrac{1}{2}\cdot \supset \cdot \zeta \subset \gamma : \cdot (x) : x \sim \epsilon \zeta \cdot \supset \cdot (\exists \delta)\cdot \delta \in \text{Simil'}(\text{Rs} \cup \text{Řs} \cup \text{Rs}^\circ)\cdot a \subset \delta \cdot x \sim \epsilon \delta)\cdot a \uparrow \beta \subset \text{Rs} \cup \text{Řs} \cup \text{Rs}^\circ\})_{po} \qquad (3)$$

According to this expression, *sense* is identical (i.e., of the same logical value) with the expression which stands to the right of the identity sign. In this expression, Rs is the only nonlogical constant (the Greek letters and x are variables; the other symbols are logical constants).

A *second thesis* of construction theory asserts that *each scientific statement is, in the final analysis, a statement about the basic relation(s)*; more precisely, each statement can be transformed into another statement which (besides logical constants) contains only the basic relation(s), where the logical value (although not the epistemic value) is retained. Let us clarify this thesis with the example of Th. 6 of the three dimensionality of the color solid. With the aid of the constructional definition of Proxcol, Th. 6 can be transformed, through substitution, into the sentence:

$$3 \text{ Dnhomvic } (\check{\epsilon} \mid \text{Sim} \mid \epsilon) \,\vDash\, \text{Color} \qquad (4)$$

Through step-by-step substitutions on the basis of the definitions of color, Colid, Colidprox, Proxpl, place, Excl, sight, sense, Sim, qual, similcirc, Ps, and a formal simplification we finally obtain from (4) the following form for Th. 6; in this form, "Rs" is the only nonlogical symbol (Q, x, and the Greek letters are variables; the other symbols are logical constants):

$$(\exists Q, \nu)\cdot 3 \text{ Dnhomvic } (\check{\epsilon} \mid Q \mid \epsilon) \,\vDash\, \text{Abstr'}\{\hat{a}\,\hat{\beta}\,((\exists \chi, \lambda, \mu)\cdot \chi\,\check{\epsilon}\mid Q\mid \epsilon\lambda\cdot$$
$$\chi\,\check{\epsilon}\mid Q\mid \epsilon\mu\cdot\lambda\,\check{\epsilon}\mid Q\mid \epsilon\mu\cdot\chi,\,\lambda,\,\mu\in\hat{\xi}\,\{\exists\,!\,\xi : (\exists \rho)\cdot\rho\,\epsilon\nu\cdot\xi=\rho-\textbf{s'}(\nu-$$
$$[\rho])\}\cdot a\,\epsilon\chi\cdot\beta\,\epsilon\lambda\cdot\mu\cap\overrightarrow{Q}'a=\mu\cap\overrightarrow{Q}'\beta)\}_{po}\cdot\nu=\text{Simil'}((\text{Ex}\cup\text{I})\,\vDash\,\hat{a}$$
$$\{(\exists\mu)\cdot\mu\,\epsilon\,\text{Abstr'}Q_{po}\cdot\text{Dnp}\,(5,\,\mu,\,a,\,\text{Vicin'}Q)\})\cdot Q=\hat{a}\,\hat{\beta}\,(a,\,\beta\,\epsilon\,\hat{\zeta}\,\{(\gamma):$$
$$\gamma\,\epsilon\,\text{Simil'}(\text{Rs}\cup\text{Řs}\cup\text{Rs}^\circ)\cdot\text{Nc'}(\zeta\cap\gamma)\,/\,\text{Nc'}\zeta>\tfrac{1}{2}\cdot\supset\cdot\zeta\subset\gamma:\cdot(x)$$
$$: x\sim\epsilon\zeta\cdot\supset\cdot(\exists\delta)\cdot\delta\,\epsilon\,\text{Simil'}(\text{Rs}\cup\text{Řs}\cup\text{Rs}^\circ)\cdot a\subset\delta\cdot x\sim\epsilon\delta\}\cdot a\uparrow\beta$$
$$\subset\text{Rs}\cup\text{Řs}\cup\text{Rs}^\circ) \qquad (5)$$

To facilitate understanding:

$$v = \text{Simil'Excl}, \quad Q = \text{Sim}$$

We can see that the expression which uses only the basic relation is already very complicated, even for a statement on a relatively low level. This complication increases very considerably for the higher levels, so that finally a retranslation is practically out of the question. Perhaps this is one of the reasons that the thesis of the reducibility of all objects and statements to one or a few basic relations does not seem very plausible at first sight. The objection that the objects of cognition form an extremely rich manifold is perfectly justified. But it does not follow from this objection that it is impossible to found this manifold on a narrow basis, but only that the structure of the system must be sufficiently complicated in order to be able to represent that manifold through the multiplicity of constructional forms in spite of the simplicity of the building stones.

The above translations were meant only as illustrative examples. Precise form in every detail is here not of the essence. Thus, the subsequent considerations are independent of the assumed number (one) and kind (Rs) of the basic relations. The example which we have carried out above shows that the empirical statements concerning the three-dimensionality of the color solid can be formulated, with our choice of basis, as a statement about *a certain, purely formal, though very complicated, property of the basic relation* Rs. In the same way, *all empirical statements of science can be expressed as statements about purely formal properties of the basic relation(s)*. This holds generally, no matter which basic relations and no matter what constructional system may be chosen.

120. *The Preliminary Time Order*

Constructional remark: We can envisage Rs_{po} as relation (extension) of a preliminary time order, which is not yet without gaps and not yet in strict serial order. We shall not introduce a new symbol for this relation.

Paraphrase: An elementary experience is called *earlier in time* than another in the sense of the preliminary time order, if an Rs-chain exists between them.

Realistic state of affairs: Cf. § 87.

Remark: The relation of complete temporal order must be a sequential relation (i.e., not only, like Rs_{po}, transitive and irreflexive, hence assymmetrical, but also connected) (§ 11). Rs_{po} is not connected: there will be pairs of elementary experiences, between which no Rs-chain exists in either direction. A complete temporal sequence can be constructed only later with the aid of the regularities of the processes of the outside world.

121. *The Derivation Relation* [99] *of an Object*

According to the central thesis of construction theory, it is in principle possible to fit each scientific object (or concept) into the constructional system. Now, every object of the constructional system can be represented by an expression which contains the basic relation as its only nonlogical constant (§ 119). We obtain the logical form of this expression by replacing the symbol "Rs" of the basic relation by a variable, for example, R. The relation of this expression to R, we call the *derivation relation* of the object in question, since it is also the relation which expresses how the object is derived from the basic relation.

If the object in question is constructed in the system as a class, for example c, then there is an expression for c which contains only Rs. Let us abbreviate this expression as $\phi(Rs)$, so that $c = \phi(Rs)$; its logical form is then $\phi(R)$. The derivation relation of c is then the relation between $\phi(R)$ and R; hence (since $\phi(R)$ is a variable class): $\hat{a} \, \check{R} \, \{a = \phi(R)\}$.

If the object has been constructed as a relation extension, for example G, then there is an expression $\psi(Rs)$ such that $G = \psi(Rs)$. In this case, the derivation relation of G is: $\hat{Q}\check{R} \, \{Q = \psi(R)\}$.

In both of the given expressions for the derivation relations, no nonlogical constants occur. Hence, we see that *the derivation relation of any object is a purely logical constant*.

> EXAMPLE. For simplicity's sake, let us consider an object of a lower level, namely, the class of the sense modalities (sense, § 115). The expression for the class *sense*, which contains only Rs, has been given earlier (§ 119 [3]). From it results the following definition for the derivation relation of sense, which we designate by Der(sense).

Der(sense) $=_{df} \lambda \, R \, \{\lambda = \text{Abstr}' \, (\hat{a} \, \beta \, \{a, \beta \, \epsilon \, \check{\zeta} \, ((\gamma) : \gamma \, \epsilon \, \text{Simil}'(R \cup \check{R} \cup R^0) \, . \, \text{Nc}'(\zeta \cap \gamma) \, / \, \text{Nc}'\zeta > \frac{1}{2} \, . \, \supset \, . \, \zeta \subset \gamma : . \, (x) : x \sim \epsilon \, \zeta \, . \, \supset \, . \, (\exists \delta) \, . \, \delta \, \epsilon \, \text{Simil}'(R \cup \check{R} \cup R^0) \, . \, a \subset \delta \, . \, x \sim \epsilon \, \delta) \, . \, a \uparrow \beta \subset R \cup \check{R} \cup R^0 \})_{po} \}$

It is a familiar fact of the theory of axiomatics that an axiomatic system (for example, a geometric system) can initially be constructed as a purely logical system, which is subsequently transformed into an

---

[99] Ableitungsrelation

empirical theory [100] (for example, a physical geometry) by replacing the primitive concepts of the axiomatic system with empirical concepts.[101] In precisely analogous fashion, *the constructional system can initially be formulated as a purely logical system,* where each construction is replaced by the corresponding derivation relation. Through the substitution of the empirical concept Rs (as the only basic concept of the system) in place of the variable R, this purely logical system can be transformed into the actual constructional system of all empirical concepts.

122. *The Stated Constructions are Merely Examples*

At this place, we shall cease to exhibit the constructions in their explicit form, namely, as constructional definitions in the language of logistics and (in part) translations into the other languages.

In concluding the first part of the constructional system, let it be emphasized again that the determination of the content of the stated constructions does not belong to the thesis of the present treatise. This thesis merely asserts the possibility, in general, of a constructional system and especially of a constructional system of the same form as we have used here; furthermore, the thesis asserts the applicability and fruitfulness of the indicated method. After the exhibition of the constructional system, we shall give a more precise statement of these assertions (§ 156). The only purpose of these constructions was to show the aim of construction theory more clearly and to illustrate the method. The detailed execution depends upon the results of the empirical sciences. If the assertions which lie at the basis of indicated constructions are not scientifically tenable, then we must replace them by those findings by which they are replaced in the sciences; these must then be formulated in the constructional language and must be fitted into the constructional system. None of this will in any way impair the possibility, in principle, of translating all scientific statements into statements within a constructional system.

---

[100] Realtheorie
[101] Realbegriffe

B

THE INTERMEDIATE LEVELS: PHYSICAL OBJECTS

123. *About the Formulation of the Further Constructional Levels*

The further constructional levels we shall put forth not in the strict symbolic form of logistics, but merely in a loose paraphrase. We shall also occasionally omit constructions if they easily result from the context; thus, we shall state only the most important steps.

The following constructions follow the route which was indicated in § 94. To begin with, we shall discuss the method of constructing three-dimensional, *physical space* (§ 124), and then we shall carry out this construction as well as the construction of the visual things which depend upon it (§§ 125–128). For the constructional system, the most important visual thing is *my body* (§ 129). It will help us to give definite descriptions of the various senses, so that with its aid we can supplement the domain of the autopsychological (§ § 130–132). Then we shall describe the construction of the *world of perception* (§ § 133–135) as well as the construction of the *world of physics* (§ 136), which is quite different from the former. Finally, we shall discuss some physical objects (persons, the expression relation; § 137 f.), which are required for the subsequent construction of the heteropsychological objects.

124. *Various Possibilities for the Construction of Physical Space*

The following constructional step, namely, the transition from the two-dimensional order of the visual field to the three-dimensional order of the space of visual things is one of the most important steps in the constructional system. Various attempts were made to solve the problem of executing this construction; we shall here mention the most important ones and shall give reasons why we deviate from them.

REFERENCES. The only older work which gives a detailed description of this problem is that of Kauffmann [Imman.] 9–31; it is not necessary to concern ourselves with it here. The first to make a more precise investigation concerning the derivation of the three-dimensional space order (the "ontogram") from the two-dimensional space order (the "phenogram") was Gerhards [Aussenwelthyp.]; he was also the first to employ mathematical techniques. Our derivation differs from that of Gerhards in the following way: we do not presuppose, and construct from individual aspects, an unchangeable outside world, but construct at once the entire four-dimensional space-time world which comprises all events.

Russell ([External W.], [Const. Matter], [Sense-Data]) constructs visual things as classes of their aspects, in fact, not merely as classes of the real, experienced aspects, but as classes of *possible aspects*. This method is tenable if, as with Russell, these aspects are taken as basic elements. We have begun our structure several levels further down; thus, in order to be able to follow the same route as Russell, we will first of all have to construct the aspects from our basic elements, namely, the elementary experiences. However, this is probably impossible for aspects which "have not been seen", or at least, it would offer very considerable difficulties. Hence, it is more advantageous for us to use a different method, namely, to construct the entire visual world at once, rather than the individual visual things. Russell's method has the advantage of greater logical simplicity. The advantage of our method lies, first of all, in the fact that we have used the autopsychological basis, which Russell himself considers a desirable goal (cf. § 64), secondly, in the circumstance that unperceived points and states of a thing are, in our system, not inferred, but constructed. This procedure, too, Russell considers desirable. (Cf. the motto preceding § 1; § 3; [Sense-Data] 157 f., 159). It must be admitted, however, that our kind of construction of physical points and of the physical space is by no means a fully satisfactory solution.

Reasons similar to those just mentioned have induced us to avoid the procedure which Whitehead ([Space], [Nat. Knowledge], [Nature]) has followed. Whitehead constructs space and time only *after* the things, as the structure of the relations which become apparent in the behavior of things to one another. He emphasizes especially that we experience, not spatial or temporal points, but extensions; from these, we must construct the points according to the method of "extensive abstraction". Unquestionably, this procedure has great advantages in method and content; however, we cannot follow it since the problem of constructing the three-dimensional things or four-dimensional events from the position relations in the sensory field, especially the visual field, offer unsurmounted difficulties. (Whitehead fails to indicate a solution to this problem.)

For the indicated problem, cf. also the discussion of Poincaré ([Wiss.], [Wert], [Letzte Ged.]) about the three dimensionality of space; furthermore, cf. Becker ([Geom.] 446 ff.) about the "constitutive steps of spatiality", following some of Husserl's ideas; also, the discussions of Carnap [Dreidimens.] and Jacoby [Ontol.] 100 ff. (The last two hold that the increase of the dimension number from two to three in the constructional step under discussion has the purpose of permitting the construction of causal regularity.)

The indicated investigations are important, since they (in contrast to some other systems) recognize and discuss the problem of the transition of the two-dimensional to the three-dimensional order. However, they are all mistaken when they assume that the two dimensionality of the visual field order must be envisaged as given; this holds also for my own [Dreidimens.]. Construction theory has shown us that this two-dimensional order, just as the three-dimensional one, must be considered derived; thus, the problem of its construction is posed. An attempt at solving this problem has been discussed in § 89 and has been put forth as part of the constructional system in § 117 (cf. also the other possibilities of a solution discussed in § 92).

It is still a question whether it is appropriate, or perhaps even necessary, to construct visual space before the construction of the visual things and their physical space. Psychologically, the three-dimensional, metric, non-Euclidean (namely, spherical), visual space forms an intermediate step between the two-dimensional order of the visual field and the three-dimensional Euclidean order of the outside world. However, it is probably appropriate for the constructional system to omit this step. For the introduction of this step does not bring about a formal simplification of construction, and the objects which are found on this intermediate level cannot be described as "real". According to our earlier considerations, such a simplifying deviation from the psychological order of the process of cognition is permissible for the constructional system (cf. § 100). (Gerhards and Russell [see above], in their construction of the three-dimensional space of visual things, likewise omit the intermediate level of visual space.)

125. *The Space-Time World*

The points of n-dimensional, real-number space, we call *world points*; they are n-tuples of numbers which serve as subjects [102] of the following assignment.[103]

To some world points, we shall assign colors (later on, also, quality classes or classes of quality classes from other sense modalities); that is to say, we shall establish a one-many relation between world points and colors such that requirements 1–12 (§ 126) are fulfilled as far as possible.

The dimension number n is not constructionally determined. We only lay down that n should be the smallest number for which the desired assignment can be carried out. From requirements 3 and 5, and the empirical theorem (Th. 5 (§ 117) about the two dimensionality of the visual field, it follows that: $n \geqq 3$; hence the dimension number of space $(n - 1)$ is at least equal to 2. From the (in realistic language) disappearance and reappearance of things in the visual field, it follows that $n \geqq 4$; hence, the dimension number of space is at least 3. Finally, it can be ascertained empirically that the construction can be executed for $n = 4$; hence, the dimension number of the order of world points is to be fixed at 4, that of space at 3.

The n numbers of each world point form an ordered set; they are called its coördinates; the first number is called its time coördinate; the other $n - 1$ numbers, its space coördinates. World points with the same time coördinates are called *simultaneous* (absolute time system). A class of world points which are all simultaneous with one another (i.e., a cross section where t is constant) is called a *space class*.

Assume that a Euclidean metric on the basis of a Pythagorean determination of distances holds in the n-dimensional number space. Let the expressions "straight line", "surface", "congruent", "angle", etc., be defined in the customary way through relations of numbers. We can then use the language of geometry since it is briefer and more intuitive. It must be noted, however, that what we have in mind are always arith-

---

[102] Unterlage
[103] Zuschreibung

metical relations between numbers, namely, between the coördinates of the world points. For, space (not in the abstract-mathematical, but in the actual, phenomenal sense), spatial position, spatial configurations, have neither been introduced as basic entities, nor have they been defined; we are only just now constructing these objects. In the constructional system, the peculiar quality of spatiality, even though it is such an essential feature of our experience of the outside world, no more occurs as a quality than do the other qualities, namely, colors, tones, emotions, etc. For the constructional system concerns itself only with the structural and, in the case of space, only with the formal properties of this structure. In doing so, the constructional system does not lose a recognizable (that is, conceptually apprehensible) object, for, according to the thesis of construction theory, the nonstructural cannot become the object of a scientific statement. The space which we here construct, even though we treat it only structurally, must nevertheless be well distinguished from the so-called "space" of pure abstract geometry, which was constructed before the introduction of the basic relation (§ 107). We presuppose and apply this abstract space as already constructed in order to be able to construct now space in the actual sense of the word, namely, *physical space*. The former, strictly speaking unspatial, order [104] is called "space" (or "abstract space") only because of its applicability to physical space (cf. also § 25).

126. *The Assignment of Colors to World Points*

The assignment of colors to the world points and the subsequent constructions which are connected with this are carried out in such a way that the following desiderata are satisfied as far as possible. They cannot be precisely satisfied because of (in realistic language) hallucinations, disturbances of the eye and the intervening medium, deformations and disintegration of bodies, etc. In § 127, we shall indicate in realistic language the empirical states of affairs on which these individual desiderata or rules of construction rest.

1. There is a series of prominent world points which we call the *points of view*.[105] They form a continuous curve in such a way that each of the $n - 1$ space coördinates is a single-valued, continuous function of the time coördinate.

2. The straight lines which proceed from a given point of view and

---

[104] Ordnungsgefüge
[105] Ausblickpunkt

which form, with the negative direction of time, the angle γ, we call the *lines of view*.

3. γ is constant and is very nearly equal to a right angle. Thus, if a point of view has the time coördinate t_1, then we can take as its lines of view the straight lines of its space class (cross section $t = t_1$) which proceed from this point.

4. A one-to-one correspondence is established between elementary experiences and some of the points of view in such a way that an experience which is later in time (Rs_{po}, cf. § 120) corresponds to a point of view with a larger time coördinate.

5. If possible, we assign to each visual sensation (§ 116) of an elementary experience a line of view of the corresponding point of view in such a way that (a) to sensations with proximate visual field places (Proxpl, § 117) we assign lines of view which form only a small angle with one another, and vice versa; and that (b) the pairs of lines of view which are assigned to the visual sensations of two definite places in different elementary experiences all form the same angle, and conversely.

6. The color of a visual sensation is assigned to a world point of the corresponding line of view. Points which are occupied in this way are called "world points seen from the given point of view" or, in short, *seen color spots*. For the choice of position of these points on their lines of view, cf. 11.

7. Furthermore, taking into consideration the requirements 8–10, we shall assign one color each to certain other world points. These world points are called *unseen color spots*. Among the points of each of the bundles of lines of view (according to 3, this means with very near approximation: among the points of each of the space classes), they form at most a two-dimensional area, usually connected surfaces.

8. An unseen color spot may not be located on a line of view between a point of view and a seen color spot.

9. The assignment of colors to unseen color spots according to 7 is carried out in such a way that, as far as possible, each seen color spot belongs to a *world line*. A world line is a continuous curve or curve segment such that precisely one world point belongs to each value of the time coördinate within a given interval; the world point may be either a seen or an unseen color spot. Within the interval, each space coördinate of the segment is a single-valued, continuous function of the time coördinate.

10. According to 7, we have to assign a color to the unseen color spots. Taking into account the colors of seen color spots, we make a pre-

liminary choice of these colors in such a way that the color of the points of a world line, considered as a function of time, shows a rate of change which is as small as possible, i.e., if possible, remains constant.

11. Aside from the requirements of number 8, the following requirements determine the position of world lines, which in turn determine the choice of position of the seen as well as the unseen color spots (according to 6) which lie upon their lines of view:

a. The world lines should have as little curvature as possible;

b. The angles between world lines and the direction of time should be as small as possible;

c. Two world lines which run through one or more pairs of proximate seen color spots should, if possible, also be proximate elsewhere, especially in the time intervals;

d. A set of world lines which form a spatially connected parallel bundle during one or several time intervals should, if possible, do the same at other times especially in the intervals between these intervals.

12. We shall later on supplement and correct the assignment; cf. § 135 (supplementation of partially observed things or events through analogy) and § 144 (utilization of the observations of others). Nevertheless, the above-indicated requirements should always be fulfilled to the largest possible extent.

127. *Formulation of the Above Points in Realistic Language*

To facilitate understanding, let us here indicate, in realistic language, the states of affairs which lie at the bottom of the indicated requirements which determine the assignment of colors to the world points.

1. The particular point in the interior of the head from which the world seems to be seen has as its world line a continuous curve in the space-time world. (The construction does not have to concern itself with binocular vision, since the determination of depth has a sufficient and more precise foundation elsewhere.)

2. The optical medium between the eye and the seen things can generally be considered homogeneous. Under this assumption, the light rays which impinge upon the eye form straight lines which enclose the angle arc tg c with the negative direction of time (c designates the speed of light).

3. The speed of light, c, is constant and very large. Thus, the light rays are very nearly the straight lines of a momentary space.

4. Each visual perception is based upon an act of seeing from one of the points of view.

5. a. Visual field places that lie next to one another always depict only points of the outside world whose lines of view form a small angle at the eye;

b. A given pair of visual field places always has the same visual angle.

6. We conclude, from a visual sensation, that a point of the outside world which lies on the corresponding line of view has the color of the visual sensation.

7. At any given time, there are many points of the outside world which have a color, but are not seen at that time. These visible, but unseen (by me), world points are, for the most part, points on the surfaces of bodies.

8. A visible, colored point of the outside world which is not seen by me at a given time cannot at that time be located in front of a seen point.

9. We must assume, if there are no reasons to the contrary, that a point of the outside world which has once been seen existed previously and will exist afterward. Its locations form a continuous world line.

10. We shall assume, if there is no reason to the contrary, that each point of the outside world retains at the other times the same or as similar as possible a color as that with which it was seen at one time.

11. Assumptions concerning the motion of points, especially during times when they are not seen, are to be made according to the following rules:

a. Changes of velocity or direction of motion are not assumed to be larger than is required by the observation; thus, if there are no reasons to the contrary, we shall assume the inertial motion (constancy of direction and velocity);

b. Velocity is not assumed to be larger than is required by the observation; thus, if there are no reasons to the contrary, we shall assume rest;

c. If we once, or repeatedly, observe two points to be next to one another, we shall assume that they are next to one another also when they are not seen;

d. If observations show several points to move as a connected surface, then we assume the same behavior while no observations are being made.

12. Inferences from the observed to the unobserved are at first scarce, later on more abundant, for example, through re-cognition of a partially

seen thing (§ 135), through an inference on the basis of a natural law (§ 135), or with the aid of observations of others (§ 144).

128. *The Visual Things*

If, in a bundle of world lines which have been constructed according to the given requirements (§§ 126, 127), the proximity relations remain at least approximately the same during a protracted stretch (of time), then the class of the corresponding world points is called a *visual thing*. If, in addition to the proximity relations, the metric relations also remain constant, then the thing is called *rigid*. The intersection of a visual thing with a space-class is called a *state* of the thing. (It is possible that it might be more appropriate to construct first the states-of-things and only afterward the things as classes of corresponding "genidentical" states-of-things; we shall not, at this point, investigate this question.)

Two world points of the same world line, we call *genidentical*; likewise, two states of the same thing.

The class of world points of a thing which are seen from a given point of view is called the "seen part" of the thing in the elementary experience to which the point of view corresponds. Since a point of view and the points which are seen from it are very nearly simultaneous, we can, in first approximation, take the seen part of a thing as a subclass of a state of the thing.

The class of those visual sensations of an elementary experience which correspond to the seen points of a given thing are called the *aspect* of the thing in that experience. Accordingly, the "seen parts" of the thing, that is, roughly speaking, parts of states of the thing, corresponds to aspects of the thing.

> REFERENCES. Concerning the concept of *genidentity* (this term stems from Lewin), cf. Lewin [Zeitl.], Russell [External W.] 108 ff. Cf. also § 159 below, especially with respect to the necessary distinction between genidentity and identity.

129. *"My Body"*

There is a certain visual thing B which fulfills the conditions listed below. These conditions and even an appropriate part of them form a constructional definite description of it; this visual thing is called *my body*.

1. Each state of B is very close to the corresponding point of view.
2. B, as all other visual things, forms an open surface when seen from

a point of view. However, in contrast to all other visual things, every total state of B also forms an open surface.

3. The world lines of B or connected areas of them are correlated with the qualities (or classes of qualities) of a certain sense class in such a way that, upon contact with the world line of another visual thing or of another part of B, another quality, called a tactile quality, occurs simultaneously in the experience in question; the so-constructed sense class is called the *tactile sense*.

4. In a similar way, certain motions of B are correlated with the qualities of another sense class; the sense class so described is called *kinesthetic sense*.

5. On the basis of B, it will later on be possible to give a constructional description of the remaining sense classes (§ 131).

The given constructional determinations are founded upon the following empirical states of affairs (in realistic language):

1. My body is always in the vicinity of my eye.

2. The surface of a body can never all be seen at the same time; thus, any part of the surface of a body which is seen at one time can never be a closed surface. However, in the case of some bodies, the entire surface is visible; thus, the visible surface is a closed surface. On the other hand, in the case of my body, even the visible surface is an open surface, since some parts of its surface, for example, the eye and the back, are not visible.

3. The places of the surface of my body correspond to the qualities (or location signs) of the tactile sense in such a way that we experience a tactile sensation of a certain quality if a corresponding part of the skin is touched by another body or by another part of my body.

4. The qualities of kinesthetic sensations correspond to certain types of motions of my body.

5. The other senses are connected in a definite way with certain parts of my body, namely, with the sense organs.

> REFERENCES. Because of its special epistemological significance, the construction of "my body" has been investigated several times, for example, by Kauffmann [Imman.] 39–54, Ziehen [Erkth.] 58, 277, 445 ff., Driesch [Ordnungsl.] 354 ff.

130. *The Tactile-Visual Things*

Earlier, we have assigned colors, i.e., classes of classes of visual qualities, to some world points. We shall now do the same in a somewhat different way with quality classes of the tactile sense, or rather, with classes of such classes, namely those which coincide in their location sign. Earlier, we discussed seen and unseen color spots; in like fashion, we now distinguish touch points. The position of the touched touch points can be determined more precisely than those of the seen color spots. For these touch points touch the corresponding part of my body; hence, if we assume the spatial position of my body as already determined, we do not have to determine any distance or dimension of depth in this case. In most cases, the touch points are also color spots, either seen or unseen. This allows us in many cases to determine more precisely the position of the world lines of the color spots. Sometimes the touch points are not color spots; in these cases, they determine new world lines. In some cases, it takes these world lines of mere touch points, together with the world lines of color spots, in order to form the closed surface of a *tactile-visual thing*. For example, this is the case for the most important tactile-visual thing, namely, for my body. A large part of the surface of my body consists of world lines to which no color spots, but only touch points, correspond. Thus, my body becomes a completely closed thing only by taking into account the qualities of the tactile sense.

> REFERENCES. The problem of assigning tactile qualities to world points to which only visual qualities (colors) were originally assigned and, furthermore, the assignment of still other sensory qualities (§ 133) can also be formulated as the problem of the mutual correlation of the various "sense spaces". This problem is discussed by Poincaré [Wert], Schlick [Raum und Zeit] 95 ff. (Method of Coincidences) and Jacoby [Ontol.].

131. *Definite Description of the Remaining Senses*

After my body has been constructed as a complete thing, namely, as a tactile-visual thing, we can, if necessary, give definite descriptions of various of its parts according to their shape or mutual position, since all spatial shape and position relations can be expressed with the aid of the already constructed space coördinates. Thus, the sense organs, which, for subsequent constructions, are the most important parts of my body, can be constructionally described. The events taking place in these organs are correlated in a certain way with certain senses. This enables us to give definite descriptions of the individual senses. For example, after spatial determinations have enabled us to distinguish ear, nose, tongue, etc., from the other parts of the body, hearing, smelling, tasting, etc., can be characterized, for example, by the fact that the quality classes of the sense classes do not, as a rule, occur if the corresponding organ is blocked off from its surroundings in a certain way.

In the case of the senses of pain, warmth, and cold, the organ, namely, the skin, coincides with that of the tactile sense of which we have given a definite description above (§ 129). The constructional definite description of these senses is possible in various ways, for example, through correlation with the stimuli in question. The qualities of the sense of pain frequently coincide with certain qualities of the tactile sense (namely, those of great intensity). The senses of warmth and cold, for example, are characterized by the fact that, under certain conditions, we frequently run through a sequence of qualities of one of them, and afterward through a sequence of qualities of the other; it is also true of them that most qualities of the one sense exclude most qualities of the other for the same part of the organ.

Thus, in one way or another, we will finally be able to distinguish, or construct, all the individual sense classes. As we have mentioned earlier (§§ 76, 85), we count among the sense classes also the domain of emotions. According to the explanation of the construction of sense classes which we have given above (§ 85), it also holds that, if there are psychological objects (for example, volitions) outside of, and irreducible to, sensations and emotions, then the various types of such entities each form one sense class. Definite descriptions of these further sense classes could be given by correlating them with other sense classes (it holds, for example, for volitions, if they exist as a special kind of entity, that they could be correlated with kinesthetic sensations), or by correlating them with processes of the body (for example, correlation between emotions and expressive motions).

After definite descriptions of the individual senses have been given, it is possible to construct the various components of the qualities which are represented in the quality classes. By a "component" we understand, for example, pitch of a tone, loudness of a tone, timbre; hue, saturation, brightness; generally: *quality* (*in the narrower sense*), with several of the senses also *intensity*, and, in the case of the senses of the skin, the *location sign*; further, the (three?) dimensions of emotions, etc. The construction of these components, as classes of quality classes of the sense modality in question, becomes possible usually through a correlation with those overt processes to which certain values or certain changes of the individual components frequently run parallel. Given the constructions which we have already stated, such overt processes can, to a large extent, already be constructionally formulated; further possibilities arise after the construction of the perceptual things, which is given below (§ 134).

132. *The Domain of the Autopsychological*

Earlier, we divided the elementary experiences into individual constituents, namely sensations, and also into general constituents, namely qualities (§§ 93, 116). In the constructions given so far, these constituents have been divided into main areas (sense classes) and have been analyzed into components (especially qualities in the narrower sense, intensity, location sign). Within their main areas, they have been assigned a qualitative and in part also a spatial order. Initially, the elementary experiences were brought into a preliminary time order (Rs_{po}, § 120); then, with the aid of the time coördinate of the point of view in the visual world (§ 126), they were placed into a complete time sequence.

The thus-ordered elementary experiences themselves, their constituents and components, and the more complex entities which are to be constructed from these, form the domain of objects of which I am conscious, or *my consciousness*. This domain forms the foundation of the domain of the *autopsychological*. The latter results, if we introduce, in addition, the "unconscious" objects. The construction of unconscious objects on the basis of conscious objects is analogous to that of unseen color spots on the basis of seen color spots (§ 126). There we made a certain assignment to world points, i.e., to coördinate quadruples; here we make an assignment only to time points, i.e., to the individual values of the time coördinate. Through the earlier construction of the seen, namely, through the mediation of the points of view, elementary experiences are assigned to certain time points. Now we assign quality classes, as well as components of qualities and more complex structures formed from them, to intermediate time points as well, even though no point of view and no elementary experience corresponds to them. The methodological tenets of construction theory require that all of these "unconscious" entities should be constructed from previously constructed, i.e., "conscious" objects. It is possible, however, that the unconscious entities are formed from the constituents of experiences and their components in a different way from the conscious entities.

The construction of unconscious objects has the following purpose: with their aid we can construct the domain of autopsychological objects as a domain in which a more thoroughgoing regularity of events holds than in the subdomain of the conscious. The construction form has a certain resemblance to that of the physical world, especially to the procedure of supplementation through analogy, which we shall discuss below (§ 135). In both cases, there are tendencies toward preserving state identity [106] and process identity [107] (thus, as it were, a psychological category of substance and a psychological category of causality). There is, however, a remarkable feature of the domain of psychological objects in which it differs from the physical world and especially the world of physical science: in the former case, thoroughgoing regularity can be obtained neither completely nor even in asymptotic approximation. Certain events (namely perceptions) occur always spontaneously and are never the result of preceding ones.

We cannot here give a detailed description of the constructional object forms. The construction (or cognitive synthesis) of the physical world is very nearly completed in prescientific thought. On the other hand, the construction of the autopsychological domain—setting aside certain insignificant beginnings—takes place only in science, indeed, in a science which stands in a very early state of development, namely psychology. Thus, it is understandable that the construction is far from complete. In this science, there is no unanimity concerning the principles which it is to follow. As concerns the majority of constructions, namely, the completion of the context through introduction of the unconscious, there is not even unanimity about the question of whether this supplementation is to be carried out at all, whether it is appropriate and permissible. The question of appropriateness must be decided by psychological research itself and will probably be decided in the near future. On the other hand, the much-debated question concerning the methodological (logical or epistemological) permissibility of the construction of the unconscious must, on the basis of construction theory, certainly be answered in the affirmative. For, the construction of the unconscious is completely analogous to the construction of unseen color spots from seen color spots; yet the permissibility of the latter construction is never denied or even questioned. Also, on the basis of this analogy, one can easily see that the construction of such supplemented domains, which contain among other things also objects which do not immediately occur in experiences, does not consist in anything but an appropriate *reorganization* of the objects which occur immediately. But perhaps the opposition to the concept of unconscious psychological events is directed less toward the postulation of such objects than against the assertion of their reality. However, even

---

[106] Zustandsgleichheit
[107] Ablaufsgleichheit

this objection cannot very well be maintained in view of the analogy with the unseen color spots and all the unperceived points of the perceptual world. (Later on, we shall concern ourselves more closely with the problem of reality, § 170 ff.)

We speak of "physical things" and their "states". In a similar way, it is customary to envisage the autopsychological entities which correspond to an individual time point—be it an elementary experience with its (quasi) constituents, or an experience supplemented by subconscious entities, or subconscious entities alone—as "states" of a persisting bearer, of a psychological thing, as it were. From the analogy of this cognitive synthesis to that of the physical things, it follows that this bearer, which we do not commonly call "psychological thing", but *the self* or *my mind,* must be constructed as *a class of autopsychological states.* It is of especial importance in this connection to keep in mind that a class is not the collection of its elements (§ 37), but a quasi object which allows us to make statements about that which the elements have in common. The obvious objection to this constructional definition is unfounded as long as we keep this in mind. The constructional definition is to reflect nothing but the structural, the ordered, in the self, which alone can be rationally apprehended. On the other hand, the question whether, at the bottom of all autopsychological objects, there lies the "self" as a final unresolvable unity, is not a question of order, but a question of essence; thus, to pose and answer this question is not the task of the constructional system, but of metaphysics (cf. § 163).

133. *The Assignment of Other Sense Qualities*

So far, we have assigned only the qualities of the visual sense and of the tactile sense to certain world points (§§ 126, 130). Since individual descriptions of the remaining senses are now also available (§ 131), we can proceed to assign their qualities or classes of their qualities to world points. Taking into account the cognitive synthesis as it actually occurs, the constructional system will not undertake this assignment with all qualities, but only with those where the assignment can be carried out in an appropriate way. This means that, for example, the assignment to individual world points of a (visual) world line does not result in too many changes of the assigned qualities in the course of time. For example, for the qualities of the sense of taste, an assignment is possible; if we assign the quality "sweet" to a certain state of a certain piece of sugar, then the assignment to "tasted points" can be extended to "untasted points" of the world lines (in analogy to the seen and unseen points, § 126). This procedure will not often lead to contradictions through the assignment of different taste qualities to points of the same world line. An assignment for the qualities of the olfactory sense is similarly successful. In the case of the auditory sense, the assignment is not quite so simple. If we have once heard a tone in a thing, then we cannot simply continue to assign this tone to it permanently, without arriving at frequent contradictions. The qualities of certain other senses, for example, the sense of balance, the kinesthetic sense, the sensations in organs, can be assigned to certain world lines or bundles of world lines, i.e., to visual things, only with great difficulty or perhaps not at all.

However, there is no clear boundary line between assignable and non-assignable sense qualities. Let us consider, for example, the emotions and perhaps also the volitions. (We consider the volitions as an independent quality domain, i.e., as a "sense" only for the sake of argument, without wishing to prejudge the necessity, or even possibility, of such a step; cf. § 85.) We do not frequently assign qualities of emotions or volitions as properties to things in the outside world. This is due to the scientific orientation of our thinking, which affects us in this way, even outside of science, in daily life. We must assume, however, that to decline this assignment is only the result of a process of abstraction and does not hold from the outset. In the uncritical conception of a child, the apple does not only taste "sourish", but also "delicious" or even "like more". This seems to mean that, not only a taste quality, but also an emotion quality and even a volition quality is assigned to it. In a similar way, a woods is "melancholy", a letter "painful", a dress "arrogant". (It must be carefully noted that these objects are not meant as subjects on the basis of empathy, but as objects with the properties in question.) It must be admitted that these assignments are completely justified, for, just as we may call sugar "sweet", since it produces a taste sensation of an appropriate quality, a melody may be called "gay", a letter "painful", an act "outrageous", since these objects produce the appropriate emotions. Furthermore, an apple looks "begging for a bite", a face looks "pushing for a punch", a noise is "to run away from", since these objects cause volitions of the appropriate kind. The assignment of qualities of emotion and volition is generally dropped as conceptual thinking develops. The reason for this perhaps does not lie so much in pronounced temporal variations of these qualities in the same thing—for these variations are here frequently less pronounced than they are, for example, with the sense of warmth, the sense of cold, and the olfactory sense;

rather, these assignments are given up because of contradictions which result later on (when the intersubjective world is constructed) between the assignments which are made by the various subjects. This would seem to justify the assumption that emotions (and volitions, if they are an independent domain) actually stand on the same level as sensations (in the narrower, customary sense). Nevertheless, they are not included among the qualities which are assigned to the outside world; they are envisaged as belonging in a certain way to the "inward" man. The only reason for this seems to be that these qualities, even if assigned to the same object, show a higher degree of variation between several subjects than the sensations in the narrower sense. However, the rejection of these qualities for the construction of perceptual things by no means holds throughout; above, we have mentioned the thinking of the child, and similar remarks can frequently be made about the world of poetry.

That we are here concerned only with differences in degree becomes obvious through the fact that, in the course of scientific development, the qualities of taste and of odor are eventually no longer assigned, and the same holds finally even for the qualities of the tactile and the visual sense. This rejection is a necessary consequence of the insight that the assignment, even of the qualities of these sense modalities varies from subject to subject and thus cannot be carried out in a unique and consistent way. In other words, the conceptual formation (and thus also the construction which follows it) of the perceptual world has only provisional validity. In the progress of knowledge (and of construction) it must give way to the strictly unambiguous but completely quality-free world of physics (cf. § 136.)

134. *Perceptual Things*

Almost without exception, it is points of the tactile-visual things to which the qualities of the remaining senses are assigned in the indicated way. After this assignment we call these things *perceptual things*. The entire space-time world, with the assignment of sense qualities to the individual world points, we call the perceptual world.

Earlier we were able to use spatial relations of shape and position to furnish definite descriptions of the individual parts of my body, taken as *visual* things (§ 131); now we can produce such descriptions on a large scale for individual objects as kinds of objects taken as *perceptual* things. On this can then be based constructional definite descriptions of individual colors, individual odors, etc. (e.g., green as the color of foliage, etc.). As we can see from etymological considerations, this construction is analogous to the actual formation of concepts and of words for the individual sensation qualities. The construction of the autopsychological domain is here supplemented by higher-level constructions. Such supplementations will occur in various other places as well, but we shall not pay any further attention to them.

135. Completion of the Perceptual World through Analogy

Assume that, for large parts of two space-time regions, the assignment of sense qualities is completely or very nearly identical, while the remaining area of one of the space-time regions shows assignments for points where no qualities of the sense in question are assigned to the corresponding points of the other area. In this case, we undertake analogous assignments in the latter area.

The remaining area may be part of the larger region in a temporal or in a spatial sense. Depending upon which of the two is the case, the application of the construction procedure of *assignment by analogy* would seem to be quite different in the two cases. In the first case, the import of the procedure can be intuitively formulated in the following way (in realistic language): if a temporally large part of a known process is repeated in equal or similar ways while it remains unobserved for the remainder of the time, then we assume (if there are no reasons to the contrary) that, during the time when no observations are made, the second process continues in a way analogous to the first, or, more briefly, the processes are subject to mutual analogy. In the second case, i.e., in the case of completion in a spatial direction, the import of the procedure can be formulated thus (in realistic language): if a spatial part of a previously perceived thing is perceived again in the same or in similar ways, while the remaining spatial area remains unobserved, then we assume (if there are no reasons to the contrary) that the unobserved spatial part contains part of a thing which is analogous to the corresponding part of the first thing; or, more briefly, the things are subject to mutual analogy.

Both ways of applying this procedure have occurred earlier when we were concerned with supplementing the seen color spots with unseen color spots so as to arrive at world lines (the first kind in § 126, rules 10, 11, c, d; the second kind in rule 11, c, d), similarly, in the supplementation of touched touch points through untouched touch points (§ 130).

In a sense, the first kind of application of the assignment by analogy can be envisaged as the application of a *postulate of causality*, the second as the application of a *postulate of substance*, or, to put it the other way around, *the two categories of causality and substance amount to the application of the same analogy construction to different coördinates.*

Even if we consider the color spots alone, the application of this procedure brings the assignments very considerably closer to completion. Further supplementations result from the mutual support of the various senses. Through such supplementations, new things and regularities become known, or old ones become better known; with the aid of this information, further supplementations become possible. Thus, we find mutual advancement between the recognition of general laws which hold for things and processes on one hand, and the supplementation of the assignment of qualities to points in the perceptual world on the other.

136. *The World of Physics*

The perceptual world is constructed through the assignment of sense qualities; from it we must distinguish the *world of physics*, where physical-state magnitudes [108] are assigned to the points of the four-dimensional number space. This construction has the purpose of formulating a domain which is determined through *mathematically expressible laws*. They are to be mathematically expressible in order to allow us to *calculate* certain elements from those other elements which determine them. Furthermore, the necessity of constructing the world of physics rests on the circumstance that only this world, but not the perceptual world (cf. § 132, conclusion), can be made intersubjective in an unequivocal, consistent manner (§§ 146–149).

It is not antecedently obvious that physics, if it wants to establish a domain of thoroughgoing regularity, has to eliminate all qualities and replace them by numbers. The opposition (which Goethe, for example, maintained against Newton in the polemical part of his *Farbenlehre*) asserts that one has to remain within the domain of the sense qualities and that one must ascertain the regularities which hold between them. This would mean that we would have to find the regularities in the domain which we called the perceptual world. Of course, laws like the natural laws of physics do not hold in this domain. One can show, however, that there must be regularities of some sort if the construction of a world of physics, which is governed by regularities, is to be possible at

---

[108] physikalische Zustandsgrössen

all. However, the regularities within the perceptual world are of a much more complicated nature than the laws of physics. At the moment, we cannot concern ourselves with these problems. There is a much more simple way to arrive at a domain of thoroughgoing regularity and calculability, and that is to construct the world of physics as a pure world of numbers.

The indicated purpose of this construction does not unambiguously determine which physical-state magnitudes must be chosen for the construction of the world of physics; at least, this is not clear at the present state of physical knowledge. There are various choices. However, as far as empirical evidence is concerned, the various resulting systems of physics have the same value. It is probable that eventually a clear decision will be made (which will be based upon empirical evidence but which will be guided by methodological principles, for example, the principle of greatest possible simplicity).

The formulation of the laws of nature depends upon the choice of state magnitudes and upon the system of physics. Nevertheless, the kind and degree of determination which is provided through the natural laws is empirically fixed and does not depend upon the system. That is to say, the assignment of all state magnitudes to all world points is determined by the assignment of the state magnitudes to the points of a three-dimensional cross section at right angles to the first coördinate (which corresponds to time).

The construction of the physical world, aside from the regularity to which it is to lead, is essentially determined through a special relation which holds between it and the perceptual world; this relation we want to call *physicoqualitative correlation*. To begin with, the world points of physics are in a one-to-one correspondence to the world points of the perceptual world. (Nevertheless, the metric of the physical world can be different from that of the perceptual world; for example, it could be the non-Euclidean metric which is required by the general theory of relativity.) Then there exists a one-many relation between the qualities and the state magnitudes in such a way that, if there is an assignment of physical-state magnitudes of any (purely numerical) structure to a physical [109] point in its neighborhood, then the quality which is correlated with this structure is always assigned to the correlated world point of the perceptual world or, at least, it can be assigned without contradiction. However, in the opposite direction, the correlation is not unique; the assignment of a quality to a world point in the perceptual world does not

---

[109] physikalisch

determine which structure of state magnitudes is to be assigned to the neighborhood of the corresponding physical world point of the world of physics; the assignment of this quality merely determines a class to which this structure must belong. It is clear that the physico-qualitative correlation cannot be free from the imprecision which attaches to the perceptual world generally.

REFERENCES. Concerning the problem of deciding between the possible systems of physics, cf. Carnap [Aufg. d. Phys.]; this article also concerns itself in more detail with the physico-qualitative correlation. About kind and degree of determination of the world of physics, cf. Carnap [Dreidimens.]. That the world of physics is completely free from sense qualities is shown by Schlick [Raum and Zeit] 93 f. and Carnap [Phys. Begr.]; the latter also gives reasons for the transition from the qualitative perceptual world to the quantitative physical world (p. 51 ff.).

137. *Biological Objects; Man*

After the world of physics has been constructed, it is possible to give a definite description of each individual event and each thing that belongs to the world. This can be accomplished through indication of place and time or through the relation to other events and things or through properties based on the assignments. We have already assumed earlier that definite descriptions of the individual sense organs of my body are given (§ 131); it is now also possible to give a constructional definite description of all the other parts and events of my body; furthermore, all other individual physical things, their parts, and events in connection with them. Accordingly, these physical things can be placed into classes or into entire systems of classes of various levels according to the properties in which they agree. In this way we obtain, for example, the inorganic and organic substances, furthermore, the inorganic and organic individual objects as well as the entire system of organisms, of plants, and of animals, as well as the system of artifacts. In such a way, the entire domain of physical objects is constructable.

Organisms are characterized through special properties of the events which take place with them or through certain "faculties" which are to be constructed on the basis of these events, for example, metabolism, procreation, regulation, etc. It is not necessary at this point to discuss these identifying properties in more detail. The only important thing is that they are physical properties, i.e., properties which we can assume to be constructed after the construction of the world of physics. The organisms with their essential properties and relations and events which are peculiar to organisms are called *biological objects*.

One can show empirically that "my body", a thing which we constructed at first as a visual thing (§ 129) and which we have then, through further assignments, placed in the perceptual world, belongs to the organisms. The class of *men* is constructed as a class of the biological classification of organisms, to which my body belongs. A constructional definite description of this class is given by indicating the degree to which its elements are to agree with my body in size, figure, motions, and other events. Outside of the thing which is called "my body", there are "other men" (as physical things) who belong to this class. This class forms an object type which is of especial importance for the constructional system. Starting from it, we shall construct the heteropsychological domain (§ 140) and thus all higher objects.

138. *The Expression Relation*

The construction of my body, its parts, its motions, and the other events which are connected with it, has already been discussed (§§ 129, 131, 137). It is relatively unimportant whether we here mean by "my body" the mere tactile-visual thing, to which we originally gave this name, or the corresponding physical thing, because the events which we need for further constructions can be satisfactorily identified through tactile and visual qualities.

For the subsequent construction of the heteropsychological (§ 140), the *expression relation* is of fundamental importance. As pointed out earlier (§ 19), by this is meant the relation between expressive motions, i.e., facial expressions, gestures, bodily motions, even organic processes, on the one hand, and the simultaneous psychological events which are "expressed" through them, on the other. This explanation is not meant to be the constructional definition of the expression relation, since it would clearly be circular. It is really meant to refer to already known facts in order to provide a clearer understanding of the word. The construction of the expression relation, on the other hand, consists in the following: to a class of autopsychological events which frequently occur simultaneously with certain recognizable physical events of my body, we correlate the class of these physical events as "expression".

The construction of the heteropsychological could also be based upon the *psychophysical relation* (§§ 19, 21), instead of the expression relation, if only this relation were somewhat better known. In this case, the relation would have to be constructed in the following way: to a class of autopsychological events which frequently occur simultaneously with certain physical events of my central nervous system, the class of these physical events is "psychophysically" correlated.

THE UPPER LEVELS:
HETEROPSYCHOLOGICAL AND
CULTURAL OBJECTS

139. *About the Presentation of Subsequent Constructional Levels*

For the subsequent levels of the constructional system, we cannot do more than give outlines showing the *possibility* of a construction of the object in question on the basis of preceding constructions.

To begin with, we shall construct the *heteropsychological objects* (§ 140) on the basis of "other persons", which are already constructed as physical things (§ 137), and with the aid of the expression relation (§ 138). Furthermore, certain events in the other persons are envisaged as "productions of signs". With their aid, we shall construct the *world of the other* (§§ 141–145). There exists a certain correspondence between the world which we have constructed up to this point, namely, "my world", and this "world of the other". Upon this correspondence the construction of the *intersubjective world* is based (§§ 146–149). Finally, it is possible, on the basis of the (auto- or hetero-) psychological objects, to construct the objects of the highest level, namely, the *cultural objects* (§ 150 f.) and *values* (§ 152). After having discussed these constructions, we shall then consider the problem of the elimination of the basic relation(s) as the only remaining aspect of the constructional system that is not purely formal (§§ 153–155). Finally, we shall summarize, in the form of theses, all those points which may be asserted after completion of the exposition of the constructional system (§ 156). These theses are thus different from the content of the system itself, which was to be no more than an example.

140. *The Domain of the Heteropsychological*

Earlier (§ 137), we have constructed "other persons" as those organisms which are similar to my body in certain ways. Thus, they have been constructed as physical things. Now we shall undertake the construction of the psychological aspects of other persons, namely, the *heteropsychological*. This construction consists in the following: on the basis of physical events in another person and with the aid of the expression relation, which has been constructed earlier (§ 138), we assign psychological events to this person. Aside from the expression relation, we shall also utilize the "production of signs", i.e., information that the other person gives me (§§ 141–144). Here we arrive at two very important points; the construction of the heteropsychological can be an assignment only to the *body* of the other, not to his mind, which, after all, cannot be constructed in any other way than through this assignment; thus, constructionally, the other mind does not even exist before this assignment is carried out. Secondly, the assigned psychological events are autopsychological events for the very same reason: the only psychological entities which have been constructed up to this point are autopsychological entities, and no other can be constructed prior to this assignment; there is no possibility of constructing non-autopsychological entities other than with the aid of precisely this assignment.

We shall supplement this assignment in order to obtain a more or less complete experience sequence of the other person by using two types of law, both of which are derived from elementary experiences, namely, state laws [110] (i.e., that constituents of elementary experiences of type *a* are generally simultaneous with others of type *b*) and process laws [111] (i.e., that experiences, or constituents of experiences or sequences of them, of type *a* are generally succeeded by others of type *b*). Thus, the entire *experience sequence of the other person consists of* nothing but *a rearrangement of my own experiences and their constituents.* It must be noted, however, that we can construct experiences for the other person which do not correspond to any of my own experiences, but the constitu-

---

[110] Zustandsgesetze
[111] Ablaufsgesetze

ents of such experiences of the other person must occur as constituents of my own experiences, for (in constructional language) there is nothing to be assigned except the elementary experiences and what is constructed from them, i.e., their quasi constituents (in the widest sense, including components, etc.); (in realistic language): as I observe expressive events in another person, I cannot infer from them something that is unknown to me in kind.

We have pointed out (§ 132) that my experiences or conscious events are supplemented through the insertion of unconscious events so as to form the complete autopsychological domain; this domain shows fairly extensive, though not altogether autonomous, regularity. In precisely analogous fashion, we now supplement the experience sequence or the consciousness of the other with unconscious events of the other so as to arrive at the complete domain of the psychological states of the other. In so doing we assume the same determining laws as in the supplementation which produced the autopsychological domain. The thus constructed "psychological states of the other", when taken as a class, may be called the *mind of the other* in analogy to "my mind". The general domain of the heteropsychological embraces all psychological events of all other persons who (i.e., whose bodies) occur as physical things in the already constructed world of physics.

From the indicated type of construction for the heteropsychological domain, it follows that there can be no heteropsychological phenomena without a body, for (in constructional language): the heteropsychological can be constructed only through the mediation of a body; in particular, of a body where certain events ("expressive events") occur which are similar to those of my body; (in realistic language): if heteropsychological objects were not connected with a body through which they express themselves, they would be in principle unrecognizable and thus could not become the objects of scientific statements. (We shall not here concern ourselves with the problem of telepathy; a closer investigation would show that even telepathic knowledge of the heteropsychological needs the mediation of a body.)

If we were to presuppose sufficient (but presently unavailable) knowledge of brain physiology (such that the correlation problem of the psychophysical relation would be solved, cf. § 21), then the psychological states of another person could be more precisely and more completely constructed with the aid of the *psychophysical relation* than with the aid of the expression relation (together with the production of signs). If the brain events of the other person were completely constructed to their last detail as parts of the world of physics, then it would be possible to construct from them, at the same time, the conscious as well as the unconscious; hence, the entire range of the psychological states of the other person. The just-indicated conclusions follow from this type of construction also.

> REFERENCES. Considering its great importance for the construction of the knowable world, the problem of the construction of the heteropsychological is not very often posed as a problem; attempts at its solution are even more rare. Actually, we have to mention only the following: Kauffmann [Imman.] 106–121; Dingler [Naturphil.] 140 ff.; Driesch [Ordnungsl.] 371 ff. (with bibliography); Ziehen [Erkth.] 277 ff.; Becher [Geisteswiss.] 119 ff., 285 ff.; Jacoby [Ontol.] 307 ff. In these and other investigations of this kind (with the exception of Kauffmann and Dingler), the heteropsychological is generally inferred, rather than constructed. This inference amounts to a violation of the construction principle of Russell (see the motto preceding § 1, and § 3). Russell himself does not apply his principle to this particular problem. For detailed discussions of the epistemological reducibility of the heteropsychological to the physical, see Carnap [Realismus].
>
> About the reduction by *behaviorism*, not only of the heteropsychological, but of all psychological phenomena to physical phenomena, cf. § 59.

141. *The Production of Signs*

Other persons, considered as physical things, exhibit certain physical manifestations other than expressive events which are of especial importance for the increase of knowledge and hence for the completion of the constructional system. These are the sign-giving manifestations, especially spoken and written words; we call them *sign productions*. They make possible a broadening of the constructional system, an increase in the number of constructable objects of almost all kinds.

Earlier, we have discussed the *sign relation* and have emphasized its difference from the expression relation (§ 19). One of its partial relations is the *relation between "sign production" and the signified*. The construction of this relation is more difficult than any of the constructions which we have hitherto undertaken. One can of course produce rules for how the meaning of sounds of a foreign language can be inferred by a comparison of these sounds with processes in the speaker. However, it is not possible to formulate these rules in such a way that the first occurrence of a sound will always allow us to infer its meaning. One can only indicate how one could make conjectures and how these conjectures, after the sounds have occurred a number of times, can be either rejected or better confirmed until they become certainties.

In order to arrive at a constructional definition of the relation of sign production, one would have to translate such rules (for the recognition of the meaning of a sign) into the constructional language. Consequently, this definition, too, would take on a very complicated form. To begin with, we would have to stipulate that a physical event in another person is considered a sign production if the following construction can be completely carried out for that event. An object is considered the designatum of a sign production of a certain person if there is a procedure which assigns the greatest weight to it in relation to that sign production. The meaning of the sign production is considered the more safely ascertained, the more the weight of the object in question surpasses the weight of the other objects for the same sign production. We can here only barely hint at the rules for the assignment of weights to the various objects for a given sign production.

> The rules would say, for example, that the weight which is assigned to a physical thing, relative to a sign production, rises if the thing is close to the body of the sign-giver at the time of the sign production; furthermore, if it stands in certain relations (namely, the stimulus relations) to the sense organs of the sign-giver, or else if it was in the proximity of the sign-giver or stood in the stimulus relation to his sense organs, not at the time of the sign production, but a short time before. Furthermore, the weight rises if the thing is in motion or if it changes its state of motion or if it undergoes a discontinuous process or if it contrasts very strongly in its physical properties with its surroundings, etc. Let this simple indication suffice to show that such rules are possible.

According to the indicated procedure, sign production is, to begin with, related to the physical. Unlike the sample rules, our rules must eventually assign weights, not only to physical bodies, but to physical objects of all kinds (events, states, properties, relations, etc.). Furthermore, and still relative to a given sign production, we shall use similar rules to assign weights to the psychological objects of the sign-giver; they are again objects of various kinds (experiences, constituents, components, etc.). Eventually, weights will also be assigned to the psychological objects of other persons, including the self. After we have later on carried out still higher-level constructions, the objects which we shall then introduce will also have weights assigned to them, according to the closer or more remote connection between the object in question and the sign-giver.

The most important assignment of weights to objects, albeit the most difficult one, arises when (in realistic language) a word is understood through its context. Relative to a given word, which occurs in a sentence, those objects are to be assigned increased weight, which stand in a close relation to the objects designated by the other words of the sentence (they could be of the same object type, they could be in spatial or temporal proximity, they could coincide in certain properties or be connected through a certain event, etc.). If the meaning of the other word has not been sufficiently ascertained, we must for each word take several objects into account, depending on their weight.

142. *Reports of Other Persons*

Taking into consideration other words for the interpretation of a given word is only the most primitive form of considering the context. A much more fruitful form follows from the circumstance that words form sentences and that sentences designate states of affairs. A sign production which forms an entire *sentence*, i.e., *which designates a state of affairs*, we call a *report*.[112] The *reporting relation* (between a report and its state of affairs) is to be constructed together with the sign production relation (between a word and the designated object), since the two constructions relate to, and support, one another. However, the *construction of the reporting relation* is still more complicated than the construction of the sign production relation for words, especially since the different possible sentence forms must be taken into consideration.

> EXAMPLE. In order to indicate the rough form of this construction, let us concern ourselves with a rather simple sentence form, namely, with sentences which consist of three words, which designate a referent, a relation and a relatum (example: "Karl hits Fritz"). In such a case, the constructional definition of the reporting relation would contain roughly the following elements: the meaning of a report is that particular state of affairs which has the greatest total weight relative to that report. The total weight is a function (perhaps the product) of individual weight factors of the state of affairs relative to the given report. For the determination of these factors, definite rules would have to be devised, which could be like or similar to the following: A state of affairs is related to two objects (in the example, Karl and Fritz) and a relation which holds between them (hitting). The first factor for the total weight of a given state of affairs relative to a given report is the weight of the first object of the state of affairs (to be determined according to the rules of § 141), relative to the first word of

---

[112] Angabe

the report ("Karl"); the second factor is the weight of the relation of the state of affairs relative to the second word of the report ("hits"); the third factor is the weight of the third object of the state of affairs, relative to the third word of the report ("Fritz"). A fourth factor, which carries much more weight than the three just-mentioned ones, could perhaps be determined in the following way. It is largest when the state of affairs obtains (i.e., if the relation in question holds between the two objects; in the example, if Karl really hits Fritz); it is smaller when it is not known whether or not the state of affairs obtains; still smaller, if the state of affairs does not obtain, even though the first object belongs to the domain and the second to the converse domain of the relation; it is still smaller if only one of these two conditions is fulfilled and still smaller if both of them remain unfulfilled, but if the objects at least belong to the object type or at least to the sphere of the domain or the converse domain, etc.

The meaning of a report is secure to the extent to which the total weight of a state of affairs which is determined according to rules of the indicated kind surpasses the total weights of the remaining states of affairs. The more or less secure correlations which are thus established for the reporting relation can now in turn be used for the sign production relation for words, namely, for the three words of the report. Now, if we have secured a pair consisting of a report and a state of affairs which stand to one another in the reporting relation, then an object is assigned greater weight relative to a word if word and object occur in corresponding positions in the report and in the state of affairs, respectively. The weight factor which is thus assigned to an object is of especial importance for the determination of its weight. This is a reflection of the special value of the "context" for the determination of the meaning of a word.

143. *Intuitive Understanding and Functional Dependency*

We have said earlier (§ 100) that the construction does not represent the actual process of cognition in its concrete manifestations, but that it is intended to give a *rational reconstruction* of the formal structure of this process. This viewpoint allows and even requires deviations of the construction from the actual process of cognition. In the last-mentioned cases, namely, in the constructional utilization of expressive motions, of sign productions, and of reports, this deviation is especially great. A child, in learning to understand the meaning of spoken words and sentences, proceeds in an associative, intuitive fashion and not (or at least only to a very inconsiderable degree) through ratiocination. To a still greater degree, the understanding of the expressive motions of another person is restricted to the intuitive procedure. It is somewhat different with a sentence. After we have already understood a sentence, we can still remember its individual parts and infer the meaning of the entire sentence from the meanings of the parts and thus provide a rational check for the intuitive understanding. On the other hand, after we have understood the facial expressions of another person, it is not possible in most cases to recollect precisely the individual expressions of the other; the impressions of purely physical events are quite fleeting, so that essentially there remains only the recollection of the apprehended meaning.

Now, there is a certain dependency between sign production and expressive motion, on the one hand, and the designated or expressed meaning, on the other; it is this dependency which is to be expressed in the construction. This dependency holds in every case, whether the understanding of an utterance is intuitive or rational. To begin with, the dependency consists in the fact that all apprehensions of heteropsychological phenomena depend upon the mediation of a sign production or an expressive motion. More than that, the entire nature of the apprehensible or the apprehended content is dependent upon the nature of the mediating utterance. In other words, the heteropsychological is (even intuitively) apprehensible only as the meaning of an utterance (of an expressive motion or a sign production). The meaning of an utterance is a unique function of the physical properties of the utterance ("function" in the mathematical, not in the psychological, sense). Since the construction states this function, the course of the process of cognition is not misrepresented by the construction (it is not falsely given out as a rational-discursive, rather than an intuitive process); the construction does not even contain a fiction to the effect that the process is rational rather than intuitive. (The latter is the case only in the language of fictitious constructive operations, which is added as an aid to understanding.) The construction itself does not indicate any process at all, but only the above-mentioned logical function.

These remarks hold, beyond the present problem, quite generally for all constructions. For the sake of brevity and intuitive obviousness, we have, in this chapter (IV, C), used the realistic language most of the time. Thus, the present context makes it especially important to note that the constructions themselves (which are not here given) have the neutral character of logical functions even with the objects which are presently under discussion.

REFERENCES. About the necessity of giving an epistemological-logical "justification" or legitimization of the recognition of the hetero-psychological, which in reality takes place through empathy or "apperceptive supplementation" (B. Erdmann), cf. Becher [Geisteswiss.] 285 ff. For a more detailed anaylsis of the sense of the epistemological reduction in general and especially of the reduction of the heteropsychological to the physical, see Carnap [Realismus].

144. *The Utilization of Reports of Other Persons*

In the process of cognition, and thus also in the constructional system, we make two different kinds of use of the reports of other persons. To begin with, a report (if it is reliable) informs me about a state of affairs, but, secondly, I also find out that this state of affairs is known to the other.

Let us consider, to begin with, the utilization of the content of reports. Before a report is utilized, its reliability must be tested. This is done, on the one hand, through a comparison with already more or less well-established states of affairs and relational laws between them and, on the other hand, by taking into consideration the trustworthiness of the author of the report, the criteria for which are discovered empirically and gradually. We shall not dwell upon the test of trustworthiness and shall presuppose that a selection of the reliable reports has already been made.

It is quite obvious that the utilization of the contents of reports makes for an extraordinary enrichment of the possibilities of construction. More precisely, the number of constructable objects in the various domains is increased many times. Only the domain of the autopsychological allows very little enlargement. Not so with the physical domain, and the construction of the domains of the heteropsychological and finally of the cultural rest almost entirely on the utilization of reports. There is no need to concern ourselves at this point with the details of this.

Let us again focus our attention on the fact that, *on no level* of the constructional system, hence not even through the utilization of the reports of other persons, *is something fundamentally new introduced into the system*, but that what we have here is *only a reorganization* (albeit a very complicated one) of the given elements. The new order which eventuates from this reorganization is not determined through something that lies outside of the given, but again only through the given itself or, more precisely, through the inventory of the basic relation(s). Thus, this utilization of reports does not lead us to abandon the autopsychological basis upon which the entire constructional system is founded. Nevertheless, we do not construct other persons as mere machines, but with all the contents of their experiences, to the extent to which they are (in realistic language) recognizable. After all, it was the thesis of construction theory that the constructional system, in spite of its autopsychological basis, would be in a position to express all legitimate statements, more precisely, all statements which can be considered valid in an empirical science or which can be posed as questions. (This does not include the statements of metaphysics.)

145. *The World of the Other*

The experiences of a given other person M (who has been constructed as a physical thing, according to § 137) are constructed according to the last-described procedure, i.e., with the aid of the expression relation and the reporting relation. It is not possible to construct these experiences either as numerous or as variegated as my own experiences, the elementary experiences, are given to me. Nevertheless, in spite of this incompleteness, we can apply the same construction forms to them which we have applied to elementary experiences from the beginning of the constructional system. More precisely, the constructional steps which were carried out earlier with the basic relation Rs are now carrried out with the analogous relation Rs_M, which holds between M's experiences. Thus, we formulate new constructional definitions by transforming the already available constructional definitions through a substitution of Rs_M for Rs and through attaching an appropriate subscript (indicating M) to the defined symbols (e.g., $color_M$, $qual_M$, etc.). Thus, we construct "M's objects" which form "*the world of M.*"

Even here we do not desert the autopsychological basis; all of "M's objects" are still objects of the one constructional system and thus go back ultimately to the basic object of that system, i.e., to a relation which holds between elementary experiences (my experiences!). However, there is a certain sense in which one can speak of *the constructional system of M*; by this is meant nothing but a certain *branch* of "the" (or "my") *constructional system* that branches off at a high level. The only reason why we can envisage this branch as a constructional system is that it mirrors the entire constructional system by virtue of a certain analogy. We call it the constructional system "of M" only because, within "the" (or "my") constructional system, it is constructed as having a certain connection with M's body.

146. *Intersubjective Correspondence*

From the indicated way of constructing the "world of M", it follows that, between this world and "my world", there exists a certain analogy; more precisely, the analogy holds between the constructional system as a whole (S) and the "constructional system of M" (S_M). It must be remembered, however, that S_M is only a partial system within S; the world of M is constructed within my world; it is not to be considered as formed by M, but as formed by me for M.

The analogy between S and S_M amounts to a very far-reaching, but not to a complete, agreement. To begin with, for almost every construction in S, there is a corresponding construction in S_M, which has an analogous definitional form and whose symbol is marked by an index M. Furthermore, corresponding assertions hold almost without exception for correspondingly constructed objects. This holds especially for the levels prior to the construction of the space-time world. Later on, however, in the construction of the physical and the heteropsychological domain, this simple agreement, which depends upon analogous construction, no longer holds; on the other hand, a new type of agreement occurs.

In § 129, it was described how "my body" was constructed first as a visual thing and then as a physical thing, which may be designated by mb. In an analogous way, we construct in S_M an object mb_M, namely, the body of M. (Note the difference between the physical thing M and mb_M. The former is constructed with myself as the vantage point; the latter, by proceeding from M's experiences.) From the analogy in constructional form it follows that mb and mb_M agree in certain properties; for example, they are both physical things. On the other hand, they disagree in many other properties. For example, if M has another hair color than I have, then we obtain two different statements about mb and mb_M, respectively.

For the remaining physical things within S, it also does not hold that they agree with the corresponding things in S_M (for the things which stand in certain spatial relations to my body do not as a rule stand in the same relations to M). But now we find an agreement of a new kind. A one-to-one correspondence holds between the spatiotemporal world of physics in S and that in S_M, in the following way: the spatiotemporal relations which hold for the physical world points in S_M also hold for the corresponding world points in S. The same is true for qualitative relations (i.e., relations which hold on the basis of assignment). For reasons to be explained later, we wish to call this correspondence *intersubjective correspondence*. An object in S_M which corresponds by virtue of analogous construction to an object O of S, we have called O_M. Now we assign the symbol O^M to the object of S_M which intersubjectively corresponds to the object O. Two intersubjectively corresponding objects of S and S_M represent (in realistic language) "the same" object, once as it is recognized by me and the other time as it is (so far as I know) recognized by M.

> EXAMPLE. The body of a third person N is not to be characterized in S_M by a construction analogous to that in S. (Thus, it should by no means be designated with N_M.) But (under favorable conditions) there is a physical thing in S_M which intersubjectively corresponds to N, hence which is to be designated by N^M. N^M then represents the person N as it is cognized by M. Within the world of physics of S_M, N^M may have an entirely different constructional definite description than N has in S; but both objects exhibit identical properties in the respective worlds of physics. In this case we also find a certain agreement relative to the constructional form in that N in S as well as N^M in S_M is constructed as "another person".

There are, in particular, two places where the constructional forms of intersubjectively corresponding objects in S and S_M deviate considerably from one another. mb (my body) and mb^M (my body from M's point of view) are indeed both physical things, but, unlike mb_M (body of M as it is seen by himself), mb^M does not have a construction form analogous to that of mb, for we construct mb in S as "my body", while mb^M is constructed in S_M in the form, "body of another person". The second deviation goes in the opposite direction: M (the body of M seen by me) and M^M (the body of M seen by himself) are indeed both physical things, but are constructed differently. There is no object in S_M which would be constructed in analogy to M (hence, no object to be designated as M_M). (The construction form of mb^M is similar, but not precisely analogous to that of M.) While M in S is constructed as "body of another person", M^M in S_M is constructed as "my body" ($M^M = mb_M$).

147. *Intersubjective Correspondence Holds for All Object Types*

Intersubjective correspondence holds not only between physical objects, but also between psychological ones. For the most part, heteropsychological objects correspond to other heteropsychological objects. In S, we assign to N, namely, the body of another person, certain heteropsychological objects: in S_M there is an object N^M, again the body of another person, which stands in intersubjective correspondence to N; certain heteropsychological objects are assigned to N^M, and these objects stand in intersubjective correspondence to the heteropsychological objects which were assigned to N in S. The psychological objects of N in S correspond to the psychological objects of N^M in S_M in their qualitative structure (provided only that both constructions can be, and are, carried out).

In the construction of the psychological, the greatest differences in the constructional forms for intersubjectively corresponding objects arise at two points which are connected with the two just-mentioned ones, namely, in the construction of the psychological objects which are assigned to mb and to M (i.e., my psychological events, states, etc., and the psychological events, states, etc., of M).

We said earlier that this intersubjective correspondence does not hold for the lower constructional levels, but only for the levels beginning with the construction of the space-time world, while for the lower levels we could only show constructional analogy. However, after the intersubjective correspondence, which was first introduced for the world of physics, has now been accomplished for the psychological world, it gives us a thoroughgoing correspondence of all objects of S and S_M. It must be noted, however, that the intersubjective correspondence does not hold on the lower levels between such objects of S as Rs, elex, qual, sense, sight, and the analogously constructed objects Rs_M, $elex_M$, etc., which relate to M and his experiences. Rather, this correspondence holds between Rs, elex, etc., and certain objects Rs^M, $elex^M$, etc.

> EXAMPLE. elex are the (i.e., "my") elementary experiences; $elex_M$ are the experiences of another person M; $elex^M$, on the other hand, are again my experiences, but in a way in which they are constructed in S_M, (in realistic language) as they are recognized by M. Of course, these, as all objects, are constructed in S (i.e., "by me"), for there are no other objects. S_M is, after all, a part of the system S. In realistic language: $elex^M$ are my experiences, not as I know them, but as they are known to the other person M on the basis of his observations and the reports which I make. More precisely, they represent my knowledge (gained through his reports and various inferences) of his awareness of my experiences. Thus, $elex^M$ represents what, to my knowledge, M knows about my experiences. Considerations precisely analogous to the correspondence of elex to $elex^M$ hold also for the other objects of the lower constructional levels.

The intersubjective correspondence between S and S_M cannot at once be obtained for all objects of the two systems, but only after certain supplementations have been carried out. For example, the world of physics of each of the two systems is always incomplete and the gaps do not generally occur at the same places. Thus, the one system will contain assignments to world points of physics where they are lacking in the other system or where the other system has different, incompatible assignments. (Contradictory assignments are relatively rare. Where they occur, special criteria, which we shall not here discuss, must bring about a decision which recognizes one of the two assignments as legitimate, while deleting the other.) If we have disagreement in assignments, it will in most cases be brought about by the fact that one system has an assignment where the other has a vacant place. In these cases, a corresponding, supplementary assignment will be made in the second system in conformity with the rules for supplementation which have been given above (§ 135). (In realistic language): initially, the corresponding objects of the two systems agree in their properties; where the agreement cannot be proved, it is introduced as an hypothesis. Once this has been done in all cases, intersubjective correspondence holds throughout the two systems.

> It has been stated that S_M is contained in S as a proper part of S, and it has also been said that the objects of both systems can be brought into a one-to-one correspondence (intersubjective correspondence). These two statements are not contradictory to one another, since neither of the two systems can be completed. The second statement means the following: for each object which is constructed in one of the systems, an intersubjectively corresponding object can be constructed in the other as soon as the latter is sufficiently enlarged.

148. *The Intersubjective World*

We have seen above that, as a rule, intersubjectively corresponding objects of S and S_M differ from one another in the way they are constructed, but that they agree in properties which do not depend on the particular form of construction; that is, that they agree in properties which could be called material [113] properties. The properties which are thus in agreement and the statements about such properties we wish to call *intersubjectively communicable* [114] (more precisely, "intersubjectively

---

[113] inhaltlich
[114] übertragbar

communicable between S and S_M"). On the other hand, properties which belong to an object only in S or only in S_M, and the statements about such properties, we call *subjective in* S or *subjective in* S_M, respectively. It is easy to see that the intersubjectively communicable statements include, for example, statements about the similarity of two qualities, furthermore, statements about color, size, odor, etc., of a given physical thing, also statements about the emotions of a given person at a given time, etc. Moreover, certain statements about constructional form are intersubjectively communicable, for example, statements concerning whether an object is to be constructed as a class or as a relation, and similar ones. However, most statements about the form of the construction of an object in S or in S_M must be described as subjective in S or in S_M, respectively. For example, this holds frequently for statements about the required order in the construction of certain objects, and for requisite supplementations (according to § 126, rules 7, 10). It also holds if the construction of a certain physical object requires arguments by analogy (according to § 135), etc.

So far, we have considered only the intersubjective correspondence between the systems S and S_M, i.e., a one-to-one correspondence of the objects of my world and the objects of the world of a given other person M. Now, everything that has been said about person M also holds for the remaining "other persons," thus, for example, for N, P, etc. Hence, there is a one-to-one intersubjective correspondence between the systems S and S_N, also between the systems S and S_P, etc. What has been said about the correspondence between S and S_M also holds for these correspondences. Now, if a one-to-one correspondence holds between S_M and S and also between S and S_N, then there exists a one-to-one correspondence between S_M and S_N, which has the same properties as the former correspondences. Thus, there exists a general one-to-one correspondence between all such systems, that is, between all the worlds of all persons (i.e., normal persons known to me), including myself. Henceforth, we shall mean by *intersubjective correspondence* this general correspondence and no longer the correspondence between two given systems. Also, in an analogous way, we shall mean from now on by *intersubjectively communicable properties* and *intersubjectively communicable statements* such as continue to hold when their object is replaced by the intersubjectively corresponding object of any other system. The class of all objects of the various systems which intersubjectively correspond to a given object of any system, we call an *intersubjective object*. Furthermore, a property of such a class, which it possesses on the basis of an intersubjectively communicable property of its elements, we call an *intersubjective property*; and a statement about an intersubjective property of an intersubjective object, we call an *intersubjective statement*.

EXAMPLES. If, e.g., the statement $f(O)$ about object O of system S is intersubjectively communicable, then this means that the corresponding statements $f(O^M)$, $f(O^N)$, etc., whose subjects O^M, O^N of systems S_M, S_N intersubjectively correspond to O, also hold. This situation is most easily expressed through an appropriate statement about the class which comprises the objects O, O^M, O^N, etc. If we designate the intersubjective correspondence by Int, then this class is to be called $\overrightarrow{\text{Int}'}\, O$, but $\overrightarrow{\text{Int}'}\, O^M$ or $\overrightarrow{\text{Int}'}\, O^N$ will do as well. By definition, the new statement, say $F\,(\overrightarrow{\text{Int}'}\, O)$, is an intersubjective statement that is derived from the intersubjectively communicable statements $f(O)$, $f(O^M)$, etc. Classes of the indicated kind, for example, $\overrightarrow{\text{Int}'}\, O$ ($\overrightarrow{\text{Int}'}\, O^M$ and $\overrightarrow{\text{Int}'}\, O^N$ are identical with it) will now be called intersubjective objects. If we start with another object, say P, then the class $\overrightarrow{\text{Int}'}\, P$ of objects P, P^M, P^N, etc., is derived in the same way.

As we can easily see from the example, the intersubjective objects are the abstraction classes (§ 73) of intersubjective correspondence. The world of these objects we call the *intersubjective world*. The indicated (quasi-analytic) procedure of the construction of an intersubjective object on the basis of the intersubjectively corresponding objects of the individual systems, we call *intersubjectivizing*.

In contrast to other conceptions (for example, Christiansen [Kantkritik]) in our system *intersubjectivizing is not based upon a fiction*. The constructional system confines itself to the reports of other persons for the construction, i.e., to begin with, for the constructional supplementation of the physical world, but then also for the construction of the heteropsychological. However, these constructions do not consist in a hypothetical inference or fictitious postulation of something that is not given, but they consist *merely in the reorganization of the given* (cf. § 140). The same holds for the construction of the intersubjective world. Within the constructional system, no metaphysical assertions are made concerning the objects which are thus constructed through reorganization.

149. *The Intersubjective World as the World of Science*

The intersubjective world (in the sense of the above-given construction) forms the actual object domain of science. But science contains not only intersubjective statements, but also nonintersubjective statements that correspond to intersubjective statements or can be transformed into intersubjective statements. This transformation is one of the tasks of science; science aims to produce a supply of exclusively intersubjective statements. This aim is rarely stated explicitly, since the transformation generally takes place in an almost imperceptible way: we generally use the same sign (word or special symbol) for different but intersubjectively corresponding objects and, in addition, we use this same sign also for the intersubjective object which corresponds to all of them (and which we have constructed as their class).

This feature of science does not radically exclude from the domain of science all statements which are not intersubjectively communicable, i.e., which are subjective. Such statements can be scientifically phrased through a reformulation which mentions the author in the statement.

It likewise holds for the objects to be constructed subsequently, especially for the cultural ones, that they have intersubjectively corresponding objects in the systems S_M, etc. Thus, even in their case, it is possible to derive intersubjective objects. In doing this, the procedure of intersubjectivizing remains always the same; thus, it is not necessary to consider it in any detail for the higher-level constructions which we shall indicate in the sequel.

150. *The Primary Cultural Objects*

Earlier, we have briefly characterized the cultural object type and have emphasized its independence from the physical and psychological object types (§ 23). For the construction of cultural objects, the manifestation relation (§ 24) is of especial and fundamental importance. This is because the primary cultural objects, i.e., those objects whose construction does not presuppose the construction of other cultural objects, are always constructed on the basis of their manifestations (cf. § 55 f.), i.e., on the basis of those psychological events in which they are actualized or become apparent. There is a certain analogy between the construction of the cultural objects on the basis of their manifestations and the construction of the physical things on the basis of the experiences in which they are perceived. We cannot here give an explicit account of these constructions. The reason for this is that the psychology (or phenomenology) of the cognition of cultural objects has not been researched and systematically described to the same degree as the psychology of perception. Thus, we give only a few examples and indicate briefly how they could be generalized. These indications may suffice, since we are here mainly concerned with the *possibility of construction* of cultural objects from psychological objects and since we are less concerned with the question precisely what forms these constructions must take.

> EXAMPLE. The custom of greeting through the lifting of one's hat would perhaps have to be constructed in the following form: "The custom of "greeting through the lifting of one's hat" is present in a society (or in some other sociological grouping) at a certain time, if, among the members of this society at that time, there is present a psychological disposition of such a kind that, in situations of such and such a sort, a voluntary act of such and such a sort takes place."

All primary cultural objects are to be constructed on the basis of their manifestation in the indicated fashion. It is the task of a logic of the cultural sciences to investigate which objects of the various cultural areas are to be constructed as *primary* cultural objects. A phenomenology of the cultural sciences would then have to investigate, for each primary cultural object, which psychological objects are its manifestations and hence must serve as a basis for its construction and how this construction is to be carried out.

151. *The Higher Cultural Objects*

The remaining cultural objects are constructed on the basis of the primary cultural objects, but psychological, and occasionally physical, objects are also used. In this case, even more than in the case of the primary cultural objects, construction theory has to await the investigations of the special sciences in order to be able to give correct, concrete examples of constructions. Thus, we confine ourselves to the indication of an example without being able to assert the correctness or appropriateness of precisely this constructional form.

> EXAMPLE. The object "state" [115] could perhaps be constructed in the following form: a relational structure of persons is called a "state" if it is characterized in such and such a way through its manifestations, namely, the psychological behavior of these persons and the dispositions

---

[115] Staat

toward such behavior, especially the disposition, on the part of some persons, to act upon the volitions of others.

Sociological groups or organizations are, among others, the most important higher cultural objects. Such a structure (for example, a tribe, a family, a club, a state, etc.) must be constructed as a relation extension, not as a class, since the order of the members within the sociological group belongs to the character of the group. That it is not permissible to construct these groups as classes follows from the possibility that the members of two different groups are identical.

The other sociological groups must be constructed in a way which is similar to that which we indicated for the state. In this and other ways, we can then construct generally all higher cultural objects on the basis of the primary cultural objects and occasionally also on the basis of objects of other previously constructed types. Thus, we can construct, either as primary or as derived objects, the cultural objects of all cultural fields; hence, the entities, properties, relations, events, states, etc., of technology, of economics, of law, of politics, of language, of art, of science, of religion, etc. Finally, the division into, and the characterization of, the individual fields can be carried out through further constructions.

REFERENCES. There seem to be hardly any attempts at a genuine construction (i.e., a construction that goes back to the given) of cultural objects, either in the literature of epistemology, of the philosophy of history, of history, or of sociology. Even delineations of the last steps of such a construction, starting from the psychological domain, are relatively rare. It seems that the only investigations which we have to mention are those by Driesch [Ordnungsl.] 421 ff., Section E, The Order Forms of the Cultural; [Wirlichk.] 194: "Thus, an *individual state* is the mental behavior of a number of individual persons as it is guided by the contents of certain books."

Through the indicated way of constructing the cultural on the basis of the psychological, as it is also found in our example of the state, the impression could arise that the cultural objects are here unduly "psychologized". In order to overcome this objection, let us again emphasize that the construction of one object on the basis of certain other objects does not amount to saying that the object is similar to those other objects; on the contrary, if the construction leads to the formation of new logical levels (as it does in the case of the cultural objects, and especially the higher levels of cultural objects, where it is very marked), the thus-constructed objects have a different mode of being, or, more precisely, they belong to a different object sphere (§§ 29, 41 f.). Thus, there is no psychologism in our way of constructing the cultural objects (cf. also § 56).

On the other hand, let it be emphasized again that the assertion that cultural objects belong to a new object sphere is not to be understood in any metaphysical sense. It follows from the given definition of the concept of an object sphere that we have here nothing but a formal-logical delineation of objects against one another. According to the conceptions of construction theory, no relation between two object types other than the formal-logical relation which depends upon the constructional forms of the types can become the subject of a scientific statement.

152. *The Domain of Values*

So far, we have given or indicated the construction of the most important object types familiar in daily life and in science, to wit: the physical, the psychological, and the cultural. In conclusion, let us briefly indicate now the construction of the *values,* at least in their general methodological form. Here, even less than with other object types, can we expect final formulations, since the domain of values, as far as the character of its objects and their recognition is concerned, is to an especially high degree problematic and subject to controversy.

The construction of values does not continue from the already discussed levels of the cultural or the heteropsychological, but connects with an earlier stage of the constructional system. We have to distinguish several types of values, for example, the ethical, the aesthetic, the religious, the biological (in the widest sense, including technological and economic values, values of individual and social hygiene), and others. The construction of values from certain experiences, namely, value experiences, is in many ways analogous to the construction of physical things from "perceptual experiences" (more precisely, from sense qualities). Let it suffice here to indicate some examples of such experiences. For the construction of ethical values, for example, we must consider (among others) experiences of conscience, experiences of duty or of responsibility, etc. For aesthetic values, we take into account experiences of (aesthetic) pleasure or other attitudes in the appreciation of art, experiences of artistic creation, etc. The particular nature of the value experiences of the different value types is investigated by the phenomenology of values; we cannot here concern ourselves with the details of this issue. Once the phenomenological analysis is carried out, we can give a constructional expression for the characteristic properties of the various value experiences with the aid of the autopsychological qualities and their components, which have been constructed earlier, especially the emotions and volitions (§ 131 f.). On the basis of those constructions, we can then form the construction of the various value types. This should not be considered a psychologizing of values, just as the construction of physical objects from sense qualities does not amount to a psychologizing of the physical. In realistic language, values themselves are not experiential or psychological, but exist independently of being experienced. They are merely recognized in the experiences (more precisely, in the value sensations [116] whose intentional objects they are). In like fashion, a physical thing is not psychological, but exists independently of perception and is merely recognized through a perception whose intentional object it is. On the other hand, construction theory does not speak this kind of realistic language, but is neutral toward the metaphysical component of realistic statements. However, construction theory provides a translation into constructional language of the indicated statement about the relation between values and value sensations. This translation is analogous to the translation of the statement concerning the relation between physical things and perceptions; that is to say, it emphasizes a purely logical relation, namely, that one object is determined through the nature of another.

This concludes the outline of the constructional system.

153. The Problem of Eliminating the Basic Relations
(§§ 153–155 may be omitted.)

Every constructional system rests upon basic relations which are introduced as undefined basic concepts. Thus, all constructed objects are complexes (§ 36) of the basic relations. All statements which occur in the constructional system are statements about nothing but the basic relations. Formally, they initially contain indeed also other objects; however, through substitution of the constructional definitions of these objects, it is possible to transform them step by step in such a way that their external sentence form, too, finally contains only the symbols of the basic relations (and logical symbols). For the present constructional system, in whose outline only one basic relation (Rs) is used, this has been discussed in § 119 in the example of theorem Th. 6 concerning the three-dimensionality of the color solid.

---

[116] Wertgefühl

However, this characteristic of the statements of a constructional system is not in harmony with the earlier thesis that statements of science are purely structural statements or that, in principle, it is possible to transform them into such statements, and that in the progress of science they should be so transformed (§ 15 f.). A purely structural statement must contain only logical symbols; in it must occur no undefined basic concepts from any empirical domain. Thus, after the constructional system has carried the formalization of scientific statements to the point where they are merely statements about a few (perhaps only one) basic relations, the problem arises whether it is possible to complete this formalization by *eliminating from the statements of science these basic relations* as the last, nonlogical objects.

That this elimination is possible becomes obvious through the following consideration. Given a constructional system which proceeds from certain basic relations, there is a possibility that this system can also be formulated with a different set of basic relations. But then the construction of each object would have to be formulated in a different way. Assume that we were to try to transform the previous constructional definitions by simply substituting the new basic relations for the old ones; it would then indeed be possible for the lower levels that the thus-transformed definitions are not meaningless or empty. But for a reasonably high level, the probability of such an accident is extremely small. It is still less likely that the empirical statements of the constructional system about constructed objects would accidentally continue to hold even after the transformation. From this it follows that the original basic relations can be characterized by saying that the objects which are constructed from them in a certain way show a certain empirical behavior; definite descriptions of the basic relations could be formulated with reference to the behavior of objects on a sufficiently high level. Thus it follows that it is possible to define, through purely logical concepts, the basic relations which were originally introduced as undefined basic concepts.

154. *"Founded" Relation Extensions*

The task of eliminating the basic relations as the only nonlogical objects of the constructional system contains one more difficulty to which we have to pay some further attention. We had assumed that, after a replacement of one set of basic relations by another, the constructional formulas of the system would not remain applicable, and the empirical statements would cease to hold. However, our assumption is justified only if the new relation extensions are not arbitrary, unconnected pair lists, but if we require of them that they correspond to some experience-able, "natural" relations (to give a preliminary, vague expression).

If no such requirement is made, then there are certainly other rela-tion extensions for which all constructional formulas can be produced. However, in such a case, the construction leads to other entities than with the original relation extensions, but, for these other entities, the same empirical statements still hold as for the original ones (that is to say, the symbols for these statements are still the same, but they now mean something different). All we have to do is to carry out a one-to-one transformation of the set of basic elements into itself and determine as the new basic relations those relation extensions whose inventory is the transformed inventory of the original basic relations. In this case, the new relation extensions have the same structure as the original ones (they are "isomorphic", cf. § 11). From this it follows that, to each originally constructed object, there corresponds precisely one new one with the same formal properties. Thus all statements of the construc-tional system continue to hold, since they concern only formal properties. However, we can then not find any sense [117] for the new basic relations; they are lists of pairs of basic elements without any (experienceable) connection. It is even more difficult to find for the constructed objects any entities which are not in some way disjointed.

In contrast to relations of this sort, we wish to call relation extensions which correspond to experienceable, "natural" relations *founded relation extensions*. Thus, the various member pairs of founded relation extensions have something in common that can be experienced.

We have seen (§ 153) that the basic relations can be eliminated only by characterizing them through the behavior of sufficiently high-level objects which are constructed from them. If this characterization is to become a definite description, it must be limited to founded relation extensions. This establishes the importance of the concept of founded relation extensions for the constructional system, for, if we take into account all relation extensions (in the formal-logical sense of arbitrary, ordered couples), then the basic relations are not the only ones which satisfy the definite descriptions, but they are the only ones among the founded relation extensions. We shall use the example of our construc-tional system to carry out such a definite description (§ 155).

The given explanation of the concept of foundedness is not meant as a definition; it is merely to make comprehensible what is meant. The

---

[117] Beziehungssinn

concept of foundedness is *undefinable*. It cannot be derived from constructed concepts, since it is the most fundamental concept of the constructional system. It also can not be derived from the (customary) basic concepts of formal logic. On the other hand, it does not belong to any definite extralogical object domain, as all other nonlogical objects do. Our considerations concerning the characterization of the basic relations of a constructional system as founded relation extensions of a certain kind hold for every constructional system of any domain whatever. It is perhaps permissible, because of this generality, to envisage the concept of foundedness as a concept of logic and to introduce it, since it is undefinable, as a *basic concept of logic*. That this concept is concerned with the *application* to object domains is not a valid objection to introducing it as a basic concept of logic. The same is true for another basic concept of logic, namely, generality: "(x) fx" means that the propositional function of fx has the value true for every argument of an object domain in which it is meaningful. Logic is not really a domain at all, but contains those statements which (as tautologies) hold for the objects of any domain whatever. From this it follows that it must concern itself precisely with those concepts which are applicable to any domain whatever. And foundedness, after all, belongs to these concepts. In view of these reasons, let us introduce the class of *founded relation extensions* as a basic concept of logic (logistic symbol: *found*) without therefore considering the problem as already solved.

155. *Elimination of the Basic Relation* Rs

Let us use our constructional system as an example in order to show how the elimination of the basic relations and thus the final formalization of the constructional system can be carried out, if we make the just-mentioned assumption that *found* can be taken as a basic concept of logic. The undefined basic relation Rs, we define in the following way: Rs is the only founded relation extension from which we can construct in a given way a certain sufficiently high-level object, still to be chosen, which shows certain empirical characteristics.

We have to choose a sufficiently high-level empirical theorem about Rs. Let us abbreviate this theorem as Th(Rs). We envisage this theorem as generated from the propositional function Th(R) through introduction of the argument Rs. "Rs" is now definitely described as that particular founded relation which satisfies Th(R). Thus, we define:

$$Rs =_{df} \iota'\{ \text{found} \cap \check{R} \, (L \, (R)) \}$$

In order to show that this can be practically carried out, we choose as our empirical statement theorem Th. 6 concerning the three-dimensionality of the color solid (§ 118). We have shown earlier how this theorem can be expressed as a statement exclusively about Rs (§ 119 [5]). Considering the complicated nature of the statement about Rs, it is perhaps permissible to assume that it is of sufficiently high level. This statement is the value for Rs of a certain propositional function Th(R), which has the following form (abbreviated):

$(\exists Q, \nu)$. 3 Dnhomvic $(\varepsilon \mid Q \mid \epsilon)$ $\rhd$ Abstr $'\{\hat{a}\,\beta\,((\exists\chi, \lambda, \mu)$ . . . .

. . . $(\exists\delta)$. $\delta\,\epsilon$ Simil' $(R \cup \check{R} \cup R^o)$. $a \subset \delta$. $x \sim \epsilon\,\delta\}$. $a \uparrow \beta \subset R \cup \check{R} \cup R^o)$

We now *define the basic relation* Rs as the only founded relation which satisfies this propositional function (abbreviated):

$Rs =_{df} \iota'\{$found $\cap \check{R}\,((\exists Q, \nu)$. 3 Dnhomvic . . .

. . . $(\exists\delta)$. $\delta\,\epsilon$ Simil' $(R \cup \check{R} \cup R^o)$. $a \subset \delta$. $x \sim \epsilon\,\delta\}$. $a \uparrow \beta \subset R \cup \check{R} \cup R^o))\}$

This expression which defines Rs *no longer contains anything but logical symbols and variables.* Since all objects and statements of the constructional system can be expressed through Rs, *it is now possible to express all objects and statements of the constructional system in a purely logical way.* Thus our aim of the complete formalization of the constructional system is achieved. We have shown that (and, through the suggestions in the outline of the constructional system, also how) all objects of science can be envisaged as structural objects, and all statements of science can be envisaged as structural statements and can be transformed into structure sentences. We had to presuppose, however, that *found* is a logical concept; here lies an unresolved problem.

156. *Theses about the Constructional System*

In concluding the presentation of the constructional system, let us again emphasize what is important in this system outline and what is not. The primary purpose in the formation of a constructional system was to illustrate, by way of an example, the actual content of construction theory, namely, to formulate the problems of forming such a system. In order to fulfill this purpose, the outline had to be given with a certain amount of detail in spite of the shortcomings in its content. These shortcomings were not so much due to difficulties which arise from some of the unsolved logical problems; rather, they arose from difficulties and as yet unresolved problems in the individual empirical sciences.

A further purpose of the outline was to show that a constructional system of all scientific objects is, in principle, possible, no matter how the details of such a system would have to be formulated. We do not only wish to assert here that it is possible in general to erect some constructional system or another; rather, we wish to defend the thesis that it is possible (though perhaps not necessary in all points) to give the following properties to the constructional system, which are also found in the system which we have tentatively outlined:

A. Formal Theses
    1. The basic elements are all of the same type.
    2. The basic order is established through relation extensions (§ 75).
    3. The basic relations are all of the same level.
    4. All basic relations are first-level relation extensions (i.e., relation extensions of basic elements).
    5. A small number of basic relations suffices.
    6. (A conjecture): One basic relation suffices (§ 82).
B. Material Theses
    7. The basic elements are experiences as unanalyzable units (§ 67 f.).
    8. "My" elementary experiences are the basic elements ("autopsychological basis" [§ 64]).
    9. (A conjecture): Rs (recollection of similarity) can be taken as the only basic relation (§ 78).
    10. The following objects occur in the indicated sequence: quality classes, sense classes, the visual sense, visual field places, colors (possibly before the visual field places), space and time order, the visual things, my body, the other autopsychological objects (possibly before the spatial order), physical objects, other persons, heteropsychological objects, cultural objects, objects of all kinds as intersubjective objects (§§ 112–151).
    11. The construction of the world of physics consists in an assignment of numbers ("state magnitudes") to the elements (world points) of a four-dimensional number array (space-time system); the assignment is based upon the distribution of the quality classes (§§ 125–136).
    12. The construction of heteropsychological objects rests upon the expression relation (including the reporting relation) or upon the psychophysical relation (§§ 140, 57 f.).

13. The construction of cultural objects rests upon the manifestation relation (§§ 55 f., 150).

Thesis 6, that only one basic relation is required, and, to a greater extent thesis 9, concerning the special nature of this basic relation, are expressly indicated as conjectures. We are considerably more certain that thesis 5 concerning the small number of basic relations is correct. All previous attempts at tables of categories or basic postulates,[118] from Aristotle to Driesch, appear to us, all of them, to be too rich (cf. § 83). The reason for this lies in the fact that the methodological tools which were used are unsatisfactory. Only the application of the logico-constructive method shows how in many cases which were considered irreducible a reduction and thus a construction is possible.

Summary

IV. Outline of a Constructional System (106–156)

A. *The Lower Levels: Autopsychological Objects (106–122)*

The only purpose of this outline is to provide an example for the clarification of construction theory. The lower levels are to be given in somewhat greater detail, on the basis of the preceding formal and material investigations. In addition to the constructional definitions, we give some theorems as examples; these are either *analytic,* that is, deducible from the definitions, or *empirical*. Like all other scientific propositions, these theorems can be translated into propositions about the basic relation alone: an analytic theorem will then result in a tautology, an empirical theorem in a proposition about an empirical, formal property of the basic relation (106).

To begin with, the logical and mathematical concepts (the latter actually form a part of the former) must be defined. They presuppose only the fundamental logical concepts, not the basic relation; they are not concepts in the sense of empirical concepts (107). On the basis of the basic relation (recollection of similarity, 108), the constructions of the following concepts are given (the constructions correspond to the derivations in §§ 67–94 and are given in the previously indicated languages, §§ 95–102): the elementary experiences (109), part similarity (110), similarity circles (111), quality classes (112), part identity (113), similarity between qualities (114), sense classes, visual sense (115), the sensations, analysis of experiences into their individual and general constituents (116), visual field places and their order in the visual field (117), the colors and their order in the color solid (118), the preliminary time order (120).

The thesis that every scientific concept is either a class or a relation exten-

---

[118] Grundsetzung

sion which can be expressed through the basic relation alone is clarified by taking the concept of the sense modalities as an example. The thesis that every scientific proposition can be transformed into a proposition about the basic relation alone is exemplified through the empirical proposition about the three-dimensionality of the color solid (119).

By the *derivation relation* of an object we understand a certain expression which indicates how the object is derived from the basic relation; it designates a purely logical concept. If we replace each construction by the corresponding derivation relation, we formulate the constructional system in the form of a purely logical system; by substituting the basic relation, this system is then transformed into the proper constructional system of all empirical concepts (121).

B. *The Intermediate Levels: Physical Objects (123–138)*

There are several ways of constructing three-dimensional space (to begin with visual things) from the two-dimensional order of the visual field (124). We choose that form which utilizes only the temporal sequence of the visual fields which occur in the experiences (we do not use kinesthetic sensations); the four-dimensional "visual world" results through the assignment of colors to the "world points" (125–127). Certain parts of this visual world are the "visual things" (128). One of these is especially important: *my body*; it has certain unique properties which allow a definite description of it (129). With its aid, definite descriptions of the other senses can be given (we include here the emotions [130, 131]). The experiences have now been analyzed into their qualitative constituents; the latter have been divided into sense modalities and components. With the aid of these entities, all conscious processes can be constructed. These are supplemented by the so-called unconscious processes in order to provide more thoroughgoing regularities. Conscious and unconscious processes together form the total domain of the *autopsychological*. The *self* is the class of autopsychological states (132).

From the visual world results the *perceptual world* of "perceptual things" through the assignment of the qualities of the remaining senses (133, 134). This assignment is supplemented by certain rules of analogy (which correspond to the categories of causality and substance [135]). The perceptual world stands in contrast to the *world of physics*, where we assign to the world points not qualities but numbers, namely, the values of physical state magnitudes. In the world of physics, strict laws hold which can be mathematically formulated, and it can be intersubjectivized in an unequivocal fashion; this constitutes an advantage over the perceptual world (136). It is possible, in the world of physics, to give definite descriptions of all physically differentiable processes and things, hence, for example, organisms, and among them especially *other persons*, and all other biological concepts (137). The expression relation and the psychophysical relation can be constructed with the aid of the processes of "my body" (138).

C. The Upper Levels: Heteropsychological and Cultural Objects
(139–156)

The construction of the *heteropsychological* consists in the assignment of psychological events to the body of another person with the aid of the expression relation. Hence, from the viewpoint of construction theory, the heteropsychological consists in a reorganization of the autopsychological. If the psychophysical relation were better known, then we could use it instead of the expression relation for a more precise and complete construction of the heteropsychological. The heteropsychological, just as the autopsychological, is supplemented through the addition of the unconscious (140). For the construction of the heteropsychological, we must use—aside from the expression relation in the narrower sense—also "sign production", namely, the linguistic expressions of other persons. The relation of sign production is constructed in analogy to the learning of a foreign language without interpreter, initially for words (141), then for sentences: "reporting relation" (142). In the actual learning of a language, understanding is, for the most part, intuitive; in the construction, this intuition is rationally reconstructed (143). The reports of other persons are now used for further constructions: all object types are enriched, but nothing that is new in principle can be brought into the system. Utilizing the reports of others does not mean that the autopsychological basis has been abandoned; after all, the reports have been constructed on that basis (144).

From the constructed experiences of another person M we can construct the "world of M" in analogy to the construction of "my world" from "my experiences". We now find two relations between the objects of M and the objects of my world: 1. the relation of analogous construction, which must be taken into account especially on the lower levels (145) and 2. the *intersubjective correspondence* between empirically identical objects (e.g., between my Berlin and that of M [146]). This correspondence can now be used for the supplementation of each of the two systems (147). A class of intersubjectively corresponding objects, one of which is in my system and the remaining in the systems of the other persons is called an "intersubjective object" (e.g., the class of the objects "Berlin" in the various systems); they form the *intersubjective world* (148). It is the proper object domain of the sciences (149).

The primary *cultural objects* (i.e., those which do not presuppose any other cultural objects for their construction) are constructed on the basis of their manifestations, i.e., on the basis of psychological objects (150). With their aid we can then construct the other cultural objects, where the sociological objects must be constructed predominantly as relations. The construction of the cultural from the psychological does not amount to "psychologizing", for the cultural objects form new object spheres (151).

With the domains of the autopsychological, the physical, the heteropsychological, and the cultural, the most important object types have been constructed. Values are mentioned as an example of a further object type. They are to be constructed on the basis of "value experiences" in analogy to the construction of the physical on the basis of sense qualities (152).

In principle, all statements of science are translatable into statements about the basic relation; can it, too, be eliminated so that all statements are pure structure statements (153)? It turns out that this is possible, but only if the concept of a *founded relation extension* is added to the fundamental concepts of logic. Founded relation-extensions are those which correspond to natural, experienceable relations. It remains problematic whether this addition is permissible (154). The elimination is clarified by means of an example (155).

The purpose of the indicated outline of a constructional system is merely to illustrate the theory. On the other hand, what is asserted as valid is stated in a few theses. The *formal* theses say the following: all basic elements are of the same level. The basic relations are on the first level; there is only a small number of them, perhaps only one. The *material* theses state: the basic elements are "my experiences" as unanalyzable units; it is possible that recollection of similarity suffices as basic relation; the following can be constructed in sequence: qualities, senses, visual sense, visual field, colors, space and time order, visual things, my body, the other autopsychological objects, the physical objects, among them other persons, heteropsychological and cultural objects, objects of all kinds as intersubjective objects. The construction of the world of physics is an array of numbers on the basis of the distribution of qualities; the construction of the heteropsychological is based on the expression and reporting relations or on the psychophysical relation; the construction of the cultural is based upon the manifestation relation (156).

PART FIVE

CLARIFICATION OF SOME
PHILOSOPHICAL PROBLEMS ON THE BASIS
OF CONSTRUCTION THEORY

157. The Constructional System as the Basis of Philosophical Investigations

After having given, in the previous section, an outline of the constructional system, we now want to show, by way of example, the value of such a system for the clarification of philosophical problems. The virtue of the constructional system in this connection does not lie in the presentation of materially new insights, which could then be used for the solution of those problems. What it achieves is actually only a uniform *ordering of concepts* which allows *a clearer formulation of the question for each problem and thus brings us closer to a solution.*

Since the given constructional system is only a preliminary outline, we do not wish to base the following considerations upon details of this system, but only upon its character as a whole. Hence, we presuppose the possibility of a unified system of concepts and the possibility of constructing this system from experiential relations as basic concepts in the following sequence: the autopsychological, the physical, the heteropsychological, the cultural. Thus we presuppose roughly what has been stated in the theses of § 156. The problems which we shall discuss are meant only as examples. In this book, the emphasis is put on construction theory itself, not upon its application; thus, we cannot give a detailed discussion of the individual problems. We must leave this for a separate discussion. It is still less feasible to give an exhaustive survey of all those problems which can be treated in connection with construction theory. We can here only suggest in what way construction theory sheds light upon various problem situations and what course a subsequent, detailed treatment would have to take.

To begin with, we shall briefly discuss some problems of essence,[119] among them the problems of identity, the self, dualism of the physical and the psychological, and causality (§§ 158–165). Furthermore, we shall consider the psychophysical problem (§§ 166–169) and the problem of reality (§§ 170–178); in both cases, we shall clearly distinguish the constructional aspect of the problem from its metaphysical aspect. Finally, we shall discuss the question of the limitation of (rational) knowledge and shall clarify the distinction between science and metaphysics (§§ 179–183).

---

[119] Wesensprobleme

SOME PROBLEMS OF ESSENCE

158. About the Difference between Individual and General Concepts

Concepts are usually divided into individual concepts and general concepts; the concept Napoleon is an individual concept; the concept mammal, a general concept. From the standpoint of construction theory, this division is not justified, or, rather, it is ambiguous, since every concept, depending upon one's point of view, can be considered either an individual concept or a general concept. We have stated this earlier (§ 5) and have derived from it the justification for speaking of *the* object which corresponds to a given concept. Now that we know the constructional forms, in particular the ascension forms (III, A, especially § 40), we realize that, just as the general concepts, (almost) *all of the so-called individual concepts are classes or relation extensions.*

EXAMPLE. Let us use for clarification the following descending sequence of objects (or concepts). The dog (species) is a class to which my dog Luchs belongs. Luchs is a class whose elements are the "states" of Luchs. An individual state of Luchs (as a perceptual thing) is a class whose elements are points of the perceptual world. One such point is a many-place relation extension whose terms are four numerical terms (namely, the space-time coördinates) and one or more sense qualities; a sense quality is a class "of my experiences". The latter are here envisaged as basic elements.

In the ordinary view, some of the concepts in this example would have to be called individual and others general. But each of them (except for the last one) is constructed as a class or relation extension, and each of them is an element of the preceding class or a term of the preceding relation extension; thus, each of them is a generality [120] of other objects.

What is the reason that, in the ordinary view, e.g., the species dog and the sense quality brown are considered something general while the dog Luchs, and a given world point, and a given experience are considered something individual, and that frequently only the latter are called "objects", while the former are called "mere concepts"?

The investigation of this and similar examples shows, to begin with, that the so-called individual objects have in common that they are temporally determined, either as belonging to a given time point or a connected time stretch. Furthermore, there is always a definite space point or a connected spatial area to which they belong, if they can be spatially determined at all. On the other hand, the sense quality brown, for example, has many unconnected space-time areas assigned to it (namely, the areas of those space-time points in which this brown is experienced, i.e., to which it is assigned during the construction of the perceptual world).

However, there are orders (though not spatio-temporal orders) in which either points or connected areas are associated with so-called general concepts. For example, to brown—if it is a precisely determined hue, etc.—there belongs a point of the color solid or, if we are concerned with brown in general, a connected part of the color solid. Similarly, the species dog is, as it were, assigned a point of the zoölogical solid (the system of animal species) and to the class of mammals there belongs a connected part of this solid.

Thus, the difference between individual and general objects (or concepts) rests upon the distinction between spatio-temporal and other orders. Usually, only objects which are individualized with respect to the first order are considered individuals. The problem of why this is so is thus reduced to the problem of finding out what distinguishes the orders of space and time from the others. We shall see later that these two orders are also fundamental for the characterization of real-typical [121]

---

[120] ein Allgemeines
[121] wirklichkeitsartig

objects (§ 172 ff.). The distinction which we wish to discover goes back to a difference between two types of relation extensions which have quality classes as terms. We shall concern ourselves only with the visual sense, since it has more bearing on this issue than any of the others. We are then concerned with the difference between place identity and color identity of two quality classes of the visual sense. Upon the first of these relation extensions rests the construction of the spatial order; upon the second rests the qualitative order of the colors, the "color solid". We have seen earlier (§ 91) that there is a formal difference between the two relation extensions which stems from the fact that different place-identical quality classes can never belong to the same elementary experience, but that different color-identical ones can. This difference was required at that juncture to differentiate the two relation extensions and thus the two orders (visual field and color solid) and to construct each of them separately (§§ 88 ff., 117 f.). We also realized, at that time, that this difference does not only have formal-logical import; since the spatial order is derived precisely from place identity, spatial order could not fulfill its peculiar role in the synthesis of cognition [122] if it were not for this formal-logical property of place identity. This role of spatial order is to serve as the principle of individuation and also (according to the subsequent discussion, § 172 ff.) as *principium realisationis,* namely, as the principle which allows us to posit something initially as real-typical, and eventually as real. We must add that similar considerations hold for temporal order, which is connected with spatial order in the construction of the physical world. The reason why temporal order can also play both of these roles, namely, that of a principle of individuation as well as that of a principle of concretion, is that temporal order also leads to a separation of the characteristics (particularly of the quality classes) of elementary experiences, since characteristics of non-identical experiences are held to be temporally different, and vice versa. In fact, temporal order can play these roles logically prior to spatial order.

The view of construction theory concerning the difference between individual and general objects can now be formulated as follows: There are two types of order—initially only for quality classes, but derivatively also for any objects whatever—which are differentiated by the fact that the relation extensions upon which they are based have a certain formal-logical distinction, which has to do with whether two quality classes can belong to the same elementary experience. The first kind comprises the

---

[122] Erkenntnissynthese

orders which we called temporal and spatial; the second kind, all others. The formal-logical properties of the relation extensions which generate the first type of order make it possible to use these orders as principles of individuation and thus also as principles of concretion [123] (which presupposes individuation). Thus, there results an ascertainable, formal distinction between such objects which are assigned (either themselves or through the mediation of their elements) to points or a connected area of orders of the first kind and objects which do not have this property. The former, we call "objects of the first type"; and the latter, "objects of the second type". It turns out that, for an object of the second type, there is always an order of the second type (i.e., such an order can be constructed) such that the object corresponds to a point or a connected partial area of this order. Thus objects of the first and of the second types behave analogously relative to their respective orders. It is of course permissible to use the customary designations "individual" and "general" for the objects of the first and second types. However, these expressions should not be thought to refer to any but the indicated differentiating properties; it must be especially noted that the so-called individual objects are in no sense logically simpler or more uniform than the general objects.

159. On Identity

The problem of identity is connected with the just-discussed problem of the distinction between individual and general objects. For its clarification, it presupposes a solution of that problem, namely, a recognition of the logical import of that distinction.

The problem of identity arises only because it is not the case that each object has only one name (in the widest sense). Thus, basically, the problem is to determine when two or more different expressions designate the same object. That there are several different expressions for the same object is not just an empirical shortcoming of the system of expressions. Rather, a multiplicity of names is logically brought about by the fact that, for each object, we may have not only a *proper name* (more than one proper name is superfluous), but that we also have *definite descriptions;* in fact, always several of them (perhaps even arbitrarily many). We have explained earlier (§ 13) that a definite description consists in the following: an object is described through an indication of overlapping classes to which it belongs, or through relations to other

---

[123] Wirklichkeitssetzung

objects, or through a purely structural description of its place in a relational structure. This description is carried to the point where it holds only for this object alone and for no other object. We have seen the fundamental importance of definite descriptions, especially for construction theory, since the constructional system consists of nothing but such descriptions in the form of constructional definitions. Moreover, definite descriptions play an important role in all other questions of epistemic and especially of scientific identification. The following are all definite descriptions which may occur in questions: "the father of Mr. A", "the birth day of Mr. A", "the species of this beetle", "the specific resistance of copper", etc. As an answer, we require other definite descriptions of the same objects, namely, names of persons, dates, numbers, etc. The questions have a point only because there are different descriptions of the same object, namely, the description in a question ("the birth date of Mr. A") and the description of the answer ("March 22, 1832"). Expressions designating the same object, we call synonymous. In this connection, we must pay attention to the distinction between nominatum and sense of an object sign; it corresponds to the distinction between logical and epistemic value of statements (§ 50). The expressions, "the birth date of Mr. A" and "March 22, 1832", have the same nominatum, for it is the same day which is designated by both of them. On the other hand, they have obviously different senses. This is shown by the fact that it is not trivial to claim that they are identical.

Substitutability is the criterion for an identical nominatum: two designations are said to be synonymous if each propositional function which is turned into a true sentence through the substitution of one of the designations does the same upon the substitution of the other. *This is the definition of logical identity.*

> EXAMPLE. The sentences, "Goethe died on March 22, 1832" and "Goethe died on the birthday of Mr. A" are both true. The same holds for all other sentences about this date. That one of these two sentences is important while the other one is not, is of no consequence in this context. All that matters for a criterion that two designations have the same nominatum, i.e., a criterion for "identity", is the truth value of the sentences involved.

Identity, in common usage and also in the usage of science, is not always taken in the strictest sense. Language often treats objects which are not identical in the strict, logical sense as identical; whether objects are envisaged as identical is frequently shown through the use of the words "the same" or simply "this". Frequently, identity does not hold for the object which is ostensibly meant, but for its kind; in these cases, the object functions as a representative of its kind.

EXAMPLES. The question, "Do you already have this book? this butterfly?" does not mean the indicated object itself, but the kind, as whose representative the object is taken. This improper identification can have various different aspects, as can be seen from the following four sentences: "The public transport system in A has the same trains as that in B." "Today, I came home on the same train as yesterday, namely, on the 6:12." "This is the same train that used to run on Route 10." "I was sitting in the train which you saw go by."

The indicated examples show that in some cases it is clear to what the identity is supposed to relate, i.e., as representatives of what kind the object is meant. For example, in the case of an animal or a plant, we mean, as a rule, the species. In different cases, depending on the context, an object is held to be the representative of entirely different classes. In these cases, the identity, which is ostensibly related to the object itself, holds only for one of these classes. This is the case in our example of the four sentences about the train. In order to be able, in these cases, to characterize the difference in the aspects of identification, we can use two different modes of approach or modes of expression. According to the first approach, we are, in these cases (for example, in the case of the four sentences), not concerned with identity, but with various other relations, which, however, are envisaged as identity (either linguistically or conceptually). According to the second approach, we are not here concerned with similarity (in this or that respect), but with identity in the strict sense, however, not with identity between the individual objects which occur here, but between objects on a higher level (classes or relation extensions), of which the objects are representatives.

EXAMPLE. Let us apply the first mode of approach to the above example of the four sentences about the train. In this case, we say that the identity, which is expressed in the form of words, does not, strictly speaking, obtain between the objects, but that various other relations hold between them, namely, (a) similarity in construction and looks, (b) the identical time of day or the identical place in the time schedule, (c) "genidentity" (cf. § 128), i.e., association of various "thing-states" [124] with one object, (d) the intersubjective correspondence between thing-states (cf. § 146). On the other hand, under the second mode of approach, we take the trains to be representatives of objects of a

---

[124] Dingzustände

higher level; these higher-level objects, for which identity holds in the strict sense, are, in our four cases, (a) the manufacturing pattern, as a class of trains; (b) the arrangement to have a daily train at 6:12 P.M., as a class of train runs; (c) the physical thing "train" as the class of its states; (d) the intersubjective object "train" as the class of those objects which are in intersubjective correspondence (§ 148), that is to say, an individual train in the intersubjective sense. It can be seen that identity in the strict sense does not hold between the objects themselves, but only between the higher-level objects which they represent. This is quite obvious in the first three cases, namely, (a) manufacturing pattern, (b) the arrangement of which I make use on both days, and (c) the physical thing at different times. It is somewhat more difficult to recognize this in case (d), where identity holds only for the intersubjective object, which is constructed as a class, but not for the individual objects which are intersubjectively correlated to one another. I can here only refer back to the earlier presentation of intersubjectivization (§§ 146–149).

The above considerations show that, with every identity statement, we must pay careful attention to whether or not identity is meant in the strict sense. One may say that, in most cases of linguistic identity (that is to say, when words like "the same" or "this" are used or even if the same word is used several times), we are concerned with improper identity. In such cases (according to the second approach), the objects are taken as representatives of strictly identical objects of a higher level; (in the first approach): instead of with identity, we are here concerned with other equivalence relations (§ 11). Relations of this kind are especially likeness of any kind, meaning the agreement in any property whatever, genidentity (§ 128), and intersubjective correspondence (§ 146 f.). The last two are frequently confused with (proper) identity; this is perhaps due to the fact that, so far, they have not received any name. In all cases where such relations hold, the higher-level object for which the identity holds is constructed from the nonidentical objects with the aid of the relation in question; it is only this construction which gives us the right to speak of identity in these cases.

REFERENCES. There are some essentially correct remarks about genidentity in the literature, in which this relation is falsely described as "identity"; these remarks receive their just recognition only after the two relations are clearly distinguished. Thus, for example, Cornelius' claim (opposed by Gomperz [Weltansch.] 163) that "identity" (where genidentity is meant) must be constructed from certain agreements between experiences is justified. Furthermore, Volkelt's critical remark against Avenarius [Gewissheit] 130, that "identity" (where, again, genidentity is meant) is not originally given and thus must not be considered "pure experience", is correct.

It is remarkable that occasionally the temporal sequence of concept formation is such that, first, a relation of the just-described sort is linguistically taken as identity, and that the higher-level object which justifies this usage is constructed only afterward. In fact, the higher-level object is constructed, as it were, precisely through this improper use of language. In this context, we must also mention the method of constructing an object on the basis of other objects by indicating under what conditions two of the latter objects are to be considered identical.

> EXAMPLES. The construction of perceptual things which rests upon genidentity can, for example, take the following form: "A perceived thing *a* and a perceived thing *b* are the same thing if *a* and *b* fulfill such and such conditions (namely, the genidentity criteria)." Likewise, animal species (and, in an analogous way, plant species) are constructed in zoölogy by speaking of "the same" animal, if such and such criteria are fulfilled. The above-mentioned four cases, where we spoke of "the same" train, can also be used as examples in this connection. An important example is formed by the characterization of the different geometrical disciplines. According to F. Klein, they can be envisaged as the theories of those properties which remain invariant, relative to various types of transformation. Consequently, the concept formation, and thus the construction, of topology can be characterized by saying that geometrical entities are considered identical (e.g., two drawn figures are considered representations of "the same" state of affairs), if they are homomorphic; we have a corresponding case in projective geometry, if they are in projective relation; correspondingly, in a metric geometry, if they are similar; lastly, in a nonexistent discipline, which corresponds to topography but is purely geometrical, we would call two figures identical if they are congruent. (The designation, homomorphism, projective relation, similarity, and congruence, are generally applied only to entities of the same system, but not to two arbitrarily chosen figures; thus, we would have to say, more precisely: "if the figures are of such a nature that they would have the relation of homomorphism, etc., if they were brought into a system".)

160. *The Essence of the Psychological, Physical, and Cultural Object Types*

Let us again briefly summarize how the nature of the most important different object types and their distinctions can be characterized on the basis of the constructional system. This is of fundamental importance for the problems which are to be considered subsequently. In order to omit unnecessary detail, we shall not, at this point, take into consideration the distinctions within the main object types. Thus, for each object type, we consider only the most important representative. Of the autopsychological object type, we consider the experiences, their individual constituents, and the qualities (of sense impressions, emotions, volitions, etc.). Of the physical object type, we consider the physical things. Of the heteropsychological objects, we consider again experiences, their individual constituents, and the qualities; of the cultural objects, we consider the primary cultural objects and general higher-level objects.

The constructional system shows that all objects can be constructed from "my elementary experiences" as basic elements. In other words (and this is what is meant by the expression "to construct"), all (scientific) statements can be transformed into statements about my experiences (more precisely, into statements about relations between my experiences) where the logical value is retained. Thus, each object which is not itself one of my experiences, is a quasi object; I use its name as a convenient abbreviation in order to speak about my experiences. In fact, within construction theory, and thus within rational science, its name is *nothing but* an abbreviation. Whether, in addition, it also designates something which "exists by itself" is a question of metaphysics which has no place in science (cf. §§ 161 and 176).

The *autopsychological objects* (that is to say, the most important ones which have been mentioned above) are in part my experiences themselves, in part classes of such experiences, which have been formed with the aid of the basic relation(s); in part, they are relation extensions of those experiences and these classes; thus, they are my experiences themselves and auxiliary expressions (quasi objects) of the next higher levels.

The *physical objects* are four-dimensional orders of qualities (or of numbers which represent the qualities); thus, they are classes of my experiences. The experiences are originally organized into classes and the latter into fourfold systems of sequences; certain subsystems of the latter are formed by the physical objects.

The *heteropsychological objects* consist of a new arrangement of the autopsychological objects in relation to certain physical objects (namely, my body and the bodies of other persons). Thus, they have in common with the physical objects that they are orders of autopsychological objects. However, the order of the autopsychological objects which leads to the physical objects (namely, the above-mentioned fourfold system of sequences) is very different from the order of the autopsychological domain, while that particular order of autopsychological objects which results in the heteropsychological objects has considerable similarity with the order of the autopsychological objects themselves. This similarity, though, does not hold for proximity in individual cases (namely, in the time order), but it holds relative to the general laws of proximateness within an order [125] (that is to say, it holds for the psychological laws of a process in time).

The *cultural objects* are orders of heteropsychological (and, to a lesser degree, also of autopsychological) objects, which are usually found several levels higher up.

161. *Constructional and Metaphysical Essence*

The indicated answers to the quest after the nature of the various object types are frequently felt to be unsatisfactory. They would be considered unsatisfactory if the question were not concerned with constructional, but with metaphysical, essence. If we ask for the *constructional essence* of an object, we wish to know the constructional context of this object within the system, especially how this object can be derived from the basic objects. On the other hand, if someone asks for the *metaphysical essence* of an object, he wishes to know what the object in question is in itself. Such a question presupposes that the object does not only exist as a certain constructional form, but also as an "object-in-itself", and this characterizes the question as belonging to metaphysics. This is frequently overlooked, and thus this same question is sometimes posed in science, which is nonmetaphysical, and where such questions have neither justification nor meaning.

We must indicate still more precisely what is to be meant by the constructional essence of an object. In science, we can, strictly speaking, not speak about the essence of an object, not even about the constructional essence of an object, and thus we cannot raise any question concerning essence. An object has an essence, and an object name has a nominatum, only in a certain improper sense, and thus the question about the nominatum of a given object name is meaningful only in this improper sense. Strictly speaking, the question should not be phrased as "What is the nominatum of this object sign?", but "Which sentences in which this object sign can occur are true?" *We can make an unambiguous assessment only of the truth or falsity of a sentence, not of the nominatum*

---
[125] Ordnungsnachbarschaft

of a sign, not even of an object sign. Thus, the indication of the essence of an object or, what amounts to the same, the indication of the nominatum of the sign of an object, consists in an indication of the truth criteria for those sentences in which the sign of this object can occur. Such criteria can be formulated in various different ways; these various ways then indicate the respective character of the essence description in question. If the constructional essence of an object is to be indicated, the criterion consists in the construction formula of the object, which is a transformation rule that allows us to translate step by step every sentence in which the sign of the object occurs into sentences about objects on a lower constructional level and, finally, into a sentence about the basic relation(s) alone. Let us consider those pairs of experiences for which the basic relation(s) hold(s) and which occur in the inventory list of the basic relation(s) as an indication of the originally given states of affairs; [126] then a criterion of the just-indicated kind consists in a reduction of all sentences about the object whose constructional nature we wish to ascertain, to such sentences as can be shown to be true or false through the originally given states of affairs.

The earlier mentioned concept of an *essential relation* (§ 20), which plays a considerable role in discussions about problems of essence (especially in connection with the problems of causality and of psychophysical parallelism) is related to the notion of metaphysical essence. An essential relation cannot be given a place in the constructional system. Thus, statements about such relations cannot be brought into a verifiable form. Thus, science cannot ask questions concerning essential relations. Hence, this concept is shown to belong to metaphysics.

REFERENCES. Cf. Hertz [Einleitg.] 129 f., about the question concerning the "nature" of force or of electricity.

162. *About Mind-Body Dualism*

Are body and mind, the physical and the psychological, two different substances (or principles or object types or aspects) of the world, or is there only *one* substance (or object type, etc.)? (This problem of dualism must be clearly distinguished from the actual "psychophysical problem", namely, the problem of the mutual dependency relations between the physical and the psychological events, which shall be discussed in more detail in the sequel [§§ 166–169].) If we consider the indicated

[126] Ur-Sachverhalte

question from the viewpoint of construction theory, then the argument for dualism would have to be phrased in roughly the following fashion. Even though construction theory places emphasis upon the fact that, in the formation of the constructional system, we proceed from a unified basis, it must nevertheless construct various object types, especially the physical and the psychological, in order to comprehend all objects of science within the system. From this it follows (and this is the argument for dualism) that, in spite of the unity of the basis, there are differences between the object types, and especially there is an important difference between the physical and the psychological. Against this, it must be said that construction theory speaks of "object types" or generally of constructed "objects" only to make a concession to the realistic mode of speech of the empirical sciences. Within the framework of construction theory it would be more fitting to speak of *order forms* and their types. When we are confronted with a monism-dualism problem within any domain whatever, we must always clearly distinguish whether the question concerns the unity or multiplicity of that which is to be ordered or of the order forms. Since there are in any case various different types of order form, in fact, an arbitrarily large number of them, the question is of import only relative to that which is to be ordered, i.e., relative to the basic elements. If the question is posed in this form, we must decide it, for the constructional system and thus for the monism-dualism problem of the physical and the psychological, in favor of monism; this results from the uniformity of the basic elements of the system.

Let us illustrate this fact through an analogy. We observe the starred sky at night; neither the moon nor clouds are visible, only stars. We can undertake to distinguish and classify the stars; we notice various "object types" which are distinguished according to type of light, brightness, color. Hence, in this case, there are distinctions in that which is to be ordered.

In contrast, let us now consider the (fictitious) case that only fixed stars of equal brightness and color are visible. If we are now asked for the number of object types, we would have to answer that we notice objects of only one type. We would not become doubtful about the justification of this answer if somebody were to object: "No, there are quite a number of different object types which can be noticed: to begin with, the stars themselves; secondly, the distances between any two stars; third, the relations in size between any two distances; fourth, the triangles of any three stars; fifth, the overlapping relation between two triangles; etc.; these object types are, in fact, entirely different from one another: a distance is not a star; a relation between two distances is not a distance; etc." Against this objection, we would reply that the enumerated different object types (except for the stars themselves) are not autonomous object types; they do not actually comprise objects, in the proper sense of the word, which can be coördinated with the stars, but only relations and relational structures among the stars. If we notice any stars at all, we always notice them at definite places and thus distances, figures, and relations are necessarily given at the same time. The question whether we notice one, two, or several types of object cannot refer to the number of ascertainable types of such order forms of the elements, for these order forms, as can be seen from the indicated five examples, are unlimited in number. Thus the question can concern only the elements themselves.

The analogy of the stars (that is to say, the second case with the propertyless stars which are connected only through relations) gives a good picture of the intention of construction theory: all objects of the empirical sciences (except for the elementary experiences themselves, which correspond to the stars) are constellations of stars, together with their relations and connections, which are formed from propertyless, but orderable, stars. The differences between the so-called object types, especially the difference between the physical and the psychological, merely indicate different types of constellation (or their connections) which are due to different modes of organization.

Let us now apply the insights which we have gained from the example to the monism-dualism problem; we see that the physical and the psychological must not be envisaged as two principles or aspects of the world. They are order forms of the one, unified domain of elements which are propertyless and merely connected through relations. There is an unlimited number of such order forms. If we were to claim that the difference between the physical and the psychological amounts to a difference between two substances or aspects of the world, then we should not stop with these two forms. In science, even today, there is already a considerable number of object types which have the same independence and thus the same claim to be considered essential aspects of the world. The old metaphysical problem of dualism is restricted to the physical and the psychological only because science recognized the independence of these two object types, more precisely, constructional forms, first. In the meantime, other object types (especially the cultural objects, the biological objects, and the values) have been recognized as independent, even though the equality of their status with that of the physical and the psychological objects is at the moment still debated (cf. also the examples of further object types in § 25). But even this enumeration of object types mentions too few, since each of them comprises objects on various constructional levels, as has been shown in the sketch of the constructional system. This aggregation is useful for a rough classification, but we must not overlook the fact that the objects on the different levels belong to different object spheres (§§ 41, 29) and thus belong to logically totally separate and independent domains. Thus, in the final analysis, it turns out that dualism is an arbitrary restriction to two important, but not fundamentally preëminent object domains. As a thesis concerning the fundamental constitution of the world, it is certainly not tenable but has to give way to a pluralism which recognizes in the world an unlimited number of aspects or substances. But these would then merely be the unlimited number of possible forms of ordering the elements on the basis of their basic relation(s). The result remains the same; *in the world of cognizable objects, there are indeed* (as in any domain, if it can be ordered at all) *an unlimited number of order forms, but only one uniform type of element which is to be ordered.*

REFERENCES. In the opinion of Natorp, whose conception is related to ours, this rejection of psychophysical dualism goes back to Kant. Natorp says [Psychol.] 148, that, according to Kant, " "matter", namely, the sensations of the inner and outer sense, are one and the same and are distinguished only through the "form", i.e., their mode of ordering." Natorp gives some further historical remarks and systematic discussions concerning the problems just treated. Moreover, our position agrees with that of Russell [Mind], where a bibliography to this problem is found (p. 22 ff.); he derives his position from William James and mentions especially the *behaviorists.* Another, but related, formulation is found in Ziehen ([Erkth.] 19 f., 43 ff. [Gegenw. Stand] 66 ff. "Binomism"). Russell ([Mind] 287 ff.) speaks of the physical and the psychological as two types of regularities for the same elements. The formulation of Mach ([Anal.] 14, [Erk.] 18) that there are different directions of investigation relative to the same matter is likewise related to the given position.

163. *The Problem of the Self*

The "self" is the class of elementary experiences. It is frequently and justly emphasized that the self is not a bundle of representations, or experiences, but a unit. This is not in opposition to our thesis, for (as we have shown in § 37 and have emphasized repeatedly) a class is not a collection, or the sum, or a bundle of its elements, but a unified expression for that which the elements have in common.

The existence of the self is not an originally given fact.[127] The *sum* does not follow from the *cogito;* it does not follow from "I experience" that "I am", but only that an experience is. The self does not belong to the expression of the basic experience at all, but is constructed only later, essentially for the purpose of delineation against the "others"; that is, only on a high constructional level, after the construction of the heteropsychological. Thus, a more fitting expression than "I experience" would be "experience" or, still better, "this experience". Thus, we ought to replace the Cartesian dictum by "this experience; therefore this experience is", and this is of course a mere tautology. The self does not belong to the original state of affairs (§ 65), as we have already indicated during the discussion of the autopsychological basis. Philosophical introspection [128] has led philosophers of various persuasions to the same result, namely, that the original processes of consciousness must not be envisaged as the activities of an acting subject, the "self".

REFERENCES. Not "I think", but "it thinks within me", says Russell [Mind] 18, and we would, just as Lichtenberg (according to Schlick [Erkenntnisl.] 147 f.) strike out the "within me". A similar denial of activity in the original state of affairs is found in Nietzsche [Wille] §§ 304, 309; Avenarius [Kritik]; Natorp [Psychol.] 41 ff.; Driesch [Ordnungsl.]; Schlick [Erkenntnisl.] 147 f. Cf. also the bibliography in § 65. Where the mistaken cleavage of the original state of affairs into self and object leads is shown in Nikolai Hartmann [Metaphysik] 38, 40, where a distinction is finally made, not only between two, but between four, layers, namely, subject, object, object image, and the transobjective.

164. *The Nature of the Intention Relation*

The intention relation holds between a content-possessing psychological process and its content, for example, between my present representation of the cathedral of Cologne and this building as the content of my representation, or that which is "intended". Thus, the domain of the relation comprises the "intending" psychological processes, such as perceptions, representations, emotions (if they are related to something), etc., which are directed toward something. We leave open the debated question whether all psychological processes belong in this category; that is, whether they are all "intentional". Now, if the intention relation

[127] Ur-Sachverhalt
[128] Selbstbesinnung

holds, for example, between a given perceptual experience of a tree and the intended tree, then by the "intended tree" we mean initially the tree "that is represented in the perception"; thus, it could also be a tree in a dream or a hallucination. Now, whether it is such an unreal tree or whether there is a real tree that corresponds to the intended tree, is a secondary question which is of no concern for the immediate character of the experience.

Now, the customary conception of the intention relation holds that such intending psychological events refer, in a peculiar way, to something beyond themselves, namely, to their "intended" or "meant" object, which is different from them. It is consequently held that the relation is of a special sort and cannot be reduced to anything else. What is correct in this conception is only that the experience and its intended object are not identical. *But the intention relation is not a relation of a unique kind* which can be found nowhere but between a psychological entity and that which is represented in it. For, from the viewpoint of construction theory, the intended tree is a certain, already very complicated ordering of experiences, namely, of those experiences of which we say that the tree is their intended object; now, these experiences are units which cannot be analyzed, but can merely be brought into different orders, in this case, into an order which represents the intended tree. From this we can see the following: the intention relation holds generally between an experience and an order of experiences, if the following two conditions are fulfilled: first, the experience must belong to this order; second, this order must be one of those constructional forms in which real-typical objects are constructed. ("Real-typical" objects are those objects for which a distinction between real and nonreal is meaningful, even before this distinction has been made [§ 172]. This agrees with the fact that, so far as the intentional object is concerned, it is not yet necessary to decide the question of reality.)

The relation between an element and a relational structure of a certain sort in which it has a place is one of the most important relations of the applied theory of relations. The *intention relation* is nothing but a subclass of this relation, namely, the relation between an experience (or constituent of an experience) and an order which has a real-typical structure. Actually, there is no objection if such a relation is formulated as "reference to something outside itself", as long as it is made clear that the expression "outside" means that the intentional object is not identical with the experience or, more precisely, that the experience stands in a more comprehensive context.

EXAMPLES. Let us mention some examples of the indicated general relation in other areas; in these cases, we can also use the expression of "referring". A given plant refers to the botanical system of plants, a given hue to the color solid, a person refers to his family, his state, or his occupational hierarchy, etc.

The intention relation belongs to the same type as the relations in the indicated examples. Of course, if a tree occurs in one of our experiences, we are usually conscious that this tree is intended, while we do not, as a rule, think of the color solid whenever we are aware of a color. But this is only a difference in degree; consciousness of the tree can occasionally be lacking, although this is rarely the case in an adult person. However, if one says that it lies in the essence of an experience to refer intentionally to something, even if one is not in each experience conscious of its intended object, then it must be replied that, from the viewpoint of construction theory, this holds quite generally; it is essential to each object that it belongs to certain order contexts; otherwise, it could not even be constructed, that is, could not exist as an object of cognition.

REFERENCES. The traditional theory of intentionality stems from Brentano and has been continued by Husserl [Phänomenol.] 64 ff.

Our position agrees essentially with that of Russell [Mind]. It is closely related to that of Jacoby ([Ontol.] 258 ff.), according to which we are here concerned with the overlapping of two systematic orders, namely, the system of consciousness and some other system, for example, the system of external reality. Jacoby puts justifiable emphasis on the fact that, through this insight, the "duplication of entities in the external world into appearance and the thing-in-itself" becomes superfluous and is disregarded (p. 257).

165. *The Nature of Causality*

There are certain laws in the perceptual world which supplement the construction of this domain to a considerable degree and without which the construction of a large part of this domain would not even be possible. These laws have the form of implications between assignments to pairs of places or place areas which have a certain relation to one another in the order of places. It will be recalled that events in the perceptual world are represented by four-dimensional areas of world points, to which (in part) qualities are assigned (cf. the construction of the perceptual world, §§ 125 f., 133 f.). Hence, such a law has the following form: "If qualities are assigned to the world points of a (four-dimensional) area in such and such a way, then qualities of such and such a kind are assigned, or must be assigned, to the world points of another area whose location stands in such and such a relation to the location of the first area." If the two areas which are thus connected through implication are simultaneous, we are concerned with a *state law;* [129] if they follow one another, with a *process law.*[130] If the two four-dimensional areas are in proximity, then we have a *proximity law.*[131] In the case of a state law, we have spatial proximity; in the case of a process law, temporal proximity. In this latter case (process law with temporal proximity), the law is called a *causal law.* Of the two four-dimensional areas which are in temporal proximity, i.e., which follow one another, and between which the dependency obtains, we call the earlier one the *cause* of the latter, while this latter area is called the *effect* of the former.

Thus, within science, causality means nothing but a functional dependency of a certain sort. We must emphasize this because time and again the opinion is advanced that, aside from the functional dependency between the two events, there must be a "real" relation or "essential relation", namely, such that the first event "produces", "generates", or "brings about", the second. It is strange that the opinion is still held, even by physicists and epistemologists, that science, in this case, physics, must not rest content with an investigation of those functional dependencies, but that it should ascertain, above all, the "real causes".

The error which lies in this opinion becomes even clearer if we consider, not the perceptual world, but the purely quantitative world of physics, with which physics is after all concerned. In the world of physics, one cannot even speak of events which stand to one another in the relation of cause and effect. The concepts "cause" and "effect" are meaningful only within the perceptual world; thus, they are infected with the imprecision which attaches to concept formations within this world. Actually, the process laws of the world of physics, i.e., the causal laws of physics, do not speak of a dependency between events, but of a dependency between a state and a certain limiting value relative to the assignment of state magnitudes [132] (namely, the temporal differential quotient of a state magnitude). It is only these causal laws, and not those of the perceptual world, which hold strictly and without exception. The causal laws in the perceptual world do not hold strictly, but only as

---

[129] Zustandsgesetz

[130] Ablaufgesetz

[131] Nachbarschaftsgesetz

[132] Zustandsgrössen

qualified by the vague clause "if no other circumstance intervenes." Thus, if we speak of strict causal laws, we can mean only the physical laws. But in this case, there is nothing present which could be called "cause" and "effect" (for nobody will wish to call a momentary state a "cause", let alone a differential quotient, an "effect"). Moreover, what is meant here can certainly not be the essential relation called "bringing about". We have frequently mentioned the metaphysical, extrascientific character of essential relations. (Cf. also the general remarks concerning problems of essence at the end of § 169, which also apply to the problem of causality.)

REFERENCES. Since Hume, it has been said frequently and clearly that, within science, *"real causation"* *must be denied.* (Let me here only refer to Mach, Verworn [Kondit.], and Vaihinger [Als Ob].) Thus, an explicit clarification from the standpoint of construction theory seems superfluous; perhaps the clearest rebuttal was given by Russell in his lecture [Cause].

B

THE PSYCHOPHYSICAL PROBLEM

166. Formulation of the Problem

In the present context, we do not mean by the psychophysical problem the question of whether to all psychological events there corresponds a simultaneous physiological event in the central nervous system (such that to similar psychological events there correspond similar physiological events). This is presupposed as an empirical hypothesis. Furthermore, we also do not mean the problem of ascertaining the types of individual brain events which correspond to the various sorts of psychological events. The solution of this "correlation problem" of the psychophysical relation (cf. § 21) is a task of physiology. The philosophical problem presupposes the solution of this problem or at least presupposes that it is solvable. We are here concerned with the problem that we have designated earlier as the "essence problem" of the psychophysical relation (§ 22); we are here asking how the parallelism of two such disparate sequences of events can be envisaged and explained. More recent philosophy of nature has again concerned itself with this ancient problem, and since then it has been one of the most frequently treated and debated philosophical problems.

REFERENCES. Du Bois-Reymond [Grenzen] 33 ff., formulates the problem in the following way: "If we make this same assumption of astronomical knowledge for the brain of man . . . then, relative to all material events which occur in it, our knowledge . . . will be complete . . . even those material events which are always, and hence probably necessarily, simultaneous with mental (in our language, "psychological") events, would be completely understood . . . however, as concerns the mental events themselves, it appears that they would be just as incomprehensible as they are now, even if we presuppose astronomical knowledge of the mental organ . . . . What conceivable connection is there between certain motions of certain atoms in my brain, on one hand, and certain, for me given, not further definable, undeniable facts such as, "I feel pain", "I feel desire". . . . It is altogether and forever incomprehensible that it is not a matter of indifference to a collection of carbon, hydrogen, nitrogen, oxygen, etc., atoms how they are situated and how they move. . . . *There is no way of comprehending how consciousness can result from their interaction.*" (Italics mine). We give the quotation in such detail since it shows, in exemplary fashion, how a problem can be clouded to the point of complete opaqueness, if a question is posed in the wrong way.

Of the extremely extensive literature concerning this problem, let me mention only the lucid discussions by Busse [Geist]; in the same book, Dürr gives an extensive bibliography; furthermore, Erdmann [Leib].

167. *The Psychophysical Problem Does Not Originate from the Heteropsychological*

Let us, first of all, find out which state of affairs is here to be explained, and in what situation we meet with this state of affairs.

Let us (just as Du Bois-Reymond) presuppose knowledge of the brain events. We express this through the fiction that we are in the possession of a "brain mirror", i.e., of an apparatus which allows us to observe a living brain in detail.

To begin with, it could appear as if the state of affairs with which the psychophysical problem is concerned could be observed in the following way: we use the brain mirror to look at the brain events of a test person, and at the same time we listen to his reports about the events of which he is conscious; furthermore, we observe his expressive motions. But this cannot be the typical case of the observation of the state of affairs in question, for here we are not confronted with two parallel sequences of events in different domains, but with two parallel *physical* sequences of events, namely, the sequence of visual observations in the brain mirror and the sequence of auditory observations of the spoken words of the test person (perhaps combined with visual observations of his expressive motions). Of course, we draw conclusions concerning the sequence of psychological events from the second sequence of physical events. But, what we *observe* are two physical sequences which show a certain complicated parallelism, but a parallelism which is in principle no more problematic than any other parallelism between physical processes. At any rate, this is not a situation in which the state of affairs in question is, as such, observed.

To facilitate understanding, we have represented the situation in realistic language. If we use constructional language, it is even more clearly evident that it is in principle impossible to observe the basic state of affairs of the psychophysical problem in another person. The two parallel sequences are constructed, on one hand, as a sequence of physical events in the body of another person, and, on the other hand, as a sequence of heteropsychological events which are constructionally assigned to this body. But the assignment of heteropsychological phenomena to the body of another person consists in assigning autopsychological events solely according to the physical behavior of this body. It is trivial and requires no further explanation that, in this case, we have a parallelism between the physical events of this body and the values which have been assigned. To pose the psychophysical problem from the vantage point of the heteropsychological would be very much like the following: somebody has accustomed himself to envisage an angry Zeus whenever he hears thunder. Eventually, he poses the question of how it could be explained that Zeus's anger and the thunder always occur simultaneously.

168. *The Basic Situation of the Psychophysical Problem*

Since the basic situation of the psychophysical problem has nothing to do with the heteropsychological, it must be related to the autopsychological. Therefore, in order to produce appropriate conditions, I have to observe my own brain through the brain mirror. In order to simplify the situation as much as possible, let us assume that auditory perceptions take place in such a way that they attract the main attention (while the visual observations through the brain mirror are only made on the side). The auditory perceptions could be produced by creating certain physical conditions, for example, by having a music box play a melody. But then we encounter a difficulty which corresponds precisely to the one discussed in connection with the heteropsychological experiment: I see brain events and I hear the tones of a music box; thus, we have again a purely physical parallelism. Thus, let us assume, instead, that I merely vividly imagine the melody. Here, now, we have really the desired situation: in imagination, I hear a melody, or, better, the same melody over and over (psychological sequence), and at the same time, I observe in the brain mirror my brain events (physical sequence); the parallelism shows itself in the fact that the same brain event always occurs during the same phase of the melody.

Let us consider the just-described basic situation from the constructional point of view. We find that the following state of affairs obtains. There is a temporal sequence of elementary experiences. If we carry out a constructional analysis of these experiences into their constituents (more precisely, into their quasi constituents), it becomes evident that there is a parallelism between two sequences of constituents; in each experience of the sequence of experiences, there is one constituent from each of the two constituent sequences; two constituents which occur together once will occur together again if one or the other of them occurs. The occurrence of two sequences of constituents of experiences which are connected with one another in such a way, we wish to call generally *parallelism of constituents*. Such a parallelism can occur, as we shall see, between the most heterogeneous sequences of constituents. In the case of the basic situation here under discussion, the parallelism of the constituents has the peculiarity that the constituents of one of the sequences (visual perceptions) can be used for the construction of real physical objects, while the constituents of the other sequence (auditory representations) cannot be used in this way; rather, the latter can be of any arbitrary kind.

There are also parallelisms of a different sort. Parallelisms between two sequences of constituents, both of which can be used for the construction of physical objects, occur frequently.

> EXAMPLES. Parallelism between different sense modalities; (in physical-realistic language): when a body visibly vibrates in a certain way, it simultaneously emits a certain sound; when a body has a certain visual shape, then it has simultaneously an analogous tactile shape. Parallelism within the same sense modality is also frequent; if a body has the visual shape of a horse, then it has simultaneously one of the horse colors; if part of a body has the visual shape of a horse head, then the entire body has simultaneously the visual shape of a horse.

Furthermore, there are parallelisms between two sequences of constituents, neither of which can be used for the construction of real physical objects, but (either for the construction of unreal physical objects or) only (as all sequences of constituents) for the construction of psychological objects.

> EXAMPLE. (In physical-realistic language): if I have the representation (not the perception) of the visual shape of a rose, then I have simultaneously the representation of the color and the fragrance of a rose; if I have the representation of the taste of an apple, then I simultaneously have a feeling of pleasure.

169. *Constructional and Metaphysical Problem*

The indicated parallelism, which takes place in the basic situation of the psychophysical problem, is distinguished from the other examples of parallelism only by the fact that one of the sequences of constituents can be used for the construction of physical objects, while the second sequence may be utilizable for the construction of physical objects, but does not have to be. From the viewpoint of construction theory, this is not an essential difference. The inherent nature of the given does not allow us to make essential distinctions between experiences or between constituents of experiences, especially not on the basis of the fact that constituents of one sort can be ordered in a certain way, while others can be ordered only in other ways. Thus, from the viewpoint of construction theory, the discernment of that basic situation does not offer anything new. *It is only another case of the frequently occurring parallelism of sequences of constituents.* It offers no more problems than this parallelism offers in general. Many more examples of such parallelisms could be mentioned, none of them any less problematic. The indicated cases, including the psychophysical situation, pose the problem: how can the occurrence of a parallelism of sequences of constituents be explained? For construction theory, and thus also *for (rational) science, the only thing to be done here is to ascertain what is the case,* namely, that it is not only the case that the given can be ordered in some way or another, but that it can be ordered to such an extent and in such a way that parallel sequences of this sort can be constructionally produced. The quest for an *explanation of these findings lies outside the range of science*; this shows itself already in the fact that this question cannot be expressed in concepts that can be constructed; for the concepts, "interpretation", "explanation", "basis", do not in this sense have any place in a constructional system of objects of cognition. (This holds for any such constructional system and not only for a constructional system of our specific kind.) Rather, the quest for an explanation of that parallelism belongs within metaphysics.

It is a familiar fact that metaphysics explains the parallelisms of the first kind through realistic or phenomenalistic postulations of physical things-in-themselves; it is one and the same thing which on one hand appears to me as the visual thing, apple, and on the other hand as the taste thing, apple. Parallelisms of the second kind can be explained through analogous postulations of psychological realities; it is one and the same psychological entity which is, on one hand, the representation of an apple and which carries with it, on the other hand, a certain emotional quality. Thus in both cases the metaphysical explanation makes use of a reification (positing as real) or a substantialization (in the sense of the category of substance). In a similar way, the parallelism of the third kind, the one that occurs in the psychophysical basic situation, can be explained through reification of things-in-themselves which have two different types of property.

To the extent to which it is necessary and possible for science, the psychophysical problem can be clarified in the indicated way on the basis of construction theory. The given suggestions must here suffice. Of course, this clarification does not go beyond the indicated state of affairs; but this does not mean that there is a gap in science: *a question which goes further cannot even be formulated within science* (i.e., formulated with scientific, that is to say, constructable, concepts, cf. § 180).

Aside from the psychophysical relation, we have noticed earlier certain other relations between different object types, each of which gives rise to a correlation problem as well as to an essence problem (§§ 20, 21, 24). In a manner similar to that used for the psychophysical problem, we could also show for these other problems that they can be posed in constructional language only as correlation problems. Their solutions, in these cases, are certain functional dependencies. On the other hand, if they are envisaged as essence problems, then they belong to the domain of metaphysics. This holds especially, for example, for the intention relation (cf. § 164), the causal relation (cf. § 165), and the manifestation and documentation relations among cultural objects.

REFERENCES. It was especially Mach [Anal.] who emphasized that in science we can ask only for functional dependencies, not for "essential relations". At present, this view is frequently argued by thinkers he has influenced.

Dingler [Naturphil.] 158 ff., also tries a solution to the psychophysical problem with the aid of the thought experiment, where the "brain mirror" is used relative to one's own brain, but shortly before the nicely prepared solution, he goes astray: he believes that the simultaneity between the picture in the brain mirror and the corresponding conscious event cannot be established because of the loss of time in the transmission through the apparatus. However, this time difference is not essential for the problem; moreover, it does not occur if the phenomena in question are static or periodic.

THE CONSTRUCTIONAL OR EMPIRICAL
PROBLEM OF REALITY

170. *Real and Nonreal Physical Objects*

The only concept of reality which occurs in the empirical sciences we shall call the *empirical concept of reality*. It is this concept which distinguishes a geographically determined mountain from a legendary or a dreamed mountain, and an experienced emotion from a simulated one. The question as to what is real, when it is formulated with the aid of constructable concepts, can only be concerned with this empirical reality; it alone can be posed and treated within the constructional system; hence, we speak here of the "constructional" or "empirical" problem of reality, in contrast to the "metaphysical" problem of reality which will be discussed in the sequel (§ 175 ff.), when we shall be concerned with a different, a "metaphysical", concept of reality. This latter concept occurs only in traditional philosophy, not in the empirical sciences.

To begin with, we consider the concept of (empirical) reality as it relates to physical objects, in particular to the most important objects, namely, physical bodies. These bodies are called *real* if they are constructed as classes of physical [133] points which are located on connected bundles of world lines and are placed within the all-comprehending four-dimensional system of the space-time world of physics (§ 136). On the

---

[133] physikalisch

other hand, things which, taken by themselves, have the same or a similar constitution as the real physical bodies, i.e., which are also four-dimensional orders of world points with physical [133] assignments, but which are not parts of the one, comprehensive, four-dimensional system of the world of physics, are called also "physical" since they have a similar constitution, but, since they do not belong to the total system, they are called *nonreal* physical things.

The construction of nonreal physical things can take place in various different ways. Generally speaking, the construction of physical things, including the real ones, leaves it initially open whether they are real or nonreal; this decision will be made only afterward depending on the possibility of placing them in the total system. This holds already for the world of perception, which is a preliminary to the world of physics.

> EXAMPLE. On the basis of a number of visual perceptions alone, we do not generally carry out an assignment to the world points of the four-dimensional system, according to the rules of § 126 ff.; rather, we establish initially a special, four-dimensional order of the colors in question which could represent a visual thing during a span of time. We must now test whether or not this visual thing can be placed in the system of the perceptual world according to the constructional forms of this system. If it can be so placed without producing a contradiction with the other constructions of perceptual things, where the assertions of other persons are frequently decisive factors, then it is legitimized as a *real* perceptual thing (i.e., initially, as a visual thing). If it cannot be so placed, then it is a *nonreal* perceptual thing.

In constructing a nonreal thing, we can decide, through a more detailed investigation, what kind of nonreal physical thing it is. If a visual thing (as in the indicated example) is constructed from visual perceptions, then it could perhaps be a *dream,* a *hallucination,* an *hypnotic suggestion,* etc. On the other hand, if the construction takes place on the basis of assertions of other persons (§ 144), then, depending upon the circumstances (i.e., the "intention" of the other), it could be a *lie,* a *piece of fiction,* an *error,* etc. (of another). However, construction can also form a physical thing in a free way, relying neither upon the experiences of the self nor upon the assertions of others. Here the object must be called an object of *one's own phantasy,* whose purpose could be (one's own) lie, invention, theoretical fiction, hypothetical assumption, or free play of phantasy.

---

[133] physikalisch

The given suggestions will suffice to make it clear that the *difference between reality and nonreality (dream, invention, etc.) retains its full meaning even in a constructional system which is based upon an auto-psychological basis, and that this distinction in no way presupposes any transcendency.*

171. Real and Nonreal Objects of Psychological and Cultural Type

For object types other than physical objects, we must envisage the difference between real and nonreal objects in much the same way as for physical objects. An object is called "psychological" if it is constituted in such a way that, taken by itself and according to its internal structure, it has the constitution of events or states that are normally called autopsychological, no matter whether this object is based on my own experiences, the assertions of others, or free stipulation. If, in addition, it can be placed within the connected and temporally ordered system of autopsychological objects, then it is called a *real autopsychological object.* If an object can be assigned to another person, who is a real physical object in the just-discussed sense, in accordance with the constructional forms appropriate to the heteropsychological (§ 140), then we call it a *real heteropsychological object.* If no placement is possible in either of these ways, then it is called a *nonreal psychological object.* We must here again distinguish, just as we did above, between a dream, a lie, etc.

For cultural objects, the distinction is logically even more simple (though empirically more difficult). An object which is constructed in such a way that, taken by itself, it has the constitution of those objects which we have called cultural, is in each case called a *cultural object,* whether it be real or not. It is called *real* if its manifestations belong to the real psychological objects; otherwise, it is called *nonreal.* The application of this criterion is simple in the case of those objects which are constructed as primary cultural objects. It becomes more complicated for the higher cultural objects, because, in these cases, we must consider the reality or nonreality of the primary cultural objects which lie at their basis. I do not wish to go into any more detail in this matter.

Through a comparison of these distinctions in the areas of the physical, the psychological, and the cultural, we find that, throughout, the following properties are used as indicators to distinguish the real from the nonreal.

1. *Every real object belongs to a comprehensive system which is governed by regularities*; that is to say, the physical objects belong to the

world of physics, the psychological objects to the psychological system of a subject, and the cultural objects belong to the cultural world.

2. *Every real object is either itself an intersubjective object or the immediate occasion for the construction of such an object.* The latter we can say of an object which belongs to the field [134] of intersubjective correspondence (§ 146 f.).

3. *Every real object has a position in the temporal order.*

172. *The Concept of Real-Typical Objects*

More difficult than the just-discussed differentiation between real and nonreal objects is the distinction between objects which are either real or nonreal, on the one hand, and objects to which this distinction does not apply, on the other; the former we call *real-typical.*

As we have seen above, the real and nonreal objects of an object domain agree in several properties; these, then, are the characteristic properties of the real-typical in the domain in question; we shall now consider them in more detail. For example, if a physical object has the properties common to real and nonreal physical objects, then it is a real-typical physical object. It may then happen that we recognize it as a real object or as a nonreal object, but it is also possible that this distinction has not yet been carried out or perhaps that it cannot be carried out on the basis of the available information. Nevertheless, we can know of it that it is real-typical.

> REFERENCES. The concept of the real-typical is called by Christiansen [Kantkritik] "empirical objectivity". "What must be the nature of an object, that we may ask of it whether or not it is real?" In Christiansen's opinion, Kant actually means real-typical objects when he speaks of "objects". Meinong, in his theory of objects, calls the real-typical objects "real".

The concept of reality is not yet a scientifically determined concept. Its boundaries are not drawn according to uniform principles, but are in part merely traditional, i.e., objectively speaking, merely accidental (just like the historical boundaries of a state). But (in contrast to the boundaries of a state) these boundaries are not uniquely determined. In the following, we attempt a rough determination of the boundaries of the real-typical in the various domains. In doing so, we shall conform to linguistic usage as it obtains in science and after the clarifying influ-

---

[134] Geltungsbereich

ence of scientific thinking also in daily life. But this use of language is frequently quite fluctuating.

In order to find, for a certain object domain, the boundary between real-typical objects and those that are not, let us, for the sake of simplicity, confine ourselves to the comprehensive system of those domains for which we have succeeded in distinguishing the real objects from the nonreal ones (§ 171): the world of physics (as a whole), the psychological world (as a whole), or the cultural world (as a whole). According to the indicated criteria of reality, the real-typical objects, if they occur within such a system, are real. Thus, if we limit ourselves to such a system, then the desired boundary of the real-typical coincides with the boundary of the real. It is permissible to make this restriction since the boundary of the real-typical, outside of such a system, is analogous to the boundary inside.

173. *The Boundary of the Real-Typical in the Physical Domain*

Let us, to begin with, find the boundary between the real-typical and the other objects for the physical object type. In doing so, we shall limit ourselves to the total system of the world of physics, within which the real-typical objects are the same as the real ones. The following discussion does not so much have the purpose of ascertaining the precise course of the boundary; rather, it is to show that this boundary is rather arbitrary and frequently vacillating.

To begin with, and according to general linguistic usage, physical bodies (which belong to the system) must be called real. From this it follows for our problem that the physical bodies, whether real or not, are real-typical. But, even here, doubts are possible in some cases (for example, in the case of a virtual optical picture). However, greater difficulties arise in another direction: we now have to ask which physical objects, other than bodies, may be called real. It is common linguistic usage to call the events in, and the states of, these bodies real. To a large extent, this holds also for the sensory-qualitative properties, although here we already find some deviation. However, for the *wholes* which are composed out of bodies, the differences in language use occur with more frequency; here we are concerned with those body-like objects which consist of bodies as their spatial parts, but which do not themselves have to be spatially connected (cf. § 36, about the concept of whole). If the individual bodies which form the whole are spatially close together, then we frequently call the whole real and sometimes even call it itself a body (for example, a pile of sand, a forest). If the individual bodies are spatially farther separated from one another, then the whole is more likely to be called real, the more similar the individual bodies are to one another.

> EXAMPLES. "My furniture", "the German coal reserves", will generally be admitted to be physical objects. On the other hand, there will already be doubts concerning an object such as "the present vegetation of central Europe" (meaning the whole, whose parts are the presently living, individual plants). The object, whose parts are certain trees, may or may not be called real, depending upon the characteristic properties of the trees: if the trees are close together, then the object is called a forest or a part of a forest, and there is hardly any doubt; if, on the other hand, we are concerned with the oaks of Europe, or with all trees in Europe which are higher than twenty meters, or with the European trees the name of whose owners begins with an A, then it becomes more and more likely that the object is no longer considered real, but a more or less arbitrary "conceptual assemblage" without a "real" object which "lies at the bottom of it".

Classes of bodies (about the distinction between class and whole, cf. § 37) are not as frequently considered real as wholes which consist of bodies. This is justified inasmuch as these classes are much more clearly distinguished from bodies, since they belong to another object sphere, while the whole belongs to the same object sphere as the bodies themselves. But, even here, the boundary does not take a simple and clear course. There are classes of bodies which are frequently considered real, namely, those whose characteristic property can be perceived through the senses or is in some other way considered easily recognizable and important. This coincides with what has been said above about properties, for a property of physical bodies is, as a rule, to be constructed as the class of those things which have this property.

> EXAMPLE. Physical substances are frequently called real, for example, the substance gold as the class of all pieces of gold (in contradistinction to the corresponding whole which is the total amount of gold in the world).

Linguistic usage is even more vacillating in the case of relation extensions of physical bodies.

> EXAMPLES. The relation extension which is characterized by one body *pushing* another is generally considered real. Occasionally, the spatial distance between two bodies is thought of as something real, but, sometimes, it is considered merely to *hold* for real bodies and to be

purely conceptual. This latter conception is even more marked in the case of the temporal distance between two body states and perhaps even more in the case of those relations between bodies which are based upon qualitative likeness or similarity.

Let us now proceed from classes to *classes of classes* and to *relations* [135] *between classes* and from relations [135] to *classes of relations* [135] and to *relations* [135] *between relations* [135]; such objects are generally no longer called real. But there are exceptions even among these objects which are two (or more) levels higher than bodies; even here, there are certain objects which are occasionally considered real. This is an especially good indication of the *arbitrary and accidental boundary of the concept of the real-typical.* (Incidentally, on these levels, linguistic usage fluctuates even with respect to the expression "physical".)

EXAMPLE. The relation [135] between one generation of animals and their immediate offspring is a relation [135] between classes of physical bodies. One finds occasionally, though not generally, that this relation [135] of *parent generation* is considered real.

174. *The Boundary of the Real-Typical in the Psychological and the Cultural Domains*

In the domain of psychological objects, common usage draws the boundary of the real-typical in a somewhat less arbitrary way than in the case of the physical objects. Generally, only experiences and the individual constituents of experiences are considered real (or nonreal, as the case may be). To these are added unconscious constituents of experiences, if they are constructed as a supplementation of the conscious ones (§ 132). Occasionally, one of the senses of a certain person is considered as something real (for example, the visual sense of Mr. N); this is done less often with a given quality class (for example, a certain blue hue, not as it is perceived on a particular occasion, but generally). In the case of relation extensions of experiences or of constituents of experiences, the boundary shows considerable fluctuation, just as in the case of the physical.

In the domain of the cultural objects, we find the boundary in an even worse condition than in the preceding two cases. Here, it is not only the case that the boundary is frequently rather erratic from a given viewpoint, but it also shows great differences between different points of

---

[135] Relation

view. Oftentimes, reality is denied to the entire domain, as if all the cultural objects were only "conceptual assemblages". However, if some cultural objects are considered real, then the boundary can be drawn on very different levels and may frequently include only a part of the objects on certain levels. The domain of the cultural objects shows a very large number of levels; thus, here there are many more possibilities for varying the boundary. Linguistic usage actually expresses many of these possibilities and thus shows very little uniformity. This can be explained mainly through the fact that the domain of the cultural has been recognized and accepted as an independent object domain only very recently.

We have here considered the concept of the real-typical, not from a substantive or systematic point of view, but only relative to linguistic usage. Here we merely find a disjointed concept which is not clearly delineated. The boundaries of this concept are subject to a certain degree of arbitrariness. It is reasonable to assume that the variations which we find here are caused mainly by subjective dispositions relative to the experiences, and by variations in interest. The terminological situation which we have described shows that it is necessary to make a clear and uniform determination of this boundary; that is to say, to determine with which concepts the distinction between real and nonreal is to be made at all. The purpose of our discussion is, mainly, to show that we are here not concerned with a question of fact, but with (the lack of) a convention. Furthermore, the discussion has the purpose of showing the urgent need for such a convention.

THE METAPHYSICAL PROBLEM
OF REALITY

175. Realism, Idealism, and Phenomenalism

We now wish to deal with a problem of reality which is quite different from the one that we have discussed so far. We have determined what constructional (empirically ascertainable) conditions must be fulfilled in order for an object to be called real in the customary usage of the empirical sciences. In addition to this "constructional" or "empirical" problem of reality, the question may arise whether or not we must ascribe "reality" in a special sense to these empirically real objects. For this special sense, there are various formulations; most commonly, it is characterized as *independence from the cognizing consciousness*. Thus, we have to differentiate two different meanings of the word "reality". Wherever it is necessary, we shall indicate them by calling the one "empirical reality" and the other "metaphysical reality". Later on we shall give a justification for this second expression (§ 176).

> EXAMPLES. The difference between the two meanings becomes clear through the following two questions: "Was the Trojan War a real event or merely an invention?" and "Are those objects which are not feigned or simulated, for example the perceived physical bodies, real, or are they merely contents of consciousness?" The first question is treated by

historical science; it is to be resolved with empirical and constructional methods, and hence there is no divergence of opinion among the adherents of the various philosophical schools. The second question is customarily transacted within the field of philosophy; it is answered in different ways by different schools; we shall see later that it is extra-constructional and hence extrascientific; it is metaphysical.

REFERENCES. We customarily use the expressions "actual" [136] and "real" [137] as synonymous. Külpe [Realis.] distinguishes the postulated, inferred (i.e., constructed) objects from the processes of consciousness. He calls the former "real", and the latter "actual"; but this seems a little too far removed from customary usage.

The second concept of reality (in the sense of independence from the cognizing subject) indicates the point where the schools of realism, idealism, and phenomenalism part company. These schools are distinguished from one another by the fact that they ascribe reality in the second sense to object domains of varying extent (within the field of the empirically real). *Realism* holds that the constructed physical and heteropsychological objects are real. Subjective *idealism* holds that the heteropsychological, but not the physical, objects are real. The more radical form of *solipsism* denies even the reality of heteropsychological objects. (Objective idealism ascribes reality to a superindividual, absolute subject, which is not constructed within our system; hence, we shall not consider this school in the present context.) *Phenomenalism* agrees with realism in maintaining that real entities exist outside of the domain of the autopsychological; on the other hand, it agrees with idealism in denying this reality to the physical; according to phenomenalism, reality must be ascribed to unrecognizable "things-in-themselves", whose appearances are the physical objects.

176. *The Metaphysical Concept of Reality*

The concept of reality (in the sense of independence from the cognizing consciousness) does not belong within (rational) science, but within metaphysics. This is now to be demonstrated. For this purpose, we investigate whether this concept can be constructed, i.e., whether it can be expressed through objects of the most important types which we have already considered, namely, the autopsychological, the physical, the heteropsychological, and the cultural. At first sight, it might appear as

---

[136] wirklich
[137] real

though this were possible. An object which I have recognized, that is, an object which has been constructed on the basis of my experience, will have to be called "independent of my consciousness" if its constitution does not depend upon my will, i.e., if an act of volition which aims at a change of the object does not result in such a change. But this does not agree with the concept of reality as it is meant by realism and idealism (the former ascribing it to, and the latter denying it of, physical bodies). For, according to the definition which we have just attempted, a physical body which I hold in my hand should not be called real, since (even in the opinion of the realists) it changes if I carry out an appropriate act of will; this would then be contradictory to the realistic position. On the other hand, this definition requires that any physical thing which lies outside of our technological reach, for example, a crater in the moon, should be acknowledged as real, since (even in the opinion of idealism) it does not change if I carry out an appropriate act of will; this then would be contradictory to the position of idealism.

One could try in various other ways to give a definition of reality (in the sense of independence of my consciousness) in such a way that the concept becomes constructable. However, one can show in each such case that the concept which is so defined does not agree with the concept as it is meant by realism as well as by idealism. It must be noted that this holds, not only of a constructional system which has the system form represented in our outline, but for any experiential constructional system, even for a system which does not proceed from an autopsychological basis, but from the experiences of all subjects or from the physical. *The (second) concept of reality cannot be constructed in an experiential constructional system; this characterizes it as a nonrational, metaphysical concept.*

REFERENCES. It seems that we agree with Russell [Scientif.] 120 ff. in the indicated conception that the concept of nonempirical reality cannot be constructed. However, this does not seem to be consistent with the fact that, in Russell, questions of the following kind are frequently posed, which (independently of how they are answered) imply a realistic persuasion: whether physical things exist when they are not observed; whether other persons exist; whether classes exist; etc. ([Scientif.] 123, [Mind] 308, [External W.] 126, [Sense-Data] 157 and elsewhere). Cf. also Weyl [Handb.] 89.

The indicated conception of the concept of reality is related to that of positivism, which goes back to Mach. Cf., for example, Ostwald [Naturphil.] 101 ff.; the concept of reality as it is defined there roughly corresponds to the constructional concept of reality. The same holds for the concept of reality as it is defined by Bavink ([Ergebn.] 26, 187); thus, Bavink is right when he describes it as neutral relative to the realism problem.

The definition of the concept of a *thing-in-itself* goes back to the concept of reality (in the sense of independence from the cognizing subject). Thus, in our conception, this concept, too, must be placed *within metaphysics*, for metaphysics is the extrascientific domain of theoretical form (§ 182).

> REFERENCES. If things-in-themselves are defined as real objects which are not given (as is done by Schlick [Erkenntnisl.] 179), then they must indeed be counted among the cognizable objects and thus must be placed within the domain of (rational) science and not within metaphysics; for then they coincide with the constructed real objects. However, it seems to us that this definition is not very practical, since it deviates altogether too much from customary usage (cf. Külpe [Realis.] II, 213). The same holds also for the characterization of constructed real objects as transcendent ([Erkenntnisl.] 180). The essential limit of transcendence, according to customary usage, lies between the recognizable (in our language, constructable) objects and the nonrecognizable (not constructable) objects. If one wishes to emphasize, through a special expression, the limit between the given objects and those objects which are constructed but not given, then the term "transgression" ("transgredient" or *transgressive* objects) may serve for this purpose; this term has been introduced by Ziehen [Erkth.] 279; Ziehen justifiably makes a sharp distinction between this concept and the concept of transcendence.

177. Construction Theory Contradicts Neither Realism, Idealism, nor Phenomenalism

The following concerns objects which are empirically real (i.e., objects which are (in constructional language) placed in the total system of the object type in question; cf. § 171; (in realistic language) objects which have been "recognized" or "determined" as "real"). Relative to these empirically real objects of the various object types, construction theory and *realism* agree in the following points: 1. Such objects can be clearly distinguished from unreal objects of the same object type (dreams, hallucinations, inventions, etc.). Only to the extent to which they can be clearly distinguished, are they used in the formation of the system of knowledge. 2. They can be intersubjectivized, i.e., in principle, they can be placed in constructional systems which belong to other persons (§ 146 ff.) and can be confirmed or corrected through the reports of other persons (§ 144); they are included in the system of knowledge only to the extent to which they can be intersubjectivized. 3. They are independent from being cognized in the sense that they exist also at times when they are not represented in my experiences or in the experiences of another. 4. They are independent of me, in the sense that a wish to change them does not result in a change of their characteristics unless a physical causal chain connects an appropriate motion of my body with the object in question. 5. They are governed by their own regularities which makes it occasionally possible to make predictions: if I put my body into an appropriate position, then an experience of a certain predictable kind takes place, whether I want it or not. However, there is agreement, not only in the points just mentioned, but in all points in which assertions are made at all by *both* theories. *Construction theory and realism do not contradict one another in any point.*

Construction theory and *subjective idealism* agree with one another in the claim that statements about objects of cognition can, in principle, all be transformed into statements about structural properties of the given (with retention of the logical value, cf. § 50). Construction theory agrees with *solipsism* in the notion that the given consists of my experiences. Construction theory agrees with *transcendental idealism* in the conception that all objects of cognition are constructed (in idealistic language: "are created in thought"); in fact, the constructed objects are objects of conceptual knowledge only *qua* logical forms which are generated in a certain way. Ultimately, this holds also for the basic elements of the constructional system. Even though these basic elements are initially introduced as unanalyzable units, eventually, in the progress of construction, different properties are attributed to them, and they are analyzed into (quasi) constituents (§ 116). It is only through this procedure, that is, only as constructed objects, that they become objects of cognition in the proper sense of the word, in particular, objects of psychology. Here again we have the situation that there is agreement between idealism in its different varieties and construction theory in all points where assertions are made by *both* theories. *Construction theory and idealism* (objective, subjective, and solipsistic idealism) *do not contradict one another in any point.*

The same holds for *phenomenalism.* For, aside from asserting the existence of "things-in-themselves", it shows no deviation from construction theory, and construction theory neither affirms nor denies the existence of things in themselves. Here again, we find agreement in all points where *both* theories make assertions. *Construction theory and phenomenalism do not contradict one another at any point.*

178. The Divergence Among the Three Schools Occurs Only Within the Field of Metaphysics

It is not particularly surprising that none of the doctrines—realism, idealism (in its different varieties), and phenomenalism—show in themselves any contradiction to construction theory, yet contradict one another. For, the three schools do, after all, agree with one another and with construction theory in the following points: ultimately, all knowledge goes back to my experiences, which are related to one another, connected, and synthesized; thus, there is a logical progress which leads, first, to the various entities of my consciousness, then to the physical objects, furthermore, with the aid of the latter, to the phenomena of consciousness of other subjects, i.e., to the heteropsychological, and, through the mediation of the heteropsychological, to the cultural objects. *But this is the theory of knowledge in its entirety.* Whatever else construction theory states about the necessary or the useful forms and methods of construction belongs to the logical, but not to the epistemological, aspect of its task. The theory of knowledge does not reach beyond what has just been indicated. How cognition can proceed from one object to another, how, in what sequence, and in which form the levels of a system of cognition can be formulated,—all this is contained in the indicated material. The theory of knowledge cannot ask any further questions.

But where do the contradictory components of realism, idealism, and phenomenalism belong, if not to the theory of knowledge? The assertions of these doctrines which stand in contradiction to one another are all related to the second concept of reality (§ 175), and this concept, as we have already seen (§ 176), belongs to metaphysics. From this it follows: *the so-called epistemological schools of realism, idealism, and phenomenalism agree within the field of epistemology. Construction theory represents the neutral foundation which they have in common. They diverge only in the field of metaphysics, that is to say (if they are meant to be epistemological schools of thought), only because of a transgression of their proper boundaries.*

It is occasionally said that there is a (usually tacit) realism at the bottom of the practical procedures of the empirical sciences, especially of physics. However, we must here clearly distinguish between a certain kind of language usage and the assertion of a thesis. The realistic orientation of the physicist shows itself primarily in the use of realistic language; this is practical and justifiable (cf. § 52). On the other hand, realism, as an explicit thesis, goes beyond this and is not permissible; it must be corrected so as to become "objectivism": the regular connections (which in natural laws are formulated as implication statements) are objective and are independent of the will of the individual; on the other hand, the ascription of the property "real" to any substance (be it matter, energy, electromagnetic field, or whatever) cannot be derived from any experience and hence would be metaphysical.

REFERENCES. The above-indicated standpoint is closely related to what Gätschenberger, [Symbola] 452, says about the reconciliation between idealists and spiritualists on the one hand, and materialists on the other: "Materialism is a translation of spiritualism"; "All philosophers are correct, but they express themselves with varying degrees of ineptness, and they cannot help this, since they use the *available* language and consequently speak in a hundred sublanguages, instead of inventing one pasigraphy." This neutral language is the goal of construction theory.

Carnap [Realismus] contains detailed expositions of the difference between the empirical and the metaphysical concept of reality and more exact reasons why the realism debate should be banished from science and placed within metaphysics.

AIMS AND LIMITS OF SCIENCE

179. *The Aims of Science*

We have repeatedly pointed out that the formation of the constructional system as a whole is the task of unified science, while construction theory is merely engaged in carrying out the appropriate logical investigations. By placing the objects of science in one unified constructional system, the different "sciences" are at the same time recognized as branches of the one science and are themselves brought into a system.

How should we determine the aim of unified science from the viewpoint of construction theory? The aim of science consists in finding and ordering the true statements about the objects of cognition (not all true statements, but a selection, made according to certain principles; we do not undertake to discuss the teleological problem of these principles at this point).

In order to be able to approach this aim, that is, in order to be able to make statements about objects at all, we must be able to construct these objects (for, otherwise, their names have no meaning). *Thus, the formation of the constructional system is the first aim of science.* It is the first aim, not in a temporal, but in a logical, sense. The historical development of science does not have to postpone the investigation of an object until this object is placed within a constructional system. For objects on higher levels, especially for biological and cultural objects, science must not wait for this to take place, if it does not want to forego, for a long time, the development of these essential fields with their important practical applications. Rather, in the actual process of science, the objects are taken from the store of everyday knowledge and are gradually purified and rationalized, while the intuitive components in the determination of these objects are not eliminated, but are rationally justified (cf. § 100). Only when this has been successfully accomplished can the object be constructed, and only when it has been carried out, in addition, for all its constructional ancestors, can the constructional system be built up to the object in question. This is the procedure as it historically takes place in actual practice. From a logical point of view, however, statements which are made about an object become statements in the strictest scientific sense only after the object has been constructed, beginning from the basic objects. For, only the construction formula of the object—as a rule of translation of statements about it into statements about the basic objects, namely, about relations between elementary experiences—gives a verifiable meaning to such statements, for verification means testing on the basis of experiences.

The first aim, then, is the construction of objects; it is followed by a second aim, namely, the investigation of the nonconstructional properties and relations of the objects. The first aim is reached through convention; [138] the second, however, through experience. (In the view of construction theory, there are no other components in cognition than these two, the conventional and the empirical; thus, there is no synthetic a priori.) It has already been said that, in the actual process of science, these two aims are almost always connected with one another. Moreover, most of the time, it is not even possible to make a selection of those properties which are most useful for the constructional definition of an object until a large number of properties of this object are known. In analogy, the construction of an object corresponds to the indication of the geographical coördinates for a place on the surface of the earth. The place is uniquely determined through these coördinates; any question about the nature of this place (perhaps about the climate, nature of the soil, etc.) has now a definite meaning. To answer all these questions is then a further aim which can never be completed and which is to be approached through experience.

---

[138] Festsetzung

REFERENCES. In the opinion of the Marburg Neo-Kantian school (cf. Natorp [Grundlagen] 18 ff.), the object is the eternal X, and its determination an aim that can never be accomplished. Against this, it must be pointed out that a finite number of characteristics suffices for the construction of the object, thus for its definite description within the field of objects in general. If such a definite description is given, then the object is no longer an X, but something that is uniquely determined, whose complete description, however, still remains a task that cannot be completed.

180. *About the Limitations of Scientific Knowledge*

Science, the system of conceptual knowledge, has no limits. But this does not mean that there is nothing outside of science and that it is all-inclusive. The total range of life has still many other dimensions outside of science, but, within its dimension, science meets no barrier. Let us consider an analogy: an infinite plane in space does not include the entire space, but it is nevertheless unlimited, without border, and is thus distinguished, for example, from a triangle within this plane. When we say that scientific knowledge is not limited, we mean: *there is no question whose answer is in principle unattainable by science.* Concerning the expression "in principle": if it is practically impossible to answer a question about a certain event, because the event is too far removed in either space or time, but if a question of a similar kind about a present event which is within reach can in fact be answered, then we call the question "practically unanswerable, but answerable in principle"; spatial and temporal remoteness, we call a "mere technical obstacle", not an "obstacle unsurmountable in principle". In like fashion, a question is said to be "answerable in principle" if it is not practically possible to answer it today, but if a state of technological resources (in the widest sense) can be envisaged which would make it possible to answer this question.

It is occasionally said that the answer to some questions cannot be conceptualized; that it cannot be formulated. But in such a case, the question itself could not have been formulated. In order to recognize this, let us investigate somewhat more closely what the answer to a question consists in. In the strictly logical sense, to pose a question is to give a statement together with the task of deciding whether this statement or its negation is true. A statement can only be given by producing its symbol, namely, a sentence, which consists of words or other symbols. Now, it happens very frequently, especially in philosophy, that a sequence of words is given which has the outward construction of a sentence and is therefore mistaken for one without being one. A string of words can fail to be a sentence in two ways: first, if it contains a word which has no meaning, or, second (and this is the more frequent case), if the individual words do indeed have meaning (i.e., if they can occur as parts of genuine, not merely apparent, sentences), but if this meaning does not fit with the context of the sentence. In a word language, it is very difficult to avoid such pseudo sentences, since, in order to recognize them, it is necessary to pay attention to the meaning of every individual word; on the other hand, in a logistic language, it is not necessary to consider the meaning, but only the "type" of the sign (which corresponds to the sphere of the object, § 29). Similarly, an ideal, logically unobjectionable, word language would require of us no more than to consider the grammatical word type and the inflection forms. The difficulty in recognizing pseudo sentences in natural language is connected with the problem of the "confusion of spheres" in the given word language which we have discussed earlier (§ 30); it is not possible for us here to concern ourselves with the particulars of this important logical problem.

Now, if it is the case that a genuine question is posed, what are the possibilities of giving an answer? In such a case, a statement is given; it is expressed through conceptual symbols [139] in formally permissible combination. Now, in principle, every legitimate concept of science has a definite place in the constructional system ("in principle", i.e., if not today, then at a conceivable state of development of scientific knowledge); otherwise, the concept cannot be acknowledged to be legitimate. Since we are here concerned only with answerability *in principle*, let us disregard the stage of scientific development as it happens to be, and let us assume that we have reached a stage where the concepts which occur in the statement in question have already been placed within the constructional system. We now replace the sign for each of these concepts as it occurs in the given sentence by the expression which defines it in its constructional definition, and we carry out, step by step, further substitutions of constructional definitions. We already know that, eventually, the sentence will have a form in which (outside of logical symbols) it contains only signs for basic relations. (This transformation has been discussed in § 119 and has been illustrated in an example.) Thus, the sentence which was given when the question was posed has now been so transformed that it expresses a definite (formal and extensional)

---

[139] Begriffszeichen

state of affairs relative to the basic relation. In keeping with the tenets of construction theory, we presuppose that it is in principle possible to recognize whether or not a given basic relation holds between two given elementary experiences. Now, the state of affairs in question is composed of nothing but such individual relation extension statements, where the number of elements which are connected through the basic relation, namely, of elementary experiences, is finite. From this it follows that it is in principle possible to ascertain in a finite number of steps whether or not the state of affairs in question obtains and hence that the posed question can in principle be answered.

Now we see more clearly what it means to say that science has no "limiting points": *the truth or falsity of each statement which is formed from scientific concepts can in principle be ascertained.*

> REFERENCES. Cf. the quotation from Wittgenstein in § 183.
>
> The requirement that only such concept words [140] should be considered legitimate which are constructed, that is, which can be translated back into expressions about basic objects is related to the requirement which is posed by *positivism* and which has, for example, been formulated by Petzold [Positiv.] 7, in the following way: "If someone is unable to descend from the highest concepts at once to the last individual facts which fall under them, then he does not even possess these concepts." Similarly, Gätschenberger [Symbola].
>
> In the thesis of the decidability of all questions, we agree with positivism as well as with idealism; cf. Becker [Geom.] 412: "According to the principle of transcendental idealism, a question which is in principle (in essence) undecidable does not have any meaning at all. No state of affairs corresponds to it, which could provide an answer for it. For there are no states of affairs which are in principle inaccessible to consciousness."

181. *Faith and Knowledge*

According to the above-indicated position, conceptual knowledge does not meet any limitations in its own field; nevertheless, it is an open question whether it is perhaps possible to gain insights in a manner which lies outside of conceptual knowledge and which is inaccessible to conceptual thinking. Such a possibility would lie, for example, in faith, perhaps on the basis of religious revelation, mystical absorption, or other types of vision (intuition).

Unquestionably, there are phenomena of faith, religious and other-

---

[140] Begriffsworte

wise, and of intuition; they play an important role, not only for practical life, but also for cognition. Moreover, it can be admitted that, in these phenomena, somehow something is "grasped", but this figurative expression should not lead to the assumption that knowledge is gained through these phenomena. What is gained is a certain attitude, a certain psychological state, which, under certain circumstances, can indeed be favorable for obtaining certain insights. Knowledge, however, can be present only when we designate and formulate, when a statement is rendered in words or other signs. Admittedly, the above-mentioned states put us occasionally in a position of asserting a statement or ascertaining its truth. But it is only this articulable, hence conceptual, ascertainment [141] which is knowledge; it must be carefully distinguished from that state itself. This conception is closely connected with our conception of a concept. A concept is the meaning of a sign which may occur in sentences.

Thus, for example, faith in a certain revelation or in the assertions of a certain person can, through further investigation, lead to knowledge, for in this case, faith means the same as holding to be true. On the other hand, if by faith is meant the inner attitude of a person as something which cannot be conceptually formulated, then we are not even within the realm of theory, and the effect of this attitude cannot be called knowledge. It is similar with intuition. Either it has an articulable result —in this case, this result is put into conceptual form through this articulation and thus has been made subject to the laws of conceptual knowledge—or else something ineffable is meant—in such a case, intuition again cannot claim to be taken as knowledge. Still less can it be maintained that, in this way, questions can be solved which cannot be answered within science. For, we cannot speak of question and answer if we are concerned with the ineffable.

We do not here wish to make either a negative or a positive value judgment about faith and intuition (in the nonrational sense). They are areas of life just like poetry and love. Like these latter areas, they can of course become *objects* of science (for there is nothing which could not become an object of science), but, as far as their content is concerned, they are altogether different from science. Those nonrational areas, on the one hand, and science, on the other hand, can neither confirm nor disprove one another.

A justification of our use of language. Occasionally, it is objected that the word "knowledge" [142] should not be used only for conceptual knowledge, but should also include other things, for example, a non-

---

[141] Feststellung
[142] Erkenntnis

rational or an intuitive grasp of certain things. Against this objection, we wish to propose the following compromise, in order to reach an agreement about a reasonable delineation of the term "knowledge". Let us proceed from those phenomena which are held to fall within the field of "knowledge" by ourselves as well as by the objectors. Let us think of the field of knowledge as comprising, in addition, all those things which stand in the relation of dependency (either positive or negative, i.e., either confirmation or contradiction) to the contents of this common area. Furthermore, add to it all those things which stand in a relation of dependency to the contents of the area as it has thus been enlarged, etc. Let us be careful and choose as the common initial field only the field of empirical knowledge (for example, "The oak is a tree", "I have three apples"), and let us pose, for example, the question whether the contents of mathematics should be called knowledge. In this case, the suggested criterion would be applied in the following way. The arithmetical statement "$3 + 2 = 5$" contradicts the following statements which belong to the field of empirical knowledge (i.e., whose affirmation and negation are empirical cognitions): "I have three apples", "You have two apples", "Together we have four apples". Thus the validity of these three statements is dependent upon the above-mentioned statement of arithmetic. Consequently, this statement belongs to the total field of knowledge (i.e., either its affirmation or its negation is a true statement; our criterion does not decide which of these two is the case, since we are not here concerned with the difference between true and false, but only with the question of what belongs to the field of knowledge). The criterion is fulfilled in a similar way, also, for all other statements of arithmetic, of analysis, and of geometry. Thus, the contents of mathematics belong to the field of knowledge; to the extent to which its validity is ascertained, it should, according to the proposed compromise, be called "knowledge". Thus, the entire area of rational science, of formal as well as of empirical science, should be called "knowledge".

Now, what about "nonrational knowledge", for example, the content of a mystical, ineffable view of God? It does not come into a relation with any knowledge within the limits that we have so far staked out; it can neither be confirmed nor disconfirmed by any of it; there is no road from the continent of rational knowledge to the island of intuition, while there is a road from the country of empirical knowledge to the country of formal knowledge, which thus show that they belong to the same continent. Thus it follows that, if our suggested compromise is accepted, then nonrational intuition and religious faith (to the extent to which they are not only a believing the truth of certain propositions, but are ineffable) cannot be called *knowledge*.

It should be favorable to the peaceful relations between the various spheres of life, if we do not designate two such heterogeneous spheres with the same name. It is only through this that contradiction and strife arise, which are not even possible as long as the complete heterogeneity is clearly seen and emphasized.

182. *Intuitive Metaphysics*

The decision of the main questions about metaphysics, namely, whether it is meaningful at all and has a right to exist and, if so, whether it is a science, apparently depends entirely on what is meant by "metaphysics". Nowadays, there is no unanimity whatever on this point. Some philosophers call metaphysics a such and such delineated area of (conceptual) science. In view of the fact that this word, through its historical past, contains for many a suggestion of the vague and speculative, it would be more appropriate not to call such areas of philosophy which are to be treated with strict scientific concepts "metaphysics". If what is in question is basic knowledge (in the sense of logical, experiential, constructional order), then the name "basic science" could be used. If we are concerned with the ultimate, most general knowledge, the name "cosmology" or a similar one could be employed.

Other philosophers use the name "metaphysics" for the result of a nonrational, purely intuitive process; this seems to be the more appropriate usage.

REFERENCES. In referring metaphysics to the area of the nonrational, we are in agreement with many metaphysicians. Cf., for example, Bergson ([Metaphysik] 5): "That science which wants to get by without symbols." This means metaphysics does not wish to grasp its object by proceeding via concepts, which are symbols, but immediately through intuition. Schlick [Metaphysik] gives an especially clear account of the difference between metaphysics and knowledge.

If the name "metaphysics" is used in this sense, then it follows immediately that metaphysics is not a science (in our sense). If someone wishes to contradict this, he should be quite clear whether he opposes our delineation of the term "metaphysics" or (as Bergson) our delineation of the term "science". We are not as much concerned with the former as we are with the latter; if it were found desirable to call "metaphysics" what we have called "basic science" or "cosmology", we should be perfectly agreeable and consequently would have to call metaphysics, too, a science; on the other hand, a deviation from our restriction of the meaning of the expressions "knowledge" and "science" to the field of the rational seems to us altogether inappropriate for the reasons given in § 181.

That intuitive metaphysics, too, uses words for its exposition should not lead to the opinion that it proceeds within the field of concepts and thus belongs to (rational) science. For, even though we may call conceptual only that which can be expressed through words or other signs, it does not follow that everything that employs words is conceptual. There are spheres of life other than conceptual knowledge in which words are used, for example, in the imposition of will from person to person, in art, in the area of myth, which stands between science and art (and to which intuitive metaphysics perhaps belongs), and in other areas. Words can be considered signs of concepts only if they are either defined or at least if they can be defined; more precisely, if they are placed within an experiential constructional system or at least if they can be so placed (cf. the quotation from Petzold in § 180).

183. *Rationalism?*

The indicated position, namely, that (rational) science not only can deal with any objects, but that it also never comes to a limit, never meets with a question that cannot in principle be answered, is occasionally called "rationalism"; however, this expression is not justified. If we take the word in the sense of the old epistemological and theoretical opposition between rationalism and empiricism, then this expression should obviously not be used to indicate our position. Since, according to construction theory, each statement of science is at bottom a statement about relations that hold between elementary experiences, it follows that each substantive (i.e., not purely formal) insight goes back to experience. Thus, the designation "empiricism" is more justified. (That it is not a raw empiricism needs hardly to be emphasized in view of the importance which construction theory attaches to the form components of cognition.)

However, the word "rationalism" is nowadays, for the most part, and perhaps also in this case, used in its modern sense, namely, in opposition to irrationalism. But even in this sense we would not wish to have it applied to construction theory. After all, the word is meant, not so much for those positions which, like ours, wish to give reason (i.e., to conceptualizing understanding) a leading role within the field of *knowledge,* but, rather, it is applied to those persuasions which wish to bestow such a position upon it with respect to *life* as a whole. But such a tendency is found neither in construction theory in general nor in the notion that conceptual knowledge is unlimited. The proud thesis that no question is in principle unsolvable for science agrees very well with the humble insight that, even after all questions have been answered, the problem which life poses for us has not yet been solved. The task of cognition is a definite, well-circumscribed, important task in life, and it can certainly be demanded that mankind should shape that aspect of life which can be shaped with the aid of knowledge by a determined application of this knowledge, that is, by using the methods of science. Even if modern movements frequently underestimate the importance of science for life, we do not wish to fall into the opposite error. Rather, we wish to admit clearly to ourselves, who are engaged in scientific work, that the mastery of life requires an effort of all our various powers; we should be wary of the shortsighted belief that the demands of life can all be met with the power of conceptual thinking alone.

To put it otherwise: for us there is no *"Ignorabimus"*; nevertheless, there are perhaps unsolvable riddles of life. This is not a contradiction. *Ignorabimus* would mean: there are questions to which it is in principle impossible to find answers. *However, the "riddles of life" are not questions, but are practical situations.* The "riddle of death" consists in the shock through the death of a fellow man or in the fear of one's own death. It has nothing to do with questions which can be asked about death, even if some men, deceiving themselves, occasionally believe that they have formulated this riddle by pronouncing such questions. In principle, these questions can be answered by biology (though presently only to a very small extent), but these answers are of no help to a grieved person, which shows that it is a self-deception to regard them as formulations of the riddle of death. Rather, the riddle consists in the task of "getting over" this life situation, of overcoming the shock, and perhaps even making it fruitful for one's later life. Our thesis that all questions can be answered has indeed a certain connection with this task of overcoming, but this connection is so remote that the thesis does not make any assertion as to whether or not it is in principle always possible to surmount such distress. We do not have to decide this here.

REFERENCES. Wittgenstein has clearly formulated the proud thesis of the omnipotence of rational science as well as the humble insight relative to its importance for practical life: "For an answer which cannot be expressed, the question too cannot be expressed. *The riddle* does not exist. If a question can be put at all, then it *can* also be answered. . . . We feel that even if *all possible* scientific questions are answered, the problems of life still have not been touched at all. Of course there is then no question left, and just this is the answer." [Abhandlg.] 262. Unfortunately, this treatise has remained almost unknown. In part, it is difficult to understand and has not been sufficiently clarified, but it is very valuable, both in its logical derivations and in the ethical attitude which it shows. Wittgenstein summarizes the import of his treatise in the following words: "What can be said at all, can be said clearly, and whereof one cannot speak, thereof one must be silent." (p. 185).

Summary

V. CLARIFICATION OF SOME PHILOSOPHICAL PROBLEMS ON THE BASIS OF CONSTRUCTION THEORY (157–183)

We wish to discuss some examples in order to show that the ordering of concepts which construction theory achieves allows a more precise formulation of the problems (157).

A. *Some Problems of Essence (158–165)*

The investigation of the traditional distinction between *individual* and *general concepts* shows that these are not two essentially different kinds of entity. The so-called individual concepts, too, must be constructed as classes or relations. The only difference is that, to an individual concept, there corresponds a connected area in the space-time order, while for the general concepts we have such a correspondence only with respect to another (qualitative) order. From a logical point of view, the former are not simpler or more uniform than the latter (158).

Identity: two signs are "synonymous", mean "the same", if they are everywhere interchangeable. In common usage we frequently call objects "the same" even if they are not strictly identical. This improper identification is based upon a strict identity, not indeed of the objects in question, but of objects on a higher level (e.g., classes to which these objects belong); among the objects themselves there holds another relation, frequently that of gen-identity or of equivalence relative to some order or to the intersubjective correlation (159).

What is the essence of the physical, the psychological, the cultural? The objects of these types are quasi objects, linguistic aids for the representation of certain relations among experiences (160). This is their constructional essence. The indication of the scientific or constructional essence of an object can only consist in the indication of criteria for the truth of those sentences in which the name of the object occurs. This can be done, for example, by giving constructional chain definitions. Questions that go beyond this cannot be answered by using constructable concepts; they are concerned with the metaphysical essence of objects and lie outside of the framework of science (161).

The problem of mind-body dualism: are there two essentially different object types? Answer: the physical and the psychological are two different forms of order (analogy: stellar constellations) of the basic elements. There is only one kind of basic element, yet there are not only two, but very many, different ways of ordering them. This is no peculiarity of the empirical world, but holds analytically of any ordered domain (162).

The *self* is the class (not the collection) of the experiences (or autopsychological states). The self does not belong to the expression of the basic experience, but is constructed only on a very high level (163).

The *intention relation* between a psychological event and that which is meant by it is not a unique, irreducible relation; rather, it is a special case of the relation between an experience and a real-typical experiential structure which includes that experience (164).

In science, *causality* means nothing but functional dependency. Strictly speaking, it does not exist in the perceptual world, but only in the world of physics. The dependency holds between a state and a certain limiting value in the assignments of state magnitudes; hence, it does not hold between events. Thus, the concepts of "cause" and "effect", which have already lost their anthropomorphic sense of "bringing about" in the perceptual world, have no meaning at all in the world of physics (165).

B. *The Psychophysical Problem (166–169)*

The psychophysical problem of traditional philosophy asks for an explanation of *psychophysical parallelism* (166). This parallelism cannot, originally, relate to the heteropsychological (167), but can be empirically observed only as a parallelism between the sequence of autopsychological events and observed processes of my own brain. However, during this observation, the brain processes occur as the contents of my own experiences. Hence we are here not concerned with a parallelism of essentially different entities, but between sequences of constituents of experiences; such parallelisms occur frequently in other contexts too (168). In science we can only ascertain that there is such a parallelism. The interpretation of this fact belongs to metaphysics. In science we cannot even pose a question that expresses this metaphysical problem (169).

C. *The Constructional or Empirical Problem of Reality (170–174)*

We can use empirical criteria in order to differentiate between a "real" thing and a "nonreal" one, e.g., a merely imagined, invented or erroneously supposed entity: the "empirical" or "constructional" concept of reality. This concept of reality retains its validity even in a system with autopsychological basis (170). There is a distinction between real and nonreal not only in the physical, but also in the psychological and cultural domains. The indicators of reality are the same in the various object domains, namely, participation in a comprehensive, law-governed system, and a position in the time order (171). Objects which are either real or nonreal we call real-typical; for all other objects, there is no sense to the question whether they are real or not (172). The boundary line of the real-typical as drawn by ordinary linguistic usage has an inconsistent, arbitrary, and wavering course (173, 174).

D. *The Metaphysical Problem of Reality (175–178)*

There is still another concept of reality, usually formulated as "independence from the cognizing consciousness". It is this concept which is meant by both realism and idealism when they affirm or deny the reality of the outside world (175). We call this concept of reality "metaphysical" since it cannot be defined through scientific, i.e., constructable concepts; the same holds for the concept of the "thing-in-itself" (176). Any question which is answered by construction theory as well as realism, idealism, and phenomenalism is answered uniformly (177). The divergences between the three schools occur only where they leave the domain of the constructable, that is, the domain of science; however, then we are no longer concerned with epistemology, but with metaphysics. The practical procedure of the empirical sciences is "realistic" only in language, not in the metaphysical sense. For the empirical sciences, realism in the proper sense is meaningless; it is to be replaced by an "objectivism" of lawlike regularities (178).

E. *Aims and Limits of Science (179–183)*

The aim of science consists in finding and ordering the true propositions. This is done, first, through the formulation of the constructional system— that is, the introduction of concepts—and, second, through the ascertainment of the empirical connections between these concepts (179). In science, there is *no question that is unanswerable* in principle. For, each question consists in putting forth a statement whose truth or falsity is to be ascertained. However, each statement can, in principle, be translated into a statement about the basic relation; and each such statement can in principle be verified through confrontation with the given (180). Faith and intuition in the nonrational (e.g., religious) sense have nothing to do with the distinction between true and false; they do not belong to the domain of theory and cognition (181). If, like many metaphysicians themselves, we mean by metaphysics not the doctrine of the logically most basic, or the highest, scientific insights (i.e., "basic science" or "cosmology"), but a domain of pure intuition, then metaphysics has nothing to do with science and the rational domain; between the two there can be neither confirmation nor contradiction (182). The indicated position is not that of rationalism, since it demands rationality only for science. For practical life the existence and importance of the remaining, nonrational spheres is acknowledged (183).

Pseudoproblems in Philosophy

THE HETEROPSYCHOLOGICAL AND THE REALISM CONTROVERSY

I. THE AIM OF EPISTEMOLOGY

A

THE MEANING OF
EPISTEMOLOGICAL ANALYSIS

1. The Problem

The aim of epistemology is the formulation of a method for the justification of cognitions.[1] Epistemology must specify how an ostensible piece of knowledge can be justified, that is, how it can be shown that it is authentic knowledge. Such a justification, however, is not absolute but relative; the content of a certain cognition is justified by relating it to the contents of other cognitions which are presumed to be valid. Hence, one content is "reduced" to another, or "epistemologically analyzed". Logic, too, teaches the derivation of the validity of certain propositions [2] (expressed by sentences) from the presupposed validity of others ("inference"). The difference is that logical derivation takes place through reorganization of concepts; in the derived proposition no new concept may occur. On the other hand, it is characteristic of an epistemological derivation that the cognition to be analyzed, that is, the sentence that is to be justified and derived, contains a concept which does not occur in the premises.[3]

In order to analyze the contents of cognitions, epistemology must in-

---

[1] Erkenntnisse
[2] Setzungen
[3] Voraussetzungen

vestigate the objects (concepts) of (empirical) science in its various subdivisions (natural and cultural sciences). It must ascertain to which other objects the cognition of any given object may be "reduced". Hence, "an analysis" of objects is undertaken where the "higher" objects are reduced to "lower" ones. Those objects which can no longer be reduced are called "(epistemologically) fundamental" objects.

But what is actually meant by this epistemological analysis? What does it mean to say that object a "is (epistemologically) reducible" to object b? Only when this question is answered is the task of epistemology clearly formulated and only then is it clear what is to be meant by "fundamental" objects.

It has frequently been emphasized that the epistemological quest for the justification or reduction of a cognition to others must be differentiated from the psychological question concerning the origin of a cognition. But this is only a negative determination. For those who are not satisfied with the expressions "given", "reducible", "fundamental", or those who want to eschew using these concepts in their philosophy, the aim of epistemology has not been formulated at all. In the following investigations we propose to give a precise formulation of this aim. It will turn out that we can formulate the purpose of epistemological analysis without having to use these expressions of traditional philosophy. We only have to go back to the concept of implication (as it is expressed in if—then—sentences). This is a fundamental concept of logic which cannot be criticized or even avoided by anyone: it is indispensable in any philosophy, nay, in any branch of science.

In the course of the development of a science it frequently happens that answers, indeed correct answers, to a question are found even before that question has been given a precise conceptual formulation. What happens in these cases is that a certain trend of concept formation is intuitively projected and maintained, but there is no recognition what the thus formed concepts actually mean. When finally a conceptual formulation for the intuitively posed question is found, the previously found answers are released from their state of suspension and are placed on the solid foundation of the scientific system.

> EXAMPLE. The inventors of the infinitesimal calculus (Leibniz and Newton) were able to answer questions concerning the derivative (the differential quotient) of common mathematical functions; for example, the derivative of the function x^3 is the function $3x^2$. However, they could not say to what question this expression is an answer, that is, what actually is to be understood by the "derivative" of a function. They could

indicate various applications (for example the direction of the tangent) but they could not give a precise definition of the concept "derivative". To be sure, they believed that they knew what they meant by this expression, but they only had an intuitive notion, not a conceptual definition. They thought that they had a definition which allowed them to have a conceptual understanding of "derivative". However, their formulations for this definition used such expressions as "infinitesimally small magnitude" and quotions of such, which, upon more precise analysis, turn out to be pseudo concepts (empty words). It took more than a century before an unobjectionable definition of the general concept of a limit and thus of a derivative was given. Only then all those mathematical results which had long since been used in mathematics were given their actual meaning.

In epistemological analysis the situation is very similar. Science has long been in the possession of a great number of results of epistemological analysis. She had the answers without being in the possession of the questions, that is to say, without being able to indicate the precise sense of these answers. Such already known answers are, for example, that the cognition of processes of consciousness of another person is "based upon" the perception of his motions and linguistic utterances; that the cognition of a physical object "goes back" to perceptions; that a given experience "consists of" the visual perception of a bell, the auditory perception of a sound and an emotional component; [4] the perception of a given sound "consists of" individual perceptions of such and such tones. One may be inclined to call the last two examples pieces of "psychological" analysis rather than epistemological analysis. It is indeed the case that analyses of this kind are a fundamental part of psychological procedure. For it is only through this procedure of concept formation that psychology determines its objects. However, we shall see later that this procedure is nothing but the epistemological analysis with whose meaning we are here concerned.

In science (and to some extent even in daily life) we are in the possession of the answers which are indicated in the above examples; but the actual *meaning* of these answers we do not know. It would be an error to interpret the "consists of . . ." as "is synthesized of . . . in the course of experience". Psychology, in this case especially Gestalt psychology, tells us that the total perception is experienced *before* the individual sensation out of which it is "synthesized". We become conscious of the latter only through a subsequent process of abstraction. Similar considerations hold for the other examples.

---

[4] Gefühlskomplex

Now it becomes apparent how important it is to give a clear formulation of the meaning of epistemological analysis. Initially, such a formulation will not produce an increase in knowledge, but only increased purity of knowledge: the results of already performed epistemological analyses can be clearly formulated. Moreover it will be seen that epistemological analysis, after a more precise definition of the concepts has been given, will become applicable in cases where the former, predominantly intuitive procedure did not succeed, though the failure of the intuitive procedure was not inevitable in these cases; perhaps there was only a lack of courage to see it through. If we use epistemological analysis in a conscious and clearly conceptualized way, we shall be able to reduce objects (contents of cognitions, concepts) to one another to a sufficiently large extent so that the possibility of a general reductional system ("constructional system") can be demonstrated: it is in principle possible to place all concepts of all the areas of science into this system, that is to say, they are reducible to one another and ultimately to a few basic concepts. (The proof for this thesis of a constructional system can only be indicated in this paper, § 6).

2. *Logical Analysis*

a. SUFFICIENT AND DISPENSABLE CONSTITUENT

Epistemological analysis is an analysis of the contents of experiences, more precisely the analysis of the theoretical content of experiences. We are concerned only with the theoretical content of the experience, that is, with the possible knowledge that is contained in the experience. (The analysis is not an actual division: the experience remains what it is: the analysis takes place in the course of a subsequent consideration of the already past and hence no longer alterable experience; hence it is only an "abstractive", conceptual analysis.)

In the following we shall try to describe briefly a method which will lead to results that are generally acknowledged to belong to epistemology (like the examples mentioned earlier). This method of analysis is that which is meant (or which ought to be meant), if one speaks of "epistemological analysis".

The first step in our procedure consists in the "logical division" of the theoretical content of an experience into two parts: one of these we call the "(epistemologically) *sufficient constituent*", the remainder we call (relative to that first constituent) the "(epistemologically) *dispens-*

able constituent". Let us consider an example. I touch a certain key which I have often seen; I recognize it by touching it, even though I do not see it at the moment. In touching the key I experience not only the representation [5] of the tactile shape of the key, but simultaneously (and not just subsequently by way of inference) the representation of its visual shape, even if I keep my eyes closed. I can make an "epistemic evaluation" of any experience I have had by stating to what extent this experience has added to my (theoretical) knowledge. This addition consists not only of the theoretical content of the experience itself, but also of whatever I can infer from this content with the aid of my earlier knowledge. The epistemic evaluation of the indicated experience with the key has the following result: "this thing has such and such a shape; this thing is the key to my house; this thing has the color of steel." The experience contains united in it the representation of a tactile shape and that of a visual shape, but when the experience is evaluated, I can actually discount the second constituent, namely the visual shape, since the first constituent already suffices, together with my previous knowledge, to let me conclude that it is a key, indeed the familiar key to my house. Hence I am in a position to infer its visual shape, its color, etc. Hence in the epistemic evaluation I do not have to draw this information out of the experience itself. For this reason we want to call the tactile shape a "sufficient constituent" of the experience, the visual shape (relative to the tactile shape) a "dispensable constituent". However, this constituent is dispensable only if we are concerned with adding to our knowledge, and it is only in this sense that the other constituent is sufficient. On the other hand, so far as the experience itself is concerned, the former constituent is not dispensable and the latter is not sufficient; for if the dispensable constituent were removed from the experience it would be an entirely different experience.

A simple consideration shows that this logical analysis is frequently ambiguous, that is, that one and the same experience can be analyzed in different ways. In our example one could very well forego the epistemic evaluation of the tactile shape. The epistemic evaluation of the visual shape would already suffice to draw out of the experience all that can be known. In this case it is particularly clear that the "dispensable" constituent can be given this name only in an epistemological sense: since the key has only been touched and not seen, we cannot, in this experience, dispense with the tactile shape without at the same time removing the experience itself; on the other hand we could dispense with the

---

[5] Vorstellung

epistemic *evaluation* of this constituent without thereby diminishing the extent of our knowledge.

b. THE CRITERION: RATIONAL RECONSTRUCTION

We must now define a method which allows us to decide in any given case whether a certain constituent of an experience is sufficient, that is, whether the rest of the experience is dispensable relative to it. For the facts are not always as simple as in the indicated example where we could easily see that a certain constituent is dispensable.

To say that a constituent *b* of an experience (e.g., the visual appearance of the key) is dispensable relative to constituent *a* (the tactile shape) is to say that *b* does not give me any information that is not already contained in *a* together with my prior knowledge. It is not necessary in such a case that I should be expressly conscious of the theoretical content of *b*; it is merely required that *a*, together with my prior knowledge, should logically contain *b*. If the theoretical content of *b* is logically contained in *a* and my prior knowledge, then it must be possible to derive it from them through inference. In our example, this derivation would look something like this: from the tactile shape (constituent *a*) together with my prior tactile perceptions I can infer that the touched object is the key to my house. And I know from prior visual perceptions that this key has a certain visual appearance: it has such and such a shape and color, both relatively permanent. From this I infer that the touched object has this visual appearance (constituent *b*). This inference of constituent *b* from constituent *a* together with my prior knowledge we call "rational reconstruction" of *b*.

It is clear that our conception of "rational reconstruction" does not claim that in the actual experience the constituent *b* is inferred from *a*. There can be no question that both constituents are simply experienced as an intuitive unit: there is not a trace of inference in such an experience. We also prefer not to use the locution "unconscious inference". But even if in the experience itself generally no rational construction is present we can still afterwards carry out a rational reconstruction—an inferential procedure whose purpose it is to investigate whether or not there is a certain logical dependency between certain constituents of the experience.

In order to gain a clearer understanding of the meaning of the rational reconstruction of a dispensable constituent of an experience, let us consider the following fiction: we imagine that the experience has, to begin with, only one constituent, namely the sufficient constituent (in the example the tactile shape of the key), and we then try to add to it through rational construction the second constituent (in the example the visual shape). If we succeed, then the latter is shown to be a dispensable constituent. It must be noted, however, that this fictional mode of expression is by no means necessary: the more precise and proper mode of expression is that which has been given earlier; using only constituent a (and my prior knowledge) rational reconstruction will arrive at the same knowledge that could have been gained by evaluating constituent b.

c. THE OVERDETERMINATENESS OF THE EXPERIENTIAL CONTENT

The logical character of the theoretical content of our experiences, due to which certain constituents are dispensable relative to others, is to be called their *overdeterminateness*. In mathematics we frequently call a problem overdetermined if more data are given than are necessary to solve the problem, so that at least one of the data is dispensable relative to the rest and can be derived constructively (either by calculation or drawing) from them. In this sense our experience is (epistemologically) overdetermined. We experience more than is necessary in order to gain the knowledge that can be obtained. This is to say, we can leave certain constituents of experiences unevaluated (fictional expression: these constituents could disappear from our experience) and our knowledge would not be diminished.

Overdeterminateness of the theoretical content of our experience leads to a problem which must here be briefly indicated. It is well known that an overdetermined problem does not permit a solution for an arbitrarily chosen set of data. It is solvable only if the data are not arbitrary but if a certain special condition is fulfilled which could be called the consistency of the data. Is it the case that the experiential contents fulfill such special conditions or is the aim of cognition unattainable? Neither of these is the case. There is a certain difference between the aim of cognition and a mathematical problem. The experiential contents do not fulfill a special condition of consistency (the fact that they fulfill the general condition of being orderable in some way or another has nothing to do with this point); if we think of a certain experience as being of a nature somewhat different than it in fact is, while the rest of them remains unchanged, then with respect to the changed course of experience the aim of cognition is by no means unobtainable; under certain circumstances it may become somewhat more difficult, since we would have to give a different form to certain laws of nature. By contrast, an overdetermined but solvable mathematical problem does not remain solvable if one of the given data is allowed to change arbitrarily. This difference between the aim of cognition and the mathematical problem rests upon the essential difference that in the case of the mathematical problem the laws according to which the solution is to be derived from the data is already determined before the problem is posed; on the other hand, in the case of the aim of cognition these laws (namely the regularities which hold among real objects, that is to say, the natural laws in the widest sense) follow from the data, the material of cognition, itself. This is the reason why, if the data are varied at a given point, the derived laws themselves suffer corresponding changes in such a way that there is no inconsistency between the altered material and the changed laws.

> EXAMPLE. Let a sequence of experiences have the following content: a brown rod, apparently made of copper, is balanced on a pivot; then a flame is held to one end of the rod, and that end tilts downward; this result is to be interpreted as an elongation of the rod. Now think of this content as being changed in this way: the rod tilts upward on the side where the flame is, while all the other constituents and the rest of my experiences remain the same. I am then forced to discredit something that I would otherwise have believed. However I have considerable freedom of choice. For example, I can assume that the staff is not made of copper; or that copper does not expand when it is heated; or that the yellow object is not a flame (combustion process); or that the flame does not heat; or that an upward tilt of the rod does not indicate shortening; or that I have hallucinated: in this latter case I have again several choices for declaring as invalid the criteria which made me believe in the first place that I had a conscious perception. I would then make that assumption which in the total system of natural laws would produce the smallest amount of change.

Since all natural laws have been derived inductively, that is to say through a comparison of experiential contents, a variation of the material at a given point can very well change the content of the laws and thus the content of reality as it is known, but cannot prevent the recognition of laws in general and hence of reality. Strictly speaking, contents of experiences cannot contradict one another; they are independent of one another in the strict logical sense. Strictly speaking there is no overdeterminateness of the total content of the experiences: they are overdetermined only in relation to the empirical-inductive regularities.

3. *Epistemological Analysis*

a. NUCLEUS AND SECONDARY PART

We make a distinction between the logical analysis of the cognitive content of an experience (into a sufficient constituent and a constituent that is dispensable relative to it) and the epistemological analysis into "nucleus" and "secondary part". The latter is a special case of the former: if the constituents a and b are to be called "(epistemological) nucleus" and "secondary part", then, to begin with, b must be a dispensable constituent relative to a. In addition—and this is why we here speak of "epistemological" division—b must epistemically "reduce" to a, that is, the cognition of b must "rest upon" the cognition of a, a must be "epistemically primary". The given expressions should give a rough idea of what is meant here; a more precise formulation of the concept of epistemological analysis can be given only through the indication of certain criteria. Before we consider these, let us go back to the earlier example. Let us designate as S the experience in which the key was merely felt but not seen, but in which the visual shape of the key is nevertheless contained as a representation; its constituents are called a (tactile shape) and b (visual appearance). If the experience is of such a nature that the key is felt and at the same time seen, then we call it S' and the new constituents a' and b'. From the preceding considerations it can easily be seen (and can be demonstrated through the method of rational reconstruction) that b is a dispensable constituent relative to a and conversely a relative to b: likewise b' is dispensable relative to a' and a' relative to b'. Hence there is a logical dependency in both cases which holds in both directions. However, things are different with the relation of epistemic dependency: it holds only in the first case, and there only in one direction. In experience S our knowledge of b (visual appearance) rests upon that of a (tactile shape) but not vice versa, while in experience S' both constituents are epistemically independent: knowledge of neither of them rests upon knowledge of the other.

b. FIRST CRITERION: JUSTIFICATION

In order to find the criterion for epistemological analysis, all we have to do is to make it clear why, in the simple example given above, we have decided that the epistemological relation between nucleus and the secondary part in experience S obtains between a and b but not between b and a, and why this relation does not hold at all between the constituents of experience S'. We asked ourselves "on what does our knowledge of *b* rest?", more precisely, "if I have had experience S, what reasons can I give for my (alleged) knowledge of the content of *b*; how can I justify it against doubts?". It is not necessary that these doubts should actually have been expressed by myself or others; it is sufficient to raise a "methodological doubt", the point of which is not a refusal to believe, but a quest for justification. The criterion for the epistemological relation between secondary part and nucleus lies in the possibility of justifying a cognition against which (real or methodological doubt) has been raised through another cognition whose validity has been admitted or hypothetically assumed.

In order to perform epistemological analysis in a concrete case, that is, in order to answer the question whether two given constituents of an experience, *a* and *b*, are nucleus and secondary part of that experience, we will, as a rule, turn to the special science which is concerned with the field in question. We will investigate whether, according to the methods customary in that field, an assertion which is based upon the content of *b* is considered demonstrated if for its justification we can refer to a cognition based on the content of *a*. In this way the epistemological decision is made dependent upon the procedure of a special science, that is to say, this procedure is presupposed as epistemologically unobjectionable; on the other hand, epistemology will gradually construct a system from which the procedures of the individual sciences will be critically surveyed. This is not a vicious circle, for this mode of approach corresponds to an essential feature of science, whose system does not arise in clearly determined steps from the given material; rather, initially the methodological principles are practically employed in the synthesis [6] of the material of cognition, and are only later on clearly recognized and made explicit; this makes it possible to standardize [7] the principles and to approach the material again with these standardized principles. In this way the interplay between the particular scientific and the epistemological investigation will lead to an integrated system of unified science.

By going back to the method of a special science in order to decide a given epistemological question, we do not introduce this special science as a presupposition for a valid system of knowledge (as in Kant's transcendental method). For we are not yet concerned with the question whether the (alleged) cognitions of the particular special science are to be considered correct or not, but with the question whether or not the

---

[6] Bearbeitung
[7] vereinheitlichen

epistemological dependency relation (nucleus–secondary part) holds between given objects of the field.

C. SECOND CRITERION: THE POSSIBILITY OF ERROR

That two constituents of an experience, *a* and *b*, stand in the relation of nucleus and secondary part becomes especially obvious when constituent *b* rests upon "an error"; that is to say, when it turns out later that the theoretical content of *b* is erroneous, that the state of affairs which is reflected in *b* does not actually hold. It is not necessary that we should actually be in error about the experience we wish to test: for epistemological analysis it will suffice if we know, on the basis of other experiences, that with experiences of this sort such an error can arise.

Let us again turn to our examples, namely the touching of the key with accompanying visual representation (S) and the simultaneous seeing and touching of the key (S'). Now consider the following case: I touch the key and think that I recognize it as my own; I believe it to be steel colored but it turns out afterward that the object that I have touched has the color of brass. Even if this case does not actually take place, I know on the basis of other experiences that it *can* take place in a case like S. This shows that the constituent *b* in S (visual shape) is a secondary part to *a* (tactile shape). On the other hand in an experience like S' such an error cannot occur: hence between *b'* and *a'* the relation secondary part–nucleus does not hold. For our problem it is of no concern what the experiential difference between S and S' actually consists in. One can assume either that in the phenomenal sphere itself there is a difference of a qualitative, experiential sort between an actual perception and a mere representation, or one may assume that it is possible, on the basis of other experiential contents (namely so far as they allow us to recognize the physical relation between the object and the sense organ in question), to decide whether or not an actual perception has taken place. For epistemological analysis it suffices that one can decide the question whether a given constituent is to be considered an actual perception or a mere representation; (i.e., the question whether an experience of type S or an experience of type S' is present).

B

APPLICATION: KNOWLEDGE OF THE HETEROPSYCHOLOGICAL

4. *Logical Analysis of the Cognition of Heteropsychological Occurrences*

The indicated relations, namely the logical relation between sufficient and dispensable constituent, and the epistemological relation between nucleus and secondary part are—especially in the case of our example—very simple and might appear trivial. However, these concepts can also be applied to cases with which conflicting philosophical theses and antitheses are connected, for example, to the problem of the cognition of the heteropsychological. It is a more and more widely accepted fact that the autopsychological and the heteropsychological have an entirely different epistemological character; at the present time this fact can be denied only if one holds to certain metaphysical persuasions. The epistemological difference between the heteropsychological and the autopsychological will become particularly clear through the investigation of the epistemological relationship between the heteropsychological and the physical.

The subsequent considerations are to demonstrate the following thesis: *the epistemological nucleus of every concrete cognition of heteropsychological occurrences consists of a perception of physical phenomena, or, to put it otherwise, the heteropsychological occurs only as an (epistemologically) secondary part of the physical.* For the purpose of this demonstration we will first undertake a logical, and then an epistemological, analysis.

Any knowledge I might have of a concrete heteropsychological fact, that is, of certain conscious (or unconscious) occurrences of another subject A, I can have acquired in different ways. Heteropsychological occurrences are discovered if A reports processes of his consciousness to me (in this case let my experience be called E_1); secondly, such facts are discovered without any report if I observe expressive motions (facial expressions, gestures), or acts of A (E_2); occasionally I can surmise the conscious processes of A if I know his character and know, in addition, that he is now subject to certain external conditions (E_3). There is no other way to gain knowledge of the heteropsychological. (We will not concern ourselves here with telepathy since at least in science it is not used as a means of gathering information about the heteropsychological.)

In each of the cases, E_1, E_2, E_3, the cognition of the heteropsychological is connected with the perception of physical facts. To begin with let us carry out a logical analysis and let us show that in all cases the perceptions of the physical occurrences (constituents a_1, a_2, a_3, respectively) are sufficient constituents, i.e., that the representations of heteropsychological occurrences (constituents b_1, b_2, b_3, respectively) occur only as dispensable constituents (in the sense of our earlier definitions).

On the basis of the preceeding considerations we ascertain that the relation "sufficient–dispensable constituent" holds between a and b by showing that a rational reconstruction of b on the basis of a and prior knowledge is possible. In case E_1 the rational reconstruction of b_1 is possible in the following way: after having understood the report of A, we isolate from this perception, for the purpose of epistemic evaluation, only the physical sign (a_1), i.e., for example, the hearing of the spoken words (as sounds) or the seeing of the written words (as marks), but not the understanding of these signs (b_1), which is also contained in the experience; from this material a_1 we then infer the theoretical content of b_1, utilizing our prior knowledge. This reconstruction presupposes, of course, that the words which occur are already known or that their meaning can be surmised. If this presupposition is not fulfilled, then no experience of kind E_1 is present; the constituent b_1 does not occur; if I get a letter in Chinese, I see nothing but black lines without finding out anything about heteropsychological occurrences. However, if the presupposition is fulfilled (i.e., if I know the word meanings), then I can infer from the perceived words (either the heard noises, or the seen figures) the meaning of the statement: and this is the content of b_1, namely the heteropsychological occurrence which is cognized in E_1.

In E_2 (perceptions of acts and expressive motions of A) the case is quite similar. (This rests upon the fact that E_1 is actually a special case of E_2.) If, for example, I see the beaming face of A (a_2) then the representation of the joy of A (b_2) is simultaneously contained in my experience without my having to infer it. However, in order to know that A is in a joyful mood, I do not have to utilize constituent b_2, since I can infer it from a_2 on the basis of prior experience concerning the meaning of facial expressions.

OBJECTION. ("baby—objection"). It is sometimes assumed that a small infant can react appropriately to the joyous or sad countenance of his mother even before he has had any experience concerning the meaning of these facial expressions. Child psychology has made no final decision concerning this assumption, and we do not have to decide its correctness. Our epistemological result would not be invalidated even if an adult, who could give a linguistic account of his experience, were able to recognize a heteropsychological occurrence without appropriate prior experience. Assume, for example, that such a person had an experience consisting of a visual perception of the knit brow of A together with fear of an outbreak of rage on the part of A. The epistemic evaluation should not be of the following sort: "A has a knit brow; A is in a rage" (or in physical language: "in a moment A will perceptively react in such and such a way"), because the second sentence cannot be considered *knowledge* of the wrath of A if only a *representation* of this wrath of A occurs in the experience. We can speak of knowledge only if there are prior experiences on the basis of which the perceiver knows that if the forehead of a person has such and such an appearance, then rage can be expected.

This case does not differ from a case where purely physical occurrences are recognized. Let us assume that a person who has never experienced, or heard about, the heat of a flame, sees one for the first time in his life (without being able to perceive its heat), and that he nevertheless has the idea that it is hot. Even such a (nativist) assumption would not contradict our empiricist conception that knowledge of the heat of the flame can be gained only through experience. For, in order to possess the content of representation that the flame is hot not merely as representational content, but as knowledge, one must have had perceptions (at least one) from which it can be inferred through induction that a thing which looks such and such generally feels hot.

In the third case, E_3 (surmise from the known character and the perceived or otherwise known present external circumstances of A) has no fundamental importance. In this case the experiencing person himself will generally be aware of the fact that this is not an original cognition but an inference or an inference-like intuitive procedure, since knowledge of the character of A is presupposed. But even in this case the psychological occurrence in A (b_3) can be reconstructed from the known physical circumstances (a_3) if the knowledge of the character of A is taken into account. Occasionally, a psychological occurrence in A (b_3) is not immediately recognized at all in such an experience, but is literally inferred.

Let it be emphasized again that the indicated method of rational reconstruction does not imply that in the actual experience b (the heteropsychological) is inferred from a (the perceived physical occurrences); we only claim that a logical dependency holds between the theoretical content of the experiential constituents a and b; this can be proved by the fact that b can be derived afterward by inference from a and prior knowledge.

5. *Epistemological Analysis of the Cognition of Heteropsychological Occurrences*

The logical analysis of experiences in which heteropsychological occurrences are recognized has shown that in all possible cases (E_1, E_2, E_3) constituent a (the perception of the physical) is epistemologically sufficient, while constituent b (the idea of the recognized heteropsychological occurrence) is dispensable relative to the former. Let us now undertake the epistemological analysis of these experiences. We shall arrive at the conclusion that in each case constituent a is the epistemological nucleus, while b is the secondary part. In order to show this we must now demonstrate that b is epistemologically, as well as logically, dependent upon a. To establish this we have previously formulated two different criteria: the justification of b on the basis of a, and the possibility of the erroneous assumption of b when a is given. Let us apply these criteria in turn to the recognition of heteropsychological occurrences.

The first method consists in ascertaining that, in order to support or justify a cognition of type b, scientific procedure demands, and is satisfied with, a reference to a corresponding experiential constituent of kind a. It is presupposed that the procedures of the particular special science can be considered epistemologically unobjectionable. In our case we have to go back to certain very general cognitional procedures of psychology, and we may suppose that our presupposition is fulfilled since the various epistemological persuasions (even those which do not agree with our thesis) have made no objection against these cognitional procedures.

If a psychologist is to justify or defend against doubt the assertion that certain psychological events have taken place within subject A, then no one will be satisfied if he claims that he has simply experienced or clearly felt them. Rather, one demands of him that he should state in which of the three ways, E_1, E_2, E_3, his knowledge was obtained. Of course in case E_1 the psychologist does not have to be able to repeat word for word what he has heard or read, though this would be the safest justification and would in any case be regarded as sufficient. However, he must at least be able to report that he has heard or read some words which were of such a nature that from them the particular psychological events of A can be inferred. Similarly in case E_2: the most satisfactory justification consists in describing observed expressive motions or other acts of A, and it is indispensable for any justification that acts of A can be indicated from which the particular psychological events of A can be inferred. Finally, in case E_3 the justification is accomplished through a description of the perceived outward circumstances of A and his already known character. (The testing and justification of the [alleged] knowledge of the character of A does not belong here; it goes back to earlier cognitive experiences of the psychologist which in turn are of type E_1 or E_2.)

The second criterion that the relation nucleus–secondary part holds between a and b is satisfied if we have evidence that in experiences of this kind b may rest upon an error. We say that "b rests upon an error" if it turns out afterward that the epistemic content of a, but not that of b, was in fact present. This criterion is indeed fulfilled for experiences in which we recognize heteropsychological occurrences. We must realize that in an experience of type E_1 the report of A can be either a lie or an error. This is always possible, no matter how unlikely it may be in a particular case. This possibility would amount to the following: the epistemic content of constituent a_1 (our knowledge of the words which we have heard or read) corresponds with reality, but the content of b_1 (our alleged knowledge of the reported psychological event of A) does not. In an experience of type E_2, pretense is always a possibility (as in the case of intentional deception or in play-acting). The case is the same as before; the perceived facial expressions and actions are real, but the (allegedly) recognized psychological events are not. Case E_3 does not require any special discussion since here we were antecedently aware that the recognition of the psychological event of A was only surmised in spite of correctly perceived outward circumstances; that is to say we were antecedently aware of the possibility of error.

We have now demonstrated that in all cases where heteropsychological occurrences are recognized, the epistemological nucleus of the experience in which the recognition takes place contains nothing but perceptions of physical events.

6. Result. Survey of the Genealogy of Concepts

Our considerations have led to the result that any recognition of heteropsychological occurrences goes back to a recognition of a physical event. That is to say any recognition of heteropsychological occurrences has as its epistemological nucleus the perception of physical events. We can also express this fact in the following way: *heteropsychological objects are "epistemologically secondary" relative to physical objects*; the latter "primary" relative to the former. ("objects" is here meant in the widest sense: entities, events, states, properties, etc.)

At this time we cannot give a detailed discussion of the philosophical consequences of this result; but let us have a quick look at the corresponding relations between the other object types. Considerations similar to the above would show that cultural objects (in the sense of cultural entities and processes) are epistemologically secondary relative to the heteropsychological and physical. It would even be easier to demonstrate this since there are hardly any emotional prejudices that would obscure this fact. One would only have to show that the recognition of cultural events (for example, of a religion) is based upon the recognition of psychological processes ("manifestations") in the bearers of that cultural process and upon the recognition of its physical "documentations".

It can furthermore be shown that physical objects are epistemologically secondary relative to autopsychological objects, since the recognition of physical objects depends upon perception.

If the investigations whose results are here sketched are actually carried out (this is the task of construction theory), one is led to the following stratified epistemological system of the four most important object types (to be read from bottom to top):

4. Cultural objects
3. Heteropsychological objects
2. Physical objects
1. Autopsychological objects

The objects within each of these levels can in turn also be organized according to their epistemological reducibility. The final result is a system of scientific objects or concepts which, from a few "basic concepts", leads in step-by-step construction to all the remaining concepts. In this system each concept which can become the object of a scientific statement has a definite place. The organization of concepts in this system has a twofold significance. To begin with, each concept is epistemologically secondary relative to the concept which stands below it (as we have indicated for the four main levels). Furthermore, each concept can be defined, that is, a definite description of it can be given by referring only to concepts which stand below it. Hence the system is also a derivational system, that is, a "genealogy of concepts". We will not consider this any further at this point.

II. ELIMINATION OF PSEUDOPROBLEMS FROM THE THEORY OF KNOWLEDGE

A

THE MEANING CRITERION

7. *Factual Content as a Criterion for the Meaningfulness of Statements*

The meaning of a statement lies in the fact that it expresses a (conceivable, not necessarily existing) state of affairs. If an (ostensible) statement does not express a (conceivable) state of affairs, then it has no meaning; it is only apparently a statement. If the statement expresses a state of affairs then it is in any event meaningful; it is true if this state of affairs exists, false if it does not exist. One can know that a statement is meaningful even before one knows whether it is true or false.

If a statement contains only concepts which are already known and recognized, then its meaning results from them. On the other hand, if a statement contains a new concept or a concept whose legitimacy (scientific applicability) is in question, then its meaning must be indicated. For this purpose it is necessary and sufficient to point out what experiential conditions must be supposed to obtain in order for the statement to be called true (not "to be true"), and under what conditions it is to be called false. To begin with, this indication is sufficient; it is not necessarily to indicate, in addition, the "meaning of the concept".

> EXAMPLE. The concept "Jupiter" can be introduced by the following stipulation: the statement "Jupiter rumbles in place p at time t" is to be called true if in place p at time t a thunder can be experienced; otherwise

it is to be called false. Through this convention the *statement* has been given a meaning even though nothing has been said about the meaning of the concept "Jupiter"; for if I now tell somebody: "Jupiter is going to rumble here at 12 o'clock" he knows what he can expect. If he satisfies proper conditions (i.e., if he goes to the described place), he can have an experience which either confirms or refutes my statement.

However, the demanded indication is also *necessary*. For if it were considered permissible in science to make a statement whose correctness can be neither definitely confirmed nor refuted by experience, then the intrusion of obviously meaningless (pseudo) statements could not possibly be prevented.

EXAMPLE. Let us consider the following sequence of sign complexes which become progressively more pointless. If the first expression of this sequence is to be considered meaningful (even if false), then it would be difficult to introduce, without being arbitrary, a criterion which allows us to divide the sequence into meaningful and meaningless expressions.

1. "Jupiter sits in this cloud (but the appearance of the cloud does not indicate his presence, nor is there any other perceptual method through which his presence can be recognized.)"; 2. "This rock is sad"; 3. "This triangle is virtuous"; 4. "Berlin horse blue"; 5. "And or of which"; 6. "bu ba bi"; 7. "—) (*——*". It will be admitted that (6) is just as meaningless as (7). For even though (6) consists of signs (namely letters) which otherwise occur in meaningful sentences, the way in which they are put together makes the entire expression meaningless. The relation between (4) and (6) is not fundamentally different; (4) is just as meaningless as (6) even though it is put together out of larger sign complexes which otherwise occur in meaningful sentences. So much is generally admitted. Now we must become clear that (3) and also (2) are just as meaningless as (4); (2) and (3) consists of words which (in contrast to (4)) are conjoined as their grammatical characters require but not as their meaning does. It might seem at first sight that there is an essential difference between (3) and (4), but such an error would be caused by a shortcoming of our ordinary language which allows the construction of grammatically unobjectionable but meaningless sentences. Consequently it can easily happen that a pseudo sentence is mistaken for a meaningful one. In some cases this has been very detrimental for philosophy; we shall see this later when we consider the theses of realism and idealism. (The logistical language does not have this shortcoming. We can decide for any given sentence stated in this language, including extralogical sentences, whether or not it is meaningful, even if only the kind (not also the meaning) of the occurring signs is

known. As a consequence, the logistical language has great importance for the testing of philosophical statements, but this feature is very little known and utilized.)

In order to give a more precise formulation to our thesis, let us first introduce some definitions. If a statement p expresses the content of an experience E, and if the statement q is either the same as p or can be derived from p and prior experiences, either through deductive or inductive arguments, then we say that q is "supported by" the experience E. A statement p is said to be "testable" if conditions can be indicated under which an experience E would occur which supports p or the contradictory of p. A statement p is said to have "factual content", if experiences which would support p or the contradictory of p are at least conceivable, and if their characteristics can be indicated. It follows from these definitions that if a statement is testable, then it has always factual content, but the converse does not generally hold. If it is impossible, not only for the moment, but in principle, to find an experience which will support a given statement then that statement does not have factual content.

EXAMPLES. The statement "in the next room is a three-legged table" is testable; for one can indicate under what circumstances (going there and looking) a perceptual experience of a certain kind would occur which would support the statement. Hence this statement has factual content. The statement "there is a certain red color whose sight causes terror" is not testable, for we do not know how to find an experience which would support this statement. Nevertheless, this statement has factual content, for we can think and describe the characteristics of an experience through which this statement would be supported. Such an experience would have to contain the visual perception of a red color and at the same time the feeling of terror about this color. The pseudo statements (1), (2), (3) of the preceding example do not have factual content.

If a statement is supported only through past experiences and can no longer be tested, then we do not place the same confidence in it as in a testable statement. In history, geography, anthropology, one frequently must be satisfied with statements of this kind; in physics it is generally required that a statement be testable. But if we neglect the degree of certainty of a statement and concentrate only on the question of its meaningfulness, then there is no difference between those statements that have been supported earlier and can no longer be tested, and those that can be tested at any given time; both kinds of statement are certainly meaningful, hence, either true or false. On the other hand there can be a difference of opinion about those statements which are neither testable nor have so far been supported. No decisive objection can be made if someone wants to be so strict as to ban all such statements from science. However it must be mentioned that the customary method of the empirical sciences, including physics, does not consider statements of this kind as meaningless, but admits them either as hypotheses, preliminary conjectures, or at least as statements that permit the formulation of certain problems. Hence we shall not adopt this strict rule and shall acknowledge statements of this kind as meaningful (but by no means as true); statements which have factual content are meaningful since it is at least conceivable that they will at one time or another be recognized as true or false. However, expressions that are not included among statements with factual content must under no circumstances be considered meaningful. A (pseudo) statement which cannot in principle be supported by an experience, and which therefore does not have any factual content would not express any conceivable state of affairs and therefore would not be a statement, but only a conglomeration of meaningless marks or noises.

All empirical sciences (natural sciences, psychology, cultural sciences) acknowledge and carry out in practice the requirement that every statement must have factual content. It makes no difference whether we are concerned with mineralogy, biology, or the science of religion: each statement which is to be considered meaningful in any one of these fields (i.e., which is either considered true or false or which is posed as a question) either goes directly back to experience, that is, the content of experiences, or it is at least indirectly connected with experience in such a way that it can be indicated which possible experience would confirm or refute it; that is to say, it is itself supported by experiences, or it is testable, or it has at least factual content. Only in the fields of philosophy (and theology) ostensible statements occur which do not have factual content; as we shall see later, the theses of realism and idealism are examples. We have not taken the strict viewpoint which requires of each statement that it should be supported or testable; rather, we consider statements meaningful even if they merely have factual content, but are neither supported nor testable. Hence we are using as liberal a criterion of meaningfulness as the most liberal-minded physicist or historian would use within his own science; therefore our refutation of the theses of realism and idealism will become all the more compelling.

8. *Theoretical Content of a Statement and Accompanying Representations*

Generally speaking, if we utter a statement or merely think one, our train of ideas [8] goes beyond the bare content of this statement. For example, if I say "that bench is small", my mental representation may depict the bench as being green, while the statement does not mention this fact. It is well known that in deductions from given premises errors frequently arise because in addition to the facts which form the content of the premises, other facts, which are mentally associated with them, are unawares used in the deduction.

Let us now distinguish two types of representations (or complexes or sequences of representations; it is not necessary to distinguish these). We call a representation "factual" if its content is meant to be a fact, that is, something which either takes place or does not take place, so that one can say either yes or no to the content of such a representation; all other representations are called "object representations." For example, if I have a representation of a certain person in a certain environment, and if I believe that this person is now in this environment, then the representation is factual; it is either true or false. On the other hand if I merely think of that person in that environment but hold no belief concerning place or time, then I have an object representation. However, a simple representation of a person without any determination of place or time can be factual if a certain property is claimed to be present, for example, that this person has hair of such and such a color. Hence it depends essentially upon a person's intention whether a representation is a factual or a mere object representation; in the first case the experience contains an act of judgment which either affirms or denies that the particular fact exists. From the indicated difference between the two types of representations the following distinction, which is important for our investigation, results: a factual representation can form the content of a statement, while an object representation cannot. The linguistic expression for the content of an object expression is a noun (which may be accompanied by an adjective, apposition, etc.). (In the terminology of Meinong's theory of objects: the content of an object representation is an "object", a content of a factual representation is an "objective".)

EXAMPLES. 1. Expression for object representations: "my son", "a person who looks such and such". 2. Expression for factual repre-

---
[8] Vorstellungsablauf

sentations: "my son looks so and so", "there exists a person who looks such and such".

We must divide the representations which one experiences as one utters or thinks a statement into stated and accompanying representations. Among the accompanying representations there may in turn occur factual representations as well as mere object representations. In the case of the statement "that bench is small" the representation of the smallness of the bench is the stated representation. The representation of the greenness of the bench is an accompanying representation; since it is a factual representation one could add it to the content of the statement by making the additional statement "that bench is green". Assume now that the utterance of the statement "that bench is small" causes in me the representation of a certain musical tone and perhaps also that of a happy mood. These representations are then mere object representations; they do not belong to the facts about the bench; hence they cannot be admitted into any statement about the bench: we cannot attribute the sound or the happy mood to the bench. If we nevertheless try (perhaps misled by a, in this case, pointless inclination to judge), then we obtain pseudo statements, meaningless collections of signs. The accompanying object representations, since they cannot become the content of statements, are beyond truth and falsity. While the theoretical content of a statement must be justified by reference to some criterion, for example the indicated criterion of factual content, the object representations which accompany a statement are not subject to any theoretical control; they are theoretically irrelevant but frequently of great practical importance. To imagine certain configurations of numbers, or the sounds of number words or point configurations when we speak or think of, e.g., the statement "2 plus 2 equals 4" facilitates greatly the learning and deductive manipulation of such statements. Diagrams in geometry play a similar role. The formalization of geometry which has been carried out during the last decade has shown that the graphic properties of the diagrams are a valuable practical aid for research or learning, but that they must not play any role in geometrical deduction.

Occasionally we do not want to leave the occurrence of accompanying object representations to chance but, because of their practical value, want to evoke them systematically in ourselves or others. This can be achieved by choosing appropriate names for the concepts or by choosing an appropriate linguistic form for the entire statement (in the case of an oral statement also through intonation, melody, accompanying gestures, etc.). After all, the choice of a name is independent of the theoretical content of a statement: it is purely conventional. This allows us to express the accompanying object representations, which are also independent of the theoretical content, in any way we deem appropriate.

EXAMPLES. Formalized geometry (cf. for example Hilbert, *Foundations of Geometry*) does not speak of spatial entities, but of indeterminate objects which are related in a certain way. However we do not customarily designate the basic objects of first, second, and third type with this neutral expression but with the words "point", "straight line", "surface", since we wish that the reader should connect representations of little black spots, of straight lines, and of thin flat slices with the statements about the basic objects. (This is done only to facilitate matters and has nothing to do with questions of theoretical validity.)

When an Indian calls his child "Black Buffalo", then whoever uses this name has the awe-inspiring or respect-evoking accompanying representation of that animal. Here an accompanying representation is expressed which cannot be expressed through a statement, since it does not reflect any fact. The Indian however thinks that, by giving this name, a certain (hoped for) fact is expressed; philosophers, as we shall see, have hoped to accomplish the same by giving suitable names to heteropsychological objects.

B

APPLICATION TO THE
REALISM CONTROVERSY

9. *The Theses of Realism and Idealism*

By the thesis of realism we shall understand the following two subtheses:
1. the perceived physical things which surround me are not only the
content of my perception, but, in addition, they exist in themselves
("reality of the external world"); 2. the bodies of other persons not only
exhibit perceivable reactions similar to those of my body, but, in addition,
these other persons have consciousness ("reality of the heteropsychological"). The thesis of idealism is identified with the corresponding
denials (the second of them however is maintained only by a certain
radical idealistic position, namely solipsism): 1. the external world is
not itself real, but only the perceptions or representations of it are ("nonreality of the external world"); 2. only my own processes of consciousness are real; the so-called conscious processes of others are merely
constructions or even fictions ("nonreality of the heteropsychological").

It is not our intention here to ask which of the two theses is correct.
(If we wanted to do this we would have to investigate the validity of the
subtheses separately.) Rather, we shall raise the more fundamental
question whether the indicated theses have any scientific meaning,
whether they have any content to which science can take either an
affirmative or a negative stand. This more fundamental question must

first be affirmatively answered before the question of the validity or invalidity of the theses can even be raised. According to our previous results, to ask whether they are meaningful is to ask: do these theses express a fact (no matter whether an existent or nonexistent one) or are they merely pseudo statements, made with the vain intention of expressing accompanying object representation in the form of statements, as if they were factual representations? We shall find that the latter is indeed the case, so that these theses have no content; they are not statements at all. Hence the question about the correctness of these theses cannot be raised. In the realism controversy, science can take neither an affirmative nor a negative position since the question has no meaning. We want to show this in the sequel.

10. *The Reality of the External World*

Two geographers, a realist and an idealist, who are sent out in order to find out if a mountain that is supposed to be somewhere in Africa is only legendary or if it really exists, will come to the same (positive or negative) result. In physics as well as geography there are certain criteria for the concept of reality in this sense—we want to call it "empirical reality"—which always lead to definite results no matter what the philosophical persuasion of the researcher. The two geographers will come to the same result not only about the existence of the mountain, but also about its other characteristics, namely position, shape, height, etc. In all empirical questions there is unanimity. Hence the choice of a philosophical viewpoint has no influence upon the content of natural science; (this does not mean that it could not have some practical influence upon the activity of the scientist).

There is disagreement between the two scientists only when they no longer speak as geographers but as philosophers, when they give a philosophical interpretation of the empirical results about which they agree. Then the realist says: "this mountain, which the two of us have found, not only has the ascertained geographical properties, but is, in addition, also real," and the "phenomenalist" (subvariety of realism) says: "the mountain which we have found is supported by something real which we cannot itself know." The idealist on the other hand says: "on the contrary, the mountain itself is not real, only our (or in the case of the "solipsist" variety of idealism: "only my") perceptions and conscious processes are real." This divergence between the two scientists does not occur in the empirical domain, for there is complete unanimity so far as the empirical facts are concerned. These two theses which are here in opposition to one another go beyond experience and have no factual content. Neither of the disputants suggests that his thesis should be tested through some joint decisive experiment, nor does any one of them give an indication of the design of an experiment through which his thesis could be supported.

Our example can easily be generalized. What is true for the mountain is true for the external world in general. Since we consider only factual content as the criterion for the meaningfulness of statements, *neither the thesis of realism that the external world is real, nor that of idealism that the external world is not real can be considered scientifically meaningful.* This does not mean that the two theses are false; rather, they have no meaning at all so that the question of their truth and falsity cannot even be posed.

> In the case of the second part of the realist thesis, which concerns the heteropsychological, we shall see that the formulation of this theoretically meaningless thesis must be considered the result of a wish to express an accompanying object representation. Perhaps the same is true for the first part of this thesis. Conceivably the realist thesis is due to certain emotional accompaniments, for example, the feeling of unfamiliarity with the mountain, the feeling that in many ways it is not subject to, or even resists, my will, and similar feelings. This problem can be only suggested at this time.

11. *The Reality of the Heteropsychological*

We have seen earlier (§ 5) that in each particular case the recognition of the heteropsychological goes back to the recognition of physical occurrences. And not only in the sense that in each case simultaneously with the recognition of a heteropsychological occurrence somehow the recognition of a physical occurrence takes place, but in such a way that the heteropsychological with all its characteristics depends upon the recognition of the corresponding physical occurrence. Hence one could translate any statement about a given heteropsychological occurrence, for example "A is now joyful", into a statement which mentions only physical occurrences, namely expressive motions, acts, words, etc. This statement could mention either those physical occurrences (expressive motions, etc.) which have led to the recognition of the joy of A, that is, it could speak of the content of perceptions that have already been experienced; or it could indicate ways of testing A's joy. In the latter case it is a conditional statement of the form: if A is now subject to such and such conditions, then such and such (physical, perceivable) reaction will take place.

Hence we are here confronted with two different languages, one of them psychological and one physical; we maintain that they both express the same theoretical content. It will be objected that in the statement "A is joyful" we express more than in the corresponding physical statement. This is indeed the case. Aside from having the advantage of much greater simplicity, the psychological language also expresses more than the physical language, but this more does not consist of additional theoretical content; it expresses only accompanying representations; these are merely object representations, that is, representations which do not stand for any fact, and hence which cannot form the content of a statement. They are expressed by choosing a certain language (while other accompanying features, which also do not belong to the theoretical content, are expressed, e.g., by the intonation, gestures, etc.). For by saying "A is joyful" and not merely "A shows facial expressions of such and such a form", I express that I have a representation of a feeling of joy, although a feeling of joy in the autopsychological sense, since I cannot know any other. However, to assume that by using the psychological instead of the physical language, that is to say, by using the expression "joy" instead of "facial expressions of such and such a form", we express a fact which goes beyond the physical state of affairs, is to confuse the theoretical content of the statement with an accompanying representation.

> With this confusion one would commit an error even more serious than that of the Indian (§ 8); for the accompanying representation of the Indian led him, even if erroneously, to the factual representation which, roughly speaking, could be expressed by the statement: "my son is as strong as a buffalo." In the present case however, we are not merely induced to make an erroneous statement, but a pseudo statement. For no fact is even conceivable or stateable which could connect the representation "feeling of joy" (in the autopsychological sense) with the behavior of A.

Let us again think of two scientists, this time psychologists; let one of them be a solipsist, the other a nonsolipsistic idealist or realist. (The dividing line runs here a somewhat different course than before, but this is not important to our discussion, since we do not want to find out which of the two opposing parties is correct; we only wish to show that the entire controversy is scientifically meaningless.) Our two scientists decide on the basis of empirical criteria of psychology whether A's joy is real or only simulated (empirical concept of reality), and thus come to an agreement (just as the above-mentioned two geographers did when the reality of the mountain was in question). However, if they then move from psychology to philosophy, a controversy arises. The solipsist claims that only the observed physical behavior of A (including his words) is real; he adds that he wants to describe this behavior with the expression "A is joyful", since the psychological language, in contrast with the physical language, not only has the advantage of brevity, but also that of stimulating a more appropriate accompanying representation; but the solipsist does not hold the consciousness of A to be real. His opponent on the other hand, claims that A shows not only the given physical behavior, through which the statement "A is joyful" is supported (witness the common findings of the two psychologists), but that, in addition, A really has consciousness.

As concerns the physical and observable, hence the only testable, both psychologists agree. There is no psychological question to which, after sufficiently extensive investigations, the two would not give the same answer. This shows that the choice of the philosophical standpoint has no influence upon the content of psychology (just as it has no influence upon natural science). (Here again the possibility of practical influence is not denied.) The divergence between the two standpoints occurs beyond the factual, in a domain where in principle no experience is possible; hence, according to our criterion, they have no scientific significance.

One could perhaps make the following objection: the two psychologists do in fact make the same utterance within psychology but they *mean* something different; when both of them say: "A is now joyful," the solipsist does not mean anything but: "A shows such and such reactions," while his opponent means, in addition, the presence of a certain feeling of joy. In order to show more clearly how things lie, let us refer to an analogous situation which has occurred several times in the development of mathematics and was caused by the critical investigations of the last century. We previously mentioned the concept of a differential quotient; now we want to use the concept of the irrational numbers as an example. Logical investigations (by Dedekind, Frege, Russell) have shown that it is not the case that, in addition to rational numbers, there are others that can be inserted into the sequence of rational numbers, but that every statement about an irrational number (for example, about $\sqrt{2}$) is an abbreviation for a statement about a class (or property) of rational numbers that produces a cut in the sequence of rational numbers. The following objection was frequently made: "but the mathematicians *mean* something different than a class of rational numbers when they speak of the irrational number $\sqrt{2}$; and similarly in the case of geometry (cf. the example in § 8): "but the mathematician, when they speak of points and straight lines, in geometry, *mean* something other than the indeterminate objects which are merely related in a certain way." These objections, and similarly the analogous objections about what the psychologists mean, are correct if by "meaning" we mean the train of representation which accompanies the conception of the statement in question. For this process can indeed be different, depending upon which mode of speech is adopted: the mode of speech involving "rational number" or that using "irrational numbers", the mode of speech which employs "basic objects of first, second, and third kind" or that using "points, straight lines, surfaces", the physical or the psychological language. However, the decisive factor is that in each of these cases the difference lies only in the accompanying object representation, not in the theoretical content of the statements. If somebody denies this, he has the obligation of formulating the meaningful, that is factual, substatements which he claims to be contained in a statement of the psychological language, but not in the corresponding statement of the physical language; that there is some information which is not contained in the statement of the physical language must be demonstrated by showing that the substatement to be formulated can be false in cases in which the physical statement is true.

Another objection ("worm—objection") points to the differences in the practical effect of the two statements. It runs something like this: the statement "this animal has consciousness" must contain more than the mere report that this animal shows certain observable reactions to given stimuli; for this statement influences my actions; for if I know that the worm feels pain, I do not step on it, while the mere observation that it writhes does not necessarily prevent me from doing so. This objection, too, is correct; from the viewpoint of practical inference the first statement contains more than the second; but again this additional content is only an object representation, namely that of the sensation of pain; hence this is a case of empathy. Empathy is not cognition; it does not produce any theoretical content or anything that can be stated; it is doing, not cognizing; it is a doing which establishes contact with the other and thus leads to a different practical orientation and consequently to different external actions. But all this is a practical, not a theoretical matter. Ethical values come into play, but there is no connection with truth and falsity. The theses "A merely behaves as if he had consciousness, while in reality he has none" and "A really has consciousness" are therefore only pseudo theses; they are not statements (in the theoretical sense); one can not judge them to be either "true" or "false". However one can respond affirmatively or negatively depending on whether or not one takes these words to express a practical position which one wants to adopt. (However, it is still questionable if a statement, that is to say a form of words which normally has theoretical content, is the most appropriate way of expressing such a practical orientation.)

Even though empathy is not cognition, it has great practical, that is heuristic, value for science (especially for psychology, the cultural sciences, and biology but occasionally also for physics). For the psychologist it is practically a necessity. There is as little chance of finding a psychologist who works without using empathy, as there is of finding a mathematician who works without the heuristic aid of perception. (Even the solipsistic psychologist employs empathy.) In spite of its extraordinary heuristic value, empathy is not, in principle, a necessity for psychology. Imagine a psychologist who does not use empathy but merely subjects the observed behavior of his subjects to rational analysis, and describes it in psychological language. He nevertheless ought to reach any result which can be obtained through empathy (even though perhaps much later); a psychologist who employs empathy must still give a rational justification, that is, a justification that does not depend upon empathy, for all the results which are obtained through empathy (cf. § 5).

Matters are different with historical accounts: frequently such an account would fail in its main purpose if one were to eschew the use of empathy altogether. For such an account is not generally scientifically oriented; its purpose is not predominantly theoretical, that is, with an aim for knowledge, but practical: it is to enrich life through participation, or is to direct actions in a certain way. To the extent to which this is so, history is not science, but practical activity which uses science as an aid; in this case the demand for the rational justification of empathy holds only for the scientific component.

It would be worth some effort to investigate the importance of the confusion of accompanying object representations with factual representations for the history of ideas; more precisely, the importance of the attempt, arising from this confusion, of expressing accompanying object representation through (pseudo) statements. Perhaps the origin of magic (as theory), mythology (including theology), and metaphysics, is to be explained in this way; not as if we could explain the content of such doctrines in this way, but some light would be shed on the strange circumstance that this content was not expressed through artistic media or through the practical conduct of life, but was given the form of a theory which has no theoretical content.

SUMMARY

I. THE AIM OF EPISTEMOLOGY

A. The Meaning of Epistemological Analysis

§ 1. Aim of epistemology: justification, "reduction" of one cognition to another, analysis of the contents of experiences. Results of analyses are available, but their meaning is not exactly known. Problem: what is the meaning of the epistemological analysis of the content of an experience, if it is to be different from genetic-psychological analysis?

§ 2. The first step of epistemological analysis consists in the logical analysis of the content of an experience into two parts: a "sufficient" and a "dispensable" constituent. The second constituent does not give any new knowledge over and above the first one; its theoretical content can be found in a "rational reconstruction" through inference from the first.

§ 3. The epistemological analysis divides the content of an experience into "nucleus" (a) and "secondary part" (b). This division is characterized by the fact that b is a dispensable part relative to a and, secondly, that b is epistemically secondary to a. Criteria for this are: 1. A (scientific) justification of the cognition of the content of b can be given only by referring to a; 2. the theoretical content of b can rest upon an error even though a has been correctly recognized.

B. Application: Knowledge of the Heteropsychological

§ 4. The recognition, in experience, of a heteropsychological occurrence always contains a constituent (a) which is connected with physical occurrences, and a constituent (b) which represents the heteropsychological. In such a case b is always dispensable relative to a, which can be shown through the method of rational reconstruction.

§ 5. Furthermore, a is always the nucleus of the experience. For, the scientific justification of the recognition of content b always refers to a; moreover, on the basis of a we can always be deceived about b.

§ 6. Result: only perceptions of physical events belong to the nucleus of experiences in which we recognize heteropsychological occurrences. The heteropsychological is "epistemically secondary" to the physical. An analysis of epistemic primacy (which is not here carried out) would show the following rank order: autopsychological, physical, heteropsychological, cultural; in addition, this analysis would lead to a complete genealogy of concepts.

II. ELIMINATION OF PSEUDOPROBLEMS FROM THE THEORY OF KNOWLEDGE

Theses:

1. Only statements with factual content are theoretically meaningful; (ostensible) statements which cannot, in principle, be supported by experience are meaningless.

2. The empirical sciences use only the empirical concept of reality.

3. Philosophy uses a nonempirical (metaphysical) concept of reality:
    a. the theses of realism and idealism concerning the external world have no factual content;
    b. the same holds for the theses of realism and solipsism about the heteropsychological.

4. The theses of realism and idealism can neither be supported nor refuted within a science; they have no scientific meaning.

5. The pseudo theses of realism and idealism express, not the theoretical content of a scientifically permissible statement, but only accompanying object representation; conceivably they express a certain practical orientation toward life.

CLASSIFICATION OF POSSIBLE OPPOSING VIEWPOINTS

Whoever wishes to contradict the indicated position, especially if he wants to claim scientific status for a thesis of realism or idealism, must take one of the following viewpoints; our reply ("Rpl.") is given in each case.

I. It is claimed that factual content is not a criterion for scientifically meaningful statements. Hence, a certain nontautological statement (which we shall call p), for example one of the theses of realism or idealism, is taken to be meaningful, even though it does not have factual content. Then it is necessary to find a new criterion for the meaningfulness of statement which is more extensive than the criterion of factual content.

This can be done in various ways; let us first classify the different conceptions of p:

1. p does not designate any fact. Rpl.: then p is meaningless; for what else but a fact can a statement express? In what sense could something be called "true" or "false" if it does not designate an existing or nonexisting fact?
2. p does designate a fact.
   a. This fact is in principle unrecognizable. Rpl.: then p is meaningless, for how can p be distinguished from a meaningless combination of signs, if the alleged content of p is something that cannot become the content of any experience?
   b. The fact, though recognizable, is not empirically recognizable (for otherwise p would have factual content). Rpl.: All knowledge rests upon experience ("experience" is taken in the widest sense, as the theoretical content of experiences of any kind).

The following classification cuts across the division 1-2:

1'. A new, expanded criterion for the meaningfulness of statements is narrow enough so that it just admits p (and certain other desired statements); on the other hand, obviously meaningless statements which are not to be given scientific status (for example, the above-mentioned statement of Jupiter hidden in a cloud, § 7), do not fulfill the criterion.

Here we can again distinguish two possibilities, not relative to the content of the criterion, but relative to the status it would have in its present form:

   a. The new criterion is already formulated. Rpl.: it must be demonstrated that obviously meaningless statements do not fulfill it.

b. It is assumed that a criterion of the indicated kind must exist, but it cannot yet be stated. Rpl.: in this case no actual position is maintained, there is only an intention to look in a certain direction for an as yet undetermined position.

2'. The new criterion is not narrowly limited in the indicated way but has a wide compass (for example: "any utterance of any person which has influence upon my actions will be considered scientifically meaningful" or something like this). Rpl.: then expressions such as a bang with the fist on the table, a cry of joy, a lyric poem must all be considered scientifically meaningful statements.

II. Factual content is taken to be a criterion. However, it is held that one of the two theses, namely realism or idealism, has factual content. We distinguish two cases depending upon the field to which the supposedly factual thesis relates:

1. The thesis relates to the heteropsychological alone. Question: Is the (alleged or denied) "reality of the heteropsychological" understood in such a way that the theoretical content of the statement "A is joyful" exceeds the theoretical content of the corresponding physical statement?

a. Yes. Rpl.: Then there exists an obligation to indicate the constituent which goes beyond this physical statement, and to show that it can be supported (i.e., the characteristics of the experiential content which would confirm or disprove it must be indicated). If the theoretical content, and not only the accompanying object representation, of a statement p exceeds that of statement q, then there is a statement r (which we call "the constituent in which p exceeds q") of the following kind: r is independent of q; the content of p includes the content of r and q (conjunction). In our case p is the statement "A is joyful," q the corresponding physical statement; now we ought to be able to find an r of the following sort: r is always true whenever p is true; r may be false when q is true; r has factual content. (For a precise formulation, the statements p, q, and r must be replaced by propositional functions with time variables.)

b. No. Rpl.: Then there is no conflict with our viewpoint. There only remains the terminological question whether in this case, one should still speak of "realism", "idealism", or "solipsism".

2. The thesis relates (in addition or exclusively) to the external world. Question: "does reality of the external world" mean that the theoretical content of the statement "Mont Blanc really exists" has a constituent in which it exceeds the theoretical content of the corresponding statements about perceptions?

    a. Yes. Rpl.: then there exists an obligation to identify that constituent and show how it can be supported (cf. 1, a).

    b. No. Rpl.: see 1, b.

For the sake of clarity, all critics are requested to admit explicitly to one of these viewpoints.

Bibliography and Index of Names
Index of Subjects

(*THE LOGICAL STRUCTURE OF THE WORLD*)

BIBLIOGRAPHY AND INDEX OF NAMES

The numbers after the names refer to sections. The expressions enclosed in brackets are the abbreviations under which the books are quoted in the text. (Where several editions are indicated, quotations are taken from those editions whose years appear without parentheses.)

(Suppl.) designates books which were subsequently added to this index and which are not discussed in the text.

Books which are especially suitable for the study of problems connected with construction theory, are designated in the following manner:

1. Suitable for the study of epistemological problems (e.g., analysis of reality, object types and their relations, the auto- and heteropsychological, relation between the physical and the psychological, etc.) :

    E I: Introductory   E II: Advanced

2. Suitable for the study of logical problems (e.g., propositions, propositional functions; classes, relations, structures; definitions; extensionality; types) :

    L I: Introductory   L II: Advanced

AHLMANN, 65, 94

    [Opt. Vorst.] "Zur Analysis des optischen Vorstellungslebens. Ein Beitrag zur Blindenpsychologie," *Archiv für die gesamte Psychologie,* 46, (1924), 193–261.

ARISTOTLE, 156

ASTER, ERNST, v., 65

[Erkenntnisl.] *Prinzipien einer Erkenntnislehre*. Leipzig, 1913.

AVENARIUS, RICHARD, 3, 64, 159, 163

[Kritik] *Kritik der reinen Erfahrung*. Leipzig (1888); 2nd ed., I, 1907, II, 1908.

[Weltbegriff] *Der Menschliche Weltbegriff*. Leipzig (1891); 3rd ed. 1912.

E I

BAUCH, BRUNO, 75

[Wahrheit] *Wahrheit, Wert und Wirklichkeit*. Leipzig, 1923.

BAVINK, BERNHARD, 176

[Ergebn.] *Allgemeine Ergebnisse und Probleme der Naturwissenschaft*. Leipzig (1914); 3rd ed. 1924.

BECHER, FRIEDRICH, 57, 58, 140, 143

[Gehirn] *Gehirn und Seele*. Heidelberg, 1911.

[Geisteswiss.] *Geisteswissenschaften und Naturwissenschaften*. Munich and Leipzig, 1921.

BECKER, OSKAR, 124, 180

[Geom.] "Beiträge zur phänomenologischen Begründung der Geometrie und ihrer physikalischen Anwendungen," *Jahrbuch für Philosophie und phänomenologische Forschung*, VI (1923), 385–560.

BEHMANN, HEINRICH, 3

[Math.] *Mathematik und Logik*. Leipzig and Berlin, 1927.

BERGSON, HENRI, 57, 182

[Metaphysik] *Einführung in die Metaphysik*. (Transl.) Jena, 1916.

[Materie] *Materie und Gedächtnis*. (Transl.) Jena, 1919.

BRENTANO, FRANZ, 164

[Klassifikation] *Von der Klassifikation der psychischen Phänomene*. Leipzig (1911), 1925.

BURKAMP, W.,

(Suppl.) *Begriff und Beziehung*. Studien zur Grundlegung der Logik. Leipzig, 1927.

BUSSE, LUDWIG, 57, 166

[Geist] *Geist und Körper, Seele und Leib*. Leipzig (1903); 2nd ed., with an appendix by Dürr, 1913.

CANTOR, GEORG, 37

CARNAP, RUDOLF,

[Raum] "Der Raum," *Kantstudien*, Erg. Heft no. 56. Berlin, 1922.

[Aufg. d. Phys.] Über die Aufgabe der Physik," *Kantstudien*, XXVIII (1923), 90–107.

[Dreidimens.] "Dreidimensionalität des Raumes und Kausalität," *Annalen der Philosophie*, IV (1924), 105–130.

[Abhäng.] "Über die Abhängigkeit der Eigenschaften des Raumes von denen der Zeit," *Kantstudien*, XXX (1925), 331–345.

[Grundlg.] *Die Grundlagen der Arithmetik*. Breslau, 1884.

[Funktion] *Funktion und Begriff*. Jena, 1891.

[Gegenst.] "Über Begriff und Gegenstand," *Vierteljahrsschrift für wissenschaftliche Philosophie*, XVI (1892), 192–205.

[Sinn] "Über Sinn und Bedeutung," *Zeitschrift für Philosophie und philosophische Kritik*, 100 (1892), 25–50.

[Grundges.] *Grundgesetze der Arithmetik*. I and II. Jena, 1893, 1903.

[Krit.] "Kritische Beleuchtung einiger Punkte in E. Schröders Vorlesungen über die Algebra der Logik," *Archiv für systematische Philosophie*, I (1895), 433–456.

FREYER, HANS, 12, 19, 56

[Obj. Geist] *Theorie des objektiven Geistes*. Leipzig and Berlin, 1923; 2nd ed. (1928).

FRISCHEISEN-KÖHLER, M., 64, 65

[Wissensch] *Wissenschaft und Wirklichkeit*. Leipzig and Berlin, 1912.

GÄTSCHENBERGER, RICHARD, 60, 65, 95, 178, 180

[Symbola] *Symbola. Anfangsgründe einer Erkenntnistheorie*. Karlsruhe, 1920.

GERHARDS, KARL, 124

[Aussenwelthyp.] "Der mathematische Kern der Aussenwelthypothese," *Naturwissenschaft*, 1922.

GOETHE, JOHANN WOLFGANG von, 136

GOMPERZ, HEINRICH, 64, 65, 67, 159

[Ereignis] "Die Welt als geordnetes Ereignis. Bemerkungen zu R. Wahles Definitiver Philosophie," *Zeitschrift fur Philosophie und philosophische Kritik*. 118 (1901); 119 (1902).

[Weltansch.] *Weltanschauungslehre*. I. *Methodologie*. Jena, 1905.

HAGEN, F. W., 67

HAMILTON, WILLIAM, 67

HARTMANN, NICOLAI, 163

[Metaphysik] *Grundzüge einer Metaphysik der Erkenntnis*. Berlin and Leipzig, 1921; 2nd ed. (1925).

HAUSDORFF, FELIX, 40

[Mengenl.] *Grundzüge der Mengenlehre*. Leipzig, 1914; 2nd ed., *Mengenlehre*, Berlin and Leipzig (1927).

HERTZ, HEINRICH, 161

[Einleitg.] Einleitung zu "Die Prinzipien der Mechanik," in *Vorreden und Einleitungen zu klassischen Werken der Mechanik*, published by the Wiener Philosophische Gesellschaft, (A. Höfler): Leipzig, 1899, pp. 121–164.

HILBERT, DAVID, 15

[Grundlagen] *Grundlagen der Geometrie*. Leipzig and Berlin (1899); 5th ed. 1922; 6th ed. (1923).

(Suppl.) H. u. ACKERMANN, *Grundzüge der theoretischen Logik.*
Berlin, 1928.   L I

HUME, DAVID, 165

HUNTINGTON, E. V., 107

HUSSERL, EDMUND, 3, 64, 65, 124, 164
[Phänomenol.] *Ideen zu einer reinen Phänomenologie und phänomeno-logischen Philosophie.* Halle, 1913.
[Log. Unt.] *Logische Untersuchungen.* Halle, I (1900), 2nd ed. 1913; II (1901), 2nd ed. 1913, 1921.

JACOBY, GÜNTHER, 64, 65, 124, 130, 140, 164
[Ontol.] *Allgemeine Ontologie der Wirklichkeit.* I, Halle, 1925.

JAMES, WILLIAM, 162

KANT, I., 67, 106, 162, 172

KAUFFMANN, MAX, 124, 129, 140
[Imman.] *Immanente Philosophie.* Leipzig, 1893.

KEYSER, CASSIUS, J., 33, 107
[Math. Phil.] *Mathematical Philosophy.* New York (1922), 1924.

KÖHLER, WOLFGANG, 36, 67
[Gestaltprobl.] "Gestaltprobleme und Anfänge einer Gestalttheorie, Übersichtsreferat," *Jahresberichte über die gesamte Physiologie,* III (on the year 1922) 1st half (1925), 512–539.

KLEIN, FELIX, 159

KÖNIG, JULIUS, 40
[Logik] *Neue Grundlagen der Logik, Arithmetik und Mengenlehre.* Leipzig, 1914.

KRONECKER, L., 42

KÜLPE, OSWALD, 3, 53, 175, 176
[Realis.] *Die Realisierung.* Leipzig, I, 1912. II, III, posthumously published by Messer, 1920, 1923.

LEIBNIZ, G. W., 3, 51, 52

LEWIN, KURT, 128
[Zeitl.] "Die zeitliche Geneseordnung," *Zeitschrift fur Physik,* XIII (1923), 62–81.

LEWIS, C. I., 3
[Survey] *A survey of Symbolic Logic.* Berkeley, 1918.

LICHTENBERG, 163

MACH, ERNST, 3, 64, 65, 67, 162, 165, 169, 176
[Anal.] *Die Analyse der Empfindungen.* Jena (1886); 8th ed. 1919. E I
[Erk.] *Erkenntnis und Irrtum.* Leipzig (1905); 4th ed. 1920.

MEINONG, ALEXIUS, von, 3, 93, 172
[Gegenstandsth.] "Über Gegenstandstheorie," 1904; in *Gesammelte Abhandlungen,* II. Leipzig, 1913, pp. 481–530.

[Stellung] *Über die Stellung der Gegenstandstheorie im System der Wissenschaften.* Leipzig, 1907.

NATORP, PAUL, 5, 64, 65, 162, 163, 179

[Grundlagen] *Die logischen Grundlagen der exakten Wissenschaften.* Leipzig and Berlin, 1910, 3rd ed. (1923).

[Psychol.] *Allgemeine Psychologie nach kritischer Methode.* Tübingen, 1912.

NEWTON, I., 136

NIETZSCHE, FRIEDRICH, 65, 67, 163

[Wille] *Der Wille zur Macht.* Leipzig, 1887.

OSTWALD, WILHELM, 3, 59, 176

[Werte] *Die Philosophie der Werte.* Leipzig, 1913.

[Naturphil.] *Moderne Naturphilosophie.* Leipzig, 1914.

PEANO, GUISEPPE, 3, 107

[Notations] *Notations de Logique Mathématique.* Torino, 1894.

[Formulaire] *Formulaire de Mathematiques.* Torino (1895), 1908.

PETZOLD, JOSEPH, 64, 180, 182

[Weltprobl.] *Das Weltproblem vom Standpunkte des relativistischen Positivismus aus, historisch-kritisch dargestellt.* Leipzig and Berlin (1906); 4th ed. 1924.

[Positiv.] "Positivistische Philosophie," *Zeitschrift für positivistische Philosophie,* I (1913) 1–16.

PIERI, M., 107

POINCARÉ, HENRI, 3, 16, 124, 130

[Wiss.] *Wissenschaft und Hypothese.* (Transl.) Leipzig and Berlin (1906). 3rd ed. 1914.

[Wert] *Der Wert der Wissenschaft.* (Transl.) Leipzig and Berlin (1906). 2nd ed. 1910.

[Letzte Ged.] *Letzte Gedanken.* (Transl.) Leipzig, 1913.

REHMKE, JOHANNES, 64

[Grundwiss.] *Philosophie als Grundwissenschaft.* Frankfurt, 1910.

REICHENBACH, HANS, 15, 62

[Erk.] *Relativitätstheorie und Erkenntnis apriori.* Berlin, 1920.

[Axiomatik] *Axiomatik der relativistischen Raum-Zeit-Lehre.* Braunschweig, 1924.

[Suppl.] *Philosophie der Raum-Zeit-Lehre.* Berlin and Leipzig, 1928.

E I

REININGER, ROBERT, 64, 67

[Erk.] *Philosophie des Erkennens.* Leipzig, 1911.

[Psychophys.] *Das psychophysische Problem.* Wien and Leipzig, 1916.

RICKERT, HEINRICH, 12, 64, 75

[Gegenst.] *Der Gegenstand der Erkenntnis.* Einführung in die Transzendentalphilosophie. Tübingen (1892); 5th ed. 1921.

[Kulturwiss.] *Kulturwissenschaft und Naturwissenschaft.* Tübingen (1899); 5th ed. 1921.

[Grenzen] *Die Grenzen der naturwissenschaftlichen Begriffsbildung.* Tübingen (1902); 4th ed. 1922.

[System] *System der Philosophie.* I. *Allgemeine Grundlegung der Philosophie.* Tübingen, 1921.

RUSSELL, BERTRAND, 3, 12, 13, 16, 27, 30, 33, 35, 38, 40, 43, 50, 59, 64, 65, 69, 73, 107, 124, 128, 140, 162–165, 176

[Principles] *The Principles of Mathematics.* Cambridge, 1903.   L II

[Types] "Mathematical Logic as based on the Theory of Types," *American Journ. Math.,* XXX (1908), 222–262.

[Princ. Math.] *Principia Mathematica. See* WHITEHEAD.

[External W.] *Our Knowledge of the External World.* London, 1914. Also (Transl.) *Unser Wissen von der Aussenwelt,* Leipzig, 1926.
E II

[Myst.] *Mysticism and Logic, and Other Essays.* London (1917), 1921
E II

[Scientif.] *On Scientific Method in Philosophy.* (1914), Also in [Myst.] 97 ff.

[Const. Matter] "The Ultimate Constituents of Matter," *The Monist,* (1915). Also in [Myst.] 125 ff.

[Sense-Data] "The Relation of Sense-Data to Physics," *Scientia* (1914). Also, in [Myst.] 145 ff.

[Cause] "On the Notion of Cause," *Proc. Aristot. Soc.* (1912). Also in [Myst.] 180 ff.

[Description] "Knowledge by Acquaintance and Knowledge by Description," *Proc. Aristot. Soc.* (1911). Also in [Myst.] 209 ff.

[Mind] *The Analysis of Mind.* London, 1921. (Transl.) *Die Analyse des Geistes.* Leipzig, 1927.

[Math. Phil.] *Einführung in die mathematische Philosophie.* (Transl.) Munich, 1923.   L I

[Suppl.] *The Analysis of Matter.* London, 1927.

[Suppl.] *An Outline of Philosophy.* London, 1927.

See also Wittgenstein

SCHELER, MAX, 58

SCHLICK, MORITZ, 15, 65, 67, 130, 136, 163, 176, 182

[Raum and Zeit] *Raum und Zeit in der gegenwärtigen Physik.* Berlin (1917); 4th ed. 1922.

[Erkenntnisl.] *Allgemeine Erkenntnislehre. Berlin* (1918); 2nd ed., 1925.
E I

[Metaphysik] "Erleben, Erkennen, Metaphysik," *Kantstudien,* XXXI (1926) 146–158.

SCHRÖDER, ERNST, 3

[Algebra] *Vorlesungen über die Algebra der Logik.* I–III, Leipzig, 1890–1895.

SCHUBERT-SOLDERN, RICHARD von, 64, 65

[Erkth.] *Grundlagen einer Erkenntnistheorie.* Leipzig, 1884.

[Solipsismus] "Über die Bedeutung des erkenntnistheoretischen Solipsismus," *Vierteljahrsschrift fur wissenschaftliche Philosophie und Soziologie,* XXX, 49–71.

SCHUPPE, WILHELM, 64, 65, 67

[Imman. Phil.] "Die immanente Philosophie," *Zeitschr. f. imm. Phil.,* II (1897), 1–35.

[Erkth.] *Grundriss der Erkenntnistheorie und Logik.* Berlin (1894); 2nd ed., 1910.

TILLICH, PAUL, 3

VAIHINGER, HANS, 165

[Als Ob] *Die Philosophie des Als Ob.* Leipzig (1911); 8th ed., 1922.

VEBLEN, O., 107

VERWORN, MAX, 165

[Kondit.] *Kausale und konditionale Weltanschauung.* Jena (1912); 2nd ed. 1918.

VOLKELT, JOHANNES, 64, 65, 159

[Gewissheit] *Gewissheit und Wahrheit.* Munich, 1918.

WAHLE, R., 65

WATSON, JOHN B., 59

WERTHEIMER, MAX, 36, 67

[Gestaltth.] *Über Gestalttheorie.* Berlin, 1925. Specially reproduced from *Symposion* I 39–60.

WEYL, HERMANN, 38, 40, 62, 73, 107, 176

[Handb.] "Philosophie der Mathematik und Naturwissenschaft" in *Handbuch der Philosophie,* ed. Bäumler and Schröter, Part II, A. Munich and Berlin, 1926. (Also published separately.) L II, E II

WHITEHEAD, ALFRED NORTH, 3, 12, 13, 27, 30, 33, 35, 40, 43, 50, 73, 107, 124

[Space] Space, Time and Relativity (Lecture, 1915.) In: W., *The Organization of Thought.* London, 1917, p. 191 ff.

[Nat. Knowledge] *An Enquiry Concerning the Principles of Natural Knowledge.* Cambridge, 1919.

[Nature] *The Concept of Nature.* Cambridge, 1920.

(Suppl.) *Science and the Modern World.* Cambridge, 1926.

WHITEHEAD, A. N. and B. RUSSELL,

[Princ. Math.] *Principia Mathematica.* Cambridge. I, 1910; II, 1912; III, 1913; 2nd ed., I, 1925 (same text, new introduction and appendix), II and III 1927 (no change). L II

WINDELBAND, WILHELM, 12

[Geschichte] *Geschichte und Naturwissenschaft.* Strassburg, 1894; 3rd ed. (1904).

WITTGENSTEIN, LUDWIG, 43, 180, 183

[Abhandlg.] "Logisch Philosophische Abhandlung." With preface by Russell. *Annalen der Nat. u. K. Philosophie,* XIV (1921), 185–262. (Also in book form as *Tractatus Logico Philosophicus* [German and English]. London, 1922.) L II

WITTMANN, 65, 67

[Raum] "Raum, Zeit and Wirklichkeit," in: Martius and Wittmann, *Die Formen der Wirklichkeit,* Leipzig, 1924, pp. 5–81.

WUNDT, WILHELM, 3, 57

[Phys. Psychol.] *Grundzüge der physiologischen Psychologie.* Leipzig (1874); 6th ed., I–III, 1908–1911.

ZIEHEN, THEODOR, 3, 64, 65, 89, 129, 140, 162, 176

[Schuppe] "Erkenntnistheoretische Auseinandersetzungen. 2. Schuppe. Der naive Realismus," *Zeitschrift fur Psychologie und Physiologie der Sinnesorgane,* XXXIII (1903) 91–128.

[Erkth.] *Erkennthnistheorie auf physiologischer und physikalischer Grundlage.* Jena, 1913.

[Gegenw. Stand] *Zum gegenwärtigen Stand der Erkenntnistheorie.* Wiesbaden, 1914.

INDEX OF SUBJECTS

(The numbers refer to sections of *Structure;* important passages are indicated by italics.)

> def. = definition (or clarification) of the expression
> der. = derivation of the concept (cf. § 84)
> constr. = construction of the expression
> (E) = example
> (R) = references